The 1911 Revolution in China

International Conference in Commemoration of
the Seventieth Anniversary of the 1911 Revolution
Tokyo, October 21–23, 1981

### Advisory Committee
Arisawa Hiromi
*Chairman*

Furushima Kazuo
Hayashi Kentarō
Ichiko Chūzō
Inoue Kiyoshi
Kaizuka Shigeki
Kawano Kenji

Kuwabara Takeo
Masuda Shirō
Saitō Akio
Shimada Kenji
Tōhata Seiichi
Yamamoto Tatsurō

### Organizing Committee

Andō Hikotarō
Andō Masashi
Banno Masataka
Etō Shinkichi
Fujii Shōzō
Hamashita Takeshi
Ishii Akira
Itō Akio
Katayama Tsuyoshi
Kishi Yōko
Kishimoto-Nakayama Mio
Kojima Shinji
Kojima Yoshio
Komatsubara Tomoko

Kubota Bunji
Matsumoto Takehiko
Nakamura Tadashi
Namiki Yorihisa
Nozawa Yutaka
Ogata Yōichi
Ono Shinji
Saeki Yūichi
Satō Kimihiko
Tanaka Masatoshi
Uchiyama Masao
Yamada Gōichi
Yamane Yukio
Yamashita Ryūzō

# The 1911 Revolution in China

## Interpretive Essays

Edited by
Etō Shinkichi and Harold Z. Schiffrin

UNIVERSITY OF TOKYO PRESS

Soc
DS
773.45
A16
1984

ROBERT MANNING
STROZIER

JAN 16 1986

Tallahassee, Florida

Publication of this volume was assisted by a grant from the Commemorative Association for the Japan World Exposition.

© 1984 UNIVERSITY OF TOKYO PRESS
ISBN 4-13-027021-4 / UTP 27210
ISBN 0-86008-349-7
Printed in Japan

All rights reserved. No part of this publication may be reproduced or transmitted in any form or by any means, electronic or mechanical, including photocopy, recording, or any information storage and retrieval system, without permission in writing from the publisher.

# Contents

List of Contributors   ix
Introduction
    Etō Shinkichi   xi

## I Ideological, Political, and Social Currents

The 1911 Revolution and the Awakening of the
Chinese Nation
    Jin Chongji ........................................3
The Issues of Anti-Imperialism, Democracy, and
Industrialization in the 1911 Revolution
    Hu Sheng ........................................19
The Slogan "Expel the Manchus" and the Nationalist
Movement in Modern Chinese History
    Zhang Kaiyuan ..................................33
The Shanghai Silk-Reeling Industry During the Period
of the 1911 Revolution
    Suzuki Tomoo ...................................49
Anti-Imperialism and Popular Resistance in the
Revolutionary Thought of Song Jiaoren
    Don C. Price ....................................61

## II Foreign Influences

*Daitō Gappō Ron* and the Chinese Response: An Inquiry
into Chinese Attitudes Toward Early Japanese Pan-Asianism
    Min Tu-ki ........................................83

The Influence of Kemuyama Sentarō's *Modern Anarchism*
on Chinese Revolutionary Movements
    Nakamura Tetsuo ...............................95
A Lesson from the Meiji Restoration: Revolution or
Constitutional Monarchy?
    Yung Ying-yue ................................105

III  Influences upon the Periphery

The Viet-Nam Quang Phuc Hoi and the 1911 Revolution
    Kawamoto Kuniye .............................115
A Protest Against the Concept of the "Middle Kingdom":
The Mongols and the 1911 Revolution
    Nakami Tatsuo ...............................129

IV  Revolutionaries in Action

The Bourgeois Revolutionaries in the Movement to Regain
Economic Rights Toward the End of the Qing Dynasty
    Li Zongyi ....................................153
The Chinese National Association and the 1911 Revolution
    Kojima Yoshio ...............................175
The 1911 Revolution in Hunan and the Popular Movement
    Shimizu Minoru ..............................193
Sun Yat-sen and the Founding of the Provisional Nanjing
Government
    Chen Xiqi ...................................209

V  The Foreign Powers

International Financial Relations Behind the
1911 Revolution: The Fall in the Value of Silver and
Reform of the Monetary System
    Hamashita Takeshi ...........................227
The 1911 Revolution and United States East Asian Policy
    Marius B. Jansen.............................257
The Issue of Imperialism and the 1911 Revolution
    Marie-Claire Bergère .........................267
The Foreign Powers and the 1911 Revolution: A Harmonious
Interval During a Period of Discord
    Harold Z. Schiffrin...........................273

The 1911 Revolution and the Foreign Powers
S.L. Tikhvinski ................................281

Glossary ............................................291
Index................................................309

# List of Contributors

| | |
|---|---|
| Marie-Claire Bergère | Professor of History, Institut National des Langues et Civilizations Orientales (Université de Paris III) |
| Chen Xiqi | Professor of History, Zhongshan University |
| Etō Shinkichi | Professor Emeritus, University of Tokyo; Professor of International Relations, Aoyama Gakuin University |
| Hamashita Takeshi | Associate Professor of Chinese History, Institute of Oriental Culture, University of Tokyo |
| Hu Sheng | Director, Research Unit on Party History, Chinese Communist Party Central Committee |
| Marius B. Jansen | Professor of Japanese History, Princeton University |
| Jin Chongji | Associate Director, Wenwu Publishing Company |
| Kawamoto Kuniye | Professor of Vietnamese History, Keiō University |
| Kojima Yoshio | Professor of Chinese Economies, Nihon University |
| Li Zongyi | Researcher, Chinese Institute of Modern History, Chinese Academy of Social Sciences |

| | |
|---|---|
| Min Tu-ki | Professor of Chinese History, College of Humanities, Seoul National University |
| Nakami Tatsuo | Lecturer of Mongol History, Institute for the Study of Languages and Cultures of Asia and Africa, Tokyo University of Foreign Studies |
| Nakamura Tetsuo | Professor of Chinese History, Kobe Gakuin University |
| Don C. Price | Professor of History, University of California, Davis |
| Harold Z. Schiffrin | Professor of Chinese Studies and Sociology, Truman Research Institute for the Advancement of Peace, Hebrew University |
| Shimizu Minoru | Associate Professor of Chinese History, Bukkyō University |
| Suzuki Tomoo | Professor of Chinese History, Gifu College of Pharmacy |
| S.L. Tikhvinski | Professor, Oriental Institute, Academy of Sciences of the USSR |
| Yung Ying-yue | Lecturer, Department of Japanese Studies, National University of Singapore |
| Zhang Kaiyuan | Professor of History, Huazhong Normal University |

# Introduction

On October 10, 1911, an anti-Qing revolutionary uprising took place in Wuchang. This set off a chain of revolts in the cities and provinces south of the Yangzi (Yangtze) and within three months brought to an end two millennia of dynastic rule in China. On January 1, 1912, the Republic of China was formally proclaimed in Nanjing (Nanking), the newly selected capital. It was the earliest republican government in Asia, though, strictly speaking, it was preceded by the short-lived government of Democratic Taiwan, which was quickly suppressed by the Japanese army.

The pre-modern imperial system of China had been based upon an autarchical agricultural society and supported by an elaborate, patrimonial bureaucracy. The destruction of the imperial system began with indigenous economic developments and the corruption of civilian and military bureaucracies, and was reinforced by Western impact on China. The political events of the eighteenth and nineteenth centuries shook the foundations of the empire, and the Qing gradually lost its capability to meet the overwhelming transformations: the White Lotus (Bailian jiao) Rebellion, the increase in opium consumption, the Opium War, the Arrow War, the Taiping Rebellion, the Sino-French War, the First Sino-Japanese War, Russian expansion to the Amur region, Primorskij krai (Maritime Province), and finally to Manchuria, the conclusion of various unequal treaties, and the cession of settlements and leased territories to the foreign powers.

The efforts by the Yangwu clique to graft Western technology and government systems onto China failed to solve the country's intrinsic problems. The political pendulum swung back toward traditional conservatism and anti-foreignism when the administrative reforms attempted by the young Guangxu Emperor, his advisor, Kang Youwei, and other officials induced a coup d'état by Empress Cixi and Yuan Shikai. The Boxer Rebellion, which started as a peasant rebellion with strong religious overtones, grew quickly in North China through the support of the conservative imperial court and provoked the armed intervention of the eight allied powers. The Qing imperial court was forced to make further concessions to the aggressive foreign powers in terms of foreign rights and interests and was reduced to "semi-colonial status."

It was too late for the Manchu government to recover the trust of the Chinese people. Their opposition to the regime sprang from various sources: some were merely anti-Manchu and wanted to restore a Han Chinese Confucian state; others were revolutionary republicans; some were socialists or anarchists, while some were mere power-hungry opportunists.

Sun Yat-sen was in Denver when he first learned of the revolution, and upon his return to China via Great Britain and France, he was elected provisional president of the new republic by the revolutionary delegates. Following the formal proclamation of the republic, the Qing lost the support of its generals and officials who clearly foresaw that their days were numbered: there was Yuan Shikai, the de facto supreme leader of the powerful Beiyang Army, who had clandestine negotiations with Sun and engineered the abdication of the Manchu emperor. In return, Yuan was made the first president of the republic, but his understanding of republicanism or Western democracy was negligible, and he sought to have himself enthroned as emperor of a new dynasty. Confronted by strong and vehement opposition both at home and abroad, Yuan was unable to carry out his plans. When he died in 1916, China was thrown into still further confusion. Civil wars among warlords continued to ravage the country, and no central power could control the ubiquitous foreign intervention in domestic politics.

In retrospect, it is true that the Chinese Revolution of 1911 failed to establish a strong and unified modern state. But it did terminate imperial despotism and open up new possibilities for government reforms. As a consequence, both the Guomindang (Nationalist) Party in Taiwan and the Chinese Communist Party on the Mainland regard the 1911 Revolution positively. Assessment of historical phenomena, however, varies greatly according to political circumstances: this is particularly true of China and can be explained by three reasons. First, historical studies in China have been traditionally characterized by strong ethical and political judgments. I recall that in 1962, while still a young scholar, I had the opportunity for the first time to meet Professor Yoshikawa Kōjirō, then professor of Chinese literature at Kyoto University. He asked me half-teasingly, "So you are interested in political history. All right, what is the leitmotif of Chinese literature?" In a few seconds, the name of Chinese literary figures—Tao Qian, Li Bo, Du Fu, Lu Xun, Shen Congwen, —quickly flashed through my mind, but I could not find a single common denominator. The prestigious professor smiled and raised another question: "Then what is the leitmotif of Japanese literature?" I still could not produce an answer. With his teasing smile he said, "In China it is politics and in Japan, love." If this is true of Chinese literature, how much more so of Chinese historical studies?

Second, the Chinese Communist Party relies on Marxist historiography. Marxism generally regards modern detached positivism as bourgeois objectivism: while modern positivist historians try to minimize overt political assessment in their research, Marxist historians do not hesitate to express their political views explicitly in their writings: they make clear-cut definitions of historical phenomena and unqualified distinctions between the just and the unjust. Third, the Chinese, particularly the intellectuals, are nationalists when they discuss the humiliations China suffered at the hands of foreign powers. Historians with nationalist tendencies are also guilty of loading their writings with political assessments.

These three reasons help explain why historical studies in the People's Republic of China regard the Chinese Revolution of 1911 as a national bourgeois revolution, as defined by Lenin, to overthrow medieval despotism and to cope with foreign aggression. Since the establishment of the People's Republic in 1949, this interpretation itself has remained basically unchanged. But the evaluation of the national bourgeoisie has varied according to the political climate: when the political pendulum swung toward the radical Left, the national bourgeoisie was discredited; when it swung toward moderation, it was evaluated positively. This fluctuation can be observed in the assessment of the 1911 Revolution by the People's Republic of China. In 1951, the fortieth anniversary of the revolution was totally disregarded because of the Korean War and the strict wartime policies of the Chinese Communist Party. The year 1961 was the fiftieth anniversary of the revolution: it was an era of moderation following the failure of the Great Leap Forward in 1958, and the anniversary was celebrated in Beijing as well as in the other major cities of China. The sixtieth anniversary came during the era of the Great Cultural Revolution when the radical left wing prevailed and was hence completely ignored.

In 1981, the seventieth anniversary of the revolution was celebrated throughout the People's Republic of China. After the death of Mao Zedong in 1976 and immediately following the arrest of the "Gang of Four," the political pendulum swung back to unprecedented moderation: the national goal was "modernization": developing the domestic market, increasing foreign trade, importing Western technology and capital, promoting rapprochement with the Guomindang in Taiwan, and pursuing policies to increase economic productivity. Consequently, the bourgeoisie was now evaluated highly, as was the 1911 Revolution. In Beijing, the largest celebration was held in the main chamber of the People's Great Hall on October 9: in a lengthy address, Party Chairman Hu Yaobang spoke highly of Sun Yat-sen and the 1911 Revolution, and also called for collaboration with Guomindang leaders for the reunification of China. The Academic Symposium to Celebrate the Seventieth Anniversary of the 1911 Revolution was held in Wuhan from October 12 to 17, with 81 Chinese scholars, selected from 200 candidates, and some 40 foreign scholars reading their papers.

The Guomindang regime of Taiwan has always proudly claimed to be the authentic disciples and successors of Sun and his comrades in the revolution. Celebrations are held annually on October 10, Taiwan's national day. Not to be out done by the People's Republic, on August 23, 1981, they organized an international conference entitled "Symposium on the History of Republican China" in Taipei with the participation of 44 foreign scholars and over 100 domestic scholars.

Sun Yat-sen spent long years of exile in Japan, and the Japanese scholars of China, in their wish to mark the anniversary with something more than a simple ceremony, organized an international scholarly conference in Tokyo. It was felt that political circumstances might allow scholars both from mainland China and Taiwan to sit together and for scholars from both South and North Korea to participate. The organizing committee invited delegates from Taiwan and North Korea in addition to the scholars whose papers are included in this book. At first, the Guomindang considered our invitation seriously and wanted to have some scholars participate in the Tokyo conference. But two groups in Japan vehemently opposed these invitations. One, an anticommunist, pro-Guomindang group, took the position that, since they support the Guomindang and are fighting for the annihilation of Communist China, they strongly object to Guomindang scholars attending a conference together with Mainland scholars. The other group, consisting of dogmatic Maoists who had enthusiastically supported the Great Cultural Revolution, argued that "it is incorrect and impermissible to use the false name of the Republic of China in the invitations to scholars in Taiwan." In the end, the Taiwan scholars did not participate, nor did the North Koreans. Deposite this unfortunate political background, the Tokyo conference, held from October 21 to 23 was well attended and resulted in intense academic discussions. The participants consisted of five Chinese scholars from mainland China, two each from the United States and the Republic of Korea, one each from the Soviet Union, France, Israel, and Singapore, 38 Japanese participants, and 170 observers.

In addition to the three above-mentioned international conferences, two other meetings should be mentioned. The first was a Japan-Taiwan conference, held in Yokohama on October 28 and 29, 1981. Entitled "The Three People's Principles and China," it was attended by 11 Taiwan and over 50 Japanese scholars. The other conference on the 1911 Revolution was held in Chicago on the evening of April 2, 1982, during the three-day annual meeting of the Association of Asian Studies. Papers were read before a packed audience by five scholars from mainland China, five from Taiwan, and myself. It was a remarkable gathering at which scholars from the Mainland and Taiwan sat together for the first time since 1947.

This book is a compilation of papers presented at the Tokyo conference. Professor Harold Z. Schiffrin assumed the task of editing the papers. I would like to express my sincere gratitude to my co-editor, without whose close collaboration this book could not have appeared in this form. The conference itself was made possible by the cooperation of many individuals and organizations. Foremost, the members of the advisory and organizing committees of the conference (whose names are listed on page ii) should be acknowledged for their cooperation. In particular, I wish to express my gratitude to Professor Arisawa Hiromi, president of the Association of Japanese-Chinese Exchange in the Humanities and Social Sciences, and Professor Andō Hikotarō, Waseda University. The Association of Japanese-Chinese Exchange in the Humanities and Social Sciences was extremely helpful in seeing to the administrative taskes related to the conference as well as to the publication of this volume. I would like to thank Kimoto Kensuke, secretary-general of the association, for his assistance at all stages, and Bamba Setsuko, also of the association, for compilation of the Glossary. Finally, I wish to acknowledge with gratitude the University of Tokyo Press for publication of this volume.

Etō Shinkichi<br>Organizing Committee

October 10, 1984

# Ideological, Political, and Social Currents

# The 1911 Revolution and the Awakening of the Chinese Nation

## Jin Chongji

China's defeat at the hands of Japan in the Sino-Japanese War of 1894–95 was a turning point in modern Chinese history. Thereafter, "Save the Nation" became the watchword for all patriots. The patriotic aim to save the nation from disaster supplied the motive force for the 1911 Revolution. It was a key element in the appeal of the anti-Qing revolution. However, there is a current of thought which contends that the real thrust of the revolution was against the Manchus. That this is a very superficial view can be easily demonstrated by referring to the changes that took place in Zhang Taiyan's thinking.

The 1911 Revolution added luster to the modern history of the awakening of the Chinese nation. Firstly, it brought about a deeper understanding of the nature and consequences of imperialist aggression; secondly, it linked the struggle against foreign invaders with the fight against reactionary rulers at home; thirdly, it pointed out that only revolutionary means could save the Chinese nation; and lastly, it confidently asserted that there was a bright future for China if the revolution was pressed forward. These were invaluable spiritual assets.

The fundamental flaw of the 1911 Revolution was that it did not adopt any proposal to wage an all-out struggle against imperialism and feudalism. Summing up the lessons from the past, Sun Yat-sen pointed out that none of the earlier revolutions had been pursued to their logical ends but had all been compromised. This is very significant and deserves much thought.

The history of modern China is saturated with misery and

suffering brought on by the colonialists. The nation was humiliated, its people were enslaved, and the fate of the nation was in the hands of alien powers. It was therefore inevitable that the Chinese people should become greatly agitated and rise up in heroic resistance. This was the deep well-spring of the burgeoning national democratic revolution in modern Chinese history. The 1911 Revolution wrote an important chapter in the history of the awakening of the Chinese nation.

After the Opium War of 1840–42, China was gradually reduced to semi-colonial, semi-feudal status, but the Qing dynasty managed to stabilize its reactionary rule for three decades after ruthlessly suppressing the revolution of the Taiping Heavenly Kingdom. Some feudal historians have even eulogized the first of these three decades as the Tongzhi Restoration (1862–74). Some bureaucrats who dealt in "foreign matters" (Westernization) raised the banners of "self-strengthening" and "seeking wealth." This caught the fancy of many at the time. Even Zheng Guanying, a progressive thinker riding the crest of ideological tendencies of the day, did not have the courage to point out that prior to the Sino-Japanese War, China was actually on the decline, and consequently entitled one of his books *Warnings to the Prosperous Age*. Just as Liang Qichao said, "Before the Sino-Japanese War broke out, our people were utterly ignorant of how dangerous China's situation was. Because of their ignorance of the approaching danger, they still remained complacent and self-satisfied. Nobody spoke about 'defending the motherland.' "[1] Many at that time were insensitive to the grave crisis the nation was facing.

The salvoes of the Sino-Japanese War and China's defeat aroused many patriotic Chinese from their slumber. In November 1894, shortly after the war broke out, that great revolutionary forerunner, Sun Yat-sen, established the Society to Restore China's Prosperity (Xingzhonghui), the first bourgeois revolutionary body in China. In the Society's manifesto, he wrote: "China is now surrounded by powerful foreign countries. Like hungry tigers and ravenous vultures they have been looking covetously at the rich mineral resources and abundant products of China. One after another, they have been seizing our territory either through piecemeal encroachment or outright annexation. China now faces the real danger of dismemberment. We, who care, must raise our voices and shout: 'Deliver our people from their misery and save the great edifice of our nation from collapse.' "[2] It is obvious that his main focus was on saving the nation from the danger of extermination. But as Sun Yat-sen was active mainly overseas, he did not assert much influence on the scholar-officials at home. Then, in 1897, Germany's seizure of Jiaozhou Bay sparked fierce contention among the Western powers to carve out spheres of influence in China. The national crisis came to a head. In one of his speeches at that time, Kang Youwei said, "In just two months we have witnessed twenty cases in which we have lost territory and sovereignty. The days are long; how shall we tide over the year? Some day China will become another Burma, another Annam, another India, another Poland. . . . What will become of our 400 million people and our several hundred thousand scholar-officials? . . . There is no other way to national salvation but to set our minds to it with firm resolution."[3]

In no time at all, national salvation became the stirring call rallying patriots across the land. The event was a landmark in the history of the awakening of the nation.

The movement for constitutional reform and modernization, established by the reformists headed by Kang Youwei, was in the vanguard of the national salvation movement and exerted great influence on patriotic intellectuals at home. Politically, the movement was extremely weak, and it was quickly suppressed by the feudal diehards. However, it played a tremendous role in emancipating the minds of the people and enlightening them. Before this, events had already made many people aware of the possibility that "the enemy could come at any time, and that the nation could be subjugated overnight." But as they had been cut off from the outside world for so long, they had no way of knowing what the situation was like abroad and the direction developments were taking. Very, very few in China knew much about the rest of the world in those days. In the movement for constitutional reform and modernization, the press and various patriotic groups did much to educate the people about the world situation and to draw their attention to the danger of China being subjugated. People were urged to transform society and save the nation from disaster. The newspaper *Shiwu bao* (Chinese Progress) "inspired and encouraged people with translations of articles from the European and American press and articles about the danger of China being partitioned by foreign countries. Its articles shook the country."[4] "The publication of a map in Tianjin showing how China was about to be partitioned has caused a tremendous stir far and wide."[5] According to Liang Qichao, the establishment of the School of Current Affairs and the Southern Study Society suddenly enlightened the people of Hunan, and "everywhere people exhorted and encouraged each other to be patriotic and to regard saving China as their bounden duty."[6] These quotes from contemporary writings faithfully mirrored what took place in China at that time.

After the failure of the Hundred Days of Reform, Kang Youwei and Liang Qichao fled to Japan, where they established the magazine *Qingyi bao* (Journal of Disinterested Criticism). Certain aspects of their early articles served a positive function. For example, Liang wrote, "It is imperative to show the people across the land the position China occupies in the world so that they may come to understand the policies of the foreign powers—both West and East—toward China." They also raised the slogan of nationalism. "Nationalism," Liang wrote, "is the most enlightened, most just, and most fair doctrine in the world. It means that we do not allow other nations to encroach upon our freedom, and that we do not encroach upon theirs. . . . What our people need most today is to be made aware of the danger of China being invaded by imperialism and to foster our intrinsic nationalism to counter it."[7] These and similar declarations had a positive impact on patriotic intellectuals.

History sometimes unfolds in mysterious ways. From the start, the political activities of Kang Youwei and other reformists were undertaken to oppose the revolution. But because they propagated patriotism, the idea of saving the country, and the socio-political theories of the Western bourgeoisie, objectively, they prepared the way for the widespread dissemination of bourgeois democratic ideas. As a result, many people were made aware of the grave national crisis and were fired with patriotism. And when they saw the bankruptcy of the reformist road, they turned to gather under the banner of the revolutionary democrats represented by Sun Yat-sen and thus joined the ranks of the revolution.

In the early years of the twentieth century, the bourgeois revolutionaries headed by Sun Yat-sen rapidly replaced the reformists and became the mainstream of the patriotic movement. What brought this about? The answer can be seen in the slogan: "Be patriotic and save the nation." There is a view which holds that the 1911 Revolution occurred only because anti-Manchuism was its goal and moving force. At first glance, this seems credible, but it is merely a superficial view.

At the time, contradictions did exist between the Han people and the Manchus. It was the principal contradiction in China when the Qing dynasty forced its way south of the Shanhaiguan Pass. Toward the end of the Qing dynasty, inequality between various nationalities still existed. But because the Qing rulers had gradually turned themselves into the chief representatives of the Han landlord class and the feudal ruling forces of other nationalities, and because the contradictions within feudal society were intensifying, the contradiction between the Han people and the Manchus had long become secondary. There are no real facts to support the assumption that in the early twentieth century, the Han-Manchu contradiction had deteriorated to such an extent that it could cause a nationwide revolutionary movement.

What was uppermost on the minds of the enlightened at the time was how to free China from imperialist aggression and oppression and lead it onto the road toward independence and prosperity. This was the prerequisite for solving other problems of lesser importance.

An analysis of the changes in Zhang Taiyan's thinking serves as an illustrative example that can help clarify this issue. From his childhood, Zhang Taiyan was deeply influenced by Han nationalist ideology. When he joined the ranks of the movement for constitutional reform and modernization after the Sino-Japanese War, he never went beyond the limits of reformism. In his view, it was dangerous for a revolution to take place in a time of serious national crisis. He said: "If the internal turmoil continues, it provides an opportunity that can be exploited by foreign invaders to their advantage. . . . If the people rose in arms, they would be fighting others of the same yellow race to the delight of the white man." Thus he came to the conclusion that "revolution means to engage in factional strife and throws society into disorder; political reform means respecting people of noble quality and combining the efforts of the talented. Now it is imperative to undertake political reform instead of revolution."[8]

His attitude remained unchanged even after the 1898 Reform Movement met defeat. In "On Guest Emperors," written in 1899, he continued to say that if the Han people rose in arms against the Manchu rulers in the presence of imperialists, both sides would suffer and end up in common ruin. "When two bulls fight each other with the bear as the instigator, both will be crippled. . . . If one gave vent to his animosity against the Manchus while territory was ceded to the white man, it could only bring harm to the Divine Land. . . . At a time when one's territory is threatened by the enemy, and the balance of power is against him, he cannot divert his attention even if he has an old score to settle."

It was only after the eight-nation allied force attacked and occupied Beijing that Zhang Taiyan changed his attitude. It dawned on him that the Qing government had yielded entirely to imperialism; it was impossible to depend on the government to make the country powerful and keep the enemy at bay. Thus, he wrote another article, "Correcting the Error of 'Guest Emperors,'" in which he said, "If the Manchus are not driven out, it will be impossible to make officials love their country and to raise the morale of the people against the enemy. With our territorial integrity encroached upon like this, China will finally be enslaved by the Western powers." Moreover, he had the courage to criticize himself: "Since 1898 I took refuge with those who worshiped the Qing rulers. In writing the article, 'On Guest Emperors,' I was deceptive and careless; I abandoned the true religion, and I grossly misjudged the situation." Facts prove that it was only intensified imperialist aggression and the Qing dynasty's betrayal of the country that forced Zhang Taiyan onto the road of revolution.

Facts also prove that the decisive factor in the burgeoning opposition to Qing rule during the 1911 Revolution was not the renewal of nationalist ideology in the Han tradition, but the serious national crisis that was then threatening China. In the minds of many Han people, this traitorous Qing government was controlled by an "alien nationality." They concluded that the reason why the Qing government clung obstinately to the policy of betrayal and capitulation, in defiance of the opposition of the people throughout China, lay in the fact that it was the government of an alien nationality which showed no concern for the destiny of the Han people and which unhesitatingly gave up China's sovereignty. At that time many people held this viewpoint, although it was not based on scientific analysis. Because of the old and newly born hatred for the Qing dynasty, the slogan "Down with the Manchus" won broad support.

Such anti-Manchu propaganda included a strong strain of narrow nationalism. Because the contradiction between the Han people and the Manchus was overemphasized, people tended to overlook the struggle against the two major enemies—imperialism and feudalism. On the other hand, such propaganda did call on people to concentrate their strength on the anti-Qing revolution, which was the key link in the chain of the national salvation movement. The surging anti-Manchu campaign was essentially a manifestation of a national awakening and of the movement to save the country from subjugation.

During the preparatory period of the 1911 Revolution, revolutionaries did much to spread the idea of revolution through their newspapers and magazines. What new concepts did they introduce in their attempt to save the country from doom? What new contributions did they make to the awakening of the modern Chinese nation? These could be summed up as follows:

1. *Compared to previous attempts, their exposure and analyses of the manifestations and nature of imperialist aggression were extremely incisive.* In 1901 an article, "On the Future of Imperialism and the Future of the Twentieth-Century World," in *Kaizhi lu* (Journal of New Learning), an early revolutionary periodical, declared that "in the present-day world imperialism is in its heyday while freedom is in danger of being wiped out. . . . In today's world, imperialism is actually the doctrine of bandits."9 In 1903 an article in *Zhejiang chao* (Tides of Zhejiang) declared that "imperialists have nationalism as their father and agitation for economic expansion

as their mother."[10] It declared that whenever an imperialist power launched aggression against others, it was supported by the entire nation and backed by the nation's economic strength. Some of these words were misleading, but most of them were helpful in raising the national consciousness of the people because they pointed out that imperialist aggression in China was not an accidental or random phenomenon but that it represented an inexorable trend whose motive force would be comprehended.

These writers emphasized exposing the imperialist economic invasion: "Economic contention is even more harmful than political. Why? Just like a man. If you cut off his hand in the morning and his foot at night, he will feel the pain and become startled. He will fight back with a vengeance and still have hopes of coming to life again. But if he is gradually drained of his marrow and blood, he will die a slow death without knowing why. All this rings true. If the political power of a country is seized but its economic power remains intact, there is the possibility that political power will change hands again. Political influence follows wherever capital can reach, and modern history has amply testified to this truth."[11] In saying so, revolutionaries at that time achieved a much more profound understanding of reality than their counterparts at the end of the nineteenth century.

Such an understanding was of extreme importance. Earlier, people's understanding of imperialist aggression was at a much more emotional stage. Therefore, patriotic and anti-imperialist feelings usually surged among the people when insults from imperialism were particularly harsh, and when the Qing government was exceptionally submissive and flagrantly betrayed the national interest. Resistance receded whenever the tense situation relaxed. As a result of this more profound understanding of the situation (though not based on scientific analysis), it was easy to arouse violent reactions to every advance of imperialism in China. People came to realize not only that imperialist aggression should be taken seriously, but that precautions should be taken against any future steps taken by the imperialists. All this laid a deeper and more lasting basis for the anti-imperialist patriotic movement.

2. *More important, the revolutionaries pointed out that, in ruling China, the Qing dynasty had become the tool of imperialism, and therefore the*

*fight against imperialism had to be closely linked with the fight against the Qing dynasty.* For a long time the Chinese people saw the foreign invaders and domestic feudal rulers as two separate entities. During the movement for constitutional reform and modernization, people hoped for a thorough reform in the Qing government so as to make China powerful and keep the foreign powers at bay. The Yihetuan (Boxer) movement even raised the slogan "Support the Qing dynasty and eliminate the foreign invaders." But things began to change in the early twentieth century.

In 1901 the *Guomin bao* (The Chinese National) pointed out that, drawing lessons from the angry resistance they met when they resorted to force to subjugate a nation, the imperialist powers had changed their tactics in China: by utilizing the Qing officials as their tools, they could "control China without dispatching even a single soldier." The paper raised a cry of warning: on no account "should government officials be depended on to ensure survival"; all illusions about them should be cast aside; reliance upon the people's own strength was the only way to guarantee China's survival.[12]

The ideological changes that took place among Chinese students studying in Japan during the twentieth century are another cogent example. During the national crisis, these students left for Japan in search of ways to save China. At first, most of their political attitudes were relatively moderate. They thought that the fundamental solution for the independence and prosperity of China was to bring the spirit of nationalism into full play and that this should start with education. The "resist Russia" incident in the summer of 1903, when tsarist Russia threatened to occupy northeast China by force, was the decisive turning point. In the eyes of a large number of patriotic youth, this appeared to be the signal for the powers to partition China. They formed an army of volunteers and demanded that the Qing government arm and lead them to resist tsarist Russia. But the decadent, reactionary government accused the students of "whipping up revolution on the pretext of opposing Russia" and then ruthlessly suppressed them. Inevitably, this incensed the patriotic students, who were essentially in accord with popular feelings of indignation. It brought about a sudden change in the political attitude of the Chinese students in Japan. Now that the demand for revolution was immediately given the highest priority, their anti-Manchu propaganda reached a new high. This transformation can be seen quite clearly by looking through magazines such as *Jiangsu* and *Zhejiang chao* before and after the "resist Russia" incident.

Shortly after this incident Chen Tianhua wrote in "Sudden Realization": "My friends, do you know if today's Qing court still belongs to the Manchus? No. It has long been in the hands of the foreigners. To be sure, the court cannot be offended, but is it also true that a court controlled by foreigners cannot be offended?" This single remark, "a court in the hands of foreigners," helped advance the consciousness of patriotic people.

Such a change in attitude was not accidental. After the eight-nation allied force invaded China, the Qing government issued a pompously worded directive to "estimate China's resources and ability, and to act accordingly to win the favor of friendly countries." For this purpose it quickened the pace in selling out China's sovereign rights while brutally suppressing the patriotic activities of the Chinese people, thus laying bare its true colors as national traitors. Now that the Qing government had cast its lot with the imperialist aggressors, it was only a natural and logical conclusion for the broad masses of people to link the anti-imperialist struggle with the struggle against the Qing dynasty. The combination of the struggle against foreign aggressors and the struggle against the reactionary rulers at home marked an important advance in the awakening of the modern Chinese nation.

3. *The revolutionaries pointed out that only by resorting to revolution could China be saved.* Once they saw clearly that the Qing government had become a tool of the imperialists, they naturally came to the conclusion that to be patriotic meant joining the ranks of revolution. Without overthrowing the traitorous Qing government, it would be impossible to save China. This was a lesson drawn from a long period of painful experience. In the debate between the *Min bao* (People's Report) and *Xinmin congbao* (New Citizen Journal), the necessity of revolution was brought home, and the fallacy spread by the reformists that revolution would cause internal strife and result in the country being partitioned was refuted. All this had a tremendous impact on the broad masses of the patriotic people.

In seeking salvation, they could not wait for a "gracious gift" from the reactionary government; nor could they depend upon superficial changes. The people realized that victory could be won only by revolutionary action. This was yet another important advance in the awakening of the modern Chinese nation.

4. *The revolutionaries also confidently pointed out that revolution would open up a bright future for the nation.* In an ebullient speech in 1905 to the Chinese students who had gathered to welcome him to Japan, Sun Yat-sen said that China, with its 5000-year-old civilization, lagged behind only in modern times, and that if China redoubled its efforts to catch up, "after one decade or two it will achieve everything that has been achieved by Western civilization and it will even surpass the West." In his introduction to *Min bao*, he even thought that "we can certainly carry out both political and social revolutions in one stroke, leaving the West far behind."

People of a semi-colonial, semi-feudal country invariably feel constrained; many suffer from a national inferiority complex. But Sun Yat-sen emerged from dark, difficult days full of confidence. He firmly believed that some day the Chinese nation would rise, independent and prosperous, and take its place among the countries of the world. Such a high sense of national self-respect and confidence is precisely what people of semi-colonial, semi-feudal countries require. In those dark years this was a tremendous spiritual force inspiring the Chinese people to forge ahead in struggle for a better future.

The people achieved a new understanding and awareness from the repeated lessons derived from the period of the 1911 Revolution. This understanding and awareness were also an invaluable spiritual legacy handed down by trailblazing thinkers and political leaders of that period. Compared to that which prevailed in the late nineteenth century, their perception and consciousness constituted a tremendous step forward.

The 1911 Revolution had many shortcomings, and it ultimately ended in failure. Once a nation acquired a new perception and a new consciousness, it could never revert to its original condition. This is the case in China. On this basis alone they would continue to advance and search for new truths to save the country. They would naturally retain the rational elements of their new understanding and consciousness. Subsequently, when these elements were enriched and enhanced, their full power would be revealed.

The 1911 Revolution made tremendous contributions to Chinese history. Just as Zhou Enlai once said: "The 1911 Revolution overthrew the rule of the Qing dynasty, ended the autocratic monarchy that had lasted for well over 2000 years in China, emancipated people's minds on a large, unprecedented scale, and opened up new avenues for the development of the revolution in the future." The 1911 Revolution achieved a great victory. Nevertheless, it was not a thoroughgoing revolution, and it did not accomplish its historic task. Post-revolutionary China remained under the heel of imperialist and feudal forces, and the fundamental problems of the Chinese revolution remained unsolved.

Why did such a nationwide movement as the 1911 Revolution fail? A major reason was the political weakness of the bourgeois revolutionaries who led the revolution. They tried their best to deliver China from the misery brought by imperialist aggression but were not courageous enough to face up to the imperialists. They timidly refrained from jeopardizing imperialist interests in China in the hope of avoiding intervention by the imperialist powers. They were correct in regarding the overthrow of the traitorous and decadent Qing dynasty as a key link in the whole chain of the national salvation movement, but they were naive to think that once the Qing dynasty was overthrown, China would automatically embark on the road to independence and prosperity."

Such weakness was evident in the debate between *Min bao* and *Xinmin congbao*. What was worse, they were even weaker in practice than in theory. The Wuchang uprising had hardly reached its third day when the newly established Hubei military government hurriedly proclaimed: "All the treaties signed by the Qing dynasty with foreign countries are still effective. . . . Indemnities will be paid in full as scheduled by various provinces. . . . All the vested interests of foreign countries in China will be protected." The same promises were made by the Nanjing provisional government in its "Proclamation to Friendly Countries." But the weakness of the revolutionaries, and their appeasement tactics were not rewarded by the imperialist powers. Having long regarded the revolution as a serious threat to their rule in China, the imperialist powers did everything possible to throttle the revolution or, failing that, to prevent it from intensifying. But, they were, after all, experienced colonialists. When they saw that the days of the Qing dynasty were numbered, they switched their support to Yuan Shikai in an attempt to keep imperialist and feudal rule intact in China. Unfortunately, the inexperienced revolutionaries did not see through this imperialist tactic.

The revolution ended up a de facto failure. Afterward, scenes shifted continuously on the stage of history: Japan presented the Twenty-One Demands, Yuan Shikai proclaimed himself emperor, and Zhang Xun tried to restore the monarchy. The situation in China went from bad to worse. When World War I came to an end, some thought this was the "victory of right over might," but they were soon disillusioned by the cynical disposition of the Shandong question at the Paris Peace Conference. The old, beaten track could lead China nowhere. A new trail had to be blazed. It was at this juncture that the October Revolution led by Lenin broke out in Russia, and a workers' movement was launched in China. The founding of the Chinese Communist Party two years after the May Fourth Movement of 1919 ushered in a new period of historical development in China.

The proclamation of the Second National Congress of the Chinese Communist Party, held in July 1922, declared in no uncertain terms that the party's fighting goal was to "overthrow international imperialist oppression and win complete independence for the Chinese nation." The Chinese people had been waging struggles and probing for solutions repeatedly for more than eight decades. Then, drawing from the positive and negative experience and lessons of the 1911 Revolution, they were able to arrive at this new understanding. It was precisely under such circumstances that the bourgeois revolutionary democrats represented by Sun Yat-sen who, despite painful setbacks, was still undauntedly searching for new ways to save the nation and the people, obtained help and sympathy from the Chinese Communist Party. The party proposed the formation of a democratic united front to combat the imperialists and feudal warlords.

Sun Yat-sen implemented the three great revolutionary policies of allying with the Soviet Union, allying with the Communist Party, and supporting the workers and peasants. Summing up the lessons derived from his experience over the years, he realized that all past revolutions had foundered in compromise and that none had been carried through to the end. He stated categorically that "if we want to shoulder once more the duties of revolution, we must plan on a thoroughgoing revolution. On no account should we follow the old disastrous road again—compromising with the enemy when the revolution was unfolding. From now on we should reject all tactics calling for compromise and concessions, and we should realize that any compromise is a great mistake for an all-out revolution."[13] On another occasion he said: "For thirteen years every step forward of the Chinese revolution has been resisted by counter-revolutionary forces, who prevent the revolution from winning complete victory. The warlords are such a counter-revolutionary force. Why are the warlords so strong? Because imperialism is behind them. But no one knew that it was necessary to defeat this force. This is why thirteen years since the revolution it has still not been successful."[14] Just before Sun Yat-sen died, Duan Qirui sent a representative to warn him to refrain from caustic language in order to avoid offending the imperialist powers. Sun Yat-sen retorted: "If I did not want to overthrow imperialism, I could not be called a revolutionary." Here, he spoke from the invaluable experience gained, not only by himself, but by the Chinese people in the long years of revolutionary struggle.

The long, tortuous struggle waged by the Chinese people finally put an end to imperialist and feudal rule in China. The national democratic revolution achieved victory. Today, when the Chinese people have stood up and become their own masters, we cherish all the more the memories of the outstanding fighters of the 1911 Revolution and the historic role they played in the awakening of the modern Chinese nation.

## Notes

1. Ai Shi Ke (Liang Qichao), "Zunhuang lun" [On revering the emperor], *Qingyi bao*, vol. 9.

2. Sun Yat-sen, "Xingzhonghui xuanyan" [Manifesto of the Society to Restore China's Prosperity], *Sun Zhongshan xuanji* [Selected works of Sun Yat-sen], vol. 1 (Beijing, 1956), p. 19.

3. Kang Youwei, "Sanyue ershiqiri Baoguohui shang yanjiang huici [Farewell speech to the Protect the Emperor Society on March 27], in *Wuxu bianfa* [The reforms of 1898], ed. Zhongguo shixuehui, vol. 4 (Shanghai, 1957), pp. 409–10.

4. Luo Zhenyu, "Zhensong laoren yigao" [Posthumous manuscript of the old man of the faithful pine] in *Wuxu bianfa*, vol. 4, p. 249.

5. Hu Sijing, "Wuxu lüshuang lu" [Record of walking carefully in 1898], vol. 8, in *Wuxu bianfa*, vol. 1, p. 359.

6. Liang Qichao, *Wuxu bianfa zhengbian ji* [Record of the coup d'etat of 1898], in *Wuxu bianfa*, vol. 8, pp. 303–4.

7. Rengong (Liang Qichao), "Guojia sixiang bianqian yitong lun" [On the similarities and differences in the changes of national thought], *Qingyi bao*, vol. 94, p. 95.

8. Zhang Taiyan, "Lun xuehui you dayi yu huangren jiyi baohu" [Study societies are of great value in urgently protecting the yellow race], *Shiwu bao*, vol. 19.

9. "Lun diguozhuyi zhi fada ji ershi shiji shijie zhi qiantu" [On the development of imperialism and the future of the twentieth-century world], *Qingyi bao quanbian* [Complete volumes of *Qingyi bao*], vol. 25, p. 170.

10. "Guohun pian" [Chapter on the national spirit], *Zhejiang chao*, no. 1, p. 13.

11. Fei Sheng, "Eluosi zhi Dongya xin zhengce" [Russia's new policy in East Asia], *Zhejiang chao*, no. 1, p. 1.

12. "Ershi shiji zhi Zhongguo" [Twentieth-century China], *Guomin bao*, no. 1 pp. 2–3.

13. Sun Yat-sen, "Zhongguo Guomindang xuanyan de zhiqu" [The objectives of the declaration of the Chinese Guomindang], *Sun Zhongshan xuanji*, vol. 2, p. 533.

14. Sun Yat-sen, "Zhongguo neiluan zhi yuanyin" [The cause of China's civil strife], *Sun Zhongshan xuanji*, vol. 2, pp. 899–900.

# The Issues of Anti-Imperialism, Democracy, and Industrialization in the 1911 Revolution

## Hu Sheng

Sun Yat-sen first publicized the Three People's Principles in 1905. He interpreted the Principle of Nationalism as "driving away the Manchus and resurrecting the Chinese nation." This interpretation remained unchanged until 1911. The Tongmenghui (Chinese League), which provided political and ideological leadership for the 1911 Revolution, did not put forward the specific question of opposing foreign imperialist aggression and oppression of China. Nevertheless, it should be acknowledged that the struggle waged by the Tongmenghui against the Qing regime was in essence a struggle against foreign imperialism.

The 1898 Reform Movement led by Kang Youwei put before Chinese people the pressing task of saving China from the crisis of being partitioned by the imperialist powers. The champions of the movement thought that this task could be fulfilled by asking the Qing emperor to carry out some political reforms. They did not call for the overthrow of the Qing dynasty, nor did they try to mobilize the peasants who were at the lowest rung of the social ladder. The masses at the bottom of society, chiefly the peasants, rose spontaneously to fight against the foreign invaders, resulting in the Yihetuan (Boxer) Movement of 1900.

Between the 1898 Reform Movement and the Yihetuan Movement on the one hand and the 1911 Revolution on the other, there was a link, and that was the almost nationwide patriotic movement for the protection of railway and mining rights, which started around 1903. It was a movement initiated mainly by the industrialists and businessmen demanding the recovery of the mines and railways, which the Qing government had ceded to foreign countries, and advocating the establishment of private companies to run mines and build railways with Chinese capital. The call for the protection of national and provincial interests against alien forces evoked a strong response from the people of various strata. In 1903, there also occurred the movements to resist France and Russia while the year 1905 saw the movement to protest the anti-Chinese drive in the United States. All these movements were characterized by mass participation, but unlike the Yihetuan Movement, they were non-violent. They were patriotic movements of a new type led by the bourgeoisie, ones which did not call for the overthrow of the Qing dynasty. We might as well say that the upper bourgeoisie (including the bourgeoisified landed gentry) who played a leading role in these movements attempted to preserve the Qing rule. But the logical development of objective reality showed that opposition to imperialism could not but give rise to sharp conflict with the Qing rulers. Patriotic movements would inevitably lead to revolutionary movements aimed at overthrowing the Qing regime.

Following the events of 1900 (the Yihetuan Movement and the invasion by the Eight-Power Allied Forces), the imperialists changed their tactics in their aggression toward China. In his article "On the New Tactics in Subjugating China" written in 1901, Liang Qichao said that, after the occupation of Beijing by the Eight-Power Allied Forces, the imperialist powers, instead of clamoring, as they had been doing for years, to carve up China, began to talk about "protecting China." He considered this as essentially new tactics in subjugating China. Even Liang Qichao was aware that "protecting China" meant in fact protecting the corrupt Qing regime. He held that the imperialist powers were merely using the "utterly ignorant and weak" Qing government as a proxy to rule the Chinese people. "The government is at once a slave of the foreign powers and the master of the people at home. Since the master is himself enslaved by others, what good can his slaves expect?"

What Liang Qichao said tallied with the actual situation. Before 1900, China had gradually been reduced to a semi-colony. Though at that time the Qing government had yielded to the pressure of imperialism, it was not yet resigned to the complete loss of its independent status. Hence the Sino-French War and the Sino-Japanese War. Moreover, compelled by the pressure of the Yihetuan Movement, the Qing court "declared war" against the foreign powers in 1900, even though this was only a fleeting and hypocritical gesture. After that year, the imperialist powers agreed among themselves to pursue an "open-door policy" toward China and a policy of "protecting China." The danger of their directly carving up China was over for the time being. The Qing government, "pardoned" by the big powers, returned to Beijing and became a lackey under the aegis of imperialism. Therefore, the Chinese people's struggle against imperialist enslavement was bound to manifest itself as an anti-Qing struggle.

Liang Qichao's view as quoted above should have logically led to a revolutionary conclusion. For a time between 1901 and 1902, he was inclined to favor a revolution for overthrowing the Qing court. But before long, he made an about-face to join his mentor Kang Youwei in singing the royalists' tune of opposing the revolution.

An argument of the royalists to justify their stand for constitutional monarchy and against the revolution was that revolution would invite intervention by the big powers and so make China face the danger of being divided up among them. In refutation of this argument, Sun Yat-sen said: "With the Manchu government serving as the flunky of the foreign powers, it is easier for them to grab Chinese land. Therefore, the only way for China to avoid its being carved up by them is to overthrow the Manchu government." Many similar views can be found in the journals published by revolutionaries at the time. Chen Tianhua, a well-known revolutionary propagandist, pointed out bluntly that the Qing court was actually "a court at the beck and call of foreigners," and that people had every reason to resist it.

It is true that, to demonstrate the need for launching a "national revolution," the revolutionaries often stressed the exposure of the national inequality between the Manchus and the Hans as well as the political and economic privileges of the Manchus. To stir up anti-Manchu sentiment, they again publicized such atrocities as the ten-day massacre in Yangzhou and the three massacres in Jiading committed by the Manchus against the Hans when they occupied the two cities in 1645. As Sun Yat-sen said, when he first advanced the Principle of Nationalism, he won response mostly from the secret societies and "seldom from the middle social strata and up." Shortly afterward, however, "progressive ideas and the Principle of Nationalism spread at a tremendous pace, finding their way into every stratum of society. Almost everyone came to realize the necessity of waging a revolution." This change took place around the year 1900. The anti-Manchu sentiment that had been fermenting for the previous two centuries or more burst into flames at that time precisely because anti-Manchuism had become a call for saving China from imperialism.

The revolutionaries led by Sun Yat-sen maintained that, since the revolution should make China an independent state, it was imperative first of all to overthrow the Qing government protected by imperialism. Thus they found themselves virtually in opposition to imperialism.

While opposing the constitutional monarchists, the bourgeois revolutionaries opposed the method of struggle adopted by the Yihetuan. They regarded the anti-imperialist struggle (such as burning of the churches) of the peasants and the urban poor without a unified leadership by an advanced class as "barbarous xenophobia" and "a spontaneous riot" and attempted to "improve it and raise it to a higher level" so that it would become "an orderly revolution." Though they were not totally ungrounded in these ideas, they could not put forward a comprehensive anti-imperialist program capable of mobilizing the masses.

In his work *On Revolutionary Army*, written in 1903, the young revolutionary Zou Rong put forward a revolutionary program calling for, among other things, "opposition to those, Chinese or foreigners, who interfere with the independence of the Chinese revolution." The "Declaration on External Relations," which the Tongmenghui had prepared for publication at the outbreak of the revolution, contained this provision: "Foreigners who support and aid the Qing government to the detriment of the National Military Government are to be treated with hostility." Generally speaking, however, the revolutionaries believed that they were not engaged in "barbarous xenophobic activities" but were carrying out a civilized and orderly revolution in emulation of the Western bourgeois revolution for freedom and independence. So, they reckoned, instead of interfering with the Chinese revolution, the big powers would sympathize with it. Although some of the revolutionaries declared that, in the case of armed intervention against the Chinese revolution by the big powers, China would firmly resist by relying on the favorable factors of a vast territory and a huge population, they pinned their hopes on the possibility that nothing of the sort would happen at all. They were certainly incapable of foreseeing that the big powers might sabotage the Chinese revolution by means other than armed intervention.

Despite all these weaknesses on the part of the revolutionaries, we should not deny the anti-imperialist character of the 1911 Revolution. Soon after the Wuchang Uprising, the Qing government found itself in a crisis of disintegration. The imperialist powers immediately came to realize that the club of the Chinese revolution that had hit their lackeys might fall on their own heads. They were worried that the mass struggle inspired by the revolution might develop into a "xenophobic movement." The imperialist powers tried to bring an early end to the 1911 Revolution by encouraging the "moderate" elements taking part in it, and they supported Yuan Shikai in his attempt to replace the Qing emperor and usurp the revolutionary gains—they did all this precisely because the 1911 Revolution was in essence a revolution of an anti-imperialist character.

In 1906, Sun Yat-sen said by way of explaining his Principle of Democracy: "For thousands of years, China has been under absolute monarchy. This form of government cannot be tolerated by the people who love equality and freedom." Therefore, he was in favor of carrying out a "political revolution" simultaneously with a "national revolution." In the sense of "overthrowing monarchy," the overthrow of the Qing government was a political revolution whose aim was to establish a "democratic constitutional government," i.e., a democratic state after the pattern of the Western capitalist countries. In the article "The Real Solution to China's Problems," written in 1904 during his exile in the United States, he said that "the old government must be replaced by a new, enlightened and progressive government," that "the outmoded Manchu monarchy must be changed and a

Chinese republic established in its place," and that "we will form our government on the model of your [U.S.] government."

The reformists led by Kang Youwei and Liang Qichao put forward the slogan of "democracy" during the 1898 Reform Movement, but what they really advocated was a compromise between monarchy and democracy, the "sharing of power between the monarch and the people." They were not fundamentally opposed to monarchy as such, which was the concentrated expression of the power of the feudal landlord class. They represented the political inclination of the upper bourgeoisie which was closely connected with the feudal landlord class. In the few years from 1905, a debate was carried on between China's constitutional monarchists and democratic revolutionaries, which revealed the following two major points of difference between them on the question of democracy:

1. Should the feudal monarchy which had prevailed for more than two thousand years be changed or not? This involved the question of the state system and form of government. In the eyes of the constitutionalists, the reform demanded by the revolutionaries had gone far beyond the question of the form of government. *Xinmin congbao*, edited by Liang Qichao, said: "Our goal is to reform the present government without shaking the foundation of the state, whereas the revolutionaries want to change the basic structure of state on account of the present government being corrupt." The constitutionalists regarded monarchy or democracy as a matter concerning the state system. They made it clear that only the form of government should be reformed, but not the state system. In other words, the foundation of the state must not be shaken.

Liang Qichao said that the political revolution they advocated should only aim at constitutional monarchy, which could be realized only by petitioning the present government. This was tantamount to abolishing revolution altogether. He added that he was against national revolution not because he liked the Manchus but because a political revolution unnecessarily required the overthrow of monarchy; and that it was a matter of secondary importance whether the reigning monarch was of Manchu or Han nationality. It can thus be seen that Liang Qichao and his like who opposed the revolution aimed at overthrowing the Qing dynasty were virtually against the overthrow of the system of monarchy of over two thousand years. Since they did not want to shake the foundation of the feudal state, they certainly did not need revolution but abhorred it.

Although some revolutionaries stressed that, since the present government was that of the Manchus, it must be opposed even if it practiced constitutional monarchy, more were of the opinion that the aim of the revolution was to terminate the 2,000-year-old system of monarchy and it must be opposed even if the reigning monarch was a Han. Since they stood for the transformation of the state of the dictatorship of the landlord class into a bourgeois democratic republic, they could not but advocate revolution. Such being their position, they constituted a dynamic force far more advanced than the constitutionalists.

2. In order to carry out the democratic revolution, the revolutionaries demanded mobilization of the forces of the masses. Sun Yat-sen said: "We must establish a national government through a revolution of the common people. This is not only the goal of our revolution, but also utterly indispensable to it." Quite a few revolutionaries expressed the view in their articles that the revolution must be conducted and led by the middle social stratum and that the lower social strata must be aroused. They held that only with the education and guidance by the middle social stratum could the lower social strata be prevented from carrying on unconscious and meaningless destructive activities. As interpreted at the time, the middle social stratum embraced the *shang* and the *shi*. *Shang*, or businessmen, might be taken to mean the middle and petty bourgeoisie, while *shi*, or intelligentsia, referred to intellectuals seeking a way out at a time when the feudal society was experiencing great turmoils and upheavals. As for the lower social strata, they included members of the secret societies, laborers, and soldiers. Of these three, members of the secret societies drew the greatest attention.

Revolution was bound to release the forces of the lower social strata. This was the fundamental reason why the bourgeois constitutionalists opposed it. In his *On the History of the French Revolution*, Kang Youwei wrote: "Revolution must necessarily rely on the destructive forces of the violent mob. But how can anyone succeed in anything through collaboration with the mob? Those who collaborate with them are bound to fail and bring disaster to their families and the country." Liang Qichao uttered many similar views in his polemics with the revolutionaries.

The revolutionaries believed that they were able to guide the lower social strata in an orderly revolution. At least they did not shy away from mobilizing the masses at the grass roots when agitating for the revolution. In fact, they did try to mobilize them. Their courage to launch a revolution was another characteristic marking them off as being a cut above the bourgeois constitutionalists.

When it came to practice, however, the revolutionaries showed serious weaknesses. The middle and petty bourgeoisie they represented were not strong social forces. Many intellectuals who were revolutionaries had little contact with the peasants or other laboring people. They did not go into the midst of the masses of laboring people from whom they could draw strength. They had contact only with a number of secret societies with lumpens as the core. So they just had their feet wetted by the foams of the onrushing waves at the sea, so to speak. With the peasants as their main force, the mass struggles against tyranny and for survival were sweeping across nearly every province on the eve of the Wuchang Uprising. Inspired by the outbreak of this uprising, they further developed, and the secret societies took advantage of the situation to greatly increase their activities. Although these struggles reflected in a way the influence of the revolutionaries, they remained spontaneous, for the revolutionaries were incapable of organizing and leading them. It should be said that it was precisely these large-scale spontaneous mass struggles that shook the Qing regime at its very foundations. In point of fact, the revolutionaries overthrew the Qing dynasty precisely by dint of such mass struggles. But they failed to push them forward and win a comparatively thoroughgoing victory.

After the Wuchang Uprising, more and more constitutionalists in the various provinces changed their stand of opposing the revolution and came over to its side. They joined the revolution not because they favored it, but because they feared it. They were motivated by the desire to put a quick end to the revolution before it could become raging flames when the masses at the grass roots were aroused. Although on the surface the cooperation between the revolutionaries on the one hand and the constitutionalists and those old forces favoring a revolution on the other added to the influence of the revolution, the revolutionaries failed to maintain their stand by cooperating with such unreliable allies. As a result, they forfeited their leading position when victory was won.

In the face of the revolution, the imperialist powers had to admit that the Qing government had outlived its usefulness as a tool. So they wanted to change horses. They could accept China becoming a democratic republic provided that power was in the hands of a representative of the big landlord or big comprador class. That was why the imperialist powers refused to recognize the Nanjing government headed by Sun Yat-sen. But when Yuan Shikai took over from the Qing court and declared himself president of the Republic of China, they gave him recognition and full support. The revolutionaries had to compromise with the reactionary forces represented by Yuan Shikai, causing failure of the already victorious revolution.

Thus, although the China of absolute monarchy became a republic, no radical change took place in the status of the various classes in the state system. Neither the bourgeois revolutionaries nor the bourgeois constitutionalists gained political power. China did not become a bourgeois democratic republic in its real sense. Although monarchy had been the concentrated expression of the rule of the feudal landlord class for more than 2000 years, the 1911 Revolution did not overthrow or shake the foundation of landlord rule. Therefore, the change from monarchy to democracy was merely one in the form of government, leaving the question of democracy and independence of China unsolved.

This notwithstanding, we should fully affirm the achievement of the 1911 Revolution in overthrowing the absolute monarchy of over 2000 years and in raising the banner of democratic republicanism. As far as the immediate result was concerned, post–1911 Chinese society was no less dark than in the late Qing dynasty. Judged from the whole process of historical development, however, the success and failure of the 1911 Revolution were of great significance in the annals of the Chinese people's struggle for liberation. As a country subject to imperialist domination and shackled by longstanding feudal traditions, China could not achieve genuine national independence and people's democracy without traversing a difficult and tortuous path, suffering defeat after defeat and waging repeated struggles."

From the experience of the Western capitalist countries, Chinese revolutionaries of the period of the 1911 Revolution realized that the capitalist system was, after all, not without imperfections. Sun Yat-sen had this to say in 1905: "In recent years, our revolutionaries are doing their best canvassing for the cause of making China a country as powerful as the European and American countries. Those countries may be powerful, but their people are really impoverished. Judged from the recurring general strikes and the increasing activities of the Anarchists and Socialists there, it may be said that a social revolution is drawing near." So the attitude to take toward such experiences of the Western countries was a question confronting China's bourgeois revolutionaries.

Some revolutionaries, such as Zhang Taiyan, maintained that the best way to prevent another social revolution was to avoid taking the road of the Western countries, i.e., that of developing capitalist industry and commerce. This reflected the view of the conservative small producers and proprietors. The revolutionaries headed by Sun Yat-sen held a different view. They considered development of capitalism inevitable but felt that its evils could be avoided and thus another revolution prevented if the Principle of the People's Livelihood was implemented in good time. He and his comrades regarded this principle as synonymous with socialism. He said: "It would be much easier to carry out the Principle of the People's Livelihood now in China than in Europe and America. For social problems are brought about by civilization and progress. If civilization is at a low level, there will not be serious social problems." But Sun Yat-sen was against the view that "civilization cannot benefit the poor, so it would be better to restore the ancient ways." He believed that "civilization and progress are the outcome of an objective process, something unavoidable." Here, by civilization and progress he meant the development of capitalist industry and commerce. He also pointed out: "Civilization brings both benefits and evils to mankind. It is imperative to make use of the benefits and avert the evils. In the European and American countries, the rich enjoy the benefits while the poor suffer from the evils. It is always the minority who monopolize civilization and happiness. Hence this world of inequality. The objective of our present revolution is to make China not only a state that belongs to the whole people but also a state that belongs to the whole society. This is something which the European and American countries are definitely incapable of achieving." Therefore, he advocated "accomplishing both the political revolution and social revolution at one stroke."

Sun Yat-sen interpreted the Principle of the People's Livelihood as equalization of landownership. At the time, it meant the nationalization of land through buying out. However, land nationalization was not socialism, and it could not "prevent" social revolution. "Why are the European and American countries incapable of solving their social problems?" Sun Yat-sen asked. And he answered like this: "It is because they have not solved the land problem." This was a misunderstanding, of course. He also said that in China after a revolution "the price of land is bound to rise more and more along with the advance of civilization." He actually meant that the development of capitalism would make the price of land go up. If the policy of equalization of landownership was really carried out and land really nationalized so that it would be impossible for the landlords to reap fabulous profits from the increased land prices, then all this would only favor the development of capitalism. The revolutionaries headed by Sun Yat-sen reasoned that the evils of capitalist development could be avoided and socialist revolution forestalled by eliminating landownership by the landlords. This view was completely at variance with historical reality. In fact, by dint of this reasoning, they considered themselves fully justified to work for the establishment of a bourgeois republic and the development of capitalist industry and commerce.

The constitutionalist Liang Qichao was feverishly opposed to the social revolution advocated by Sun Yat-sen. He maintained that, instead of waging a social revolution, measures should be taken by the present government to encourage the capitalists to promote production. He also refuted the viewpoint that nationalization of land meant socialism, pointing out that its adherents knew nothing about socialism at all. Although these arguments showed that Liang Qichao's understanding of socialism was closer to the point, his difference with the revolutionaries was, as a matter of fact, not over the question of whether to practice socialism or not.

Both the revolutionaries and the constitutionalists called for the development of capitalist industry and commerce, on which they had no difference at all. The divergence of views between the two sides lay in the fact that one advocated creating conditions for the development of capitalism through a democratic revolution aimed at overthrowing the Qing dynasty while the other favored the maintenance of this dynasty with the emperor as its head, hoping that it would encourage the capitalists and the development of capitalism.

That China should learn from the West and develop modern industry was not a new idea in the period of the 1911 Revolution. Between the 1860s and the early 1890s, there were as yet few factories and mines in China run by foreign capital. This offered a good opportunity for the growth of Chinese national capital. During the latter half of this period, more and more private capital was invested in modern industry. However, the expansion of Chinese national capital was impeded in those years because industry was controlled and monopolized by the feudal government and bureaucracy.

The demand for the freedom of private investment in modern industry was made as a counterpoise to the control and monopoly by the feudal government and bureaucracy. It had been strongly voiced during the abortive 1898 Reform Movement. After the events in 1900, the Qing government began superficially to pursue a policy of encouraging private capital, but the method was nothing more than giving the merchant investors official titles of different grades. In fact, no specific measures were taken to protect private capital at all. By that time, foreign capital had made deep inroads into such sectors of the economy as industry, mining, transport, and communications. It was unrealistic to expect the Qing government—a government which had long become a tool of imperialism and which was clinging fast to the system of feudal rule—to take earnest and effective measures to encourage and protect private industry and commerce.

 The above was the historical background against which the

revolutionaries of the period of the 1911 Revolution advanced the view that only through revolution could there be development of national industry and commerce, a view which was correct in principle. But the 1911 Revolution actually failed to stimulate the growth of China's national industry.

In the first few months after his removal from the office as Provisional President of the Republic of China, Sun Yat-sen said: "With the founding of the Republic of China, the Principle of Nationalism and the Principle of Democracy have been realized. Only the Principle of the People's Livelihood remains to be implemented." At the time, by the Principle of the People's Livelihood he actually meant the development of capitalist industry and commerce. And he still thought that equalization of landownership could protect the people from the evils of capitalism. He said: "The weakness of China is rooted in the poverty of its people. As I see it, the big powers have become rich through the development of industry. Now that we have won initial success in practicing republicanism, we should take industrial development as the remedy to the problem of poverty and make it the most important current policy." Therefore, Sun Yat-sen indicated that he would devote himself to the development of industry; first of all, the building of railways (200,000 kilometers within ten years). He then predicted: "In ten years' time, China will certainly have over 100,000 big capitalists. Then we should encourage state socialism as the only way to nip the evil in the bud. . . . Developed industry and commerce will inevitably lead to increased land prices. . . . A few decades later, China will have dozens of cities like Shanghai. . . . With equalization of landownership, the capitalists are bound to give up speculation in landed property and go in for industry and commerce. This will mean an infinitely bright future for Chinese society."

However, objective reality forced Sun Yat-sen to quickly discard these predictions verging on illusion and plunge himself once again into the revolution, fight against Yuan Shikai, the Northern warlords and imperialism standing behind them, and continue the struggle for China's independence and democracy.

The revolutionaries of the period of the 1911 Revolution did not succeed in establishing a bourgeois republic and carrying out capitalist industrialization as they had wished. Nonetheless the idea they put forward was an important one; namely, that only through revolution could China attain independence, democracy, and develop its industry. This has been verified and developed through the last seventy years of Chinese history.

# The Slogan "Expel the Manchus" and the Nationalist Movement in Modern Chinese History

## Zhang Kaiyuan

This article examines the social and historical background and the substance and consequences of the question of "expelling the Manchus" from the perspective of the nationalist movement in modern Chinese history. The modern Chinese nationalist movement can be divided into two phases: The first was the pre-1900 period, when the social basis of the movement consisted mainly of the peasantry, and the nuclear force consisted of members of the landlord class who were committed to social reform and resistance to foreign aggression. It also included intellectuals with bourgeois inclinations who had fought their way out of the ranks of the feudal literati and bureaucracy. During this period, "Expel the Manchus" was not the principal political slogan of the nationalist movement. The second phase was the post-1901 period, when national capitalism first developed and the number of the national bourgeoisie and bourgeois and petty-bourgeois intellectuals grew steadily. They became most active in the movement, and the slogan "Expel the Manchus" quickly became the keynote of revolutionary fervor.

In the early twentieth century, "Expel the Manchus" had become the watchword for the fight against imperialism, feudalism, and autocratic monarchy. This slogan spearheaded the popular struggle against the Qing dynasty, which had become an imperialist lackey. It marked the emergence of the Chinese nationalist movement into a regular bourgeois democratic movement. The slogan's role in mobilizing the people should not be underestimated. The fundamental factor behind the failure of the

1911 Revolution against imperialism and feudalism was the inherent weakness of the national bourgeoisie. The slogan itself was not at fault. It cannot be denied that in many anti-Manchu propagandistic articles, there was a pronounced feudal, Han chauvinistic quality, and that relations between nationalities in China were described erroneously. These distortions must be analyzed and repudiated. But, in the final analysis these backward ideas did not represent the main current of the nationalist movement and do not negate the revolutionary brilliance of this militant slogan.

The anti-Manchu slogan during the 1911 Revolution has always provoked much controversy. Many scholars at home and abroad have decried it as racist or racist revanchist, overlooking or, at least, underestimating its progressive and revolutionary nature. The slogan was an angry protest against the Qing policy of national oppression and national discrimination and also a landmark of a new period in the development of the modern Chinese nationalist movement. It was a stirring, militant slogan that reflected the common wish of the Chinese people and, after careful consideration, it was put forward by the revolutionary democrats of the early twentieth century.

The nationalist movement dealt with here refers only to the modern Chinese nationalist movement, a nationalist movement within the bourgeois sphere. If the establishment of a national state which could best meet the needs of capitalist development was a tendency of every nationalist movement of modern times, then such a tendency emerged in China after the Opium War of 1840.

Foreign capitalist aggression invariably arouses popular resistance in colonial or semi-colonial countries; it also invariably stimulates the birth and development of indigenous capitalism and corresponding cultural and ideological changes. In other words, it will inevitably produce a nationalist movement in the oppressed country. Regardless of the extent to which the nationalist movements of these countries contain backward racial and religious aspects, and regardless of the degree to which modern ideas have affected the political consciousness of leaders and participants, the tendency of these movements will eventually be to establish a national state that can best meet the needs of capitalist development. Broadly speaking, from the Opium War to the 1911 Revolution, all national wars, peasant uprisings, political reforms, and entrepreneurial initiatives, as well as the reform movement and the revolutionary struggles, were all part of the modern Chinese nationalist movement.

From its inception, the modern Chinese nationalist movement faced powerful enemies from abroad. Deep-rooted feudalism provided the social foundation for the colonial rule of imperialism in China. Therefore, a salient feature of the nationalist movement was that it was always closely linked with the struggle against imperialism and its "running dogs." The Qing government, a faithful "running dog" of the imperialists, betrayed national interests to foreign countries even as it carried on national oppression at home. Thus, "expel the Manchus" became the movement's most urgent task and the slogan for mobilizing the people. "Expel the Manchus" entailed gaining national sovereignty and independence, sweeping away the biggest stumbling block from the road to the advancement of national capitalism and setting up a national government that could best meet the requirements for developing capitalism. If these historical conditions are not taken into account, then the issue of "expelling the Manchus" will be evaluated erroneously.

The nationalism movement in modern Chinese history can be roughly divided into two periods of development. Before 1900, because national capitalism was still in its nascent stage, the social foundation of this movement was mainly the peasantry, the active force being those landlords committed to social reform and resistance to foreign aggression, and bourgeois-oriented intellectuals who had split off from the ranks of the feudal ruling class. In the sixty years after the Opium War, China witnessed five national wars, one peasant uprising, the Westernization movement, and unceasing struggles against foreign missionaries. "Subdue the aliens," "Defend the motherland," and "Support the Qing and destroy the foreigners" were political slogans during this stage of the nationalist movement. The old banner, "Overthrow the Qing, restore the Ming," raised by the anti-Manchu landlord class during the late Ming and early Qing dynasties, gradually became obsolete following the aggression against China by capitalist countries. Though to some extent this banner still influenced many secret societies and even endowed the peasant movement of the Taiping Heavenly Kingdom with some characteristics of a large-scale nationalist struggle, this slogan had nothing to do with the several large-scale national wars that took place in modern times. The situation after 1900 was totally different. Although the peasantry remained the principal social basis of the nationalist movement, nascent national capitalism, the national bourgeoisie, and the growing numbers of bourgeois and petty-bourgeois intellectuals began to emerge as the most active force in the movement. After the signing of the Boxer Protocol in 1901, the Qing dynasty exposed itself as a "running dog" of the imperialists and lost all standing with the people. Taking advantage of the people's deep resentment of the Manchu aristocracy, revolutionaries again raised the banner of "expelling the Manchus" and gave it new color and vitality. When it became a rallying call in the three-pronged struggle against imperialism, feudalism, and autocratic monarchy in the early twentieth century, the slogan became totally different in essence from the slogan of "Overthrow the Qing, restore the Ming."

The appearance of the slogan "Expel the Manchus" marked a new highwater mark in the awakening of the Chinese nation. The oath taken in 1814 by members of the Society to Restore China's Prosperity—"Drive out foreign invaders, restore the Middle Kingdom, and establish the republic"—shows that the slogan "Expel the Manchus" was from the very beginning linked with the militant goal to establish a bourgeois republic. But, just as Sun Yat-sent had said, "The persuader urged in real earnest, but the listener did not listen." Since the anti-Manchu propaganda of the Society to Restore China's Prosperity failed to attain any tangible results at home or abroad, at that time it did not represent the main current of the Chinese nationalist movement.

Anti-Manchu propaganda achieved quick and fruitful results only after 1901, when social contradictions in China came to a head and conditions were becoming ripe for revolution. In his "On Settling Old Scores with the Manchus," published in *Guomin bao* (The Chinese National), Zhang Taiyan unequivocally linked the necessity of expelling the Manchus with upholding national independence and fighting for social progress. "Without expelling the Manchus, it will be well-nigh impossible to encourage the intellectuals to assert themselves and the people to fight the enemy and make sacrifices for the motherland, let alone turn China into an independent, free country." In that same year, "On the Yihetuan (Boxer) Movement's Contributions to China," published in *Kaizhi lu* (Journal of New Learning), Zhang took an even more commendable stand and expressed the revolutionary anti-Qing idea that the militant strength of the populace must be mobilized to win national independence and democratic rights. The author extolled the indelible exploits of the Yihetuan Movement to save the nation. He pointed out emphatically: "Though the Boxers, who rose up in arms, failed to destory the foreign invaders, they nevertheless opened up a brilliant chapter in Chinese history. Without the efforts of the Boxers and their allies, how would it be possible to overthrow this entrenched, barbarous regime which has lasted for more than 200 years and eliminate the stubborn and uncivilized Manchus who hold innumerable official posts without doing a stroke of work? How would it be possible for our people to avenge a more than 200-year-old insult and enjoy the beginnings of democratic rights?" Zhang went on to declaim: "The world entered the twentieth century to the crash of thunder. Raising high the arms we bear, we hold up the banner of freedom." These ideas, though not entirely correct, mirrored the new features which appeared in the modern nationalist movement.

Only by taking this specific historical situation into consideration is one able to understand the profound meaning of the Meeting in Commemoration of the 242nd Anniversary of the Doom of China, held in Japan in spring 1902, and discover the actual political appeal in Zhang Taiyan's proclamation, which he wrote in his classical and elegant style. Sun Yat-sen attended this sensational anti-Qing meeting, and he also urged Liu Chengyu to finish his *History of Wars Waged by the Taiping Heavenly Kingdom*. In the preface Sun wrote for this book, he persuaded the readers to realize that the "Taiping Heavenly Kingdom is different from the Ming dynasty founded by Zhu Yuanzhang in that so many Han people have devoted themselves to the cause of restoring their national identity." All this shows that the revolutionary pioneers of the time were unanimous in using the slogan "Expel the

Manchus" to mobilize the people in the anti-Qing revolution. The Meeting in Commemoration of the 242nd Anniversary of the Doom of China was the earliest public gathering to arouse the Chinese people to drive out the Manchus. In early 1903 Ma Junwu and Liu Chengyu delivered anti-Manchu speeches at a New Year's gathering of Chinese students in Tokyo. Then Zhang Taiyan wrote *Refuting Kang Youwei* and *On Revolution*, and Zou Rong published *The Revolutionary Army*. All these served as calls to arms against the Qing dynasty, and they were based on the slogan "Expel the Manchus." The influence they produced both at home and abroad was wide in scope and profound in depth and found a deep response in the hearts of the suffering Chinese people. Leafing through the progressive publications of the first six months of 1903, one finds that "Expel the Manchus" clearly formed the basis of revolutionary opinion. The following remarks indicate the sincerity of this feeling: "By the time of the 1898 Reform Movement, Gang and Rong and their company had usurped political power, and the nation with such an ancient history was pushed to the verge of extinction. Then the Han people finally saw that it would not do to leave their destiny in the hands of these arrogant nonentities and that as people with lofty ideals, they must rely on themselves. It is under such circumstances that the idea of waging revolution for independence and expelling the Manchus came to be known to all."[1] Every way to save the country was tried, and every reformist plan failed, and all lofty, naive hopes were dashed. It was then that the slogan "Expel the Manchus" was raised. Only by thoroughly smashing that arrogant and inferior feudal dynasty could the ancient motherland be saved.

The slogan "Expel the Manchus" was not vaguely tinged with bourgeois nationalism as certain scholars in China and abroad maintain but was consciously brought into the orbit of bourgeois nationalism by lofty-minded patriots of early-twentieth-century China. At the turn of the century, progressive intellectuals began to study the characteristics of this new age and the origin and nature of the domestic and foreign policies of imperialism which dominated the world. They studied in particular the future of the Chinese nation in this new century. They refused to let the imperialist powers come one after another to carve up their motherland, and to allow the Qing government to sell out their motherland bit by bit. They searched, seriously and anxiously, for ways to arouse their compatriots to struggle to save China from subjugation and turn it once again into a strong country, to "set up a national state to be governed under a republican constitution." After much careful study and extensive reading they finally focused on nationalism, that vital link which could bind the nation together spiritually. They proclamied this to the people: "To achieve this lofty goal, the most important thing is to organize the people into a huge army. To do this it is imperative to have a philosophy to bind the army together so that morale will not be sapped in desperate times and victory will be consolidated. After a long search we have finally found a philosophy which best suits the nature of our nation. This philosophy is none other than nationalism."[2]

For all its prematurity and ambiguity, an article carried in the second issue of *Zhejiang chao* (Tides of Zhejiang) faithfully demonstrated these patriots' understanding of bourgeois nationalism and the importance they attached to it. The author wrote that "nationalism, like its progenitors, appeared in the nineteenth century. The Vienna Peace Conference marked the transition from liberalism to nationalism. Every major event or issue in recent history—from the Second French Revolution, the momentous changes that swept across Europe, the wars between Austria and Italy, Germany and Austria, and Austria-Hungary, and between Germany and France, the East European issue, Irish autonomy, the Anglo-Afghan and American-Spanish wars, the Meiji Restoration of Japan, and the Yihetuan Movement of China—was the result of that tremendous force, nationalism. The history of the nineteenth century is indeed the history of the development of nationalism." Whether or not the bourgeois world outlook can provide a scientific interpretation of this development of nationalism, two aspects of it deserve attention: 1) patriots of the early twentieth century regarded the French Revolution as the fountainhead of nationalism; and 2) they saw the Yihetuan Movement as the beginning of nationalism in China.

The patriots of that time answered these two questions in their own words: 1) "Why do we say that nationalism originated with the French Revolution? The answer is that nationalism is incompatible with any form of autocratic political system. Nationalism aims at achieving reunification of a sovereign state and is achieved not by force but by unity of thinking, based on equality of the people instead of one submitting to the other. Can that be possible under an autocratic system?"[3] 2) "Did not the Boxers know that an army hopelessly outnumbered by the enemy has little chance of success and that the weak cannot possibly beat the strong? But the truth is that they were filled with love for their country and were driven beyond forbearance. Therefore, they defied death and fought the enemy, one against eight, hoping eventually to repel the enemy and win national independence. . . . If the Boxers had succeeded in defeating the enemy and had returned in triumph, then idealists would have seized the opportunity to guide them in assuming national responsibilities. They would have recaptured the people's right to freedom. They would have reversed the course of events and carried out the beneficial reforms of republicanism, established popular sovereignty and independence, and swept aside the decadence of autocracy. On this occasion, the Boxers tried to drive out the foreigners. But who knows, if they had succeeded in overthrowing the Manchu government, would not the Boxers have been great advocates of reform?"[4]

In the early years of the twentieth century, the Chinese revolutionary democrats had already learned to use the bourgeois views of freedom and equality in looking at the question of nationalism. Therefore, they could certainly distinguish their nationalism from the Yihetuan's total exclusivism. They categorized the Yihetuan phenomenon as "embryonic" nationalism. When they took over the Yihetuan's anti-imperialist and patriotic traditions, they threw away the dross of feudal backwardness that had been mingled with it. They sharply criticized the slogan "Support the Qing and exterminate the foreigners" and acutely discerned that total exclusivism was naive and untenable.

A backward ideology is usually connected with a backward economy and an advanced ideology with an advanced economy. If the small-scale peasant economy was the economic basis producing exclusivism, bourgeois nationalism is then the product of incipient national capitalism. Lenin said, "The economic basis of these movements is the fact that in order to achieve complete victory for commodity production, the bourgeoisie must capture the home market, must have politically united territories with a population speaking the same language, and all obstacles to the development of that language and to its consolidation in literature must be removed."[5] Here we can see that from the very beginning the bourgeois revolutionaries' advocacy of "expelling the Manchus" was closely linked with "capturing the home market." The Hong Kong Society to Restore China's Prosperity cried out in alarm: "China is now surrounded by powerful foreign countries. Like hungry tigers and ravenous vultures they have been looking covetously at the rich mineral products and abundant products of China. One after another, they have been seizing our territory, either through piecemeal encroachment, or outright annexation. China now faces the real danger of dismemberment." It propagated the goal of "gathering all idealistic Chinese at home and abroad to study ways to enrich and strengthen China, to revitalize it and preserve its national prestige." In expounding the cause of the revolution, Zou Rong's *Gemingjun* (The Revolutionary Army) put the stress on exposing the heavy feudal exploitation and oppression by the Manchu nobility which seriously impeded "the complete victory of commodity production." *Tiantao*, edited by Zhang Taiyan, also carried such messages as "Establish a national state that can satisfy the requirements of modern capitalism to the largest extent." For example, in the article "A Circular to the Han People," the Qing government's prohibition of mining and its heavy taxes were severely taken to task. It pointed out that "the Manchus' policy is to exploit the people as much as possible, and this is what is driving the Han people to wretched poverty." All this explained the economic reason for the contradiction between the Manchus and the Han people, and the salient feature of anti-Manchuism in the early years of the twentieth century. If survivors of the Ming dynasty remembered the emperor and the days with nostalgia, as they advocated "Down with the Qing, restore the Ming," the bourgeois slogan "Revolution must drive out the Manchus" was a clear demand for profits from railway building and mining enterprises, and the hope of establishing a new democratic republic able to protect the home market.

Since the Qin and Han dynasties, the Han people had essentially achieved unity in language, but it did not mean that the nationalist movement led by the bourgeoisie had already assumed the formidable responsibility of completely eliminating "all obstacles to the development of that language and to its consolidation in literature." It was just as Lenin said: "Language is the most important means of human intercourse. Unity and unimpeded development of language are the most important conditions for genuinely free and extensive commerce on a scale commensurate with modern capitalism, for a free and broad grouping of the population in all its various classes and, lastly, for the establishment of a close connection between the market and each and every proprietor, big or little, and between seller and buyer."[6] Although the idealistic revolutionaries who emerged as national heroes at that time were not in the status of capitalist lackeys, the movement to write in the vernacular which they promoted and their research on dialects and other aspects of linguistics directly or indirectly created conditions for the large-scale development of modern capitalism. For instance, the quintessence of Chinese culture which Zhang Taiyan used to "inflame the national spirit" to drive out the Manchus referred primarily to language and its writing system. He opposed Europeanization and attacked the notion that Chinese are always inferior to Westerners and therefore deprecate themselves and say that China is doomed. After comparing the Chinese language with Western languages and after he made a sociological analysis of the meaning of Chinese characters, he agreed to "selectively add" new words to the Chinese language in order to accommodate new things. But he emphasized that the new words must correspond to "the six categories of Chinese characters," and he was against "using these words at random" in order to ensure the purity and healthy development of the Chinese language.[7] He linked the question of language with patriotic national purity and held that the fact that there were Qing writings which were totally different in form and structure from the Chinese was a reason for expelling the Manchus. Although all these views and propositions did not openly advocate capturing the home market, they clearly illustrated the aspirations of unifying and developing the Han language in order to attain national independence and prosperity.

In the past, people too often saw only the negative aspects of the exhortation to expel the Manchus. They focused mainly on its feudal, backward aspect and did little to affirm its advanced, positive side because anti-Manchuism was expressed in old and even obsolete language. Actually, this is quite unfair. Most of the exponents of "expelling the Manchus" were actors in modern plays still dressed in ancient costumes. When he advocated "inflaming the national spirit through the quintessence of Chinese culture," Zhang Taiyan first stated: "Why do we promote the quintessence of Chinese culture? It does not mean that we ask people to believe in Confucius but that we ask them to love the history of the Han people." Language was considered the first of three parts which were included in history in its broadest sense. Later, the National Culture Society repeated and developed this principle. They explained over and over again that advocating national learning did not mean opposition to new learning, but that those who stand for national learning should also acquire new learning. What they did oppose were those comprador scholars who advocated the total abolition of national learning and considered national learning useless after learning a few Western words and learning to fawn on Westerners. They held that genuine new learning and genuine national learning can and do supplement each other and that there is no genuine new learning which cannot go along with the national learning. They invited Zhang Taiyan to lecture on national learning in Tokyo and asked that his first topic be on the origin of the Chinese language.[8] Language most easily arouses people's love for their country and for their native home. Lenin asserted that "love of our language and our country" are among the main ingredients of the sense of national pride.[9] It must be acknowledged that the emphasis which proponents of expelling the Manchus gave to the preservation and development of the Chinese language in the early twentieth century was closely connected with the upsurge of the modern nationalist movement.

In the past, the slogan "Expel the Manchus" was censured for obscuring the goal of the anti-imperialist struggle. Actually, this was far from their intention. From recourse to voluminous sources we can conclude that the movement to expel the Manchus was not only directed against domestic feudal rule and national oppression but also against the Qing government's backstage supporters, who imposed colonial rule upon China. Early in 1903, the relationship between "expel the Manchus" and "opposing imperialism" was stated clearly in the article, "Four Guests Discuss Politics," in the third issue of the *Zhejiang chao*. "All those who follow the white man are slaves; the Manchus follow the white man and we follow the Manchus, so we are the slaves of slaves. Some do not merely want to be slaves but want to be the slaves of slaves. How do we account for this?" At the time, this was the general feeling of idealistic patriots. Unfortunately, however, scholars subsequently overlooked this.

Revolutionary movements have their particular targets of attack during different historical periods. Struggle calls for the study of tactics. Unlike the more rash and careless leaders or participants of sudden spontaneous struggles, the thoughtful revolutionary does not divide his forces to attack two enemies simultaneously. This principle was expounded very clearly by Zhang Taiyan, despite his extreme views on expelling the Manchus. In his "Questions and Answers Concerning the Law of the Revolutionary Army," issued in the summer of 1908, he said: "In the national revolution, the Manchus are our main enemy and the Westerners our secondary enemy. When alien forces interfere in our government, the latter becomes our main enemy. In terms of politics and society, the Westerners bring more disasters upon the Han people than the Manchus. . . . Weighing the pros and the cons, the revolutionary army has only to show some tolerance to prevent the Manchus and the whites from collaborating to eliminate us. The army law takes into account the pros and the cons. It is not entirely a matter of right and wrong."[10] This weighing of the pros and the cons was done out of tactical considerations. Under the historical conditions prevailing when the imperialist powers were busily pitted against each other, and China's domestic contradictions then became more acute, it is understandable that the bourgeois revolutionaries took "Expel the Manchus" instead of "Expel the foreigners" as their militant slogan. In retrospect, we can see that in the first two or three years of the twentieth century, the Chinese people's militant slogan changed from "Support the Qing, exterminate foreigners" to "Overthrow the Qing, eliminate the foreigners"; from "Resist the French" and "Resist the Russians," finally to the revolutionary slogan "Expel the Manchus." This resulted from unconscious or fairly conscious adaptation to objective situations, i.e., changes in the manifestation of major social contradictions. Militant slogans have to be adapted to changing objective situations. Otherwise, the subjective and objective are not linked but are separate, just as an article strays from its main subject. Of the several slogans, the least tactical was "Overthrow the Qing and exterminate the foreigners." Despite all their heroism, victory was impossible if expelling the Qing and eliminating the foreigners were attempted at the same time.

Some scholars make too much of the notion that the slogan "Expel the Manchus" obscured the class alignment, and argue that it seriously hindered the anti-imperialist struggle of the 1911 Revolution. I do not think that this view is in accord with the historical reality and that it is asking too much of the militant slogan "Drive out the Manchus." It is true that the Chinese bourgeois revolutionaries in the early years of the twentieth century were not sufficiently clear on class theory and knew very little about the Marxist theory of class struggle. However, most of their views and writings about expelling the Manchus have at least objectively revealed the class content of this militant slogan. Early in 1906, Sun Yat-sen clearly pointed out: "In its anti-Manchu aspect our struggle to overthrow the Qing government is a national revolution, while in its antimonarchical sense it is a political revolution. The two cannot be achieved separately."[11] The aim of expelling the Manchus was to overthrow the feudal monarchy headed by the Manchu nobility. It can be said that the target of this struggle was clearly defined and concentrated. Later Zhang Taiyan made it even clearer in his "Talk on Expelling the Manchus": "Expelling the Manchus means expelling the imperial family, expelling its officials, and expelling its army. This does not mean expelling all Manchus, only the Manchus who are in the Han government. Today's government has been illegally usurped by the Manchus. This is common knowledge, and I need not be more specific. It is sufficient simply to say, 'Expel the Manchus.'"[12] Here, two points were made clear: First, "expelling the Manchus" meant opposing the Qing government and its troops but not the ordinary Manchus; second, it was a shortened expression for opposing the Qing government, which was common knowledge and did not have to be specifically elaborated. Like Sun Yat-sen, Zhang Taiyan held that the aim of expelling the Manchus was to overthrow the Qing government, including the feudal officials, but it was not anti-Manchu. The Manchu imperial family was China's largest feudal group, and the Qing government was the state apparatus of the feudal landlord class, representing the most backward, most decadent, and most reactionary relations of production. In this sense, expelling the Manchus was an extremely important component of the anti-feudal struggle. Under those historical conditions, without expelling the Manchus there would be no struggle against feudalism, just as without expelling the Manchus there would be no struggle against imperialism. Separating expelling the Manchus from anti-feudalism and putting them in opposition is obviously incorrect.

After the overthrow of the Qing government, the bourgeois revolutionaries were not able to carry the anti-feudal struggle to the end. This was not because the "Expel the Manchus" slogan was wrong, but because of the inherent weakness of the national bourgeoisie. This does not mean that the bourgeois revolution did not wage an anti-feudal struggle or even that it did not demand opposition to feudalism; it only means that it was unable to wage a thorough struggle against feudalism, let alone accomplish the historic task of eliminating feudalism. In all fairness, even after 1912, the national bourgeoisie did not stop its struggle against feudalism. This is borne out in the series of progressive laws and decrees and political, economic, and cultural policies issued by the Nanjing provisional government, reforms initiated by local governments in the hands of revolutionaries in the various provinces, the struggle led by Song Jiaoren to realize parliamentary rule, the vigorous development of national capitalism advocated and promoted by Sun Yat-sen and Huang Xing, the punitive expedition against Yuan Shikai, the war to defend the republic, and the war to safeguard the constitution launched by Sun Yat-sen after 1913. All these were anti-feudal in nature. In the period of the old democratic revolution, when the national bourgeoisie led the modern Chinese nationalist movement, it did not lack the ability to raise new, basic political slogans in keeping with historical developments. The problem was that they never touched the foundations of feudalism, never launched a large-scale reform in the countryside, and did not eliminate the feudal ownership of land. Because of this, they were unable to arouse the broad peasantry and win them over as allies. This resulted in a string of defeats. The inherent weakness of the national bourgeoisie was the cause of its defeat.

An explanation is needed here. If we say that the slogan "Expel the Manchus" was not at fault, it is not meant that at that time all the propaganda devoted to expelling the Manchus was correct. The propaganda was in fact full of feudal Han chauvinism; nationality relations in China were distorted and abusive; insulting language was heaped on ethnic groups other than the Han. Essential analysis and criticism of these erroneous things in the past have been made and will continue to be made in order to restore the original features of history and eliminate remnant Han chauvinism. All these analyses and criticism, however, are not meant to negate the revolutionary spirit and the justness of the slogan "Expel the Manchus." They will, however, show more scientifically the revolutionary spirit and justness of the slogan. While commenting on the slogan, the fact remains (and it is an extremely important one in history) that the Han nationality was the oppressed nationality throughout the Qing dynasty. (This, of course, does not include the handful of upper-class Han people who had been accepted into the ruling clique.) "Expel the Manchus" was a slogan of the movement to resist national oppression and shake off the yoke of feudalism. Zhang Taiyan, who advocated active national revenge, also once clearly stated: "Revenge should be exacted in just resistance, not in indiscriminate, vengeful killing."[13] Although at that time the revolutionaries had used the most abusive language in propagating anti-Manchuism in order to arouse the people's hatred for the Qing empire, the essential content of their ideas, views, and activities were against oppression. In his "Critical Remarks on the National Question," Lenin declared: "Combat all national oppression? Yes, of course!" He also emphasized: "The principle of nationality is historically inevitable in bourgeois society and, taking this society into due account, the Marxist fully recognizes the historical legitimacy of national movements."[14] This was said two years before the outbreak of the 1911 Revolution. This Marxist principle certainly applies in evaluating the slogan "Expel the Manchus."

"Expel the Manchus" now belongs to past history, and people can evaluate it from different angles. One point, at least, is commonly agreed on by most, and that is, the slogan represented the trend of the modern Chinese nationalist movement seventy years ago and the revolutionary forerunners who had fought bravely for the cause of liberation by holding high this slogan will always be respected by future generations, for they had accomplished the most urgent historical task of the time. We are now seriously summing up and drawing lessons from their experiences, but there is no reason to expect them to have accomplished in the first struggle tasks that belong to the second or even the third struggle. China in the early twentieth century faced very powerful imperialist forces, and feudal rule was very deeply entrenched. Every step forward required fierce struggle and exacted a high price. In retrospect, we see that only a decade or so after the slogan "Expel the Manchus" was raised, its aim was accomplished. In little over a decade, our forerunners destroyed a feudal dynasty which had ruled China for 268 years. This was a remarkable victory, which our nation takes pride in. We have every reason to respect and to commemorate these forerunners and what they accomplished.

## Notes

1. "Yizai Man xuesheng! Yizai Han xuesheng!" [Separate Manchu scholars! Separate Chinese scholars!], *Su bao*, 14 March 1903.
2. Jing Chang, "Zhengti jinhua lun" [On the evolution of the form of government], *Jiangsu*, no. 3.
3. "Minzuzhuyi lun" [On nationalism], *Zhejiang chao*, no. 2.
4. "Yihetuan you gong yu Zhongguo shuo" [Speaking about the Boxers' benefit to China], reprinted in Zhang Nan and Wang Renzhi, *Xinhai geming qian shinianjian shilun xuanji* [Selected articles on current events written during the ten-year period preceding the 1911 Revolution], vol. I-1 (Hong Kong, 1962), vol. 1, pp. 58-62.
5. V. Lenin, "The Right of Nations to Self-determination," *Selected Works*, vol. 1, part 2 (Moscow, 1952) p. 318.
6. Ibid., pp. 318-19.
7. Zhang Taiyan, "Yanshuo lu" [Record of speeches], *Min bao*, no. 6.
8. Guoxue jiangxihui faqi ren, "Guoxue jiangxihui xu" [Preface to the National Learning Study Society], *Min bao*, no. 7
9. V. Lenin, "The National Pride of the Great Russians," *Selected Works*, vol. 1, part 2, p. 408.
10. *Min bao*, no. 22.
11. Sun Yat-sen, "Sanmin zhuyi yu Zhongguo de qiantu," *Sun Zhongshan xuanji* [Selected works of Sun Yat-sen], vol. 1, p. 75.
12. *Min bao*, no. 21.
13. "Pai-Man pingyi."
14. V. Lenin, *Selected Works*, vol. 20, pp. 17-18.

# The Shanghai Silk-Reeling Industry During the Period of the 1911 Revolution

## Suzuki Tomoo

In considering the role of national capital in modern China, we should study the silk-reeling as well as the cotton-spinning industries. This paper deals with the silk-reeling industry in Shanghai as a case study of the activities of the national capitalists and the national bourgeoisie in China during the period of the 1911 Revolution. By 1911 the silk-reeling industry in Shanghai had expanded to such an extent that there were 49 factories, 13,738 boilers, 40,000 to 50,000 women workers, and an annual production of 20,000 piculs.[1] The object of this report is to clarify how the capitalists (investors) in this industry, who had such great influence, behaved at the time of the 1911 Revolution. First, I will describe the process through which the modern silk-reeling industry that began in Shanghai grew into a flourishing business.

## The Establishment of Shanghai's Silk-Reeling Industry

Although attempts to establish modern silk filatures in Shanghai began in the 1860s, it was only in the early 1880s that they temporarily bore fruit. Foreign firms (*yanghang*), seeking to conform to the modern European and American silk-weaving industry which was using power-looms, took the initiative in establishing modern silk filatures in Shanghai. From 1878 to 1882, an American concern, Russell and Co. (Qichang yanghang), and British concerns, Jardine, Matheson and Co. (Yihe yanghang) and Iverson and Co. (Gongping yanghang) opened silk filatures in Shanghai.

Chinese comprador-merchants were influential investors in the British factories. Also, in Shanghai in 1881, Huang Zongxian, a silk-merchant from Huzhou, established the first silk filature (Gongheyong sichang) to be operated with national capital and tried to compete with foreign firms.[2]

In 1882, four silk filatures were established in Shanghai, and their vigorous purchasing of cocoons in the cocoon-producing centers in Jiangsu and Zhejiang provoked a nationwide movement against introducing the modern silk-reeling industry. Foreign firms and comprador-merchants in Shanghai launched themselves into the newly emerged raw-silk-producing district, Wuxi, near Shanghai, and opened cocoon wholesalers (*jianhang*) with large-scale pupa-killing and drying facilities. The guild of raw-silk wholesalers (*sihang*) dealing in traditional silk threads went so far as to use force to disrupt the operation of these new wholesalers.[3] Also, in Shanghai, where modern silk filatures were established, the leading merchants dealing in the sale of traditional silk threads united at Silk Industry Hall (Siye huiguan) and started a movement against the establishment of a modern silk-reeling industry. Furthermore, officials specializing in "foreign matters" began to impose severe regulations upon this industry in Shanghai, fearing that as foreign firms were taking the initiative in the establishment of modern silk filatures, the system of appropriating tax revenues in Jiangsu and Zhejiang could be disrupted. In the autumn of 1882, they ordered two silk filatures owned by Iverson and Co. and Russell and Co., registered under their foreign names, to close down. (The factory owned by Jardine, Matheson and Co. was left untouched because it was under the name of a Chinese merchant.) They also made regulations to control the supply of raw silk to the Shanghai silk-reeling industries. Although foreign opposition forced them to withdraw the order closing the Iverson and Co. and Russell and Co. factories—which they conceded to be exceptions—they enforced the policy of controlling cocoons despite resistance from foreign powers. The officials also controlled the establishment of more wholesalers supported by foreign powers by adopting a licensing system for cocoon wholesale operations. (The establishment of the latter in Zhejiang was hampered by the 1883 regulation [*jianjuan zhangcheng*],[4] which required applicants to obtain a joint guarantee from a local raw silk wholesaler.) They imposed a tax (*jianjuan*) on cocoon wholesalers, heavier than the *sijuan* (tariff on raw silk) imposed on raw silk wholesalers. (In those days *sijuan* was 5 yuan per picul of dried cocoons; *jianjuan* was 6.9 yuan in Jiangsu and 12 yuan in Zhejiang.) Such bureaucratic regulations, together with the disruptions caused by the raw silk wholesalers and the resistance of silkworm-growing farms in Huzhou and Jiaxing districts,[5] major traditional raw-silk-producing centers, greatly impeded the development of silk-reeling in Shanghai. Thus for about ten years after the first modern factories began operations, the silk-reeling industry in Shanghai was not able to expand since both foreign and national capital interests had difficulties in securing a supply of cocoons.

## The New Situation after the Sino-Japanese War

The Sino-Japanese War of 1894–95 marked the great turning point for the silk-reeling industry. After the war it was expected that the foreign powers, which had obtained the right to establish industries in China, would launch the full-scale development of the silk-reeling industry at the treaty ports in Jiangsu and Zhejiang. Then, in Shanghai, influential Chinese merchants, such as those engaged in selling raw silk, suddenly showed active interest in opening silk filatures. Qing officials in Jiangsu and Zhejiang, with Zhang Zhidong, Liu Kuiyi, and Liao Shoufeng as the central figures, encouraged the establishment of silk filatures with national capital in order to develop new financial resources and to prevent monopolization by the foreign powers in Shanghai. A rush for establishing such factories broke out.[6]

As the number of silk filatures in Shanghai increased, a brisk trade in cocoons was carried out at cocoon-producing centers like Wuxi and Shaoxing (especially in the districts of Sheng and Xinchang). Business at Wuxi was particularly prosperous, and after the war, owners of silk filatures and compradors in foreign firms and dried-cocoon merchants (*yujianshang*) rushed there from Shanghai and applied to local authorities for permission to open wholesale cocoon enterprises.

In response, the authorities prohibited foreign firms from operating wholesale cocoon businesses at Wuxi. Guarantees were required that each enterprise was operated by a Chinese merchant with Chinese capital. On one hand, they tightened the regulations against cocoon transactions and increased the tax per picul of dried cocoons from 6.9 yuan to 9 yuan, and, on the other, they approved applications made by the Shanghai silk-filature investors, compradors, and dried-cocoon merchants to establish wholesale cocoon firms. This led to a rush for opening wholesale businesses at Wuxi in response to the boom in silk-reeling factories in Shanghai.

In this way, Shanghai became packed with silk filatures based on national capital. Although it was difficult for foreign firms to increase silk filatures on their own by exercising their newly obtained right to establish industries in China, they welcomed the increase of these silk filatures since they wanted to buy raw silk of high quality in large quantities from Jiangsu and Zhejiang. For this reason, the foreign firms did not hinder the merchants in Shanghai when they opened silk filatures; on the contrary, they assisted such merchants by sending foreign engineers or "women instructors" in compliance with the requests made by the factories, and by operating warehouses and insurance companies which were indispensable to the silk filatures based on national capital.

Foreign firms even "helped" by furnishing funds to buy cocoons for domestic silk filatures. Since in those days the cocoon harvest was limited to the spring crop, the Shanghai factories had to buy most of their annual requirement at this time, the end of the fourth lunar month. For this reason, factory managers had to raise a large amount of money to buy cocoons at one time. Few had such funds, and it was hardly expected that the Qing authorities would provide the necessary capital. Thus domestic silk-filature capitalists were virtually dependent upon loans from foreign firms.

In financial terms, therefore, the domestic silk filature capital interests that grew in Shanghai after the Sino-Japanese War were gradually subordinated to foreign powers. In addition, these foreign powers monopolized the export of machine-made threads produced in Shanghai. They forced the domestic silk-filature capitalists in Shanghai and the silk-thread merchants (*sihao*) to sell such threads at extremely unprofitable rates. Therefore, the domestic silk-reeling industry was in effect under the control of foreign powers.[7] Furthermore, as foreign powers placed the cocoon wholesalers at Wuxi and Shaoxing under their control through the provision of cocoon funds, the sericulture farmers were also eventually subordinated to the foreigners through the silk-filature capitalists and cocoon wholesalers. Cocoon wholesalers at Wuxi and Shaoxing obtained the support of the local authorities and gentry for their cocoon-buying activities by paying a large amount of tax and by making substantial donations to the Local Public Welfare Enterprise headed by the gentry. These cocoon wholesalers gradually incorporated local ruffians and gentry who had been their rivals and had obstructed them at the beginning of cocoon transactions. At the beginning of the twentieth century, this gave rise to the formation of a multilayered oppressive system consisting of a combination of foreign powers and local authorities, domestic silk filature capitalists, dried-cocoon merchants, cocoon wholesalers, and local landowners and ruffians, who were against the sericulture farmers in Wuxi and Shaoxing. On the eve of the 1911 Revolution, this newly organized system of oppression headed by the foreign powers was gradually reinforced, as it became deeply rooted in the soil of newly emerging cocoon-producing centers in places such as Jiangyin, Liyang, Yixing, and Jintan in Jiangsu; and Sushan and Zhuji in Zhejiang.

## The Silk-Reeling Capitalists

At the end of the nineteenth century, the domestic silk-filature capitalists in Shanghai had formed a guild, and in 1909 they established Jiang-Zhe sijianye gongsuo, the General Guild of the Jiangsu-Zhejiang Silk-Reeling and Cocoon Industry,[8] in association with the guild of cocoon wholesalers in the two provinces. The directors were the influential members of the Shanghai silk-industry guild, Yang Xinzhi, Shen Lianfang, Huang Jinshen, and Gu Jingzhai. Its office was established in the American concession the following year, 1910.[9] Yang Xinzhi, who represented the Shanghai silk-industry guild, was an influential merchant who sold raw silk from Huzhou. Before the Sino-Japanese War, he had managed Taixingxiang sihao, a silk company, in Shanghai. After the war, he opened a silk filature named Xinchangheng sichang and proved his ability in silk-reeling management as a comprador of Russell and Co. and Yanhengchang sichang. At the same time, he expanded his business and dealt in cocoon transactions. Thus, his Taixingxiang silk company also became influential in the dried-cocoon wholesale business.[10] Similarly, many merchants among the silk-filature capitalists in Shanghai were simultaneously raw-silk dealers and dried-cocoon wholesalers; others were involved with foreign-owned factories and banks and, at the same time, served as compradors. Thus, even at the time of the 1911 Revolution, they were not yet established as independent industrial capitalists.

Under the Qing dynasty, the position of domestic silk-filature capitalists vis-à-vis the foreign powers and the authorities was also weak. Though the industry was supposed to have reached its take-off point at the time of the 1911 Revolution, it was still under the financial control of foreign powers. The silk company (*sihao*), in which these capitalists were integrated,[11] was forced by the foreign firms to carry out disadvantageous commercial procedures. The Qing authorities imposed a severe tax on domestic silk-reeling firms when they purchased cocoons and did not provide them with a single protective measure to help develop exports. The domestic capitalists in Shanghai were subordinated to the foreign powers and the Qing authorities but were, in their turn, second-class partners in the exploitation of silkworm-growing farmers and women workers.

But it was not easy for domestic silk filature interests to subdue these farmers and women workers. Though these capitalists tried to join with foreign powers, Qing officials, and local gentry in using force to purchase raw material, the silkworm-growing farmers and women workers offered strong resistance. The farmers in particular were difficult to handle.[12] They were not only mercenary but were also adept at bargaining and very insolent. If they were forced to sell cocoons unprofitably, they would abuse the buyers, and if the latter were persistent, they would attack them or set fire to their houses.[13] When the price of cocoons was not satisfactory, they arbitrarily reduced the supply. On the eve of the 1911 Revolution, they found new ways of resisting, such as installing drying furnaces or storing dried cocoons obtained by commissioning cocoon factories only to kill and dry cocoons. (In this way they hoarded the goods until better prices could be obtained.)[14] Such resistance made it difficult for silk-filature capitalists in Shanghai to keep buying cocoons at low prices. It was necessary for these capitalists to reduce cocoon prices to such an extent that they could extract a large amount of tax and purchasing fees. But they were unsuccessful because of the farmers' resistance.[15]

By the eve of the 1911 Revolution, domestic silk-filature capitalists were further frustrated by the resistance of female workers. Since silk-filature capitalists in Shanghai applied a strict bonus-penalty system to silk-reeling laborers, they also strongly enforced a procedure for suspending the payment of wages for two or three weeks in order to collect penalties.[16] But by the eve of the 1911 Revolution, silk-reeling workers in Shanghai began to resist this system. These women workers demanded the repayment of suspended wages at the end of December and April. When not satisfied, they even resorted to strikes.[17]

Regardless of what factory they worked in, women silk-reeling workers in Shanghai were united against the plans of silk-filature capitalists to reduce wages and extend working hours. In Shanghai, each year at the end of May or the beginning of June, the Sijianye gongsuo office assessed the wages of women workers (maximum daily wage for silk-reeling workers) for the late summer (June to December) term just before the new cocoon season. In 1911, when this office decided to leave the wages for the late summer term of the year unchanged, the women laborers in the Zhabei district factories and foreign concessions went on strike to demand higher wages. Approximately two thousand women began a general strike in the Jinchang, Changlun, Jinhua, and Xiehe factories since Lü Hesheng, owner of Xiehe factory, was about to implement a policy of reduced wages and increased hours. They tried to achieve their demand for higher wages by exerting pressure on Lü Hesheng and by presenting a written petition to the police authorities who subsequently requested the employer to reconsider the wages of women laborers. Sijianye gongsuo did not immediately comply, but under pressure from press commentary and the closely united workers, they were forced to concede and finally in early July agreed to increase the maximum daily wage for women workers after August 1 by 3.12 percent.[18]

Against such resistance, there were fewer opportunities for silk-filature capitalists in Shanghai to buy cocoons through pressure by using foreign powers, government authorities, and the landed gentry in the cocoon-producing centers. At that time, because of stiff Japanese competition in the American market, the silk industry in Shanghai fell into a steep recession. Under these circumstances, silk-filature capitalists became more united than ever and tried all possible means in order to break the deadlock. Just after the conclusion of the strike, on July 24, these capitalists invited representatives of the Chinese press in Shanghai to the office of the Sijianye gongsuo and to the silk filatures and explained their situation. The aim of the invitation was to win the support of the press, which had criticized the manufacturers during the strike, and to present the capitalists' case to the public at home and abroad. The leaders of the Sijianye gongsuo, such as Yang Xinzhi, Huang Jinshen, and Shen Lianfang, explained that the Shanghai manufacturers were burdened with numerous taxes and payments, including a heavy tax of 80 yuan per picul of raw silk, which their Japanese competitors did not have to pay.

They explained the necessity of the bonus and penalty system for women workers since the raw silk produced at their factories was highly expensive. They also requested the press to give full consideration to the situation of the silk-filature capitalists, arguing that they had to carry out a strict wage policy.[19] In addition to this public relations effort, the silk-filature capitalists began demanding the reduction of tax burdens. When a new Chinese government under Cheng Dequan was formed in Jiangsu after the 1911 Revolution, the Sijianye gongsuo made the provincial assembly agree to reduce these taxes and tariff fees on raw silk and cocoons by 20 percent in order to relieve the silk-manufacturing industry (including the traditional sector) which was hurt as a result of the revolution. In 1912, at the approach of the new cocoon season, Yang Xinzhi persistently requested Governor-general Cheng Dequan to make a special reduction of the tax, claiming that the silk-filature industry, which competed with Japanese manufacturers, deserved special protection that other industries did not need. Thus he convinced the government to agree to reduce the tax, which had been already reduced from 9 yuan to 7.2 yuan per picul of dried cocoons, to 6 yuan.[20] Subsequently, at the end of August 1911, the Sijianye gongsuo decided to reduce the daily wage for women workers, which had previously been agreed upon, from 0.33 yuan to 0.3 yuan, claiming that its situation had been suddenly aggravated by the Wuchang Uprising. And with the approval of the authorities, they unilaterally informed women workers of this reduction.[21] With the arrival of the new cocoon season (the time for wage negotiations) in 1912, the first year of the republic, Sijianye gongsuo decided to reduce the maximum wage for women laborers to 0.32 yuan, which was practically the same rate as before the strike in 1911. Soon, under the influence of Wu Juting and others who belonged to the Chinese Republican Workers Party, about thirty women workers formed a labor union, Shanghai Female Silk Filature Workers Mutual Benevolent Association (Shanghai saosi nügong tongrengonghui). The Sijianye gongsuo immediately requested the municipal office in Zhabei and the British authorities in the international concession to issue a notice prohibiting women workers from joining the union. The union was then virtually dissolved after the issue of the order.[22]

If we consider the activities of the Sijianye gongsuo at the time of the 1911 Revolution, together with the fact that Yang Xinzhi was a supporter of the leading revolutionary, Chen Qimei,[23] we may conclude that the silk-filature capitalists in Shanghai were strongly united in support of their class interests and in trying to cope with the rapid political and economic changes. At the time of the 1911 Revolution, their behavior was peculiar to the bourgeoisie in semi-feudal and semi-colonial China.

[Translated by Okui Yaeko]

## Notes

1. "Sichang duifu Tongrenhui" [Silk-reeling factory owners vs. Tongrenhui, the women workers' union], *Minli bao*, 15 July 1912. "Shina no sanshi-gyō" [Silk-reeling industries in China], Rinji Sangyō Chōsa Kyoku data, vol. 16, p. 54. On the development of silk-reeling industries in Shanghai up to the 1920s, see Soda Saburō, "Chūgoku ni okeru kindai seishi-gyō no tenkai" [The development of the modern silk-reeling industry in China], *Rekishigaku kenkyū*, no. 489.
2. Suzuki Tomoo, "Shanghai kikai seishi-gyō no seiritsu" [The establishment of the modern silk-reeling industries in Shanghai] in *Nakajima Satoshi sensei koki kinen ronbun-shū* [Anthology in honor of Professor Nakajima Satoshi's seventieth birthday], vol. 1, (Tokyo: Kyūko shoin, 1980). Hereafter, views expressed in this section are based on this article, unless stated otherwise.
3. "Xishan jinxin" [Recent news from Wuxi], *Shen bao*, 8 June 1882.
4. "Zheli" [*Lijin* taxes in Zhejiang], in *Zhejiang tongzhi* [Zhejiang gazetteer], *lijin mengao* [Section on *lijin*], p. 56.

5. Hata Korehito, "Shin-matsu Koshū no sanshi-gyō to kiito no yushutsu" [The silk-reeling industry at Huzhou in the late Qing and the export of silk thread] in *Nakajima Satoshi sensei koki kinen ronbun-shū*, vol. 2.

6. Suzuki Tomoo, "Shin-matsu Mushaku ni okeru mayu torihiki no hattatsu to gaikoku shihon" [The development of cocoon transactions and foreign capital interests in Wuxi in the late Qing], *Tōyō gakuhō*, no. 63–1.2. Hereafter, views expressed in this section are based on this article, unless stated otherwise.

7. "Lun Shanghai sichang shibai zhi yuanyou ji qibujiu zhifa jinggao sishang" [Reasons for the failure of Shanghai's silk-reeling factory management, methods of saving it, and a warning to factory managers], *Shi bao*, 12 Jan. 1913.

8. Uehara Shigemi, *Shina sanshi-gyō taikan* [A general view of the silk-reeling industry in China] (Tokyo: Sanshi Dōgyō Kumiai Chūōkai, 1929), p. 397.

9. "Baojie canguan Hufu sichang ji" [Report on the inspection of Shanghai silk-reeling factories by the media], *Minli bao*, 18 Sept. 1911.

10. "Shin-koku sanshi-gyō shisatsu fukumei-sho" [A report on the inspection of silk-reeling industries during the Qing] (Tokyo: Ministry of Agriculture and Trade, Bureau of Agriculture, 1898), p. 44; Tōa Dōbunkai, *Shin-koku shōgyō sōran* [A general view of commerce in China] (Tokyo: Maruzen, 1906), vol. 3, pp. 332–33; Kōnosu Hisashi, *Shina sanshi-gyō no kenkyū* [A study on the silk-reeling industry in China] (Tokyo: Maruyamasha Shosekibu, 1919), p. 279; Matsushita Kenzaburō, *Shina seishi-gyō chōsa fukumeisho* [A report on the investigation of the silk-reeling industry in China] (Tokyo: Ministry of Agriculture and Trade, Bureau of Agriculture, 1921), p. 150.

11. Soda, "Chūgoku ni okeru kindai seishi-gyō no tenkai."

12. Suzuki, "Shin-matsu Mushaku ni okeru mayu torihiki no hattatsu to gaikoku shihon."

13. Takayanagi Toyosaburō, "Shin-koku shin kaikō jō shisatsu hōkokusho" [A report on the inspection of newly opened ports in China] (Nagoya: Nagoya Chamber of Commerce and Industry, 1896), p. 80.

14. "On the production of cocoons in China," *Tsūshō isan*, vol. 38 (1911); Ono Shinobu, "Mushaku no seishi-gyō" [The silk-reeling industry in Wuxi], *Mantetsu chōsa geppō*, vol. 21., no. 10.

15. Suzuki, "Shin-matsu Mushaku ni okeru mayu torihiki no hattatsu to gaikoku shihon."

16. "Baojie canguan Hufu sichang ji," second series, *Minli bao*, 19 Sept. 1911.

17. "Niangzijun tongmeng bagong" [Women workers' strike], *Minli bao*, 21 Jan. 1911.

18. *Minli bao*, 7, 9, 10, 11, 12, 15, and 31 Aug. 1911.

19. "Baojie canguan Hufu sichang ji," *Minli bao*, 18–20 Sept. 1911.

20. "Jianshou jian sijuan shiyu" [Decree on the reduction of cocoon and thread tax], *Minli bao*, 28 May 1912.

21. "Shanghai sichang jianye zonggongsuo qi" [Greetings written between Shanghai silk-reeling factory owners and the union of cocoon merchants], *Minli bao*, 26 Oct. 1911.

22. "Sichang duifu Tongrenhui"; "Saosi nügong Tongrengonghui zhi guibing" [The end of Tongrengonghui, the women silk-reeling factory workers' union], *Shen bao*, 18 July 1912. On the activities of Zhonghua minguo gongdang, see Kojima Yoshio, "Shingai kakumei ki ni okeru kōtō to nōtō" [Workers' and peasants' parties at the time of the 1911 Revolution], *Rekishi hyōron*, no. 256; Li Shiyue, "Xinhai geming qianhou de Zhongguo gongren yundong he Zhongguo minguo gongdang" [Chinese workers' movement and Chinese workers' party around the time of the 1911 Revolution] *Shixue jikan*, no. 1 (1957).

23. Zhongguo renmin zhengzhi xiesheng huiyi quanguo weiyuanhui wenshi ziliao yanjiu weiyuanhui, ed., *Xinhai geming huiyi lu* [Reminiscences of the 1911 Revolution] (Beijing: Zhonghua shuju, 1962), vol. 4, pp. 10–11. Yang Pusheng, a younger

## THE SHANGHAI SILK-REELING INDUSTRY 59

brother of Yang Xinzhi, was deeply involved in the revolutionary movement under the presidency of Chen Qimei. Yang was elected general secretary together with Song Jiaoren, Chen Qimei, Tan Renfeng, and Pan Zuyi at a meeting of the Central China Office of the Chinese League held at Huzhou gongxue in Shanghai in July 1911. Yang Xinzhi was one of the advocates of Huzhou gongxue; see Matsumoto Hidenori, "Chūbu Dōmeikai to Shingai Kakumei" [The Central China Office of the Chinese League and the 1911 Revolution], in *Shingai kakumei no kenkyū* [Studies on the 1911 Revolution], ed. Onogawa Hidemi and Shimade Kenji (Tokyo: Chikuma shobō, 1978) and "Ji Shanghai zhishi yu geming yundong" [A report on the revolutionary movements and Shanghai patriots] in Feng Ziyou, *Geming yishi*, vol. 2. Yang Pusheng was also elected one of eleven staff officers of Hujun dudufu, established in November 1911 (*Minli bao*, 7 Nov. 1911). The brothers Yang Xinzhi and Yang Pusheng seem to have formed a connection with Chen Qimei from 1903 to 1906 when he was working as assistant cashier for Tongkangtai sizhan (owned by Yang Zhongshi, probably a relative of the Yang brothers) before he studied in Japan. Statements by Huang Dezhao quoted in *Minguo renwuzhuan* [Biographical dictionary of the Republic of China], ed. Li Xin and Sun Sibai, (Beijing: Zhonghua shuju, 1978) vol. 1 provide us with much information about Chen Qimei although Huang does not refer to the connection between the Yang brothers and Chen.

# Anti-Imperialism and Popular Resistance in the Revolutionary Thought of Song Jiaoren

Don C. Price

Students of modern Chinese history are well aware of the anxiety and outrage that foreign imperialism evoked among Chinese in the late Qing. In fact, many have tended to view the impulse to resist imperialism as the most powerful motivation behind both the reform and the revolutionary movements. On the other hand, the propaganda of the major revolutionary organization before 1911, the Tongmenghui, adopted a markedly moderate position and tone on the question of anti-imperialist resistance. Anti-imperialism was not one of Sun Yat-sen's Three Principles of the People, nor was it one of the Six Major Principles of the major party organ, the *Min bao*.[1] The revolutionary party, in short, made no effort to mobilize a broad base of support under the banner of anti-imperialism and seems to have avoided defining the revolution as an anti-imperialist revolution. Why? At first glance, we seem to be confronted with a strange discrepancy between the impulse to revolution and the policies articulated by the revolutionaries.

The Soviet scholar A. M. Grigor'ev has considered this problem at some length, concluding that aside from immediate tactical considerations, the revolutionaries' failure to summon the nation to an anti-imperialist struggle is to be explained on a deeper level by their limited perspective on the problem of China's national liberation. Specifically, they understood, first, that direct anti-imperialist resistance would require mobilization of the "popular masses" but were deeply suspicious of them, fearing a repetition of the Boxer fiasco. Thus, to avoid a "people's war," it was necessary to eschew demands for struggle against the foreign aggressors.[2]

And, second, they misunderstood the nature of imperialism, expecting that armed conflict and intervention could be avoided as long as China offered no "barbaric" provocations, whereas the development of China's vast human and natural domestic resources after a revolution would enable it to "squeeze out" the imperialists.[3]

The citations from pre-1911 revolutionary literature which Grigor'ev adduces testify to the patronizing, if not hostile, attitude of some revolutionaries toward the "lower classes," as well as an apparently excessive optimism about the course of China's liberation and the possibility of forestalling imperialist interference. Nevertheless, closer case studies of the early revolutionaries should yield a more concrete understanding of their anti-imperialist thought and perhaps a more accurate picture of their perspective on their tasks and the resources available for accomplishing them. In this investigation of Song Jiaoren's anti-imperialism, his assumptions about the role of the state and his expectations regarding popular mobilization, as well as his views on international relations, emerge as particularly important.

Song was born in 1882 into a modest landlord family in Taoyuan county, northwestern Hunan, at some distance from major political, cultural, and commercial centers. By age 19, he had become a *xiucai*, recovering for his family the gentry status which his grandfather had previously earned.[4] Although his early interests in Chinese geography, institutional history, and military strategy were somewhat unusual among examination candidates, there is little evidence that he was influenced by Kang Youwei's or Yan Fu's ideas of progressive world history, ideas that circulated in the more important cultural centers in Hunan after 1898.

On the other hand, there is some reason to think that Song cherished anti-Manchu sentiments from a rather early age. A cousin with whom Song maintained cordial relations preserved the poetry of a distant ancestor who is said to have distinguished sharply between Han and Manchu.[5] And Song's elder brother, who had close contacts with traditionally anti-Manchu local secret societies, is also reported to have shared this animus.[6] These fragmentary bits of information, hitherto disregarded by students of Song's career, lend substance and background to the reports of Song's schoolmates at the local academy, the Zhangjiang shuyuan, where he studied until 1902. As they recalled, Song had early voiced ambitions of overthrowing the Manchus, and in one account, outlined a rudimentary plan for the conquest of China from within.[7]

While it is impossible to reconstruct the early stages of Song's revolutionary thought with any precision, it is useful to reflect on the skimpy evidence which is available. The curriculum of Song's academy was partially modernized in 1899, in what must have been an echo of the reform movement of 1896–98, itself inspired by the shocks of the Sino-Japanese War and the ensuing scramble for concessions. Song's relations with the master who inaugurated this curriculum were cordial and confidential, and Song's own efforts on behalf of educational reform were probably likewise prompted by the thought that China's salvation demanded an understanding of the modern world, or at least the more useful elements of modern learning.[8] "To manage the affairs of the realm one must begin with [an understanding of] Europe and Asia" was the first line of a couplet which he wrote and hung on the lintel of his study door.[9] It is also worth noting that one of Song's academy schoolmates recalled his planning to "overthrow the autocracy and establish a republic," a goal which may conceivably indicate the presence in Song's early revolutionary thought of a real dissatisfaction with traditional Chinese political institutions, as incompatible with the requirements of political equity.[10] But as we shall see, Song's concern for republicanism in any significant sense remained for several years subordinate to his concern for restoring China's strength and dignity.

In 1903, Song entered a modern school in Wuchang recently established by Zhang Zhidong, the Wenputong zhongxuetang. It was in that year that he met Huang Xing, who enlisted him into his first overt revolutionary activity, the Huaxinghui plot. One of the most popular propaganda tracts which Huang used to recruit comrades was Chen Tianhua's *Meng huitou*, which began its analysis of China's present crisis with a review of foreign aggression against China.[11] Recruitment efforts must have been boosted by the climate among the students in Wuchang and elsewhere at the time. As Grigor'ev noted, some Chinese students in China and Japan volunteered to go to Manchuria to fight Russia in 1903, belying his argument that direct anti-imperialist resistance was assumed to require mobilization of the "popular masses." Among other places, such a proposal was made at a large rally in Wuchang at a time when Song was probably in the city.[12] And it was in this year or the next that Song must have recruited one acquaintance to the revolutionary movement with the argument that otherwise "400,000,000 noble sons of Huang Di might forever be the slaves of an alien race and 90,000 *li* would be delivered up entirely to the foreign powers."[13]

Song's task in the Huaxinghui plot was to recruit members from the military in Wuchang and to raise and command a force in his native prefecture of Changde. The uprising, planned for November 1904, was to consist of a bombing of the ceremonies in celebration of the Empress Dowager's seventieth birthday at the Changsha yamen, followed by the seizure of the city by revolutionary forces composed of soldiers in the local army and secret society members. This uprising was to be followed immediately by secret society uprisings elsewhere in Hunan, under the direction of Huaxinghui members, and was ultimately supported by prearrangement with coordinated revolutionary action in other provinces. In Wuchang, Song was elected secretary of the Science Study Group, a front organization that recruited members from the New Army as well as civilian students and cadets. In his own native area, one account, probably exaggerated, credits Song's elder brother with helping him to secure the support of some 30,000 secret society members in a matter of days.[14]

Before the effectiveness of this strategy could be tested, the authorities learned of the plot and moved swiftly to crush it. The strategy itself is worth considering, however. Upon his election as head of the Huaxinghui, Huang Xing is said to have argued in essence that the revolution must draw on elements that needed little but catalyzation and coordination to rise up. Those elements, in Hunan, were military students, some townspeople, and secret society members. "Just like charged explosives, they wait only for us to light the fuse and they will explode."[15] Other clues to the strategic thinking behind this plot may be found in an article in the radical journal *Youxue yibian*, published in Japan by Huang Xing and others. This article explicitly urged China's otherwise powerless intellectuals to assume responsibility for its salvation by propagandizing the cause of revolution among the lower classes, joining ranks with the secret societies, urban labor, and the military.¹⁶ In fact, Chen Tianhua's revolutionary tracts, which were written in a very self-consciously colloquial sytle, were intended in part for a lower-class audience, and were explicitly addressed to the poor and to secret society members, among others.¹⁷ Thus, Chen's denunciation of the Boxers and Yang Dusheng's criticism of lower-class xenophobia must be viewed in a broader context of radical thought, one in which lower-class support for revolutionary action was seen to be indispensable. As was clearly recognized by Ou Jujia, Chen Tianhua, and Huang Xing, one of the virtues of secret societies, and in effect, a precondition for revolution, was their anti-Manchuism, which predisposed them favorably to revolutionary propaganda and action. Ou, the author of the revolutionary pamphlet *New Guangdong*, also valued the secret societies' disdain for government authority, and Chen Tianhua admired their fighting spirit.¹⁸

Against this background, Song's role in the Huaxinghui plot implied a responsibility for mobilizing and guiding popular forces whose participation would be essential to the undertaking. If this was not to be a "people's war" in the sense of a direct counterattack against modern imperialism, it did not shrink from rallying commoners against an older alien regime of conquest. And if only a portion of the people were to be mobilized at first, it was because that portion seemed to be readily available, and sufficient. Why delay?

As Song fled central China in late 1904, he composed a heroic song, lamenting his country's long and humiliating subjection to the Manchus, and the failure of the insurrectionary plot. Despite his avowed inclination to stay behind and martyr himself, he decided that too few would remain to carry on the cause, and resolved to try again.¹⁹ Presumably the thousands of secret society members who had stood ready to rise up remained dependent on the elite leadership of a small number of men like Song, too valuable to be wasted. The fragmentary evidence on Song's thinking down to this point suggests an unarticulated assumption that China's plight arose from internal weaknesses and misgovernment which must be rectified by the restoration of an elite Han regime before the nation's power could be effectively deployed against foreign aggression.

This kind of thinking can be seen more clearly in Song's writings in Japan. The clarity may reflect not only the greater quantity of evidence for this later period, but also new elements in his thought which emerge then—especially his firsthand observations of Japan at war. But in any case, it is only after Song arrived in Japan that we begin to have an extensive direct record of his evolving ideas as regards both the mobilization of popular forces and resistance to imperialism. Let us begin with the former issue, although it must first be placed in the context of China's international plight.

Song's first long published article, "A History of Aggression by the Han Race," was written in February of 1905 and appeared in June in the first (and only surviving) issue of *Twentieth-Century China*, a journal that he himself organized. The journal as a whole, and Song's article in particular, reflects an overwhelming preoccupation with China's national weakness and the oppression to which it had consequently been exposed—a problem which had troubled reformers and revolutionaries for years. Song was not reluctant to view the problem as one in which armed counterattack would be appropriate, but the question was how to overcome existing weaknesses and rebuild the necessary military strength. The sources of weakness had often been traced to some character defect in the Chinese people, variously identified as a lack of competitiveness, self-reliance, aggressiveness, or popular spirit.[20] Song merely adopted a variant of this idea when he pinpointed the character defect as an atrophy of China's "martial spirit." Disturbed, as others had been, by foreign characterization of the Chinese as a "servile race," he countered with a review of Chinese aggressive expansionism through history, down to the recent past—a proud record by no means inferior to that of other nations. But as was natural, he observed, success bred complacency, and finally debility. Song's hope in this article was that the former martial vigor of the Han race could be revived. An element of popular nationalism can be seen in such statements as "History is an account of a people's advance and a guide for its future development," and such nationalism flowed in part from Song's determination to distinguish the proud legacy of the Han people from that of their Manchu rulers. But whether independently, or as a result of this anti-Manchuism, Song Jiaoren was led to consider the potential of this "divinely intelligent and powerful clan, 450,000,000 strong."[21]

Part of this attention to popular virtues as the source of national strength can be attributed to the example of public patriotism in Japan at war with Russia. Song was impressed by patriotic exhibits in Asakusa park on New Year's day, 1905, and in May (after his article was written) by the massive crowds at a three-day commemoration for the war dead at Yasukuni shrine.[22] Later, in 1906, he was to meditate on such gems of Western wisdom as "The strength of a nation depends on the quality of its people," or declare it no wonder that Japan was so strong, seeing how seriously its people took their responsibilities.[23] By this time, Song's search for national strength had gone far beyond the simple factor of martial spirit, but it is clear that in 1905 he felt China's effective resistance to imperialism would depend on its people, of whom he wanted to make patriots and soldiers somewhat on the Japanese model.[24] In fact, he himself was initially inclined to study military science in Japan and was dissuaded only by the energetic urgings of his friends.[25]

On the other hand, it may be asked whether there is not some connection between the focus on martial spirit shortly after Song arrived in Japan and the hints of an appreciation of that spirit before he left China—in reports of his own youthful military games, interest in military strategy during his academy years, his heroic ambitions, and the example of his beloved elder brother, who won respect among the secret societies for his attainments in swordsmanship.[26] Two of the three books which he mentioned reading in his diary before he reached Tokyo were the late Qing outlaw/knight errant novel *Seven Swords and Thirteen Knights* and the most noted romance of outlawry in Chinese fiction, *The Water Margin*.[27] In fact, Song signed his article on Han aggression with the pseudonym Gongming, the name of one of the *Water Margin* heroes.

It is against this background that we must interpret a shorter article which Song published at the same time, "Twentieth-Century Liangshanpo." Liangshanpo was the lair of the *Water Margin* bandits, whose legacy of heroic outlawry some modern progressives disdained.[28] But Song clearly did not. His article dealt with the "mounted bandits" of Manchuria, communities which, as Song explained it, had taken up arms in self-defense against Russian depredations. Song's view of these bandits was not simplistic, and he pointed out that many of them had allied with either Russian or Japanese forces in Manchuria, or took orders from Manchurian officials. He compared their behavior to that of members of a household subject to brigands' depredations, who rather than uniting for self-protection, sought advantage against their fellows by courting the brigands (i.e., the Japanese or Russians), or sought safety by courting the brigands' accomplices (i.e., the Qing government), or sought the assistance of one group of brigands against another. That the descendants of Han and Tang conquerors should resort to such devices Song found shameless, especially since their territory was ten times larger than the Boers' and their numbers five times those of Mazzini's followers. Lacking any concept of "freedom and independence," however, they could only curry favor with their oppressors.[29]

But these harsh strictures were intended in part to pinpoint a remediable defect in the bandits' consciousness, and in part to qualify Song's sympathetic view of them. He was at pains to point out that they were not Manchus and were constrained by the weakness and incompetence of the government to resort to their outlawry, which he compared to the *Water Margin* bandits' "chivalry" and "heroism." The overall impression he gives is one of misdirected but valuable potential. Song mentioned without comment the fact that local authorities in Manchuria called the mounted bandits "secret societies," thus raising the question whether he himself saw any similarity between them and the secret societies among which the Huaxinghui had recruited in Hunan. A certain amount of banditry was generally recognized to be characteristic of secret societies, and this is why, according to Song's account, the authorities used this term for the mounted bandits. For Song's purposes, the important similarity was probably that both bandits and secret societies included an element of armed defiance of official authority, whereas the significant difference was that the Manchurian bandits had no tradition of "freedom and independence," no anti-Manchu tradition.

By the spring of 1907 Song himself had decided to try to enlist these forces in the revolutionary cause and made a trip to Manchuria for the purpose. By this time he had learned a great deal more about these bandits, their history, resources, and territory, especially a semi-autonomous regime in an area on the Korean border called Jiandao. His sources of information included not only books and periodicals, but reports of Japanese adventurers who were prepared to assist Chinese revolutionaries in mounting an uprising there. Song's decision to go to Manchuria may have involved a number of factors including a new geographical strategy focusing on Beijing, and a split in the Tongmenghui between Song and Huang Xing on the one hand and Sun Yat-sen and his followers on the other.[30] For the purposes of the present inquiry, however, what is important is that Song chose a staging area where promising popular resistance already existed and planned to recruit these bandits as his main forces. The last entry in his diary, which broke off just as the Manchurian venture was getting underway, records Song's buying of two Chinese knight errant novels and a letter which he had composed, addressed to the bandit leaders. The letter is interesting in the approach Song takes, offering as representative of a larger revolutionary movement to supply advisers to the bandits, pointing out the potential force at their disposal if they could unite their bands, and also urging them to remember, and revive, their centuries-old resistance to tyranny, especially that of the Qing:

> When the Qing soldiers entered the pass to take over China, they were even crueler, slaughtering the people and seizing their property. Their harsh rule and oppressive exactions were worse than the Ming's, and the mounted warrior bands were ever more vigorous in resistance to the government, while increasing numbers of northerners followed in joining the mounted warriors for self-protection. The irreconcilable enmity between mounted warriors and government has continued to the present, resulting in your current flourishing condition, which we regard as China's great good fortune. But with the long passage of time, your original purpose has gradually been forgotten, your respective bands have been dispersed and lack coordination, so that it is impossible to accomplish a great undertaking, and you are still, despite your great numbers, no different from outlaws. . . . If we can join together to promote our great righteous cause, it will be a blessing not only for us, but for our 400 million Chinese brethren.[31]

While we must bear in mind that this letter was composed as a complimentary appeal, it nevertheless reflects a strategy based on an appreciation of those elements of the population that had already taken up arms against the authorities. Song's own role he saw as providing leadership, guidance, and direction. The prospects for such a strategy were no doubt enhanced in Song's eyes by other recent examples in which somewhat similar popular forces were mobilized for higher purposes. For example, an article from a Shanghai revolutionary paper reprinted in Song's magazine told how Lu Yafa, an upright man of modest learning, had managed to carve out a small territory and establish a popular, progressive regime there with secret society forces which he had converted from their outlawry.[32] (In fact, the account of Lu's road-building and attraction of merchants, manufacturers, and students may have inspired one of the alternatives which Song envisioned for the development of Jiandao.)[33] Further encouragement came from the Ping-Liu-Li uprising in Jiangxi and Hunan in late 1906. Song surmised, correctly, that this uprising involved not only the secret societies which the Huaxinghui had enlisted two years earlier, but also revolutionary leaders who had worked closely with Song.[34] According to reports which he read in the Japanese press, this uprising was impressive not only for its scope, but also its discipline:

> The revolutionaries are well entrenched, and their undertaking civilized. Since the uprising they have issued currency and announced prohibitions. They have 3000 modern rifles and 4000 muskets. . . . They have occupied Liling, Pingxiang, and Liuyang, and countless people have rallied to them. It is reported that aside from calling for the expulsion of the Manchus and magnates, they have not disturbed scholars, merchants, or commoners and have been particularly energetic in protecting foreigners and churches, so that even in the midst of the disturbance the people are able to carry on their normal occupations unafraid.[35]

Clearly, Song was pleased with this news and saw no insurmountable difficulty in raising a sizable popular force not only without appealing to xenophobia but while actively restraining it. In view of reports that the powers were sending gunboats up the Yangzi, Song surely approved of this restraint. More surely, he attributed the "civilized" quality of this uprising to the leadership of revolutionary intellectuals.

Song's views on mobilizing the martial potential of the people for an uprising seem to have remained fairly consistent from 1904 to 1907, but his views on the leadership required to mobilize it properly underwent an extremely interesting development. He had come to Japan a hero in defeat and continued to be preoccupied with the role of heroes in history, as we can see from his readings in Japan, down to 1906.[36] On the other hand, the strength which he witnessed in Japan was less dependent on heroes than on popular nationalism and civic virtues, cultivated by public exhibits and ceremonies like those at which the emperor himself paid personal homage to his fallen soldiers.[37] At first Song was impressed by the martial spirit of Japan, later by the individual sense of civic responsibility of its lower officials. This shift was also bound up with Song's attention to the qualifications for leadership of China's new progressive elite—the students and exiles in Japan. He (and others) were struck by a real crisis of conscience in the famous incident of late 1905 when the Japanese authorities proclaimed regulations governing the Chinese students. The insult implicit in these regulations was made explicit in newspaper articles on the occasion, one of which described the students as "dissolute and contemptible." There was a terrific uproar in the Chinese student community, thousands boycotting classes and hundreds returning to China in protest. But for some, the bitter words were taken to heart and became the occasion for deeper reflection on the qualification of China's students and exiles to lead in the revival of their country. One close associate of Song's, the immensely popular revolutionary pamphleteer Chen Tianhua, committed suicide, leaving behind a note that it was his purpose to arouse the Chinese from their torpor and moral decline, lest they vindicate their critics and bear the blame for China's ruin. Among the various character defects against which Chen specifically warned was an irresponsible vainglory that might tempt ambitious revolutionaries to borrow the strength of secret societies to achieve quick and dramatic success. Revolution, he urged, should be motivated purely by a sense of unavoidable duty.[38]

Song published Chen's suicide letter in the *Min bao* along with his own colophon, in which he promised that Chen's comrades would not forget his injunctions.[39] The following months were for Song a period of intense self-scrutiny and frustrating Confucian self-cultivation, in the mode of Wang Yangming.[40] Whether Song was particularly stung by Chen's warnings about revolutionary vainglory and secret societies, or simply by his overall attack on selfishness, irresponsibility, and lack of self-control, we cannot say. By the summer of 1906, Song's self-cultivation effort had collapsed in a nervous breakdown. The failure of his quest for heroic moral purity was a serious blow to the thought that virtuous leadership by outstanding men like himself might stimulate the moral regeneration of China. It may also have weakened the force of Chen's injunction against relying heavily on secret societies and bandits. In any event, it was only a few months after abandoning his self-cultivation that Song embarked on his Manchurian venture. Other revolutionary comrades in Manchuria argued strongly against his efforts to enlist the mounted bandits, describing them as a crowd of shiftless, thieving rascals, but Song did not heed them.[41] In fact, his letters to the bandit chiefs suggest that he was irresistibly tempted by the prospect of dramatic results—a speedy approach to Beijing.[42]

How, then, was this venture to contribute to the goals of national strengthening and anti-imperialist resistance? Simply by leading to the establishment of an effective nationalist regime. In abandoning his heroic self-image, Song did not lose sight of the importance of competent national leadership and seems rather to have focused ever more clearly on government policy as the key to mobilizing and using national strength. His "Proclamation of the Revolutionary Forces of Liaodong," written for the Manchurian venture, illustrates this thinking clearly. This appeal for popular support stressed not only the domestic evils of the Qing regime but encroachments and oppression by the foreigners as well. And while no excuse was made for the foreigners, the blame for China's victimization at their hands was assigned to the weakness and incompetence of its government. The Qing had not only ceded territory; they had kept the population of Manchuria sparse and illiterate, and its defenses weak. "In this world," Song wrote, "a country cannot be strong without arms." But the Qing had deliberately rejected anything but mounted archery of the increasingly decrepit banners until too late for modernization to be of any avail.⁴³ The sequence of tasks was clear. Revolution must use such popular forces as were available and appeal among other things to anti-imperialist sentiment, but it must lead these forces to eliminate the root of China's weakness by overthrowing the present government. Then there could be national strengthening under a new government and, finally, successful recovery and defense of national rights. There was as yet no hint that imperialism could be resisted without military strength.

But the ultimately unsuccessful plans for an uprising in Manchuria were followed by another Manchurian episode which began to suggest to Song the extent to which national rights could be protected without recourse to arms. Song's chauvinistic 1905 article about the history of Han aggression had pictured the world as a battleground in which nations rose (at the expense of others) and fell, in a ceaseless struggle. Despite his use of the term "evolution," this picture had little in common with a Darwinian or Spencerian conception of worldwide progress. By late 1906, however, Song's readings in anthropology, psychology, and biology had convinced him that human society around the world was in the midst of a progressive evolutionary process.⁴⁴ Simultaneously, his attention was attracted by Japanese and international socialism, and the 1905 revolution in Russia.⁴⁵ Apparently such contemporary world developments, together with his new evolutionary world view, somewhat modified his Han chauvinism and inspired a belief in social and political progress in general. This in turn might suggest that the ruthlessness of international competition was progressively mitigated by a constant elevation of standards of international relations. This idea, which became an important theme in Tongmenghui propaganda, did not mean that the foreign powers would not try to exploit China, but it suggested that diplomacy and international law could be used to thwart them, compensating for military weakness.⁴⁶ And it was an idea confirmed for Song by the success of his own efforts in 1908.

Song's efforts to start a revolution in Manchuria had been undertaken with the encouragement and support of Japanese who, unbeknownst to him, were interested in claiming the Jiandao area for Korea (and ultimately, Japan). Song learned of this plan only late in 1907, after his efforts to organize an uprising had collapsed, owing to a breach of secrecy. He had first fled to Dalian, and then decided to pursue the prospects of revolutionary organizational activity with Han Dengju, whom he had long known from newspaper accounts to be the chief of Jiandao. When Han told him of recent Japanese reconnaissance activity in Jiandao and their designs on this territory, Song first infiltrated the local Japanese organization, which hoped to promote these aims by falsification of international boundary evidence, and photographed their documents. Then he returned to Tokyo for further investigations into the history and geography of the territory, as well as relevant points in international law.[47] The fruits of this research were embodied in a book entitled *The Jiandao Question*, completed in July 1908, and designed to instruct the Qing government on how Japan's offensive might be countered by diplomacy. In his advice on the handling of this problem, Song pointed out that "only when states reached the point of breaking relations would territory be seized by naked force," and even asserted that "real power lies not in military dominance, but in public opinion."[48] Thus China, armed with an unassailable legal and historical claim to Jiandao, needed only to bring the case before a mediator, or the Hague court, in order to frustrate Japan's plot. Song's newfound faith in the power of international public opinion was vindicated, and thanks in considerable measure to his research, the issue was ultimately settled in China's favor.

At some point over the following two years, Song became aware of the extent to which Japanese "friends" of the Chinese revolution, including some of his associates in the Manchurian venture, had been involved in Japan's efforts to expand its own territory at China's expense.[49] Upon his return to China in early 1911, Song began to write for the Shanghai revolutionary newspaper, the *Minli bao*. A number of his articles dealing with foreign relations identified Japan as the major source of international trouble in East Asia and China's major past and future enemy.[50] Recently, he claimed, Japan had shifted from a policy of military expansion to one of economic aggression, in emulation of various European powers.[51] But unlike the Europeans, whose economic motives could, he felt, be turned to China's advantage, Japan's motives were really political, not economic. Song himself professed to favor foreign loans to boost capital-poor China's economic development, provided the conditions were right and the creditors carefully chosen. The danger with the loans which the Qing government had just negotiated with Japan was that the Japanese government was mobilizing all its economic resources, far beyond their natural demand for outlets, in a deliberate long-range plot to gain unilateral control of China's national finances.[52]

Song's treatment of the Japanese threat fell into a Chinese pattern of analysis, dating back at least to the 1890s, of distinguishing between the economic imperialism and expansionism of nations like Britain and the United States, which Song regarded as a natural part of the "great progressive trends of the world," and the imperialism of conquest, characteristic of Russia and Germany.[53] Although the former was at times held to be more insidious, it was also thought to be more amenable to control. One of Song's major points in his writings on Japan was to show that Japan never really belonged in the camp favoring China's preservation but had always been bent on conquest. Loans were now merely the latest means to that end.[54]

Song's other *bête noir* was Russia, linked with Japan since 1907 in an accord that gave each a free hand in their respective spheres of influence. By early 1911, a Russian ultimatum on the revision of a treaty governing Sino-Russian relations in Mongolia and Xinjiang threatened to precipitate another crisis. Song's recommendation was remarkably similar to the advice he had given three years earlier on Jiandao. He did not fear naked aggression and was confident that China could effectively invoke international law in the court of world opinion to resist Russia's demands. Even the "wily" Russians could not flout accepted principles of international behavior, he argued.[55]

In the case of both Japan and Russia, Song could blame the disadvantageous developments of 1911 on China's lack of a government competent and motivated to protect the national interests. The problem was therefore one of national leadership. Whereas before he blamed the Manchus for China's weakness, he now blamed them for disastrous, criminal incompetence in foreign relations. In either case the government was the root of the evil, and in either case it would have seemed illogical to attempt resistance without first eliminating the existing government.

Despite the effectiveness which he attributed to astute diplomacy, Song did not rule out the danger of foreign military action in China. Like many other revolutionaries, he was sensitive to the threat of foreign intervention in the event of prolonged disorder in China, and the impact of this concern has been noted in an excellent, detailed analysis of his political strategy between 1911 and 1913.[56] On the eve of the revolution, Song particularly stressed this problem in his analysis of the lessons of the Portuguese revolution of 1910. To avoid foreign intervention or internal financial collapse, a revolutionary regime would, he argued, have to seize power quickly, minimize the scope and duration of fighting, rely on the existing army, and preserve the status quo as much as possible, appealing to the powers' interest in stability.[57] Here it is important to note that Song was not only shifting his attention from popular uprisings to insurrection within the regular army. At the same time, he indirectly revealed a new caution about the role which military power itself might play. By 1911, Japan had ceased to be a model for China, in Song's eyes, for he saw Japan's political and social progress blocked by what amounted to a military tyranny, and the roots of this abnormal situation he traced to the role played by military leaders in the Meiji Restoration.[58] Other Chinese revolutionaries may have been less sensitive to this danger, but for Song it was perhaps another reason for hoping that the revolutionary struggle would be a short one, in which progressive civilian political forces could quickly assume power.

As it turned out, Song's wariness of the military was well founded. The main weakness of Song's analysis was his failure, at least before October 1911, to consider that a military leader hostile to the purposes of the revolution might be supported both by a very powerful contingent of the armed forces and by foreign powers, like Britain, which hoped to preserve stability and protect their interests through him—an unbeatable combination. This, of course, is precisely what happened in China, and Song paid for this disappointing lesson with his life.

In any case, Song Jiaoren's revolutionary strategy by 1911 emphasized the role of regular military and elite civilian elements, with a relative deemphasis on secret societies. His propaganda in the *Minli bao* was designed to woo constitutionalists to the cause of revolution, and the predominant role of New Army elements in the overall constellation of forces in Song's Tongmenghui, Central China branch, distinguished it from the earlier Huaxinghui conspiracy. We have seen other shifts in his thinking over those seven years which are important for his view of mass mobilization and resistance to imperialism. National martial spirit and military power seemed to him at first the key to the restoration and survival of China, but by 1911, the military was reduced to a largely internal role, and one which, moreover, he hoped to circumscribe. Deemphasis on the military was linked to an increasingly sophisticated (but not entirely accurate) view of modern international affairs, in which diplomacy and sound policy could maneuver within the balance of powers and compensate for military weakness. On the other hand, Song became more aware of the danger of foreign intervention, unless the revolution were skillfully executed.

This review tells us much more about Song Jiaoren's evolving strategy than it can tell us about the Tongmenghui program or revolutionary thought as a whole, for Song was in some ways unique. Nevertheless, it suggests a different perspective from which to view Tongmenghui propaganda. Direct armed resistance to imperialism was proposed only infrequently, and perhaps quixotically, as by the students in 1903, but it was not automatically assumed to require broad popular mobilization. Moreover, despite the bitter lessons of the Boxer fiasco, it was precisely such potentially rebellious popular elements—secret societies and bandits—that revolutionaries hoped to mobilize for their uprisings. And although they were to be mobilized against the Manchus, rather than the imperialists, anti-imperialist sentiments, among others, could be used to arouse them. Finally, optimism about the peaceful recovery of China's rights did not always stifle the impulse to vindicate its honor by force of arms, and the danger of armed foreign intervention in the event of disorder was a matter of grave concern.

If optimism about the foreigners and unwillingness to mobilize the lower classes cannot fully explain the failure to envision China's revolution as an anti-imperialist people's war, there are other reasons to be sought in the thinking of some early revolutionaries. For one thing, the persistent accusations that the Qing government was to blame for China's plight suggests an equally persistent assumption that a country's people must be mobilized by a state in order to be strong. Here the contrast in Song's view between Japan and Manchuria under the Qing is quite suggestive. The task of establishing an effective nationalist government was thus the first priority, and that, it was widely hoped, could be accomplished most quickly by enlisting popular forces already inclined to revolt. Even so, anti-imperialism was only one of the revolutionaries' goals, and as incorrigible obstacles to the others (social and political progress) as well, the Manchus would have to be overthrown sooner or later, and in such a way as not to imperil the realization of these goals. Finally, if the imperialists were to be attacked directly, they could use the Manchus against the revolution; but it could be hoped that they might observe neutrality while a revolution replaced the Manchus with a government which would embark on the restoration of China. That such considerations were prominent in the thinking of the revolutionaries is not, of course, to say that they were entirely correct.

Anti-imperialism became a major theme in post–May Fourth propaganda, and in the late 1930s it was used to build up revolutionary forces in the countryside. But by then, the balance of foreign interests in China had collapsed in war. More important, the modus vivendi between the two enemies of revolution—foreign imperialism and domestically conservative regimes—was now replaced by fighting, which weakened both of them. Foreign troops clearly bent on conquest now occupied vast stretches of Chinese soil, and revolutionary cadres had spent arduous years learning to organize peasants to struggle against a different enemy —the landlord. Before 1911, in the absence of these three conditions, it is not surprising that thoughts of mobilizing the masses before a successful domestic revolution, in a direct challenge to foreign power, hardly occurred to the revolutionaries.

## Notes

1. [Hu] Hanmin, "*Min bao* zhi liu da zhuyi" [The six major principles of the *Min bao*], *Min bao* 3:1–22 (5 April 1906). Cf. Mary C. Wright, "Introduction," in *China in Revolution* (New Haven: Yale University Press, 1968) ed. Wright, pp. 4–21.

2. A. M. Grigor'ev, *Antiimperialisticheskaya programma kitaiskikh burzhuaznykh revolyusionerov (1905–1985)* [The anti-imperialist program of Chinese bourgeois revolutionaries] (Moscow: Nauka, 1966), pp. 76–79.

3. Ibid., pp. 80–83.

4. For book-length studies of Song's political career, see Wu Xiangxiang, *Song*

*Jiaoren: Zhongguo minzhu xianzheng de xianqu* [Song Jiaoren: forerunner of Chinese democracy and constitution] (Taibei: Wenxing, 1964) and K. S. Liew, *Struggle for Democracy: Sung Chiao-jen and the 1911 Chinese Revolution* (Berkeley and Los Angeles: University of California Press, 1971).

5. Song Jiaoren, *Wo zhi lishi* [My history] (Taoyuan: Sanyu yizhong nongxiao, 1919), entry for 1905/6/20. Song Zhenlü and Huang Zhenya, "Song Jiaoren xiansheng jiashi ji anzang dizhi kao," [Song Jiaoren's family background and burial place], in *Geming wenxian* [Documents on the revolution], ed. Zhongguo Guomindang zhongyang weiyuanhui dangshi shiliao bianzuan weiyuanhui, combined vols. 42, 43 (Taibei: Zheng zhong, 1968), p. 313.

6. "Song xiansheng Shiqing shilüe" [A brief account of Song Shiqing], *Minli bao*, 7 April 1913.

7. Feng Weiying, "Zhuan," in Song, *Wo zhi lishi*, pp. 33–36.

8. Qu Fangmei, "Ku Song xiansheng zhi aisheng" [Lament for Mr. Song], *Minli bao*, 28 April 1913. Luo Runzhang, "Song mu Wan taifuren qizhi shou xu" [On the seventieth birthday of Song's mother Madame Wan], *Minli bao*, 21 April 1913. Huxi aishi ke, "Yufu tongshi," *Geming wenxian* 42, 43:12.

9. "Yufu tongshi," pp. 10–11.

10. Sun Anren, "Xu" [Preface], in Song, *Wo zhi lishi*, p. 21. Even in this account, the context suggests that Song viewed republican government (whatever the term might have meant to him then) primarily as a necessity for national survival.

11. *Meng huitou*, in *Xinhai geming* [The 1911 revolution], ed. Zhongguo shixuehui, vol. 2 (Shanghai: Shanghai Renmin 1956), p. 146.

12. Liew, *Struggle for Democracy*, p. 27.

13. "Yufu tongshi," p. 12.

14. "Song xiansheng Shiqing shilüe."

15. Liu Kuiyi, *Huang Xing zhuanji* [Biography of Huang Xing] (Taibei, 1952), p. 3.

16. "Minzuzhuyi zhi jiaoyu" [Education in nationalism], *Youxue yibian* (10 Sept. 1903), pp. 7–8.

17. *Jingshi zhong* (Tocsin), in *Xinhai geming*, 2: 141–42.

18. Ibid. Also, Ou Jujia, *Xin Guangdong* [New Guangdong], in *Ou Jujia xiansheng zhuan* [Biography of Ou Jujia], ed. Li Shaoling (Taibei, 1960), pp. 76–84.

19. Song, *Wo zhi lishi*, 1904/10/4.

20. Yan Fu and Liang Qichao voiced influential criticisms of the Chinese national character. See also Shangxin ren (Mai Menghua), "Zhongguo minqi zhi keyong" [The usefulness of the Chinese people's spirit], *Qingyi bao* 57 (14 Oct. 1900); and Ou, *Xin Guangdong*, pp. 72–73.

21. Gongming (pseud.), "Hanzu qinlüe shi," *Ershishiji zhi Zhina* [Twentieth century China] 1:31 (1 May 1905).

22. Song, *Wo zhi lishi*, 1905/1/1; 1905/5/3.

23. Ibid., 1906/2/21; 1906/8/16.

24. See "Guomin yu zhanzheng zhi guanxi" [The relation between citizenry and war], *Ershi shiji zhi Zhina* 1:43–50. Song was quite favorably impressed by this article, originally in Japanese, and edited it extensively before publishing it over the pseudonym Shangwu sheng (Admirer of the military). See Song, *Wo zhi lishi*, 1905/3/14.

25. Song, *Wo zhi lishi*, 1905/1/14; 1906/1/16.

26. "Song xiansheng Shiqing shilüe."

27. Song, *Wo zhi lishi*, 1904/11/16; 1904/12/9.

28. E.g., "Zhongguo miewang lun" [The fall of China], in *Guominbao huibian* [*Guominbao* anthology] (photographic reprint, Taibei: Wenhai, 1968). This article was originally published in 1901.

29. Jie (pseud.), "Ershishiji zhi Liangshanpo," [Twentieth-century Liangshanpo] *Ershishiji zhi Zhina* 1:112–15.

30. Matsumoto Hidenori, "Sō Kyōjin to Kantō mondai" [Song Jiaoren and the Jiandao question], prepared for the Conference on the 1911 Revolution in Commem-

oration of the 70th Anniversary, Wuhan, China, Oct. 1981. This is the most detailed examination to date of Song's Manchuria-related activities.

31. Song, *Wo zhi lishi*, 1907/4/9.
32. "Shibai yingxiong Lu Yafa zhuan" [Biography of the failed hero Lu Yafa], *Ershi shiji zhi Zhina* 1:73–76.
33. Song, *Wo zhi lishi*, 1906/9/25.
34. Ibid., 1906/12/12.
35. Ibid., 1907/1/7.
36. His readings on heroes began with the purchase of *Sekai jū ijin* [Ten great men of the world] and *Tōzai nijūshi ketsu* [Twenty-four heroes, East and West], on 3 Feb. 1905, and continued with similar items for more than a year. On 31 Jan. 1906, he bought *Eiyū sūhairon*, a translation of Thomas Carlyle's *On Heroes and Hero Worship*.
37. Song, *Wo zhi lishi*, 1905/1/1; 1905/5/3.
38. "Chen Xingtai xiansheng jueming shu" [Chen Tianhua's suicide note], *Min bao* 2:4.
39. Ibid., p. 9.
40. Song, *Wo zhi lishi*, 1906/1/4 to 1906/6/23 passim.
41. Ning Wu, "Dongbei xinhai geming jianshu" [A brief account of the 1911 Revolution in the Northeast], in *Xinhai geming huiyilu* [Memoirs on the 1911 revolution] ed. Zhongguo renmin zhengzhi xieshang huiyi quanguo weiyuanhui: Wenshi ziliao yanjiu weiyuanhui (Beijing: Zhonghua shuju, 1963) vol. 5, p. 53.
42. Song, *Wo zhi lishi*, 1907/4/9.
43. "Liaodong yijun xiwen" [Proclamation of the Liaodong Righteous Army], *Min bao* 20:105–9 (25 April 1904). For identification of this proclamation as Song's, see Matsumoto, "Sō Kyōjin to Kantō mondai," n. 36.
44. For a fuller discussion of this intellectual development, see Don C. Price, "Sung Chiao-jen, Confucianism and Revolution," *Ch'ing-shih wen-t'i* 3:7:57–61 (Nov. 1977).
45. As can be seen in Song's diary and the following translations by him: Qiangzhai (pseud.), "Yiqianjiubailingwunian Luguo zhi geming" [Russia's 1905 revolution], *Min bao* 3, 7 (5 April and 5 Sept. 1906) and "Wanguo shehuidang dahui lueshi." [A brief history of the Convention of the Socialist International], *Min bao* 5 (26 June 1906).
46. Cf. [Hu] Hanmin, "Paiwai yu guojifa" [Anti-Foreignism and international law], *Min bao* 4, 6–10, 13 (1 May 1906–5 May 1907).
47. Matsumoto, "Sō Kyōjin to Kantō mondai," pp. 40–42, 57.
48. *Jiandao wenti* [The Jiandao question], in *Song Jiaoren ji* [Collected works of Song Jiaoren], ed. Chen Xulu (Beijing: Zhonghua, 1981) 1:133.
49. See author's note to Yufu (Song Jiaoren), "Dongya zuijin ershinian shiju lun" [The past twenty years' situation in East Asia], *Minli bao*, 9 Feb. 1911.
50. Ibid., 8 Feb. 1911.
51. Yufu, "Zhengfu jie Rizhaikuan shizhaoyuan lun" [On the government's taking a ten-million-dollar loan from Japan], *Minli bao*, 30, 31 March 1911.
52. Yufu, "Zailun zhengfu jie Ribenzhai shizhaoyuan" [More on the government's taking a ten-million-dollar loan from Japan], *Minli bao*, 8 April 1911.
53. "Dongya zuijin ershi nian shiju lun," 8 Feb. 1911. Cf. Don C. Price, *Russia and the Roots of the Chinese Revolution* (Cambridge, Mass.: Harvard University Press, 1974), chs. 3, 6.
54. "Zailun zhengfu jie Ribenzhai shizhaoyuan," 7 April 1911.
55. Yufu, "Er bai nian lai zhi E huan pian" [Two hundred years' trouble from Russia], *Minli bao*, 2 March 1911.
56. Kubota Bunji, "Shingai kakumei to Son Bun, Sō Kyōjin—Chūgoku kakumei dōmeikai no kaitai katei" [Sun Yat-Sen and Song Jiaoren in the 1911 Revolution: the disintegration of the Chinese League], *Rekishigaku kenkyū* 408:1–17 (May 1974).
57. Yufu, "Puguo gaige zhi da chenggong" [The great success of the Portuguese reform], *Minli bao*, 25, 28 Sept. 1911.
58. Yufu, "Riben neige gengdie ganyan" [Thoughts on the changes in the Japanese cabinet], *Minli bao*, 5 Sept. 1911.

# Foreign Influences

# *Daitō Gappō Ron* and the Chinese Response: An Inquiry into Chinese Attitudes Toward Early Japanese Pan-Asianism

## Min Tu-ki

It is understood that some Japanese Pan-Asianists aided Chinese revolutionaries in many ways. Still under discussion, however, is how to characterize the nature of Japanese Pan-Asianism and Chinese responses toward it. This paper is an attempt to study the Chinese reformists' case.

Though not a prominent figure, Tarui Tōkichi (1850–1922) is quite often mentioned in discussions of the formative period of Japanese pan-Asianism.[1] The son of a timber merchant, Tarui was born in Nara prefecture. He went to Tokyo to study with a Kokugaku (national learning) master, Inoue Yorikuni, who believed in the distinctiveness and superiority of Japan. Later, in 1875, he worked for the newspaper *Hyōron Shinbun,* which was known for its radical views on the civil rights of ex-samurai. His unsuccessful memorial to the government and his relationship with those who criticized the ruling oligarchy for their alleged distortion of the ideals of the Meiji Restoration made him side with the advocates of the Korean expedition (Seikan ron).[2] In 1878, he sailed in search of an uninhabited island to use as a base for his cherished dream of a Korean expedition. In his autobiography he wrote: "When I first heard of the uninhabited island . . . I felt it was lucky for Japan. I had been of the opinion that unless our country first of all conquered Korea, the way for development could not be paved. If we were fortunate enough to discover an uninhabited island, we would be able to make it a center for our operations [for conquest], to which we could draw comrades, one after another, to build a base for the Korean expedition."[3] But the dream failed.

In 1882, he formed a party, Tōyō Shakaitō (Eastern Socialist Party), which was almost immediately banned by the government. After his party was suppressed, he met Tōyama Mitsuru (1855–1944), the representative of the chauvinistic Asianist group, Gen'yōsha who exerted great influence on Tarui's perception of pan-Asianism.[4]

In 1885, Tarui took part in the Osaka Incident, which aimed to force reforms in Korea. The plotters of the incident thought that this adventure would eventually lead to war with Korea and reforms in both Korea and Japan. For Tarui, this adventure was a step toward materialization of his 1878 dream of a Korean expedition. The only difference was that this time he intended to force reforms in Korea instead of conquering it. The participants in the adventure sought an opportunity in Korea to carry through reforms that had been obstructed in Japan. Success in Korea would have political consequences in Japan, for if the Tokyo government failed to implement programs elsewhere in Asia, it would have lost its claim to leadership in Asia. Ōi Kentarō, the principal plotter of the incident, thus worked out the theories of aid and tutelage for Asia,[5] and like most pan-Asianists during this period, he took for granted that Japan was the sole leader of Asia.

Tarui, who had been in and out of jail for anti-government activities since the banning of the Tōyō Shakaitō, was elected to the Diet in 1892. In 1893, while holding office, he published *Daitō gappō ron* under the pen name of Morimoto Tōkichi. Originally, the first draft was written in Japanese in 1885, and in 1891 it was published serially in classical Chinese, in *Jiyū byōdō keirin* magazine.[6] Two years later, an enlarged version with four additional chapters was published as a book.

The tract called for the formation of a Japanese-Korean confederation, and in an attempt to show neutrality and fairness, Tarui chose the name Daitō (Great East). The idea of a confederation must have been inspired by Western examples.[7] In arguing in favor of the confederation, Tarui made the following points: (1) as proved by the examples of Germany and Great Britain, confederation is the ideal way to create a powerful country; (2) the Yellow race must unite to safeguard itself against the colonialism of the White race, and specifically, the danger of the Russian advance in East Asia; (3) Japan is a "wonderland" of distinctive virtues of imperial rule and "perfect constitutionalism," virtues which are instrumental in making Japan the leader of the anti-White front; (4) since the virtue of harmony (*shinwa*) is the cardinal feature of Eastern morality, it is natural that this virtue be adopted as the moral principle of the confederation; and 5) the confederation is to be formed on equal terms, despite differences in historical background and national strength. He reasoned that Korea was weak and poor while Japan was a strong and wealthy nation, and once united it would be obligatory for Japan to protect the Korean peninsula against the threat of Russia. Tarui also advised China to form an alliance with the Daitō confederation for the purpose of safeguarding the Yellow race against White (i.e., Russian) expansionism. The alliance would eventually develop into a greater confederation of all Asian nations. Furthermore, the Sino-Daitō alliance would help Qing China tighten domestic control and prepare it for the anticipated insurrection of the Han people.

The historical assessment of *Daitō gappō ron* could not be summarized more aptly than Tarui's own statement in 1910 when Japan was on the verge of proclaiming the annexation of Korea, not a confederation on equal terms. The preface to the second printing of *Daitō gappō ron* reads: "I am proud of my foresight in seeing that Japan's relations with Korea have developed into the governing of Korea by a Japanese resident-general, and I believe that even if Korea is annexed by Japan, Korea will not be allowed to participate in the governing process as long as it needs subsidies."[8] A modern scholar has argued that this statement reflected retrogression from Tarui's original idea of confederation on equal terms or from its democratic nature, because of the persistent contradictions between his thought and behavior.[9] If we consider, however, his personal background when he wrote the tract and the contradictions in his perception of the weakness and poverty of Korea, it is more natural to see his 1910 statement as a logical result. Tarui's seemingly sophisticated argument for a confederation based on Japanese superiority resulted from his understanding of the historical and contemporary situation and his ideas on the Eastern morality of harmony and the Western idea of equal sovereignty. It was nothing more than a rhetorical mask for his idea of Asian expansionism.[10]

*Daitō gappō ron* might serve as an excuse for pro-Japanese activities by some Korean collaborationists who worked for the Japanese annexation of Korea and for their own personal benefit.[11] It is, however, puzzling that contemporary Chinese reformers responded to the tract with keen interest around the time of the 1898 Reform Movement. In 1897 Kang Youwei set up the Great Unity Translation and Publishing Company (Dadong yishuju) in Shanghai.[12] This company published many books on the subject of reform, including *E Da Bide bianfaji* (Record of Institutional Reforms of Peter the Great of Russia), *Huangchao Jingshiwen xinbian* (New Collection of Essays on Statecraft in the Qing), *Riben shumuji* (Bibliography of Japanese Books), and *Nanhai xiansheng qishangshuji* (Record of the Seven Memorials Submitted by Kang Youwei). Among the company's books listed in the *Bibliography of Japanese Books,* which was published in 1897, appeared the title of *Dadong hebang xinyi* (New Exposition of the Great East Confederation) (hereafter *Xinyi*), with the price tag of 25 cents (2 jiao and 5 *fen*). The *Record of the Seven Memorials Submitted by Kang Youwei*, published in 1898, also listed *Xinyi*. It is almost certain that the Great Unity Translation and Publishing Company had published a title similar to Tarui's before 1898. I have so far failed to locate the Great Unity Translation Company's edition of *Xinyi*. But I have found a copy published by the Shanghai Translation and Publishing Bureau (Shanghai yishuju) with Morimoto Tōkichi as the author and Chen Gaodi of Dongwan as the collator. Chen Gaodi was a disciple of Kang Youwei and worked for the Great Unity Translation and Publishing Company.[13] The Shanghai Translation and Publishing Bureau is probably the successor to the Great Unity Translation and Publishing Company following Liang Qichao's appointment as head of the governmental Shanghai Translation and Publishing Bureau on July 3 of 1898.[14] We know that when Kang Youwei was appointed director of the Guanbaoju (Office of the Government Gazette), he tried to have the *Shiwu bao* (China Progress) reorganized as a government publication.

In view of the fact that Tarui devoted the last chapter of his tract to the advocacy of an alliance between China and the Daitō confederation, which meant Japan in reality, it is possible to surmise that Kang Youwei and his followers responded positively to the idea of alliance, since he published the reprint of Tarui's tract at the time when the idea of a Chinese alliance with Japan and Great Britain was prevalent among some high officials and the reformists. It should be noted, however, that *Xinyi* was not just a reprint of Tarui's original text but was a slightly modified version by the collator. *Xinyi's* size is smaller than the original, and most of the pages have the same number of characters per page. But the collator made some modifications by removing Japanese symbols for reading classical Chinese and deleted several lines or pages, replacing them with handwritten characters. The inserted characters or lines equal the number of deleted characters or lines. There are 31 deletions, in addition to cases where Zhongguo (China) replaced references to Shinkoku (Qing) or Kando (land of the Hans). Tarui's description of the domestic situation of Qing China, which emphasized possible conflict between the Manchus and the Han people, was replaced by some passages that were quite irrelevant to the original text, such as equality of sexes (*Gappō ron,* p. 73; *Xinyi,* p. 37b) or the necessity of worshiping Confucius (*Gappō ron,* p. 139; *Xinyi,* p. 69a). With regard to Sino-Korean relations, Tarui advised Koreans not to be grateful for Ming China's military aid against Toyotomi Hideyoshi's invading army since the Chinese intervened only for their own interests. His assertion that China treated Korea like a slave (*Gappō ron,* pp. 99–101) was completely deleted, and no lines were inserted. The passages that warned Koreans of China's inability to help Korea were replaced by passages explaining the benevolent relationship between Korea and China throughout thousands of years of history (*Gappō ron,* p. 81; *Xinyi,* p. 41a). Like many Japanese pan-Asianists, Tarui declared proudly that Japan was a paradise in the world (*sekai no rakudo*) (*Gappō ron,* p. 87) and a nation with an unbroken line of emperors (*Gappō ron,* pp. 88, 92), as well as a nation with the distinctive history of never having been subjugated by any foreign country (*Gappō ron,* pp. 78, 88). These passages were either deleted or changed to a more modest style (*Xinyi,* pp. 39b, 44b). Also, the expression which may have alluded to Japan's role as "big brother" to China was toned down (*Gappō ron,* pp. 67, 74; *Xinyi,* pp. 34a, 37b). It is interesting to note that whereas Tarui advised the Chinese to change but did not elaborate, the collator inserted specific proposals, such as reform of the examination system and governmental organization, establishment of a parliamentary system, and development of a modern school system (*Gappō ron*, p. 44; *Xinyi*, p. 22b).

One of the underlying themes of Tarui's tract was to protect the Yellow race from the aggression of the White race. The confederation of Japan and Korea was proposed as a first step to form a united front of the Yellow race in the future. The alliance of the Daitō confederation, actually Japan, with China was regarded as the second step toward the Asian confederation, which might include Burma, Vietnam, the Malay peninsula, India, and Siam (*Gappō ron*, pp. 141–42; *Xinyi*, p. 70a). Japanese leadership or guidance,[15] expressed in *Gappō ron*, appears in *Xinyi* without any changes. It clearly shows that the publisher and collator did not object to the basic idea of Asian solidarity, a confederation of Japan and Korea, and the proposed alliance between China and the Daitō confederation. The other point on which the publisher and the collator of *Xinyi* agreed with Tarui was the imminent danger of Russian aggression in East Asia. A whole chapter was exclusively devoted to the description of the present situation of Russia, whereas the other White nations were rather lightly treated in a chapter on the international situation. In the chapter "Russian Situation" (*Gappō ron*, pp. 56–66; *Xinyi*, pp. 28b–33b), Tarui introduced the 15-point will of Peter the Great as evidence of Russian intentions to invade East Asia. Not only did the collator of *Xinyi* make no change in this chapter, but he actually added material in another chapter by inserting passages on the Russian menace to Korea, modifying the original which criticized the inability of Qing China to protect Korea from the Western powers (*Gappō ron*, p. 81; *Xinyi*, p. 41a).

What, then, made Kang and his followers sympathetic to the ideas brought forth in *Daitō gappō ron*? One may attribute it, first of all, to the prevalent opinion in favor of a Chinese alliance with Japan and Great Britain at a time when the international situation became increasingly threatening to China's survival. After the Triple Intervention of 1895, Chinese diplomacy relied mainly on Russia to counteract the Japanese move toward China. The German occupation of Jiaozhou (November 14, 1897) and the ensuing Russian demand for the Liaodong peninsula (March

3, 1898), however, changed the diplomatic climate significantly. Influential governors-general like Zhang Zhidong and Liu Kunyi, as well as many other reformers, then turned to Great Britain to block the Russian and German moves and to earn time to reform China. A Chinese alliance with Japan was also sought to complement the alliance with Great Britain. Japan, too, promoted an alliance with China on the basis of the common menace from Russia: the Japanese Army General Staff was eager to stir up pro-Japanese sentiment among the reformers and such influential high officials as Zhang Zhidong and Liu Kunyi; the Japanese minister to Peking offered friendly terms to invite Chinese students to Japan.[16] Not only because of these Japanese moves, but because of their aspirations to learn from Japan in order to make China strong, the reformers tended to advocate alliance with Japan. The most conspicuous advocacy of an alliance with Japan and Great Britain to resist Russia was made by Kang Youwei. Shocked by the German occupation of Jiaozhou and influenced partially by the Japanese General Staff's agents, Kang had his friends, the censors Yang Shenxiu and Chen Qizhang, memorialize the throne in favor of allying with Japan and Great Britain. In the meantime, he himself tried to persuade Grand Secretary Weng Tonghe,[17] and he distributed among officials pamphlets he had written expounding the inevitability of an alliance with Great Britain and Japan.[18] To cite other examples of the advocacy of the alliance in early 1898, Zhang Binglin sent a letter to Li Hongzhang in the hope of convincing Li to ally with Japan and even proposed that the government cede Weihaiwei to Japan in order to counteract German activities in Shandong.[19] A radical reformer in Hunan, Tang Caichang, published an article urging an alliance with Japan and Great Britain.[20] Wen Ti, a Manchu censor who had kept close contact with Kang Youwei at the time, submitted a memorial to deter the Russian scheme and advocated allying with Japan and Great Britain.[21]

Even before the German and Russian thrust, there were some reformers who advocated a Chinese alliance with Great Britain or Japan because of the traditional fear of Russia's southward advance. For example, in 1896 and 1897 Chen Chi, a longtime protégé of Weng Tonghe, proposed a triple alliance of China, Great Britain, and Japan.[22] As an editorial columnist for *Shiwu bao*, Zhang

Binglin wrote an article in early 1897 favoring the Sino-Japanese alliance on the grounds that both countries belong to the same Yellow race, and therefore must unite to protect Asia from Russian aggression.[23] It was in this milieu that *Daitō gappō ron* was reprinted. Obviously, the reprinted (lithographed) version of *Daitō gappō ron*, i.e., *Dadong hebang xinyi*, aimed at widely disseminating the idea of allying with Japan. *Xinyi* must have gone into a second printing within a year.[24]

Although the Chinese reformers advocated allying with Japan and Great Britain, they were also well aware that an alliance with powerful countries would pose the danger that China might become another India, Burma, Persia, or the Ryūkyūs.[25] However, in order to deter the imminent danger from Germany and Russia and prevent the possible partition of China, they preferred to ally with the "latent" danger rather than the serious one.[26] As mentioned previously, the secondary aim of the reformers' idea of alliance was to earn time for reforms in China. The reform plan emphasized the adoption of a constitutional system for China as proposed in the modification inserted in *Xinyi*. Tarui's boasting of the Japanese constitutional system[27] appealed to the reformers who favored constitutionalism, and conceivably they must have felt an affinity with Tarui's conviction.

The Chinese response to *Daitō gappō ron* was not confined only to the ideal of diplomatic alliance and reform. The practical proposals submitted by some reformers in September 1898, just prior to the coup d'etat by the conservatives, were also indebted to Tarui's proposal for confederation and alliance. Hong Ruchong, a minor official in the central government, memorialized that the Qing court should take measures to ally or federate (*lianhe* or *lianbang*) with Japan to withstand Russia.[28] He emphasized in the memorial that Japan was a nation of the same stock (*zulei*), and Chinese talent should be combined with Japan's new system (*xinfa*). Liang Qichao pointed to Hong's *lianhe* or *lianbang* as the idea of confederation (*hebang*, *gappō* in Japanese), and it was regarded as one of the proposals which gave the conservatives ammunition against the anti-reform movement.[29] Hong enumerated many advantages of confederation for saving nations, citing the examples of Norway and Sweden, Hungary and Austria, Italy, and Germany.[30]

Again in his memorial of September 20, Yang Shenxiu urged the confederation (*hebang*) of China with three friendly nations, i.e., Great Britain, Japan, and the United States. Yang endorsed Hong's proposal of *hebang* as the most important. He also pointed to Timothy Richard as another advocate of Chinese confederation of the three nations. Even though the "word *hebang* did not sound good," Yang maintained that it was worthy of pursuing.[31] On the very next day, Song Bolu, another spokesman for the reformist cause, submitted a memorial pleading for the idea of *hebang* as proposed by Timothy Richard. Song was more explicit than Yang Shenxiu in expounding Richard's idea: China, Japan, the United States, and Great Britain should nominate one hundred delegates each to form a council of four hundred members to deal with military affairs, the tax system, diplomacy, and military strengthening (in China).[32] Song did not seem to care for the consequences of Richard's proposal which in reality intended to put China under the three powers' joint control. To support the idea of *hebang*, he asserted mistakenly that Great Britain and Russia were already at war. According to Song, the only way to deter Russian annexation of China through the war was for a league (confederation) with the three powers.

Despite discrepancies in their interpretations of *hebang*, it seems that the concept pervaded the minds of many reformers. In his *Chronological Autobiography,* Kang Youwei mentioned *hebang* in describing the fate of the Hundred Days' Reform: "The Japanese Minister to Beijing and I had tried to organize large meetings [in Beijing and provincial capitals] to support the *hebang* of the two countries."[33]

What was the origin of the idea of *hebang*? Presumably it came from *Xinyi*. One is reminded that Hong Ruchong cited in his memorial many examples of confederation that were found in *Xinyi*. It is also possible that the 1893 edition of *Daitō gappō ron* by itself influenced the reformer because of its classical Chinese style and because it was sold at the branches of a Japanese store, Rakuzendo, in Shanghai, Tianjin, Hankou, Chongqing, and Fuzhou, which were managed by another Japanese pan-Asianist, Arao Sei, and Kishida Ginko.[34] An editorial appeared in the *Guowen bao* in 1898 that reads, "Since the Chinese were not able to understand the idea of *Taidong hebang*[35] (which demonstrated how to resist Russia), war between China and Japan became inevitable."[36] Judging from this editorial, it seems that the ideal of *Daitō gappō* was known to some Chinese even before the Sino-Japanese War, i.e., before *Xinyi* was published. This may be true, but it is more conceivable that the idea described in *Daitō gappō ron* was spread mainly through *Dadong hebang xinyi*.

We may infer the salient features of early Japanese pan-Asianism from Tarui: (1) it was based upon their belief in the superiority of the Japanese imperial polity; (2) the idea of Asian solidarity stemmed from racial sentiment that was aroused by the aggression of the White race; (3) Japanese leadership or guidance was taken for granted to resist the White menace, which specifically meant the Russian menace; (4) the idea of liberty or constitutionalism served as the rationale for Japanese expansion. Above all, the ideas served as the rationale to harmonize conflicts between the interests of Japan and other Asian nations. *Daitō gappō ron* may be considered a typical example of early Japanese pan-Asianism, and Tarui's concept of the Daitō confederation revealed the expansionist character of his pan-Asianism. Although Chinese acceptance of the proposals for a Korean-Japanese confederation and a Sino-Japanese (Daitō) alliance cannot be explained in terms of the logical context of *Daitō gappō ron* itself, it can be better understood as a Chinese response to the imminent danger of partition. The Chinese reformers accepted Tarui's pan-Asianism, not because they acknowledged traditional Japanese superiority, but because they saw it as a way of saving China in a critical international situation. For them, imminent danger had to be dealt with immediately by making use of the "latent" danger. Yet, the situation was too pressing for them to recognize seriously the nature of that danger.

## Notes

1. For a brief biography of Tarui, see foreword by Okamoto Kansuke in *Daitō gappō ron* (Tokyo: Morimoto Tōkichi, 1893) and Tadashi Suzuki, "Profile of an Asian-Minded Man, Tarui Tōkichi," *Developing Economies* VI-1 (March 1968). Also see Marius Jansen, "Japanese Views of China During the Meiji Period" in *Approaches to Modern Chinese History,* ed. Albert Feuerwerker (Berkeley and Los Angeles: University of California Press, 1967).

2. As Suzuki pointed out in his paper, Tarui's opposition to the government was not maintained consistently. Suzuki argued that such a contradiction between thought and behavior never left Tarui all his life (Suzuki, "Profile," p. 82).
3. Ibid.
4. Ibid., p. 83.
5. Marius Jansen, *The Japanese and Sun Yat-sen* (Stanford: Stanford University Press, 1970), p. 41.
6. Suzuki, "Profile," p. 83.
7. *Daitō gappō ron*, pp. 114, 130.
8. Suzuki, "Profile," p. 84.
9. Ibid., pp. 82, 98.
10. Tarui proposed *equal* terms of confederation between a strong and wealthy country (Japan), and a weak and poor country (Korea). Did Tarui really think that the equal terms might work as he proposed? If Tarui wished his idea to remain a utopian ideal, one may call it just a product of imagination. But Tarui wrote the tract as a sort of political guide for Japanese Pan-Asianism. Hence his 1910 statement. It seems unnecessary to discuss whether Tarui's idea retrogressed or not.
11. Kageyama Masaharu, "Translator's Note," in *Gendai yaku Daitō gappō ron* [*Daitō gappō ron* in modern Japanese], tr. Kageyama Masaharu (Tokyo: Daitōjuku Shuppanbu, 1963).
12. Jung-pang Lo, *K'ang Yu-wei: A Biography and a Symposium* (Tucson: University of Arizona Press, 1967), p. 153. Ding Wenjiang, *Liang Renjiang xiansheng nianpu changpian chugao* [Draft of a chronological biography of Liang Qichao] (Taibei: Shijie shuju, 1959), p. 39. Richard Howard stated that it is not clear when in 1897 the Great Unity Translation and Publishing Company was founded (Lo, *K'ang Yu-wei*, p. 307). One source gives the date vaguely as autumn or winter in the year of Dingyou (23rd year of Guangxu, i.e., 1897) (Ding, *Chugao*, p. 39). However, the first issue of *Zhixin bao* (China Reformer), a magazine edited by loyal followers of Kang Youwei in Macao, which was published as early as 22 February 1897, identifies Great Unity Translation and Publishing Company at Nicheng bridge, Damalu, Shanghai, as a sales agency for *Zhixin bao*.
13. Jiang Guilin, "Kang Nanhai xiansheng dizi kaolüe" [A brief study on the disciples of Kang Youwei], *Dalu zazhi*, vol. 61, no. 3, p. 35.
14. Liang Renjiang dashiji stated: in the year of Wuxu (1898), the emperor ordered the reorganization of the Great Unity Translation and Publishing Company into the Official Bureau of Publication (Guanshuju). Before reorganizing it, the coup d'etat took place (Ding, *Chugao*, p. 39). According to the official record, Zongli yamen memorialized to the throne on 28 June 1898, after reviewing the two respective proposals of Yang Shenxiu and Li Shengduo who urged the establishment of an agency for translation and publishing. Zongli yamen urged in the memorial to establish an official bureau for translation and publishing (yishuguanju) by reorganizing the one run by Liang Qichao in Shanghai (i.e., the Great Unity Translation and Publishing Company). Zongli yamen also proposed that the reorganized bureau should be administered by the *guandu shangban* system (official supervision and merchant management). The proposal was approved by the emperor (Guojia danganju, *Wuxu bianfa dangan shiliao*, pp. 448–50). On July 3, Liang Qichao was appointed director of the [Official Bureau of] Translation and Publishing (Jian et al., eds., *Wuxu bianfa* [Reform movement of 1898] (Shanghai: Shanghai renmin chubanshe, 1956), II, p. 29).

The Great Unity Translation and Publishing Company probably published the first printing of *Daitō gappō ron,* and the second printing must have been brought out after July 3 by Shanghai Translation and Publishing Bureau, which might have been hastily renamed by the staff of the Great Unity Translation and Publishing Company before the official authorization. In the author's note added to the 1910 second printing of *Daitō gappō ron,* Tarui made the following remark: "A Chinese named Liang Qichao *translated* my book and published it in Shanghai with his own preface.

It is said that 100,000 copies were sold" (Sakurai Yoshiyuki, "Tōyō shakaitō Tarui Tōkichi to *Daitō gappō ron*" [Tarui Tōkichi of Tōyō Shakaitō and *Daitō gappō ron*] in *Meiji to Chōsen* [Meiji and Korea] (Tokyo: Sakurai Yoshiyuki sensei kanreki kinenkai, 1964), p. 24. Although Tarui's information was inaccurate, one can sense from this statement that Liang Qichao might have been involved in publishing *Daitō gappō ron*. There is one question unsolved, however, in regard to *Xinyi*'s publication. The first printing of *Daitō gappō ron* was made in the 26th year of Meiji (1893), and the preface by Kagetsu Jokyō was dated *kishi* (*guisi* in Chinese) of Meiji, i.e., 26th year of Meiji. Curiously, however, the date of Kagetsu's preface in *Xinyi* was changed intentionally to the 30th year of Meiji, i.e., 1897. All the dates in Kagetsu's preface were also changed: 18th year of Meiji to 21st year of Meiji; 23rd year of Meiji to 25th year; 25th year of Meiji to 28th year. No systematic method was followed in changing the dating, and the intention of the *Xinyi* collator is unknown.

15. Jansen, *The Japanese and Sun Yat-sen*, pp. 41, 43.

16. On the arguments to ally with Great Britain and Japan, see Wang Shuhuai, *Wairen yu wuxu bianfa* [Foreigners and the 1898 Reform Movement] (Taibei: Institute of Modern History, Academia Sinica, 1965), p. 123ff.

17. Jian, *Wuxu bianfa*, IV, p. 141.

18. Ibid., pp. 138–39.

19. Tang Zhijun, *Zhang Taiyan xiansheng nianpu changpian* [Draft of a chronological biography of Zhang Binglin] (Beijing: Zhonghua shuju, 1979) pp. 61–63.

20. *Xiang bao leizuan* [Classified writings from *Xiang bao*] (1902; reprint ed., Taibei: Datong shuju, 1969), pp. 197–204.

21. Jian, *Wuxu bianfa*, I, p. 521; IV, pp. 141–42. *Wanguo gongbao*, vol. X, no. 5 (July 1898).

22. Chen Chi, *Yongshu neipian* [A book of ordinary argument] (1898 edition; Wenhai reprint ed., Taibei: Tailien guofeng chubanshe, 1970), pp. 144–46. (Chen Chi, "Ying-Ri yiyuelü bao Zhongguo shuo" [Great Britain and Japan must take measures to protect China], *Zhixin bao* [China reformer], no. 23, 6th month of the 23rd year of Guangzu)).

23. *Shiwu bao*, no. 18 (1st month of the 23rd year of Guangxu).

24. *Xinyi* was probably published before July 1898 and once after. See note 14.

25. For example, Tang Caichang, "Lun Zhongguo yi yu Ying-Ri lianmeng" [China must ally itself promptly with Great Britain and Japan], in *Xiang bao leizuan*, pp. 19–204.

26. Tang Caichang, "Liuyang bagong Tang Caichang gongni michou daji yuken daizouzhe" [Tang Caichang's essay in the form of a memorial to propose a secret plan for the nation], *Xiang bao leizuan*, p. 643.

27. *Daitō gappō ron*, p. 114. *Xinyi*, p. 56b.

28. Jian, *Wuxu bianfa*, II, pp. 362–66.

29. Liang Qichao, *Wuxu Zhengbianji* [Record of the coup d'etat of 1898] (reprint ed., Taibei: Wenhai chubanshe, 1964), p. 151. Guojia danganju (National Bureau of Archives), ed., *Wuxu bianfa dangan shiliao* [Archival sources on the 1898 Reform Movement] (Beijing: Zhonghua shuju, 1958), p. 470.

30. Jian, *Wuxu bianfa*, II, pp. 362–66.

31. Guojia danganju, *Wuxu bianfa dangan ziliao*, p. 15.

32. Ibid., p. 170.

33. Jian, *Wuxu bianfa*, p. 144.

34. Kageyama, "Translator's Note," in Kageyama, *Gendai yaku*, p. 1; and Jansen, *The Japanese and Sun Yat-sen*, pp. 50–51.

35. Da (大) and Tai (泰) are interchangeable in Chinese.

36. Shen Zuxian et al., *Rongan diziji* (1913; reprint ed., Taibei: Wenxing shudian, 1962). The cause of the Great East Confederation is also mentioned in an article in *Guowen bao* (27th day of the 6th month of the 24th year of Guangxu). See *Wuxu bianfa*, III, p. 391.

# The Influence of Kemuyama Sentarō's *Modern Anarchism* on Chinese Revolutionary Movements

Nakamura Tetsuo

For the first twenty years or so of the twentieth century, anarchism served a radical function as a revolutionary idea preceding Marxism, not only in Japan but also in China. However, as far as the period before the 1911 Revolution is concerned, roles played by people who devoted themselves solely to anarchism were not particularly remarkable. As pointed out by R. A. Scalapino, it was during the period of the May Fourth Movement that the more fervent anarchists appeared, and their activities played an important part in the history of the Chinese revolution.[1] Before the 1911 Revolution, people paid more attention to Narodnism (*mincui zhuyi*) as expounded by Tan Bian[2] than to the pure anarchism (*wuzhengfu zhuyi*) referred to by Scalapino. More precisely, the various activities of the Junguomin Jiaoyuhui (Militant People's Educational Association), Huaxinghui (Society for China's Revival), and Guangfuhui (Restoration Society) began to reflect the fact that intellectuals holding radical anti-Manchu principles accepted the strategies advocated by Narodnaya Volya (Minyidang), one of the Russian Narodniki groups. In this context, we would like to summarize the contents of *Modern Anarchism* (Kinsei Museifushugi) by Kemuyama Sentarō and to evaluate the influence of this book, which gave the Chinese intellectuals an opportunity to learn about Narodnaya Volya.

From the beginning of the twentieth century, elementary books on socialism and publications expressing the political ideas of Kōtoku Shūsui became available in Japan. Kemuyama's book was written from a somewhat academic viewpoint and was not meant to be pro-anarchist propaganda. The book, published on 28 April 1902, by the publishing department of the Tokyo Specialist School (later re-named Waseda University) consisted of two main parts. The first presented a systematic description of the Russian Narodniki. The second, entitled "Anarchism in European Countries and the U.S.A.," introduced the leading anarchists and described the spread of anarchism to various countries. It was undoubtedly the first part that attracted the radical intellectuals, who may well have considered it to be a detailed study of the subject. Its contents were as follows:

I. Nihilism in Russia
   1. Origin of Nihilism
   2. Inspirers of Nihilism
      a. Alexandr Herzen
      b. Nicholas Chernyshevsky
      c. Michael Bakunin
   3. History of Revolutionary Movements
      a. Period of Revolutionary Literature (from the beginning of the nineteenth century until 1863)
      b. Period of Agitational Tours
         i) 1863 to 1870
         ii) 1870 to 1877
      c. Period of Terrorist Assassinations
         i) 1878 to autumn 1879
         ii) Autumn 1879 to March 1881
         iii) March 1881 to May 1883
   4. Various Nihilist Organizational Facilities
      a. Secret Printing Press
      b. Arsenal for Making Explosives
      c. Counterfeiting Section (to forge official documents)
      d. Voluntary Red Cross (to help party members)
      e. Secret Agents
   5. Movements of Nihilist Refugees in Western Europe
   6. Notable Women Nihilists
      a. Vera Zasulich
      b. Sofia Perovskaya
      c. Gesya Gelfman
   7. Imprisonment and Siberian Exile of State Criminals

According to Onogawa Hidemi, the first Chinese translation of a Japanese work on the Russian Narodniks appeared in 1903.[3] Both Tan and Onogawa believe that *Ziyouxue* (Freedom's Blood) by Jin Yi (published in 1904) is the first systematic study in Chinese of the Russian Narodniks. According to Kemuyama, Jin Yi (pseudonym for Jin Tianhe) studied the history of the Russian Narodniks (see ad columns in *Jingzhong ribao*, 20 May 1904). *Wuzhengfu zhuyi* (Anarchism), translated by Zhang Ji, appeared in 1903. Tan ascribes the original of this translation to an Italian, but it is not known how Zhang Ji came to know the original. I suggest that the first systematic study of the Narodniks was Kemuyama's book, published as *Eluosi xuwudang* (The Russian Nihilist Party) in Chinese in the summer of 1903. I regret, however, that the only historical proof of the existence of this translation is advertisements in the *Hubei xueshengjie* (nos. 5 and 6, 27 May and 24 July 1903). The first advertisement announced the completion of the translation of *Eluosi xuwudang*. The second announced its publication. None of the advertisements gave the name of the translator, and only a group called Da Hunan-bei tongmenghui (The Greater Hunan-Hubei League) was given as the publisher. However, in the case of *Qing-E zhi Jianglai* (The Future of the Qing Dynasty and Russia) and *Han Xue* (Sinology), translated by Sanhuyimin (pseudonym for Yang Yulin) and published by the same group, the prices are given. Furthermore, it was written that these two books were sold at large bookshops in Shanghai. From this we can assume that *Eluosi xuwudang* was not intended for open sale but was considered a secret publication. The advertisement for the book stated that it was meant to serve as a guide book for members of revolutionary parties: "This book was written by a Japanese, Kemuyama Sentarō, and deals with the cause of the Russian Nihilists in full detail. It was translated into Chinese to serve as a reference book for every revolutionary organization in China."

Although it is difficult to determine exactly who the translator was, however, we can at least assume that it undertaken by a group in which Yang Yulin figured prominently, first because of his previously mentioned translations for the Greater Hunan-Hubei League and, secondly, Yang's *Xin Hunan* (New Hunan) contains expressions that are exactly the same as those used by

Kemuyama. For example, Yang wrote that the history of the Narodniks developed from the "Period of Revolutionary Literature" to the "Period of Agitational Tours," and then to the "Period of Terrorist Assassinations." In addition, according to Feng Ziyou's *Geming yishi* (vol. II, p. 125), Yang studied at Waseda University after working for Kōbun Shoin, another reason for attributing the translation to Yang.

By the time the translation was published, two excellent political critiques of the Narodniks had already appeared. An essay entitled "Eren yaoqiu lixian zhi tiexue zhuyi" (The Blood and Iron Demand of the Russian People for a Constitution) was published serially in the science column of the *Zhejiang chao* (Nos. 4 and 5, 16 May and 15 June 1903). The contents are as follows:

1. Introduction
2. The Beginning of Russian Constitutionalism
3. The Organization of the Minyidang
4. Assassination Attempts
5. The Memorial of the Minyidang
6. The Rise of Counter-revolution
7. The Continuous Resistance of the Minyidang
8. The Administrative Reforms of the Russian Government
9. Conclusion

Comparison of this essay and Kemuyama's book reveals the dependence of the former on the latter, as in translating Narodnaya Volya as Minyidang. The Minyidang's party program contained in Chapter 3 corresponds with pages 133–34 in Kemuyama's book. The memorial is the summarized translation from the passages on pages 170–80. The organizing policy of Minyidang is also an abridged translation of pages 187–88 in Kemuyama's book. This might give the impression that the essay was merely adapted from Kemuyama's book. It is actually an excellent political essay containing original ideas. The author simply collected material from Kemuyama's book. Although the title suggests that the article glorifies the Narodniks, this is not the case. The conclusion compares conditions in Russia and China. While in Russia, problems of religion and land interests had great significance, China had a racial problem. The author regretted that China has not solved its racial problems while Russia was united as a large nation and was trying to play an active part in world affairs.

The article "Xuwudang" in *Su bao* (19 June 1903) gave this problem deeper consideration:

> The purpose of Nihilists in Russia is for nothing but the reformation of state and society, which are still not perfected, and the promotion of people's happiness. They are not worried about the feelings among different races or the loss of their nation. If the so-called Nihilists were ruled by a foreign race and divided by the great powers and experienced the same situation as we do now in China, how would their means and policies change? I would not say anything but merely resort to a single policy in confronting the government.

What does this "single policy" refer to? In order to understand it, it is necessary to refer to the activities of the Militant People's Educational Association, which were taking place at this time.

The author of "The Blood and Iron Demand of the Russian People for a Constitution" was Dong Hongyi (Xunshi), whose pen name was Dutou. He studied at Waseda with Wang Jiaju (Weiren), the editor of *Zhejiang chao*. Both were members of the Qingnianhui (Youth Association) and also influential members of the Militant People's Educational Association. Zhang Ji, who also studied at Waseda, was active in the terrorist group together with Yang Yulin.

In the light of present research, it can be concluded that Kemuyama's *Modern Anarchism* was translated mainly by the Youth Association, whose major figures were former Waseda students and had a great influence upon the activities of the Militant People's Educational Association.

In dealing with the activities of the Militant People's Educational Association, some problems require careful attention. As pointed out by Jin Chongji and Hu Shengwu, the association had originally been an open organization called Ju-E yiyongdui (Resist Russia Military Corps) or Xuesheng Jun (Student Army).[4] Subsequently, it was dissolved and reorganized into a secret society. On 5 July 1903, radical students proposed to change the slogan of the association. I have named this group the Later-Period Militant People's Educational Association.[5] The following is a summary of the activities of the organization from the time when the Resist Russia Military Corps was formed (April 1903) until its reorganization as the Later-Period Militant People's Educational Association.

| | |
|---|---|
| 29 April | A mass meeting of Chinese students resolves to form the Resist Russia Military Corps. |
| 2 May | The organization's formal name, Student Army, and its regulations established. |
| 9 May | The Japanese government prohibits the use of the above name. Wang Jiaju and other students reprimanded at Kanda police station. |
| 10 May | Executive meeting held at Foreign Student Hall votes to change the name. |
| 11 May | The organization renamed Militant People's Educational Association at mass meeting of foreign students. It decided that its aims would be to foster a militant spirit and to promote patriotism. Members of the Youth Association form an overwhelming majority of the leadership. |
| 14 May | Niu Yongjian leaves Yokohama for a meeting with Yuan Shikai. Meanwhile Wang Jingfang informs Cai Jun, the Chinese minister to Japan, that the renamed organization is actually a revolutionary group using resistance to Russia as a pretext. |
| 25 May | The *Su bao* article "The Establishment of the Tokyo Militant People's Educational Association" includes the statement that patriotic activity is based upon "the principle of blood and iron." |
| 27 May | The Qing dynasty starts to take oppressive measures. |
| 5 June | *Su bao* reports the news about the Qing dynasty's oppressive measures. |
| 5 July | Reception in honor of Niu Yongjian and others. Qin Yuliu and fifteen other students present a written proposal for reorganization and suggest changing the present slogan into promoting *minzu zhuyi* (nationalism). More than one hundred people leave the party. Wang Jingfang takes the initiative. |

27 July      Wang Jiaju and Dong Hongyi summoned to the Metropolitan Police Office and forced to submit documents pledging the dissolution of the Educational Association.

After the July 5 proposal to reorganize, articles on the Educational Association disappeared from the various student magazines. According to the Japanese Ministry of Foreign Affairs records, desertions occurred rapidly after July 5. July 13 is regarded as the day when the Educational Association was virtually disbanded. Although there were many who actually did leave, the disbandment simply camouflaged the secret, reorganized party from repression by the Chinese and Japanese governments.

Feng Ziyou is the only source for the organizational system of the secret party. Summing up his records, this secret organization consisted of three organs: propaganda, assassinations, and uprisings (*Geming yishi*, vol. 1, p. 182). Members who were assigned the duty of organizing uprisings in their respective provinces on returning to China were called *shixing yuan* (operations officers). Huang Xing from Hunan, Cheng Jiacheng from Anhui, and Gong Baoquan from Zhejiang were influential *shixing yuan* (*Geming yishi*, vol. 2, p. 87). The designation *shixing yuan* deserves attention since it corresponds closely with Kemuyama's translation of executive members in Narodnaya Volya. However, did the three organs for propaganda, assassinations, and uprisings actually exist?

As a representative of the propaganda division, we can name Chen Tianhua, the author of the famous revolutionary pamphlets *Menghuitou* (Sudden Realization) and *Jingshizhong* (Alarm to Rouse the Age). Moreover, Yang Yulin, who translated Kemuyama's work, wrote *Xin Hunan*, "Minzu zhuyi zhi jiaoyu" (Nationalist Education), and other important tracts.

Huang Xing represented the uprisings division and was the central figure in the establishment of the Huaxinghui, whose inaugural meeting was held on 15 February 1904. They cooperated with the Gelaohui, a secret society consisting of lower-class elements, and established organs to appeal to noncommissioned officers and soldiers in the Wuchang New Army.

The representatives of the assassination division were Yang Yulin and Su Peng. According to Su's reminiscences, "Liuxi yiyu," the first arsenal for producing bombs was set up in Yokohama in the summer of 1903. But because of a bubonic plague in Yokohama, the police inspected the arsenal in November, and two terrorists were reported to have suffered serious eye injuries because of the explosion caused by the hasty disposal of chemicals. In the summer of 1904, Yang Yulin established a secret group in Tianjin and infiltrated Beijing. His plan to assassinate the empress dowager, Cixi, and the Guangxu Emperor failed, and he returned to Shanghai (Cai Yuanpei, "Yang Dusheng xiansheng taohai ji"). The other terrorists who had joined this attempt were Su Peng, Zhou Laisu, Zhang Ji, and He Haiqiao (*Geming yishi*, vol. 2, p. 126). Cai Yuanpei and Tao Chengzhang, who was a member of the Zhejiang Student Association set up by Wang Jiaju in Tokyo, joined this assassination squad. They then established the Guangfuhui in Shanghai in October 1904. Members of the Restoration Society were strongly inclined toward assassination tactics.

How to carry on practical revolutionary activities was a pressing question for the radical intellectuals who formed these secret organizations. In this respect, the experiences of Narodnaya Volya, which had been introduced by Kemuyama, were extremely helpful. This is especially true of the "Preparatory Tasks Assigned to the Party," prepared by Narodnaya Volya in 1883 (pp. 187–88 in Kemuyama's translation), consisting of the following six tasks:

1. To form a secret party and arm its members; to set up headquarters maintaining close contact with local bodies.
2. Local bodies are to, first, infiltrate into the bureaucracy and military; second, extend their influence among peasants; third, establish close contacts with local liberals and constitutionalists; fourth, prepare equipment necessary for the revolution; and fifth, members are to become thoroughly acquainted with local geographical and political situations.
3. To increase their influence by winning over urban laborers.
4. To elaborate a plan to win over military people, especially the commissioned officers.
5. To be assiduous in studies and in acquiring technical skills, and to gain influence among the youth and students.
6. To increase sympathy for Russian revolutionary operations

in foreign countries and to win their cooperation, direct or indirect.

This document influenced not only the period of the Militant People's Educational Association, but the activities of the subsequently established Tongmenghui (Chinese League).

With the establishment of the Society for China's Revival and the Restoration Society, the historical mission of the Military People's Educational Association was accomplished. However, if one central organ was to command the allegiance of all local bodies throughout China, then these two societies would have to cooperate with Sun Yat-sen's Society to Restore China's Prosperity. Regarding this as a top priority, Huang Xing and other leaders of of the Society for China's Revival approached Sun Yat-sen and established the Chinese League in 1905. But the Restoration Society took a negative attitude toward the League. Since the Restoration Society assumed an active role in setting up the terrorist group, it apparently preferred a central revolution, namely the assassination attempt in Beijing.

The importance of the collaboration between Huang Xing and Sun Yat-sen was that it led to revising the Educational Association's policy which, under the influence of Narodnaya Volya, had stressed the primacy of achieving civil rights (political freedom). In other words, the Zhejiang group paid little attention to economic issues, such as the problem of landlordism. This was made clear in the critical article "The Blood and Iron Demand of the Russian People for a Constitution." In order to solve the land problem, Sun Yat-sen formulated the proposal known as "equalization of land rights." Thus, it can be said that the establishment of the Chinese League had great political significance. However, the Restoration Society did not agree with equalization of land rights, which became part of Sun's Three Principles of the People. Nor did the young Hunan and Hubei intellectuals who had joined the revolutionary movement under the influence of Huaxinghui agree with this policy. They formed the Gongjinhui (Progressive Association) and began acting independently. While from a doctrinal standpoint it is possible to criticize such an attitude, actually the problem of political freedom constituted the first step toward undermining the absolute monarchy, just as in the case of Russia.

In China, after 1906 the political struggle focused on the constitutional government. This being the case, Narodnaya Volya's policy of giving priority to civil rights continued to have a practical meaning in China even after the formation of the Chinese League. Although it had some internal troubles, the League as a whole seems to have followed the course paved by the Narodniks which had been introduced by Kemuyama. This reminds us of Lenin's reference to Sun Yat-sen as a Chinese Narodnik. It also reminds us of the fact that Zhou Shuren (Lu Xun) concentrated on the first stage, the "Period of Revolutionary Literature," and not the stage of "Terrorist Assassinations." It may well be said that Qiu Jin was a Chinese Sofia Perovskaya. While retaining their particular characteristics, the revolutionary intellectuals of this period seem to have behaved as Chinese Narodniks.

[Translated by Okui Yaeko]

## Notes

1. R. A. Scalapino and G. T. Yu, *The Chinese Anarchist Movement* (1961; reprint ed., Westport, Conn.: Greenwood Press, 1980).
2. Tan Bian, "Eguo mincui zhuyi dui Tongmenghui de yingxiang" [The influence of Russian Narodnism on the Tongmenghui], *Lishi Yanjiu*, vol. 1, 1959.
3. Onogawa Hidemi, "Ryū Shibai to museifushugi" [Liu Shipei and anarchism], *Tōhō Gakuhō* (Kyoto), no. 36.
4. Jin Chongji and Hu Shengwu, "Junguomin jiaoyuhui shishi kaobian" [The history of the Militant People's Educational Association], *Guangming ribao*, 21 Nov. 1962.
5. Nakamura Tetsuo, "Kyoga Giyūtai to Gunkokumin Kyōikukai" [The Resist Russia Military Corps and Militant People's Educational Association], *Tōyō Gakuhō*, vol. 54, no. 1; idem., "Kakōkai to Kōfukukai no seiritsu katei" [The process of the establishment of Huaxinghui and Guangfuhui], *Shirin*, vol. 55, no. 2.

# A Lesson from the Meiji Restoration: Revolution or Constitutional Monarchy?

## A Study of Chinese Students in Japan During the Late Qing Period

### Yung Ying-yue

It is an established fact that many Japan-trained Chinese students contributed, either directly or indirectly, to the 1911 Revolution. It is safe to assume that these students had in some way been influenced by Japan, and since the students shared the view that modern Japan began with the Meiji Restoration, the question arises whether the Meiji Restoration set a working model for modernizing China.

The purpose of this paper is to examine the Chinese students' assessment of the Meiji Restoration. What did they view as the character and significance of the Restoration? Did their views regarding the Restoration play a decisive role in determining their support for revolution or advocacy of constitutional monarchy? Moreover, did their views influence the behavioral patterns and activities of the Chinese students in Japan? If they did, in what ways?

The Chinese students in Japan can be roughly divided according to their life-styles into the following three categories: (1) activists engaged mainly in political movements; (2) bookworms who concentrated on school work; and (3) loafers or delinquents. The student activists should be subdivided into the revolutionary and reformist camps, and they are the object of this study. However, it should be noted that in times of crisis, or when a crisis was perceived by students in general, the second and third groups could become followers of the activists.[1]

Immediately upon their arrival in Japan, the student activists directed their attention to the Meiji Restoration. After the Hundred Days' Reform fiasco in 1898, many of the reformers fled to Japan and formed the vocal group among the students. They cited the example of the Meiji Restoration to warn the Qing government. In their opinion, the Japanese lost their three-century-old faith in the Tokugawa government because of its resistance to implement a thorough reform, leading to the decay of its political power.[2] On the other hand, the Meiji era was a period of revolution. The movement to revere the emperor and overthrow the shogunate, and the abolition of the feudal domains (*han*) and the establishment of prefectures were revolutionary undertakings. The continuity of the Japanese imperial line was a monument to its ability to bend with the tide of revolution and to accept changes. Thus the student activists warned that if the Qing dynasty were to oppose the revolution, it would bring about its own end.[3]

The reformers—both exiles and students—were interested in how, during the Meiji Restoration, Western values, namely competition, destruction, progress, rights, etc., were important in the development of Japan into a modern state. For example, Liang Qichao felt that the *sonnō-jōi* movement, the overthrow of the *bakufu*, and the abolition of the *han* and the establishment of prefectures were all major destructive forces which, in the years preceding 1874 and 1875, severed Japan from its past. And, by introducing Western culture, after 1890 Japan was able to progress significantly.[4] Liang believed that if Japan had not undergone destruction, it would have had the same fate as Korea.[5]

The Chinese students also noticed Japanese public opinion and the role it played. The Japanese people, regardless of whether they were officials, warriors, farmers, workers, merchants, or monks, recognized clearly their national rights. When an American warship wanted to survey Japan's coastline, the whole country was stirred into resentment. It was this feeling of resentment which became the motive force of the *sonnō-jōi* movement. Again, during the Triple Intervention the same resentment prepared the way toward military expansion.[6] It was also this spirit of the people, like that of Yoshida Shōin, which made the breakthrough that paved the way for present-day Japan.[7] One reformer, Yang Du, saw Japan's progress from a different angle. In his opinion, Japan went through a process of learning from Chinese civilization to Western civilization, and to preserving the national spirit.[8]

Hence the students argued that if China wanted to stand up as a nation-state, it should learn from Japan's Meiji Restoration. Namely, the Qing government should let the people participate in national affairs. It should have a constitution, two political parties similar to the Jiyūtō and Kaishintō in Japan, and a political system based on the separation of the three powers (executive, legislative, and judicial). These were the general opinions of the student activists in the early days.[9]

However, beginning in 1903 a split developed because Liang Qichao, the leader of the reformers, turned openly against the revolutionaries. The main reason was that he could not betray his mentor, Kang Youwei, and join the revolutionary camp. Also, his experience during his visit to the United States convinced him that it was too early, not only for revolution, but also for republicanism in China.[10]

In their organ, *Xinmin congbao*, Liang Qichao and his reformist student group wrote that Japan had been under a system of "enlightened absolutism" since the Meiji Restoration, and that it was under this political system that Japan had been able to educate its people and turn them into citizens in the modern sense. If Japan had adopted a republican form, the remarkable progress and the advancement of democracy of present-day Japan would never have been achieved.[11]

Moreover, a two-party system existed in Japan, both parties functioning within the framework of the state.[12] Even when both parties conducted a most heated dispute with the government, as soon as imperial decrees were issued to declare wars upon China and Russia, the disputes terminated immediately, and the targets of attack were shifted to the foreigners.[13] If this had not been the case, if the Jiyūtō had insisted on the establishment of a republican state, and the Kaishintō had insisted on constitutional monarchy, the two parties would not have been able to coexist and would have fought until one was annihilated. Japan would have been ruined, not by the *bakufu*, but by foreign powers.[14]

The Chinese revolutionaries and reformers cannot be treated as parallels to the Jiyūtō and Kaishintō of Japan. The revolutionaries refused to admit the existence of a Chinese state and government. They called themselves the "ruined people." Besides, they wanted to overthrow the Qing government and set up a republican state. This would mean the destruction of China's basic foundations.[15]

In criticizing the revolutionaries, the reformers continued to take examples from Japan. They said that although Japan had a system of enlightened absolutism for more than twenty years, and the people's rights had improved, and that the country had a constitution for more than ten years, Japan was still unable to allow anything more than limited suffrage. If the revolutionaries in China proposed to introduce constitutional democracy based on universal suffrage after the revolution, then they must have been dreaming and talking nonsense.[16]

On the other hand, the revolutionaries also referred to the Meiji Restoration to refute the reformers' arguments. According to them, the Meiji Restoration was the successful culmination of the movement to overthrow the *bakufu* and reinstate the monarchy. But in the case of China, the emperor had been exterminated by the Manchus more than 200 years earlier; thus the Qing government was the equivalent of the Tokugawa *bakufu*. If the Meiji Restoration were to be taken as model, then the Qing government must be overthrown first.[17] Moreover, the emperor of Japan came from a line unbroken for ages and was loved by the people, so that the people were willing to accept both enlightened absolutism and constitutional monarchy. In China, the Manchu government was regarded as a bitter enemy by the Chinese people. It would be completely out of the question to keep the Manchus in power.[18] Furthermore, the overthrow of the *bakufu* should have proved to the Chinese that if the people wanted their government to comply with their demands, they first had to show the government that they had the force to control it. In China, the only force able to do this was the revolutionary army.[19]

There should be a certain sequence to revolution. In Japan, Itō Hirobumi had risen to his present status because of what had been accomplished by patriots like Saigō Takamori. Only after a new government came into power could there be new policies. New policies were totally impossible under the old government.[20] Japan's *bakufu* government was destroyed by personalities like Saigō and Yoshida Shōin. This paved the way for the self-administration of districts, towns, and villages, and the establishment of the constitution.[21] Thus, the revolutionaries asserted, in order to achieve what the reformers set out to do, there must first be a thorough destruction of the established political system, as taught by the lesson from the Meiji Restoration.

In short, both reformers and revolutionaries looked upon the example of Japan for solutions to China's problem. Their views of the Meiji Restoration differed according to their respective ideologies, drawing upon those points which supported their own views. Yet, it could also be argued that their beliefs—either in revolution or constitutional monarchy—were actually derived from, or strengthened by, what each saw as the lesson of the Restoration.

The students' views of the Restoration affected their life-styles as well as their activities. Having come to the conclusion that the Meiji Restoration was a process of total destruction, the student revolutionaries had no interest in pursuing academic studies. They were more inclined to engage in political movements and such activities as meetings, debates, demonstrations, and journalism. Some even participated in secret military training and learned how to make bombs. Generally, their behavior was not that which one would expect from an overseas student.[22]

Though less militant, the student reformers were also occupied in propaganda campaigns advocating constitutional monarchy and refuting the revolutionaries.[23] To them, the Meiji Restoration had been an institutional reform that led Japan to modernization. As in the case of the revolutionaries, however, they were convinced of the validity and inevitability of immediate political action for bringing about changes in China, so much so that they were less concerned with pursuing their studies.

Both the revolutionary and the reformist students were convinced that institutional changes would be the key to modernizing China, the difference between them being that the former wanted a radical and thorough change, and the latter, a gradual and partial change. This is to suggest that, in a sense, both groups emphasized the institutional aspect of modernization and neglected the other, namely, the cultural aspect in general, and the educational aspect in particular.

Many of the student activists had shown that they realized the important role played by education. Yet with their persistent involvement in political activities, they could afford little time and energy for academic work. A large number of Japan-trained students returned to become teachers and administrators in the new educational system, but it is doubtful whether many of these were former activist students. And if some were, it is even more doubtful that they could have been effective as teachers for transmitting Western learning. This task was left to the ordinary students who, because they led normal student lives during their stay in Japan, have been ignored by history.

The relative placing of Chinese learning and Western learning, or, in other words, how to deal with the conflict between the two learnings, has been the greatest problem to Chinese intellectuals since the late Qing period. Modern Chinese history has revealed to us that institutional changes alone were not able to resolve this issue. Despite their intention to learn from the Meiji Restoration, the revolutionary and reformist students in Japan tended to observe merely the institutional aspect, and failed to see the other ways, no less important, in which the Japanese coped with and assimilated Western culture.

## Notes

1. Yung Ying-yue, "Shin-matsu ni okeru Nihon ryūgaku" [Chinese students in Japan during the late Qing period], Ph.D. dissertation, University of Tokyo, 1981. See chap. 6.

2. Liang Qichao, "Jinggao dangdaozhe" [A respectful warning to the authorities], *Xinmin congbao*, vol. 18 in *Xinhai geming qian shinianjian shilun xuanji* [An anthology of articles on contemporary affairs from the decade before the 1911 Revolution] (hereafter cited as *Shilun xuanji*) (Beijing: Sanlian shudian, 1962), vol. 1, p. 224.

3. Liang Qichao, "Shige" [Explaining the meaning of revolution], *Xinmin congbao*, vol. 22 in *Shilun xuanji*, vol. 1, p. 243.

4. Liang Qichao, "Shizhong dexing xiangfan xiangcheng yi" [An interpretation of the contradictory and complementary relationships in the ten virtues], *Qingyi bao*, vol. 1 in *Shilun xuanji*, vol. 1, p. 15. Also "Xinmin shuo" [On new people], *Xinmin congbao*, vol. 2 in *Shilun xuanji*, vol. 1, p. 151.

5. "Xinmin shuo," p. 150.

6. Ibid., pp. 130–31.

7. Ibid., n. 156.

8. Yang Du, "*Youxue yipian* xu" [Preface to *Youxue yipian*], *Youxue yipian*, vol. 1 in *Shilun xuanji*, vol. 1, pp. 247–48.

9. Liang Qichao, "*Datong ribao* yuanqi" [The origin of *Datong ribao*], *Xinmin congbao*, vols. 38–39 in *Shilun xuanji*, vol. 1, p. 366. Also "Lun lifaquan" [On legislative authority], *Xinmin congbao*, vol. 2 in *Shilun xuanji*, vol. 1, p. 157.

10. Zhang Pengyuan, *Liang Qichao yu Qingji geming* [Liang Qichao and the revolution in the Qing period] (Taibei: Institute of Modern History, Academia Sinica, 1969), pp. 134, 167–75.

11. Liang Qichao, "Kaiming zhuanzhi lun" [On enlightened despotism], *Xinmin congbao*, vols. 75, 77 in *Shilun xuanji*, vol. 2 (Beijing: Sanlian shudian, 1963), p. 186.
12. Yu Zhi, "Lun Zhongguo xianzai zhi dangpai ji jianglai zhi zhengdang" [On contemporary and future political parties in China], *Xinmin congbao*, vol. 92 in *Shilun xuanji*, vol. 2, p. 609.
13. Ibid., p. 620.
14. Ibid., p. 609.
15. Ibid.
16. Liang Qichao, "Da moubao disihao duiyu benbao zhi bolun" [Our reply to the rebuttal against our newspaper in the no. 4 issue of a certain newspaper], *Xinmin congbao*, vol. 79 in *Shilun xuanji*, vol. 2, p. 271.
17. Chen Tianhua, "Lun Zhongguo yi gaichuang minzhu zhengti" [China should alter to a democratic political system], *Min bao*, vol. 1 in *Shilun xuanji*, vol. 2, p. 125.
18. Zhang Binglin, "Zheng chou Man lun" [Orthodox theory on despising the Manchus], *Guomin bao*, vol. 4 in *Shilun xuanji*, vol. 1, p. 98. Also Wang Jingwei, "Bo *Xinmin congbao* zuijin zhi feigeming lun" [To rebut the recent anti-revolution theory in *Xinmin congbao*], *Min bao*, vol. 4 in *Shilun xuanji*, vol. 2, pp. 409, 417.
19. Wang, "Bo *Xinmin congbao* zuijin zhi," p. 417.
20. Fei Sheng, "Jinshi erda xueshuo zhi pinglun" [Discussion on the two recent theories], *Zhejiang chao*, vols. 8–9 in *Shilun xuanji*, vol. 1, pp. 522–23.
21. Yang Dusheng, "Xin Hunan" [New Hunan], in *Shilun xuanji*, vol. 1, p. 640. Also Liu Shipei, "Lun jilie de haochu" [On the merits of violence], *Zhongguo baihua bao*, vol. 6 in *Shilun xuanji*, vol. 1, p. 888.
22. Yung, "Shin-matsu ni okeru Nihon ryūgaku."
23. Ibid.

# Influences upon the Periphery

# The Viet-Nam Quang Phuc Hoi and the 1911 Revolution

Kawamoto Kuniye

The early twentieth century saw the rise of nationalist movements among the oppressed peoples of Asia. And it was the Russo-Japanese War (1904–5) and China's 1911 Revolution that aroused their nationalist consciousness, although the significance of these two historical events was quite different. Vietnam provides an important case study of these new nationalist movements.

The Vietnamese nationalist movement, which rose in the early 1900s, originated with the Duy Tan Hoi (Weixinhui, Reformation Society), a political party for independence organized by Phan Boi Chau (Pan Peizhu) and the Phong Trao Dong Du (Dongyou Fengchao, Eastern Study Movement), a political campaign launched by the Vietnamese leaders belonging to the Duy Tan Hoi. The leaders visited Japan in an attempt to establish an alliance with the Japanese. Just as the Chinese in the late nineteenth and early twentieth centuries regarded Tokyo as their center for pre-revolutionary activities, the Vietnamese revolutionaries considered their study in Japan—which came several years after that of the Chinese—as a vital stage in their revolutionary movement. The Vietnamese admitted that the movement began in the wake of Japan's victory over Russia. However, as will be discussed below, the Vietnamese political movement involving Japan, which grew rapidly in the short period between 1905 and 1909, was destined to end without achieving any significant progress. After their unsuccessful movement in Japan, the Vietnamese revolutionaries were forced to seek political asylum in China and Thailand. This means that the Duy Tan Hoi's political movement waned both at home and abroad.

The successful 1911 Revolution, which originated with the Wuchang Uprising, had a tremendous impact upon all Asian peoples. It helped revive the Vietnamese revolutionary party which had then been moribund and resulted in the organization of a new party, the Viet-Nam Quang Phuc Hoi (Yuenan Guangfuhui, Vietnam Restoration Society). This was of profound significance for the history of the movement. What is important is that the 1911 Revolution transformed the Vietnamese anti-French independence struggle from a campaign to establish a constitutional government to a movement for realizing a democratic, republican system. The question arises: to what extent was the conversion of their revolutionary philosophy reflected in their activities?

In this paper I will focus on the ideological relations between the Chinese Revolutionary League (Zhongguo geming tongmenghui) and the Vietnamese Duy Tan Hoi, the detailed talks between the two, the formation of the Viet-Nam Quang Phuc Hoi after the 1911 Revolution, and the process leading to the failure of the Vietnamese party. First, I will discuss the Vietnamese reaction to the 1911 Revolution and how Viet-Nam Quang Phuc Hoi was established.

There are two basic sources for the activities of the Vietnamese revolutionary party led by Phan Boi Chau: *Prison Notes* (1913)[1] and *Chronological Biography of Phan Boi Chau*.[2] According to these sources, Phan Boi Chau went to Japan in 1905, and Ky Ngoai Hau Cuong De, a member of the Nguyen imperial family, whom Phan and his comrades recommended to assume the chairmanship of their party, arrived the following year. Their movement became active gradually. Between 1907 and 1908, about 300 Vietnamese students left their French-occupied homeland for Japan. The high point of their activities was the establishment of the Tan Viet-Nam Cong Hien Hoi (Xin Yuenan gongxianhui, New Vietnam Public Offering Society), a branch organization of the Duy Tan Hoi. However, following the agreement between Japan and France in 1907 concerning French Indo-China, the Japanese government's interference with Vietnamese activities gradually increased. In September 1908, the Ministry of Interior ordered the Vietnamese students to disband, and their movement quickly disintegrated. Most of them left Japan, and, according to official documents, Phan Boi Chau was deported. In March 1909, he left for China, his second country of exile, where he visited various regions, as well as Hong Kong, Singapore, and Bangkok to make preparations for reconstituting his revolutionary group and instigating armed revolt. Until the spring of 1911, he lived chiefly in Guangzhou, acting as a central figure among the Vietnamese who had sought refuge in South China.

According to his memoirs, Phan Boi Chau became convinced that their activities in Guangzhou had little influence over the revolutionary movement in their home country mainly because of a lack of funds. Therefore, in February 1911 he took refuge in Thailand, where his comrades were engaged in agriculture. Before he went to China, Phan Boi Chau had obtained permission from the Bangkok government for Vietnamese revolutionaries to develop and cultivate farmland in the northeastern part of Thailand. After the spring of 1911, he reportedly spent his days writing and farming in Banchieng, Udon-Tani Prefecture.

In October 1911, he learned of the success of the 1911 Revolution when Phan Ba Ngoc, who had stayed in Japan with him, came to Banchieng from Hong Kong. The news made a great impact, alleviating the frustration he felt in being forced to leave Japan. Now he had hopes of revitalizing his independence movement. Without analyzing the relations between the Vietnamese revolutionary party and the Chinese revolutionaries, and without realizing the lack of solidarity between the Vietnamese and Chinese parties in the post-revolutionary period, Phan Boi Chau simply concluded that the success of the Chinese revolution marked the first step toward the Vietnamese revolution. He did not analyze the nature of the Chinese revolution and the actual developments leading to its success at this stage. This is clear from *Prison Notes*, written during his imprisonment in Guangzhou.

According to Phan, immediately after learning of the 1911 Revolution, he sent a letter of congratulations to Zhang Binglin, Chen Qimei, and Xie Yingbo, adding that he hoped to return to China. Although these Chinese revolutionary leaders were old friends of Phan since their days in Japan, their relations were rather informal and did not reflect official ties between the Vietnamese and Chinese revolutionary parties. Therefore, the letters sent from Zhang Binglin and others to Phan advising him to visit China can only be considered private communications. Phan and other Vietnamese revolutionaries regarded the letters as an official invitation from the Chinese Revolutionary League, as is apparent from Phan's memoirs. At this point, Phan believed that having succeeded in their revolution, his Chinese friends would naturally come to the rescue of the Vietnamese revolution.

Phan's shortsighted view of international relations and lack of understanding can be seen elsewhere. One thousand copies of *Lien A So Ngon* [Lian Ya chuyan, My opinion to league the Asian nations], written before leaving Banchieng, were printed in Bangkok by Xiao Focheng, chief editor of *Huaxian xinbao*, who was working for the Thai branch of the Chinese Revolutionary League. The book won the attention of the Japanese in Bangkok, and three hundred copies were bought by the Japanese association there. After distributing some copies to the Chinese in Thailand, Phan took most of the remaining copies to China with the intention of presenting them to Chinese political leaders as a post-revolution proposal. In this book, Phan assumed that post-revolutionary China would surely become a major power in Asia, second only to Japan. He also assumed that Japan and China would join hands and rally their military strength against the European imperialist forces in Asia. This would not only prevent further imperialist encroachment but would pave the way for Vietnamese, Indian, and Filipino independence. From this standpoint, Phan insisted on an alliance between Japan and China for the benefit of Vietnamese independence. Although he had been forced to leave Japan because of the Franco-Japanese treaty, even at this juncture Phan still pinned his hopes on Japan. His unrealistic appraisal provided no viable prospect for the Vietnamese revolution he so fervently desired.

But, it is a historical fact that the 1911 Revolution transformed the Vietnamese conception of independence and influenced the establishment of the Viet-Nam Quang Phuc Hoi, which became the foundation of the government-in-exile in Guangzhou. The Duy Tan Hoi was virtually disbanded, and like the Chinese Revolutionary League, the Vietnamese movement now based itself on republican ideas.

In January 1912, Phan and three other Vietnamese revolutionaries went from Thailand to Guangzhou. There they were joined by most of the members of the Duy Tan Hoi who had lived in China after leaving Japan and by the others who had lived in Thailand. There was strong disagreement over how to reconstruct their independence movement. At first, the idea of capitalizing on the success of the Chinese revolution so that the Vietnamese revolution could be carried out with Chinese help gained momentum. But at the time when more than one hundred Vietnamese revolutionaries lived in Guangzhou, a predominant view emerged that it would be better to reorganize the revolutionary group on the basis of republican ideology, according to the example set by the 1911 Revolution. It was agreed to hold a general meeting of all Vietnamese living in Guangzhou. The meeting was held in Shahe, and Phan presented the reorganization proposal, which was said to have sparked a sharp controversy. A majority of those present adopted a resolution calling for the dissolution of the Duy Tan Hoi, which had aimed at establishing a constitutional government headed by the imperial family. Instead, it was decided to form a new party, the Viet-Nam Quang Phuc Hoi, in March 1912.

In the first half of the twentieth century, one of the tactics of the Vietnamese struggle for independence was to secretly send a large number of young students to Tokyo from the French-occupied colony. The idea was to have them obtain an ordinary education as well as military training. Eventually, most of them became revolutionaries. This was the only accomplishment of the Duy Tan Hoi, an organization established in 1904 under the leadership of Phan, a member of the scholar-gentry under the feudal Vietnamese government which was perpetuated even after the French colonized Vietnam.

Revolution was not incorporated into the several initial strategies worked out by the Duy Tan Hoi. As was appropriate for an organization led by a person of Phan's class origin, the Duy Tan Hoi was established in order to continue the anti-French struggle of the late nineteenth century. Its prime objectives were to fight the French, overthrow the puppet Vietnamese emperor, and restore the Nguyen (Ruan) dynasty. The movement hoped to receive arms and troops from foreign countries. The search for foreign aid was based on the Vietnamese defeat by the French at the end of the nineteenth century. Phan's proposal to resort to foreign aid as the most effective strategy won unanimous support from the members of the Duy Tan Hoi.

According to Phan, the Vietnamese requested Japanese help because they also was of the Yellow race and because since the Meiji Restoration, Japan had become a rising country. The Vietnamese asked for Japanese help, Phan wrote, because they believed that Japan, which had defeated Russia, would be increasingly interested in promoting economic and industrial development throughout Asia. They assumed that Japan would be sympathetic to their struggle against France, for the elimination of European influence would benefit Japan.

However, it is questionable whether Phan's naive reasoning explains the overture to the Japanese. It is highly probable that at least he hoped for foreign assistance to revive the Nguyen dynasty. Theoretically, it is easy to explain why he opted for Japanese military help at that particular time. However, the plan to form an anti-French revolutionary group, which was noticeable from around 1901, materialized quickly in 1904 apparently because Japan's victory over Russia had a profound impact on the Vietnamese. Phan said: "The Japanese victory has opened an entirely new world to us." It is unknown to what extent the Vietnamese obtained information concerning Japanese industrialization after the Meiji Restoration, but Japan's modernization apparently influenced them gradually. The Russo-Japanese War merely provided a good opportunity for the Vietnamese to renew their assessment of the results of Japan's modernization.

In his *Prison Notes*, Phan wrote: "Before the French invasion, we knew only China. After the French came, France was the only country we knew, besides China. The Vietnamese never dreamed of the changing world and new trends. . . . Japan's victory greatly influenced us and changed our thinking." But there were other reasons for which Duy Tan Hoi decided to depend upon Japan.

As mentioned previously, Phan's memoirs are the only source for studying the progress and deterioration of the Duy Tan Hoi. Largely because of its elusive literary style, the memoirs are not always reliable. In 1905, soon after the decision to depend on

Japan was made, Phan left Vietnam illegally and went to Japan. Two factors, which Phan declined to reveal, motivated the decision.

One was the country they would opt for had to be a modern monarchy, since Phan and his followers were anxious to take over the royalist movement and revive the Nguyen dynasty. For this reason, they could only choose Japan, which was a constitutional monarchy headed by an emperor. Furthermore, geographical proximity made Japan accessible.

Another reason is that, once the decision was taken, the Vietnamese were quick in dispatching their representatives to Japan because of the possibility of contacting exiled Chinese intellectuals and activists. At that time, Japan and the Japanese were quite unknown to the Vietnamese. The members of the Duy Tan Hoi probably felt that holding detailed political talks with the Chinese exiles would be effective in advancing their movement. Immediately after landing in Japan, Phan sought to contact Liang Qichao and a few days later a meeting with this non-revolutionary Chinese monarchist was arranged. Phan and his colleagues wanted to achieve one of the prime objectives of Duy Tan Hoi, namely, to attain independence from France by reviving the Nguyen dynasty. However, as is clear from Phan's activities while en route to Japan, their interest was not always limited to pro-monarchist Chinese.

The Vietnamese independence movement's intention to seek Japan's military assistance was, in a sense, a strategic if not expedient policy. However strategic it may have been, what prompted them to choose Japan was, of course, Japan's victory over Russia. If the Vietnamese who had started preparations for forming a political party around 1901 had not been impressed by the outcome of the Russo-Japanese War, they would not have depended on Japan for support. Phan asserted: "The problem of arms (in the struggle against France) will not be resolved without foreign assistance. In the light of history, geography, and race, China seems the best choice. But China has already conceded its sovereignty to France under the Tianjin treaty following the war of 1884. Those who fled to China, expecting help after the anti-French rising of 1885–86 had failed, were disappointed." He wrote that he had told his followers of the importance of relying on Japan, the victor of the war against Russia.

Between 1902 and 1903, preceding the establishment of Duy Tan Hoi, Phan Boi Chau, a native of Nghe An, went to Hue to study at the Quoc-tu-giam (Guozijian, National College). It is assumed that he read the books of Liang Qichao and Kang Youwei, which indicates that he had been interested in the Chinese exiles in Japan at an early date. In fact, before sailing to Japan in 1906 via Shanghai, Phan stopped at Guangdong and Hong Kong, and sought to meet Xu Qin, editor of the monarchist newspaper *Shang bao*, and Feng Ziyou at the office of the revolutionaryo rgan *Zhongguo ribao* in Hong Kong. Xu Qin refused to give him an interview, but Feng Ziyou welcomed him. Feng spoke candidly and, according to Phan's *Chronological Biography*, made a proposal concerning the Vietnamese revolution. Phan's interview with Feng was the first he had with a Chinese on his trip abroad. What they discussed concerning his future activities in Japan is not recorded. But Phan said that he had the impression that Feng would work in some form or other to help the Vietnamese revolution.

Despite such an exchange with Feng Ziyou, Phan visited Liang Qichao soon after his arrival in Japan. It is possible that Phan did not understand the relative influence of the contesting Chinese groups in Tokyo. Phan's memoirs do not sufficiently explain why he sought advice from Liang Qichao concerning his activities in Japan. Presumably, when Phan met Japanese politicians to request assistance for his plan to win independence and follow the example of Japan's constitutional monarchy, Liang Qichao served as his patron, and to some degree this facilitated Phan's activities in Japan.

But by seeking Liang Qichao's opinion on how to proceed with the independence movement, Phan was forced to change his policy accordingly. During the early part of Phan's stay in Japan, Liang Qichao told him that in order to win independence in Vietnam, it would be necessary to enlighten the people, develop their capacity for internal development, and rely on Guangdong and Guangxi for arms and war supplies. Support from Japan should be confined to the diplomatic field. This led Phan to drastically change the basic policy of Duy Tan Hoi, as indicated in various sources. The subsequent activities of Phan and his comrades were mainly limited to helping young Vietnamese escape from their country and study in Japan, and to soliciting wealthy Vietnamese for the funds to subsidize these students' study. To attain these two goals, they published propaganda material for home consumption. As mentioned previously, the result was that the Phong Trao Dong Du flourished in Tokyo as if it were Duy Tan Hoi's sole activity, but it subsequently deteriorated.

The sudden switch in Duy Tan Hoi's activities coincided with the establishment of the Chinese Revolutionary League. According to Phan's writings, there were virtually no relations between the Tokyo headquarters of Duy Tan Hoi and the Chinese Revolutionary League, except for the somewhat official contacts between Phan and the Chinese leaders. On the advice of the well-known Japanese politician Inukai Tsuyoshi, Phan met Sun Yat-sen twice in Yokohama. This does not mean that Phan had no contact at all with the Chinese up to that year, for he had also met Yin Chengxian from Yunnan who introduced him to Zhao Shen, Yang Zhenhong, and others, all editors of *Yunnan*, an influential magazine among the Chinese in Tokyo. Surprisingly, Phan contributed several articles to the magazine. The reason for this was not, as is sometimes believed, that Phan had joined the Chinese Revolutionary League. Actually Phan was thinking of future strategy and felt that the Vietnamese revolution should be achieved in collaboration with the people of Yunnan and Guangxi. It was probably in 1907 that Phan proposed solidarity between the Vietnamese and the people of the two provinces, and established the Yunnan-Guangxi-Vietnam League among the students in Japan. Details about the association, however, are unknown.

Although Phan had other personal contacts with members of the Chinese League, it is difficult to cite specific contacts except those with the Yunnan people. Phan, whose main concern was the Vietnamese revolution, believed that joining the Chinese League would not always be advantageous to his activities in Japan. His memoirs relating to his meeting with Sun Yat-sen clearly indicate this.

Phan wrote that his meeting with Sun in Yokohama in 1906 was not fruitful. Their disagreement, according to Phan, stemmed chiefly from Phan's monarchist ideas. The two, Phan said, also differed widely on strategic priorities. Sun bitterly attacked the "fraudulent" nature of the constitutional monarchist party, since he was very conscious of Liang Qichao's influence in *Prison Notes*. At the same time, Sun reputedly told him that the Vietnamese revolutionary party should join the Chinese Revolutionary League. He said that when the League succeeded in its revolution, it would be ready to provide all-out support to the oppressed peoples of Asia, adding that the Vietnamese would be the first to receive such aid. On the other hand, Phan insisted that the Chinese revolutionaries should first help the Vietnamese achieve their revolution, and when the Vietnamese won independence, northern Vietnam could serve as the base for a thrust into Guangdong and Guangxi, from where the revolution would spread throughout China. The two men talked at crosspurposes, Phan said. The reason for disagreement should be attributed to their different lines of reasoning. While Sun urged the Vietnamese to join the Chinese party, Phan, though he understood the meaning of establishing a democratic republican system, turned down Sun's proposal. Phan was to later try to strengthen the ties between Duy Tan Hoi members and the students and to commit the party to the idea of constitutional monarchy, clear evidence of his belief that support for a democratic republican government would be harmful to Vietnamese activities in Japan. It was inevitable that that at this point his talks with Sun were unsuccessful.

According to Phan's memoirs, except for contacts with the Yunnan people, he associated to a lesser degree with the members of the Chinese Revolutionary League. However, there were some interesting examples, as will be discussed.

When Phan arrived in Japan, it was the year in which several revolutionary parties, such as Xingzhonghui, Huaxinghui, and Guangfuhui, joined forces to establish the Chinese Revolutionary League. During the summer and fall, Phan, after secretly returning home, went back to Japan at the height of the conflict between the monarchists and revolutionaries. It is not known how Phan reacted to the bitter theoretical dispute between the exiled Chinese political leaders because he wrote nothing about it. However, apparently because of his concern for Liang Qichao or because of his declaration to Japanese politicians that he and his comrades would try to establish a constitutional monarchist government, Phan refused the help offered by the Chinese League.

In May 1905, Phan secretly returned from Japan to Vietnam, but by the end of the year, he was in Japan once more in the company of several young compatriots. At the advice of Liang Qichao, he and his group rented a house in Yokohama, but they had no means of subsistence. Liang extended moral but no financial support. When the hunger became unbearable, one student went to the *Min bao* office for help, and Zhang Binglin agreed to take in three Vietnamese students. But Phan never showed any intention of associating with the League, despite his contact with another revolutionary, Tang Jiaodun.

According to his memoirs, however, Phan maintained "friendly" relations with a number of revolutionary party members with regard to other affairs of Duy Tan Hoi between 1905 and 1909. For instance, Japanese authorities seized 200,000 piasters remitted from Saigon for financing the activities of Vietnamese students in Japan. This raised the fear that the organization in Vietnam in charge of sending students to Japan might be dissolved under French colonial pressure. Phan then consulted with Huang Xing and asked him to have the money sent to him via Feng Ziyou, who was a former member of the finance committee of the revolutionary group in Saigon.

In his memoirs, Phan said that in 1908, the Tōa Dōmeikai (Dongya Tongmenghui, East Asian League) was established in Tokyo with the aim of liberating the oppressed Asian peoples and that it was managed jointly by Phan, Zhang Ji, Zhang Binglin, and Jing Meijiu. This indicates that he had contact with the members of the Yazhou heqinhui (Asian Solidarity Association), an organization set up chiefly by Zhang Binglin and Zhang Ji to promote anarchism as advocated in the *Tianyi bao*, established by Liu Shipei in the summer of 1907. (In his memoirs Phan erroneously dated it 1908.)

Phan and his comrades left Japan in March 1909, still determined to support the Duy Tan Hoi. They never agreed on the republican concept. Officially, they did not participate in the Chinese Revolutionary League as requested by Sun Yat-sen. However, in my opinion, as exemplified in their connection with

Yazhou heqinhui, they gradually changed their ideas as a result of Japan's indifference. Immediately after the 1911 Revolution, Phan came to believe that the success of the revolution constituted the first step toward liberating Vietnam. He assumed that the organization of Viet-Nam Quang Phuc Hoi and the disbandment of Duy Tan Hoi would develop the nationalist movement. He apparently nourished these thoughts while still in Japan.

The initial objectives of Viet-Nam Quang Phuc Hoi were: 1) establishing a republic through revolution; 2) having its members secretly infiltrate Vietnam to set up a local organization; and 3) creating an organization for maintaining contact with the Chinese revolutionary party. Together with these goals, it defined details for the party's management and issued a party manifesto. It was a movement that was more realistic than the Duy Tan Hoi.

Apparently, Viet-Nam Quang Phuc Hoi originated under the influence of the 1911 Revolution. But, like Duy Tan Hoi, it suffered frequent setbacks. Long Jiguang, who invaded Guangdong during Yuan Shikai's campaign against the 1913 Second Revolulution, suppressed the organization, and it was finally destroyed.

Yuan's repression of the organization was quite understandable in view of the situation at that time. But the fact that the organization faced Yuan's offensive in Guangdong without any meaningful resistance illustrates the vulnerability of Viet-Nam Quang Phuc Hoi's leadership after 1912. The organization had not been idle. Immediately after its establishment, Phan met Huang Xing, Chen Qimei, and Hu Hanmin in order to seek their opinion on how to coordinate activities with the Chinese revolutionary party. Here again, it should be pointed out that, like the disagreement with Sun Yat-sen, Phan's talks ended in failure since he turned down their advice. The break seems mainly to have been due to the attitude of Phan and his comrades: they wanted to advance their independence movement quickly. Phan himself said: "I think that the impulsiveness of the movement was further influenced by such persons as Deng Jingya and Su Shaolou bringing about futile results to the organization." To be more specific, Phan spent most of his efforts organizing the ineffective Chan Hoa Hung A Hoi (Zhenhua xingyahui, Invigorate China, Revive Asia Society) at the advice of Deng Jingya and others and placed great emphasis on producing and distributing worthless bonds for the

Viet-Nam Quang Phuc Hoi while neglecting the consolidation of the party's structure.

[Translated by Okui Yaeko]

**Notes**

1. Phan wrote *Nguc trung thu* [Prison notes] in prison in Guangdong in 1913. It was written in classical Chinese and published in Shanghai in the same year, but no copies survive. A Japanese translation by Ga Morizō, entitled *Gokuchūki*, appeared in the monthly *Nippon oyobi Nipponjin* [Japan and the Japanese], no. 179, June 1929. This translation was republished by Nanmeikai, a Japanese publisher in Shanghai, in 1932. A Vietnamese version by Dao Trinh Nhat, based on the Japanese translation and entitled *Doi cach mang Phan Boi Chau* [The revolutionary life of Phan Boi Chau], was published in Hanoi by Nippon Bunka Kaikan in 1945.

2. Phan wrote *Chronological Biography of Phan Boi Chau* in classical Chinese during the period of his house arrest in Hue between 1937 and 1940. The first Vietnamese version, by Anh Minh and entitled *Tu phan* [Self-criticism], was published in Hue in 1946. A book by the same title, translated by Pham Trong Diem and Tong Quang Phiet, based on a manuscript by Tran Ngoc Huynh, was published by N.x.b. Van Su Dia in Hanoi in 1955. The second edition of this last publication was republished by the same publisher as *Phan Boi Chau nien bieu* [Chronological biography of Phan Boi Chau] in 1957.

# A Protest Against the Concept of the "Middle Kingdom": The Mongols and the 1911 Revolution

## Nakami Tatsuo

When the 1911 Revolution in China erupted, the political leaders of Khalkha Mongolia declared their independence and established the Bogdo Khân government. The question of Mongol independence was, for the Mongols, more precisely a question of how to establish and maintain their independence as a nation. However, for the infant Republic of China, this declaration of independence was, along with the Tibet problem, the first major "ethnic minority problem" that confronted the government. Furthermore, the Mongol problem would inevitably expand into the sphere of international relations, involving such Imperialist Powers as Japan and Russia.

In this paper, I should like to focus on two crucial aspects of this problem:

(1) How did the Mongol political leadership of the time perceive the 1911 Revolution and what significance did this revolution have for the Mongols?

(2) How did the Republic of China and Russia respond to the Mongols' having posed the problem as one of independence? What influence did international relations have on the subsequent development of the problem?

After dealing with these two issues, I will use the result of that inquiry to see how an understanding of the Mongol problem of independence can contribute to our understanding of the 1911 Revolution itself and the political conditions in the late Qing and the early Republic of China.[1]

Before moving on to the main subject of inquiry, it would be profitable to sketch the relationship between the Mongols and the Qing dynasty in the early Qing. When the Qing dynasty established political and military dominance in Mongolia, the basic relationship was conceived of as conforming to an ideal type, a relationship between a Manchu emperor lord and his Mongol vassals. This relationship provided the framework in which a broad range of other important relations—political, religious, economic, cultural, etc.—was set. The actual Mongol position in the Qing imperial structure was simply that of an "unsophisticated and submissive ally." Therefore, to prevent the Mongols from reuniting and becoming a military menace, the Qing dynasty put the Mongols under strong superintendence. Moreover, the Manchu court discouraged the Han Chinese from coming into too close contact with Mongol society, a policy that included encouraging the Mongols to maintain their own independent social structure.

However, the Manchu court had to be strong enough to maintain such a status quo between itself, the Mongols, and the Han Chinese, and after the middle nineteenth century it no longer was. By that time, the Qing imperial structure was undergoing changes as a result of attacks on two fronts: the external encroachment on its sovereignty by the Imperialist Powers and the internal threat posed by the growing strength and influence of the Han Chinese. Within the framework of the Qing control system, Mongol society too was gradually but surely changing, becoming very different from what it was in the era before Qing dominance.[2] In particular, the penetration of the Han Chinese influence must be noted. The Han Chinese merchants pushed into Mongolia and established commercial networks there in the eighteenth and nineteenth centuries. The Mongol nomads, who had always been exploited by princes and lamas, were now driven to the extremes of poverty by the added pressure of economic exploitation by the Han Chinese merchants. The result of this rampant exploitation was social unrest and a growing sense of dissatisfaction and opposition among the nomads. In Inner Mongolia, the migration of Han Chinese immigrants into the area in ever-increasing numbers was an additional factor contributing to social unrest. Pasture land was rapidly being swallowed up and converted into farmland. Given these dramatic developments in both Inner and Outer Mongolia, and the social disruption they caused, it became clear that if nothing were done the independent social structure of the Mongols would gradually but inevitably move toward complete dissolution.

It is important to note the fact that, although fundamental changes were occurring both in Mongolia and in the Qing regime itself, the Qing response to these changes in terms of its official policy toward Mongolia, at least toward Outer Mongolia, was slow. In fact, the waves of transformation in the Qing imperial structure did not much affect official Mongol policy until the beginning of the twentieth century. The 1906 reform of the Qing bureaucracy provided the perfect occasion for a drastic change of that policy: a revision that aimed at reforming Mongolia radically.

This new government policy had a number of important objectives. One of these was to strengthen and reform the administrative structure and to promote both human and natural resources in Mongolia. At the same time, the government wished to strengthen its border defenses in Mongolia against possible Russian encroachment by deploying its newly restructured military forces there. In addition to this, it planned to transplant the overpopulation of the Han Chinese from China proper there to agronomize it, that is, turn Mongolia into a farming region. It was the Han Chinese who assumed the responsibility and received the rewards for implementing this policy, while the Mongols were forced to bear its financial burden. The princes and lamas of Khalkha Mongolia regarded this new policy as one that threatened to destroy the Mongols' independent social structure and their ecological environment. Thus, this sense of impending crisis gave new impetus to the independence movement, as well as to the already active anti-Qing movement, both of which were then erupting with explosive force.

The crucial factor in all this was the personalities of the leaders of these movements. They feared the transformations taking place in the Qing regime and reacted violently to "externally imposed reforms" implemented by the Han Chinese bureaucrats. Now, does this sort of reaction by itself prove that they were merely a reactionary ruling class who sought only to preserve the traditional pattern of authority and social structure? In considering the Mongol political leadership of the time, it is important to pay particular attention to the faction that advocated independence as a goal. They themselves were quite aware of the necessity for some sort of reforms or "modernization" in the excessively conservative Mongol social structure. However, they could not countenance sacrificing the Mongols on the altar of reform, especially when those reforms would be imposed by an outside power like the Han Chinese for their own advantage. This faction, which even included some secularist lamas who advocated a reform of Lamaism, was acquainted with foreign thought and was well informed. Its members were convinced that, in order to confront and deal successfully with the impending crisis, they had no choice but to work for reunification of the Mongols and restore political sovereignty. However, it was evident to all that the Mongols were deficient in real military and political strength. How were such deficiencies made up? Moreover, they needed to develop a more compelling and concrete rationale for independence which could convince those who were hesitant to take aggressive action.

The political tension in Mongolia reached a climax on March 11, 1910, with the arrival in Urga of the new *Amban* (*Kulun banshi dachen* or Qing resident commissioner at Urga) Sandowa (Sandô, Sanduo) to whom the enforcement of the new policy had been entrusted. Until this point, the political leaders of Khalkha Mongolia had hoped they would be able to change the policy through negotiations with the Qing government, but his arrival showed that their negotiations had ultimately proven fruitless. The various anti-Qing movements and protests against the new policy had heretofore been random and local in character, but these now began to solidify and become organized. The growing protest movement not only organized most of the Khalkha Mongol princes and lamas around the Living Buddha in Urga, Jebzundamba Khutukhta, but it also included people from Inner Mongolia who had a similar sense of the crisis.

The political confusion grew greater each day. Consequently, in the summer of 1911, the political leadership of Khalkha Mongolia decided to send a delegation to Russia to ask for support. What did they have in mind when they sent off this delegation? What sort of aid were they seeking from Russia? Even today, there is no unanimity of opinion about the answers to these questions. We can, however, find some important clues in the letter to the Tsar of Russia from Jebzundamba and four Khans of Khalkha Mongolia (the original is in Mongolian).[3] The letter states that the Mongols, "submitting to the Manchu Emperor," have "dwelt in peace" for more than 200 years, but that "recently the Han Chinese bureaucrats have grabbed the political power [of the Qing] and have brought confusion and discord to the affairs of state." In particular, the letter goes on to say, "we cannot bear" the new policy of the government which was designed to "search out ways to turn Mongol land into farmland, which, if accomplished, will inevitably destroy our traditional way of life." "We followed the Manchu Emperor because he was a believer in Lamaism and a man of great compassion, but this turned out to be all talk and no substance, with the result that our suffering has only increased over the years." In essence, then, this letter points out that Mongol social order and stability, which had heretofore been supported by the traditional Qing-Mongol relationship, was confronted by a serious crisis with the transformation of the Qing regime as a result of the political ascendancy of the Han Chinese bureaucrats, specifically by the new Mongol policy. Perceiving the situation in this way, just what was it they wanted of Russia?

On this point, the following passages are of some significance. "If we follow the example of small nations who have depended on large nations and you cooperate with us, then we will not have to suffer the loss of our traditional way of life, Lamaism will continue to exist and prosper, and we will be able to dwell in peace and tranquillity." "We have now related all these matters to you [Russia] openly and freely and ask for your assistance and protection." Ultimately, rather than being a concrete petition with specific requests, the letter was intended to seek support from Russia only in some abstract sense, after detailing the crises which confronted the Mongols and, in particular, the political tensions caused by the new Qing policy. Why did the letter take this form rather than being something more substantial?

To be sure, the princes and lamas who planned the delegation shared a common awareness of the crisis confronting them. However, even after an exhaustive comparative analysis of a variety of documents, there is nothing to suggest that any consensus about the ideal status for the Mongols emerged among the participants in the plan to send the delegation. The most radical of them were advocates of independence, while some hoped for Russian support through intervention, and there were still others who argued in favor of compromise with the Qing regime. It was because of this welter of irreconcilable views that the letter took the above-mentioned form. However, the delegation tended to be composed largely of the most radical and aggressive types who were more willing to risk their lives on the dangerous mission to Russia to plead the cause they passionately believed in. Since it was dominated by radicals, when the delegation reached St. Petersburg, they asked the Russian government for assistance in achieving *their* goal, that of independence. This disparity between what the delegates asked for and what was in the letter caused Russia no small amount of confusion and embarrassment.[4]

What about the Russian government who received this request for "support" from the Mongols? How did it interpret the problem explained by the delegation, and what measures was it prepared to take in response to the request? In order to answer these questions, we must first discover what position Mongolia occupied in the overall framework of Russian foreign policy at the time.

After the Russo-Japanese War of 1904-5, the emphasis in Russian foreign policy shifted to Europe, with a consequent decrease in the importance of East Asia in the scale of priorities. While still planning to expand its sphere of influence and interests in East Asia, Russia was basically concerned with normalizing its relations with Japan, Britain, and the other Imperialist Powers. Thus, in 1907 the First Russo-Japanese Entente and the Anglo-Russian Entente were signed. Russia's special interests in Outer Mongolia were recognized by Japan in the former agreement. However, this did not mean that Russia harbored a particularly strong desire to expand into Outer Mongolia. Even in its East Asian diplomacy, Mongolia was for Russia "off the beaten track."[5]

This, then, was the environment in which the Mongol problem surfaced. Russia had perceived the traditional political situation in Mongolia to be one in which Mongolia, while a dependency of the Qing, continued to hold on to its "autonomy." Now, however, Russia judged, the new Qing policy toward Mongolia was intended to destroy that "autonomy" and assimilate Mongolia as a province of China proper. It was no wonder that virulent political unrest had erupted there. However, Russia was dubious about the possibility of the Mongols actually achieving independence. Given this analysis of the situation, the Russian government concluded that since its main concern was with the West, it could not risk an intervention in Mongolia if that would weaken its position in what it considered a more crucial area. On the other hand, if the establishment of Qing administrative organizations, colonization, the laying of railroad tracks, and military troop disposition based on this new policy were all implemented in Mongolia, the traditional balance of power on the Sino-Russian border would be destroyed, because Russia shared a border with Outer Mongolia and had, in fact, economic interests in the area. Considering this, Russia judged, support of the Mongol cause coincided with Russia's own interests and would be significant in terms of its own border defense structure.

The result of all these deliberations was that Russia refused to take positive action (in particular it refused the military aid requested by the delegation) but did settle on a fundamental policy line, i.e., "from the standpoint of a mediator between the Qing Empire and Mongolia, Russia supports the desire of the Mongols to maintain their autonomy through diplomatic channels without severing their relations to their lord, the Great Qing Emperor." Concretely, the Russian government, through its legation in Beijing, formally requested the Qing government to abandon the new policy. At the same time, it decided to try to convince the Mongol delegation of "the impossibility of effecting complete independence from China" and to promise the Mongols its moral support in the struggle to maintain their "independent institutions."[6] Thus, Russia hoped to accomplish its purpose—while avoiding a full-scale intervention in the Mongol problem, bringing a halt to the implementation of the new Qing policy in Mongolia.

Because the Qing government basically acceded to the request by the Russian government to revoke the new policy, it looked, at least temporarily, as though easing of the tensions between the Qing and Mongolia would take place. But just at that point, the Wuchang Uprising occurred. For the Mongols, the 1911 Revolution signaled not only the collapse of the Qing governmental system but also the dissolution of their dependency on and subjugation by the Manchu emperor. It held out the possibility of their being released from all the bonds which had hitherto severely restricted them. It held for them the promise of political freedom: the restoration of political sovereignty and the reunification of the Mongols. The 1911 Revolution gave those radicals who had long been advocating independence a decisive rationale for independence which could be understood and supported by all the Mongols including those who had been reluctant to take positive action before. In this sense, the 1911 Revolution can be viewed as a catalyst in the development of the Mongol independence movement. Yet, aside from what the radicals themselves thought, was this rationale really sufficient to gain the approval of the Han Chinese or the Imperialist Powers, and did they really have the ability required to achieve independence and maintain it? The aquisition of a solid rationale still left these important concrete questions unanswered.

The Mongols' move toward independence quickly shifted into high gear after the Wuchang Uprising. In November 1911, Qing officials in Urga were driven out. On December 1, 1911, the princes and lamas of Khalkha Mongolia declared their independence and organized the Bogdo Khân government. On the 29th of December, Jebzundamba Khutukhta was installed as emperor. At this time, the Bogdo Khân government controlled only the four Khalkha *Aimaɣ*s around Urga. However, the Bogdo Khân government was joined by many Inner Mongols who assumed important positions in it.[7] The new government aimed at creating an independent sovereign state including not only Outer but also Inner Mongolia, the "Great Mongol State" [*yeke Mongɣol ulus*]. News of the events in Khalkha spread rapidly to other regions, and by the beginning of 1912 the Bogdo Khân government had gained control of all Outer Mongolia and the Barga region. And in Inner Mongolia as well, there were groups acting in concert with the Bogdo Khân government. Thus, the Mongol independence movement proceeded on its course at an ever-accelerating pace. On the other hand, since China proper was in the midst of a maelstrom of political confusion, the Beijing government—still the Qing government—was not in a position to develop any concrete countermeasures to thwart these developments in Mongolia.

How did Russia view this Mongol declaration of independence? Just after the declaration, on December 21, 1911, in a letter to I. Y. Korostovets, the Russian minister to Beijing, Foreign Minister S. Sazonov wrote: "The Mongols have declared their independence but they probably do not clearly understand just what that means." In other words, he did not attach much value to the Mongol action. He confirmed that Russia must maintain its position as intermediary in the Mongol problem and that "Russia's position in Mongolia must be decided, as in the past, by treaty with the Beijing government."[8]

In a concrete response to the situation, the Russian government decided to pursue a mediating role and instructed its legation in Beijing to conclude "a treaty between the Chinese and the Mongols which would assure the autonomy of Mongolia."[9] Basically, it was hoped that this treaty would secure the recognition by China of three specific clauses: 1) China would not deploy troops in Mongolia; 2) China would not colonize Mongolia; and 3) Chinese administrative organizations would not be established in Mongolia. In return, the treaty would state that the Mongols must recognize the "sovereignty of China in Mongolia" and allow a representative of the Chinese government to officially reside there. Since this draft was produced almost immediately after the outbreak of the Mongol independence problem, it is worth attending to in some detail.

First of all, note that Russia maintained that these three clauses severely restricting Chinese activities in Mongolia were absolutely necessary to the settlement of the Mongol problem. Next, note that the "Chinese rights" in Mongolia were clearly and formally to be "sovereignty." Part of the reason for this may have been that, at the time the treaty was drafted (late 1911), the Qing government still existed, at least formally. Later, as political conditions in both China proper and Mongolia fell into disarray, this notion of "Chinese rights" changed. A similar change later occurred in the interpretation of the concept of "autonomy," which also appears frequently in the document. As noted previously, when the Mongol delegation went to Russia in the summer of 1911, the Russian government had seen the Mongol political situation in terms of the Mongol princes having traditionally maintained their "autonomy" within the Qing system. Here "autonomy" meant that, within the structure of the Qing political system, each Mongol prince maintaining his own individual, relatively autonomous status. Thus, when Russia put pressure on the Qing government to maintain Mongolian "autonomy," it meant a restoration of the conditions prevailing prior to the implementation of the new policy. But the situation had now changed, for with the collapse of the Qing political system, the Mongols had established their own political authority. Furthermore, even though the Qing had collapsed in China proper, the new government had not yet fully established itself. Until a new form of government (in fact, this would be the Republic of China) was established and until the power base of the Bogdo Khân regime was fully stabilized, the political situation was much too fluid to allow for any concrete meaning to be applied to what Russia referred to as "Mongolian autonomy," to define the locus of responsibility or the exact form of that autonomy.

Immediately after the Mongols declared their independence, Russia commenced the mediatory work designed to settle the situation. However, Russia had to do so with utmost care for there was a rival power, with which it did not want to come into conflict —Japan, which had its own interests in Inner Mongolia. It was precisely because of the Japanese presence that Russia had, from the very first, tried to limit the scope of the Mongol problem to Outer Mongolia. Russia thought of Inner Mongolia as being under "special circumstances" because of Japan's interests there.[10] Thus without paying any regard to Mongol aspirations for the formation of a Great Mongol State uniting both Inner and Outer Mongolia, Russia and Japan were already in the process of restricting the powers of the Bogdo Khân government.

The direct occasion for the adjustment and balancing of Russian and Japanese interests in Inner Mongolia was a Russian communiqué on the Mongol problem issued January 11, 1912.[11] The reason the Russian government thought it necessary to issue this communiqué was that the press in various countries at that time suggested strongly that there was a Russian plot behind the Mongol independence declaration, and even that Russia had a secret desire to eventually annex Mongolia. Russia hoped that this communiqué would make clear its position on the Mongol problem, allay suspicions of any dark intentions, and make clear its position as a mediator between the Beijing government and the

Bogdo Khân government. In fact, however, the communiqué provoked quite different reactions.

On the one hand, the Beijing government hardened its position on the problem because of the phrasing at the end of the communiqué which stated that, if the Beijing government were to completely reject the proposed mediation, Russia would have no alternative but to establish direct bilateral relations with Mongolia. Russia had used this phrasing with the intent of applying pressure on the Beijing government to accept the principle of Russian mediation, but the effect was precisely the opposite of that intended. It actually invited Beijing's refusal of Russian mediation. On the other hand, Japan displayed great interest in resolving whether or not the ambiguous term "Mongolia" used throughout the text of the communiqué was intended to include Inner Mongolia. Japan had already acknowledged that Outer Mongolia was under the Russian sphere of influence, but there was no agreement between Japan and Russia on the status of Inner Mongolia. The Japanese foreign minister was eager to pursue negotiations to clarify Japanese and Russian spheres of influence in Inner Mongolia, while the Russian government, as noted previously, had tried to limit the Mongol problem to Outer Mongolia precisely because of the delicate nature of its relations with Japan. Ultimately, the third round of Russo-Japanese negotiations, starting on January 16, 1912, began as a result of Japan's inquiry concerning the use of the term "Mongolia" in the communiqué. The negotiations went rather smoothly since they were conducted in a cooperative atmosphere, with both sides searching for a "balance" in East Asia.

In May of 1912, there were indications that the Mongol problem would be brought to a new stage of development. At that time, the Russian minister to Beijing, on the basis of an analysis of the situation in China, proposed that a more aggressive policy than the original Russian plan for mediation be adapted.[12] By this time, the Russo-Japanese Entente negotiations had reached agreement in principle. Russia was gradually moving toward a new perception of the situation. Thus, Russia abandoned its former policy of seeking a general negotiated settlement between the Republic of China and the Bogdo Khân's Mongolia through Russian mediation and began to look for other policy options. Furthermore, although the details of the actual situation and the life expectancy of the Bogdo Khân regime had not been clear when it took power in late 1911, by now the government had at least consolidated its power and established effective control over all of Outer Mongolia and part of Inner Mongolia as well. On the other hand, although the locus of political power was still not fully clear in China proper in late 1911, by this time Yuan Shikai's Republic of China government had finally been established, and it clearly had its sights set on asserting for itself a Qing-style political domination of Mongolia.

At this stage of the problem, there was a significant change of nuance in the concept of "autonomy" which Russia had always used in reference to Mongolia. Previously, as mentioned above, the term "autonomy" referred to relatively autonomous conditions under which the individual Mongol princes acted within the Qing administrative framework. Now, however, the phrase "Mongolian autonomy" had come to refer to the status of the political administration of the Bogdo Khân government rather than of the individual princes. This change in nuance was accompanied by a Russian move to clarify the political status of the Bogdo Khân government in international law. A few years later, Russia described this change as one "from rule by a general assembly of individual princes to rule by the unified authority of an emperor and his council."[13] In the past, Russia had left room for acknowledging the Republic of China's legal status in Outer Mongolia as "sovereignty," but now it argued that its status must be acknowledged as only "suzerainty." This shift in terminology signaled a new, more aggressive Russian strategy.

In June 1912, Russia for the last time offered its plan for Russian mediation which contained the three restrictive clauses, but again it was immediately rejected by the Beijing government. Why did China reject this proposal? Although the Yuan Shikai government was in place, its domestic authority was still weak. Certainly its prestige and authority would be greatly enhanced if it could establish relations with the Imperialist Powers and thereby acquire their recognition. In particular, the settlement of the Mongol problem was indispensable to the normal relations with Russia. Nonetheless, the Beijing government was strongly suspicious of the sincerity of Russia's motives in Mongolia. Beijing itself had no ideological base or principles upon which to base a

Mongol policy adapted to the new situation in Mongolia. It had only a desire to restore the Qing administrative system. Moreover, there was strong sentiment in the country for crushing Mongol independence by military force. Most of the Han Chinese thought it only right and proper that the Mongols be subject to the authority of the Republic of China. Thus, if the Yuan government were to show itself too conciliatory on the Mongol problem, it risked a violent eruption of internal opposition based on naive Great Han Nationalism. Thus the Yuan government concluded that a weak stand on the Mongol problem would seriously damage its domestic leadership and stability.

The solution of the Mongol problem by a Russian-mediated Sino-Mongol treaty was thus brought to a standstill by the final Chinese rejection. Meanwhile, the Russo-Japanese Entente was formally signed on July 8, 1912, fixing the Japanese and Russian spheres of influence in Inner Mongolia.

Given these changes in the political situation, Russia convened a special Council of Ministers on August 15 to settle on a new policy to deal with the Mongol problem.[14] It concluded that the best policy would be to "conclude a bilateral diplomatic document with Khalkha [the Bogdo Khân government] since the indecisive policy on the Mongol problem is harmful to Russia." It was urged that in the "diplomatic document" Russia guarantee the autonomy of the Bogdo Khân regime and implement the three restrictive clauses of the earlier plan. In return, Russia requested the Bogdo Khân government to pledge that it would not enter into any agreement with another country which might violate the spirit of these clauses, and further that it would acknowledge Russia's broad economic interests in the region by signing the commercial protocol appended to the agreement. Russia also stipulated that the regional application of the agreement would be restricted to Outer Mongolia.

Thus, at this council, the Russian government formulated a new strategy. Russia would negotiate separately with the Bogdo Khân government and acknowledge its autonomy in Outer Mongolia. Moreover, Russia decided to demand from the Bogdo Khân government guarantees of Russia's superior position in the economic sphere in Outer Mongolia. However, the adoption of this new policy did not by any means imply that Russia had abandoned completely its former basic aims for the solution of the Mongol problem—namely, the establishment of an accord between China and Mongolia in which the autonomy of the latter would be recognized through Russia's mediation. As to what was referred to as the "political significance" of the "diplomatic document" which Russia wanted to conclude with the Bogdo Khân government, Russia pointed out that it would "make the Chinese seriously recognize the fact that there really is a separate bilateral agreement between the Mongols and us [the Russians], and what the implications of this are for Sino-Russian relations." Essentially, Russia, having seen China's intransigent position, recognized that the time was not ripe for Sino-Mongol negotiations to be mediated by Russia. Thus it adapted the strategy of taking the seemingly easier course of opening negotiations directly with the Bogdo Khân government. It intended then to utilize whatever was gained by this as a lever to dislodge the Chinese from their intransigent position and then wait for China to take a new position. Russia had thus shifted from the formula of seeking a single general solution to the problem toward a two-stage solution formula, in which it would first approach Bogdo Khân's Mongolia and then deal with the Beijing government afterward.

This, then, was the process whereby the basic principles of the Russian solution to the Mongol problem were decided upon and systematized. In the final analysis, the basic principles had remained unchanged throughout the process: the autonomy of Outer Mongolia under the Bogdo Khân government, but under the *suzerainty* of the Republic of China; the guarantee of this autonomy through the three restrictive clauses; and the acquisition of sweeping economic rights and interests in Outer Mongolia by Russia.

Now, I would like to give a brief account of the events that occurred following the implementation of this latest strategy by Russia. Although Russo-Mongol negotiations began in the fall of 1912, the gulf separating their positions was immense. The Bogdo Khân government's goal was nothing less than a fully sovereign state uniting all of Mongolia, while Russia, for its part, was willing to recognize an autonomous government only in Outer Mongolia. During the negotiations, the Bogdo Khân government pressed Russia for clarifications of its concepts of autonomy, of the nature of the relationship with the Republic of China, and of the territory and national boundaries under discussion. Further, as an independent state, it protested the concession of excessive rights and interests to Russia. But Russia was not diverted by such protests from its judgment that a final solution to the Mongol problem could only be achieved through negotiation with China. If Russia simply accepted the demands of the Bogdo Khân government, the latter would set up an independent state under Russian protection. However, since world opinion was in favor of the protection of Chinese territorial integrity, there was danger that the other Imperialist Powers would be angered by the Russian action. Thus, Russia had to maintain a rigid stance and not accede to the Mongol demands.

For the Mongols, there were really only two options: "cooperate with Russia and maintain autonomy or affiliate with Yuan Shikai and revert to the previous state [of subjugation]."[15] Given only these two options, they felt compelled to choose the Russian proposal as the lesser of two evils, and they signed the Russo-Mongol Agreement on November 3, 1912. However, this did not solve all their problems because this agreement did not make the scope of its application sufficiently clear. Where the Russian text of the agreement refers to "Mongolia" and an "autonomous organization," the corresponding passages in the Mongolian text have "the Mongol State" and "a self-constituted, self-governing organization." Needless to say, the implications of these terms are not precisely identical.[16] In any sense, the agreement was signed, and the Bogdo Khân regime wanted to use it to prove that it had been recognized as a sovereign state. It could then go on to use the agreement to gain similar recognition from the other Imperialist Powers. Moreover, it initiated military activity in Inner Mongolia to expand the territory under its actual control.[17]

From the Russian point of view, however, this agreement was nothing more than one step in the process of achieving a final solution to the problem. The Bogdo Khân regime would have to rely on Russia's power to maintain itself, and it would thus be easy, Russia thought, to apply pressure at any time it wished. For this reason, Russia was most concerned with the economic benefits it would gain from the Commercial Protocol attached to the agreement and the shock the Republic of China would experience upon learning that it had actually been signed.

Nevertheless, the discrepancy in understanding between Russia and the Bogdo Khân government about what had been accomplished in the agreement affected the development of the Russian formula for a two-stage solution to the Mongol problem. The key to the success of the Russian formula depended on unanimity in the understanding of the principles underlying a solution of the problem between Russia and Mongolia in the first stage of the formula, which was the Russo-Mongol Agreement. But, although the negotiations and the agreement itself failed to achieve that unanimity, the first stage of the Russian plan achieved qualified success in that it did draw the Beijing government into a willingness to enter into negotiations.

The ensuing Sino-Russian negotiations,[18] however, did not proceed smoothly at all, because of the tough stance China took in emphatically proclaiming its sovereignty over Mongolia. The negotiations were complicated by the plight in which the Yuan Shikai government found itself. On the one hand, it wanted to strengthen its position vis-à-vis its domestic rivals by normalizing relations with Russia and obtaining its support. On the other hand, it had to be extremely prudent in its handling of the Mongol problem, for it did not want to provoke mass opposition. Later, Yuan Shikai, after he had suppressed the Second Revolution in September 1913 and established a dictatorship, no longer had to worry about this dilemma, and he decided to move toward an accord with Russia. However, when accord was reached, the actual agreement (the Russo-Chinese Declaration of November 5, 1913) did nothing but acknowledge the principles by which Russia and China could jointly reach a solution of the Mongol problem. Thus, Russia was forced to set up a tripartite conference of Yuan's government, the Bogdo Khân government, and itself as the final step in the process of finding a solution.

This conference was convened in Kiakhta in September 1914 and was to proceed from the somewhat unstable foundation of two documents which were not fully consistent with each other: the Russo-Mongol Agreement and the Russo-Chinese Declaration. The conference was often on the brink of disaster because of differences in the intentions and expectations of the participants. The fact that it did not break apart is a tribute to the skill with which Russia controlled the course of negotiations. In the end,

Russia was successful in forging an agreement which effectively implemented the principles it had originally enunciated years before. The success of the Kiakhta Agreement, which was signed on July 7, 1915, was in marked contrast with the failure of the Simla Conference, involving Britain, China, and Tibet, which was convened at about the same time to seek a solution to the Tibet problem.

The reason that so many years were required to reach a final solution of the Mongol problem was that the three parties concerned had completely different images of what Mongolia was and what it should be. For the Bogdo Khân government, the goal was the formation of a fully sovereign state which would include Inner Mongolia within its boundaries. The Beijing government thought of Mongolia as being part of China and desired to reassert the Qing dynasty pattern of administrative control. Russia, for its part, planned for Outer Mongolia to be autonomous under China's suzerainty.

However, among these three parties, Russia had by far the strongest bargaining position and prevailed over the others. Since the Bogdo Khân regime depended for its very existence on Russia, it had no alternative but to acknowledge the solution proposed by Russia in order to salvage anything at all of what it had gained by declaring its independence. The Beijing government, too, had little choice but to approve the Russian plan, because it did not want to suffer a complete loss of control over Mongolia and because it wanted to better its relations with Russia, one of the Imperialist Powers.

Russia had carefully analyzed the Mongol problem in the framework of its overall foreign policy and only then had set about deciding the principles for a solution. Russia's foreign policy objectives were most strongly oriented toward Europe and it did not want to be forced to assume added responsibilities in East Asia. Thus it had absolutely no desire to support or underwrite the sort of fully sovereign state envisioned by the Bogdo Khân government. Moreover, by not lending its support to the establishment of such a state, it would be able to proceed without having to rashly move against the tide of world opinion that was gathering in support of China's territorial integrity and sovereignty. The restriction of the Bogdo Khân's territory to Outer Mongolia also was necessary in order to appease Japan. Russian special interests in Outer Mongolia were acknowledged by the other Imperialist Powers. This recognition made it easy for Russia to make a slightly aggressive policy and demand economic concessions in Outer Mongolia.

Thus, the international relations of the time were reflected in Russian policy toward Mongolia and were the decisive factor in determining it. Moreover, as noted previously, Russia was able to take the overwhelming leadership in the solution of the Mongol problem and prevailed over the other two parties. Consequently, the international relations of the time were reflected in the Mongol problem directly through Russian policy and became the decisive factor in achieving its settlement.

Finally, I should like to see whether this investigation of the Mongol independence problem which emerged at the height of the 1911 Revolution can add anything to our understanding of the revolution itself and of political conditions in the late Qing and early Republican periods.

It is important to point out, I think, the different images that the Mongols and the Han Chinese had of the concept of "Zhongguo" (the Middle Kingdom), more specifically, the fact that the Mongols lacked this concept completely.

For the Han Chinese, the 1911 Revolution meant the final expulsion of a Manchu emperor from the seat of power and the collapse of the old system symbolized by the existence of a Manchu emperor. Yet, even though the name of the country changed from the Qing Empire (Qingguo) to the Republic of China and the new form of the government reflected the change in name, the Han Chinese still thought of "Zhongguo" (the Middle Kingdom) as an entity that maintained its existence throughout the changes. It was as though they thought that both the Qing Empire and the Republic of China were but different manifestations or incarnations of the same "Zhongguo."

The Mongols, however, had never had this concept of "Zhongguo" (the Middle Kingdom) which was so dear to the hearts and minds of the Han Chinese. The closest term to the concept of "Zhongguo" in Mongolian was "Kitad" (Kyatad). But rather than being an abstract concept like "Zhongguo," their term "Kitad" was nothing more than a geographic name which referred to the original habitat of the Han Chinese. Quite naturally, it did not include Mongolia, Tibet, Manchuria, Turkestan, etc. Thus, it was not possible for the Mongols to identify "Kitad" with the Qing Empire ("Čin ulus") for they regarded both "Kitad" and Mongolia as being the same level of entity under the umbrella of the Qing Empire. The Han Chinese tried to introduce the "Zhongguo" concept into the Mongolian world view just after the establishment of the Republic by coining a new term in Mongolian, "Dundatu ulus," which was a direct translation of the Chinese "Zhongguo," but the perception gap persisted.

In conclusion then, it seems clear that the 1911 Revolution and the Mongol declaration of independence basically had their origins in the same set of causal circumstances. From about the middle nineteenth century, the Qing government was shaken by two new political challenges: the rising power and influence of the Han Chinese and the encroachment of the Imperialist Powers. These changes in the political environment eventually transformed the Qing political structure itself. In China proper, a logical consequence of this transformation was the 1911 Revolution. When the effect of the changes in the Qing structure reached Mongolia, the Mongols felt themselves to be threatened as a nation and began to grope for a restoration of their political sovereignty and ethnic unity. In this context, the 1911 Revolution became a catalyst for Mongol aspirations, moving them in the direction of independence. Yet, since the Han Chinese had regarded the Qing Empire as being identical with "Zhongguo," they naturally thought that the newest incarnation, the Republic of China, would inherit the former's sovereignty over Mongolia, and they thought that Mongolia should naturally be part of the new "Zhongguo" (the Middle Kingdom).

On the other hand, since they lacked the very concept of "Zhongguo," the Mongols thought that with the disappearance of the Qing regime both "Kitad" and Mongolia should be free to choose their own separate destinies. There was thus a decisive and fateful gap between the perceptions of the two nations. In the end, this gap was only closed because of the skillful diplomatic maneuvering of Russia. By acknowledging that Mongolia was under the suzerainty of the Republic of China, Russia demonstrated to the Han Chinese that it regarded Mongolia to be part of "Zhongguo" (the

Middle Kingdom), thus satisfying the honor of the Republic. On the other hand, it was also able to help the Bogdo Khân government satisfy at least part of its desire for independence from "Waifan-bu" (outer vassal) status under the Qing imperial structure by clarifying the status of Mongolia as autonomous under international law.

Seen in this way, then, the Mongol independence problem was a powerful and significant protest by one of the non-Han minorities against the concept of "Zhongguo" (the Middle Kingdom) so central to the world view of the Han Chinese.

[Translated by Robert J. J. Wargo and Beverly Nelson]

## Notes

I wish to thank Professor Nakai Hideki of Hokkaido University for his valuable comments.

M.O.: *Mezhdunarodnye otnosheniya v epokhu imperializma, dokumenty iz arkhivov Tsarskogo i Vremennogo pravitel'stv, 1873–1917.* [International relations in the age of imperialism: documents from the archives of the Tsarist and the Provisionary governments] (Moscow: Gosudarstvennoe izdatel'stvo politicheskoy literatury, 1931–40), 19 vols.

1. In this article, the focus is placed mainly on the Mongols' activities in Outer Mongolia around the Khalkha region. The reason for this is that the Mongols in Outer Mongolia, where regional integrity still existed to some extent, were successful in unifying opinion and acting in concert in the midst of political transformation. Meanwhile, in Inner Mongolia, even if some leaders wanted to carry out some political activity, there was no political or regional integrity to base such movements on. It is significant that there was no centripetal force to promote integration of the Mongols in Inner Mongolia. Moreover, in fact, the Mongols themselves in Inner Mongolia were reduced to minority status except in a few regions because of the enormous number of Han Chinese immigrants. For the responses of the Mongols in Inner Mongolia to the 1911 Revolution and the Mongol declaration of independence, see my article, "Gunsannorubu to Uchi Mongoru no meiun" [Prince Gungsunnorbu and the fate of Inner Mongolia] in *Nairiku Ajia, Nishi Ajia no shakai to bunka* [Society and culture of Inner Asia and the Muslim world], ed. Mori Masao (Tokyo: Yamakawa Shuppan-sha, 1983), pp. 411–35.

2. For Mongolia under the Qing dominance, see Joseph Fletcher's excellent articles in *The Cambridge History of China*, vol. 18, *Late Ch'ing, Part I*, ed. John K. Fairbank (Cambridge, Mass.: Harvard University Press, 1978), pp. 48–57, 352–59.

3. The Mongolian text is in L. Dindüb, *Mongyol-un tobči teüke* [A brief history of the Mongols) (Ulan Bator: Mongyol keblel-ün quriy-a, 1934), pp. 4–15.

4. Kotwicz to a Mongol high officer, correspondence, 6 October (23 September), 1911, in Russian, *V. Kotvichyn khuwyn arkhivaas oldson Mongolyn tüükhend kholbogdokh zarim bichig* [The Mongol historical materials from W. Kotwicz's papers] (Ulan Bator: Sh. U.A.-yn khevlel, 1972), no. 8, pp. 41–46.

5. A. Popov, "Tsarskaya Rossiya i Mongoliya v 1913–1914 gg." [Tsarist Russia and Mongolia in 1913–1914], *Krasny arkhiv*, vol. 6(37), (1929), p. 9.

6. The Journals of the Special Conference on the Far Eastern Problem, 17 Aug. 1911, *M.O.*, ser. II, vol. 18, pt. 1 (Moscow, 1938), no. 329, pp. 339–41.

7. For roles and activities of the Inner Mongols under the Bogdo Khân regime, see my articles: "Haisan to Otai: Bogudo Hān seiken-ka ni okeru Minami-Mongorujin" [Khaisan and Udai: Two Inner Mongols under the Bogdo Khân regime], *Tōyō Gakuhō*, vol. 57, nos. 1–2 (Jan. 1976), pp. 125–70; "The Minority's Groping: Further Light on Khaisan and Udai," *Journal of Asian and African Studies*, no. 20 (1980), pp. 108–10.

8. S.S. Grigortsevich, *Dal'nevostochnaya politika imperialisticheskikh derzhav v 1906–1917 gg.* [The Far Eastern policy of the Imperialist Powers in 1906–1917), (Tomsk: Izdatel'stvo Tomskogo universiteta, 1965), p. 402.

9. Sazonov to Shekine, telegram, 23 (10) Dec. 1911, *M.O.*, ser. II, vol. 19, pt. 1, (Moscow, 1938), no. 253, p. 234.

10. Ibid., p. 235.

11. E.D. Grimm, *Sbornik dogovor i drugikh dokumentov; po istorii mezhdunarodnykh otnosheny na D. Vostoke* [Collection of agreements and other documents on the history of international relations in the Far East, 1842–1925] (Moscow: Institut Vostokovedenie, 1927), no. 73, pp. 178–79.

12. Krupensky to Sazonov, dispatch, 14 (1) May 1912, *M.O.*, ser. II, vol. 20, pt. 1 (Moscow, 1939), no. 5, pp. 4–5.

13. Sazonov to Krupensky, telegram, 28 (15) June 1913, *Sbornik diplomaticheskikh dokumentov po Mongol'skomu voprosu (23 Avgusta 1912 g.–2 Noyabrya 1913 g.)* [Collection of diplomatic documents on the Mongol problem, 6 September (23 August) 1912–15 (2) November, 1913] (St. Petersburg: Ministerstvo inostrannykh del, 1914), p. 66.

14. The Special Journal of the Council of Ministers, 15 Aug. 1912, *M.O.*, ser. II, vol. 20, pt. 2 (Moscow, 1940), no. 472, pp. 6–11.

15. Iwan J. Korostovetz, *Von Chinggis Khan zur Sowjetrepublik* (Berlin & Leipzig: Walter de Gruyter & Co., 1926), p. 173.

16. Sh. Sandag, "Avtonomi yum uu, tusgaar togtnol yum uu?" [Autonomy or independence?], *Sh.U.A.-yn medee*, 1971, no. 1, pp. 20–21.

17. Nakami Tatsuo, "Bogudo Hān seiken no taigai kōshō doryoku to teikoku-shugi rekkyō" [Independent Mongolia and the Imperialist Powers], *Ajia Afurika Gengo Bunka Kenkyū*, vol. 17 (1979), pp. 1–58.

18. For these Sino-Russian negotiations, see my article, "1913 nen no Ro-Chū sengen: Chūka-minkoku no seiritsu to Mongoru mondai" [On the Russo-Chinese declaration of November 5, 1913: The emergence of the Republic of China and the Mongol problem], *Kokusai Seiji*, no. 66 (Nov. 1980), pp. 109–27.

# Revolutionaries in Action

# The Bourgeois Revolutionaries in the Movement to Regain Economic Rights Toward the End of the Qing Dynasty

## Li Zongyi

The movement to regain economic rights was an anti-imperialist, patriotic struggle launched in China in the early twentieth century. The two main political groups of the Chinese bourgeoisie—the revolutionaries and the constitutionalists—were both deeply involved in this struggle. While the leading role of the constitutionalists in this movement is a recognized historical fact, the role played by the revolutionaries is often overlooked. In fact, although the Tongmenghui (Chinese League) failed to incorporate the promotion of this movement into its general program of action, a considerable number of its members, aware of the necessity and urgency to expand the revolutionary forces on this front, took part in the struggle and played an important role.

The positive role played by the revolutionaries was first manifested in the mobilization of public opinion. In their publications, they repeatedly put forward slogans fired with strong patriotic sentiments to awaken the entire nation. Secondly, their role was manifested in the actual struggle. It can be said that members of the revolutionary party took part in each round of the struggle in China. Although individual roles in the struggle varied, they were always a firm and active force that occupied a significant position in the struggle. Keenly aware that the recovery of economic rights alone could not lead to a fundamental solution of the national crisis, they called on the people to rise up to overthrow the Qing government and strive for higher revolutionary goals. In so doing, they played the part of radicals.

In a semi-colonial and semi-feudal society, the struggle for national independence is a factor making for revolution which is independent of man's subjective will. No matter how desperately the constitutionalists tried to stem the surging tide of revolution, time and again the ruthless struggle exposed the traitorous and brutal features of the Qing government, thus irresistibly propelling the vast number of patriots toward the revolution. Thanks to the vigorous agitation of the revolutionaries, the movement to preserve railway rights in Sichuan rapidly developed into a people's uprising, and the anti-imperialist, patriotic struggle turned into a high tide of revolt against the Qing dynasty, thus heralding the 1911 Revolution.

The 1911 Revolution was initiated and led by the Chinese bourgeois revolutionaries. The decade preceding the 1911 Revolution was a most important decade for the bourgeois revolutionaries. During this period, with the steady progress of the democratic revolution, an uninterrupted movement to regain economic rights emerged throughout China. It grew more intense in a wave-like manner and finally led to the movement for the preservation of railway rights in Sichuan which shook the entire nation. In this series of patriotic movements, what was the position and role of the bourgeois revolutionaries and how did they promote this agitation and make it part of the revolution? In this article, I will try to probe this subject, since it has seldom been discussed in previous studies.

The movement to recover economic rights which began in the early twentieth century was justified resistance to the imperialist powers' economic aggression against China. Its object was to recover various economic rights that were seized by imperialist powers, particularly the right to build railways and open mines, so as to enable China to develop its own railway and mining industries. The upsurge of this anti-imperialist, patriotic movement was an important hallmark of the new awakening of the Chinese nation. As distinguished from the previous patriotic movements, its salient feature was that it was directly linked to the historical demand to develop capitalism in China. Therefore, it had a new social content.

The recovery of economic rights was a form of struggle launched by the Chinese bourgeoisie for national independence. This clarion call was backed by the bourgeoisie's pressing demand for developing the national capitalist economy. Under the historical conditions of the time, their demand conformed to the progressive trend of China's social development. Consequently they had the support of the broad masses who were subjected to imperialist oppression. This was the basic reason why the struggle to regain economic rights in certain areas could have developed into vigorous patriotic movements. In a sense, through the slogan of recovering economic rights, the bourgeoisie drew people from various walks of life into political activities.

The movement was a united action of people from various walks of life led by the bourgeoisie. Both revolutionaries and constitutionalists, the two large political groups of the Chinese bourgeoisie, became deeply involved in the struggle. Relying on their own political and economic strengths, the constitutionalist businessmen who had vital interests in the economic rights of their respective provinces put forward specific proposals for regaining these rights. They campaigned for this cause and often claimed to be representatives of the people of their provinces. In the country as a whole, they indisputably played leading roles. However, the active role of the revolutionaries should not be overlooked. In the past, we knew very little about the role of the revolutionaries, and our knowledge was very vague. It was mainly because the scholars on this subject focused on the lack of anti-imperialist content in the political program of the Tongmenghui and overlooked the difference between the revolutionaries' political perception and their actual social practice. In fact, although the Tongmenghui failed to incorporate the movement to regain economic rights into its general program of action, there were quite a number of revolutionaries who realized the necessity and urgency to expand revolutionary forces through this anti-imperialist, patriotic struggle. Moreover, they participated in this struggle and played a very important and active role in it.

The role of the bourgeois revolutionaries in the movement to regain economic rights was first manifested in the mobilization of public opinion. The books and journals published by them contained many articles advocating the recovery of economic rights. In particular, journals like the *Tides of Zhejiang (Zhejiang chao)*, *Students of Hubei (Hubei xueshengjie)*, *Journal of Yunnan (Yun-*

*nan zazhi)*, *Jincheng*, *Sichuan*, *Vernacular Paper of Anhui (Anhui suhua bao)*, *Shenzhou Daily (Shenzhou ribao)*, and *Minli bao* provided extremely penetrating and candid exposures of imperialist aggression against China. By analyzing the changes in the strategy of the imperialist powers in their aggression against China at the turn of the century, these journals pointed out that the time had passed when the imperialist powers used cannons to extort trading rights and that the powers had now switched mainly to seizing concessions, railways, mining properties, and commercial and industrial enterprises. They added that imperialism "relied on its policy of economic aggression" with "intentions much more malicious than before."[1] Issuing slogans such as "China belongs to the Chinese people" and "The railways and mines of a province belong to the people of that province," the revolutionary periodicals called on the people to "regain economic rights and resist foreign aggression." These slogans that aimed at awakening the entire nation echoed strong patriotic sentiments.

Every publication that spread revolutionary ideas not only lamented the danger of China's being subjected to conquest by imperialist powers, but virtually all of them issued direct calls for the recovery of China's economic rights. The *Journal of Yunnan* played a major role in the struggle to regain mining rights in Kunming and six other prefectures in Yunnan province and to foil the French attempt to build the Yunnan-Vietnam railway. The journal *Jincheng* listed "recovery of the railway and mining rights" as one of its "six cardinal principles," and almost every issue carried articles commenting on the subject. *Min bao*, the Tongmenghui organ, also showed much concern over the same subject. The current affairs column in *Min bao* devoted a number of articles to the movement to recover economic rights. While pointing out the inability of this movement to solve the "fundamental domestic issues" and calling on the people to strive for higher goals, it voiced strong support for the struggles going on in various parts of the country. For instance, it exhorted the people of Shanxi to "struggle hard and never give up hope"[2] with regard to the Shanxi mines; it denounced Yuan Shuxun,[3] governor of Shandong, and Zhang Zhidong, governor-general of Hunan and Hubei, for selling mining rights; and it praised the formation of the Guangdong-Hankou Railway Company for demonstrating "the might of our people" and "winning the admiration of the world," etc.[4] The second issue of *Min bao* published an article by the important Tongmenghui leader, Chen Tianhua, on the eve of his suicide. Chen wrote that the development of the movement to regain China's economic rights testified to the "progress of the Chinese nation." Revolutionaries, he wrote, should be adept at promoting this struggle so as to attain the aim of "changing the state system, enlightening the people and nurturing talented industrialists." He also wrote: "Once our sovereign rights are regained, it will still be possible to absorb foreign capital in order to promote Chinese civilization."[5] These remarks of Chen Tianhua more or less reflected the ideas of some of the Tongmenghui leaders. In addition, *Min bao* published serially Hu Hanmin's article, "Opposing Foreigners and International Law." Running to tens of thousands of words, the article strongly refuted the imperialist powers' slanderous characterization of the Chinese people's recovery of their economic rights as xenophobia. Hu pointed out that "during recent years our people's concept of 'opposing foreigners' is vastly different from that of the past. Formerly it meant shutting the country off from all foreign influences, since anything or anyone that was not Chinese was considered barbarian. But now opposing foreigners means that we claim our own rights." Chen Tianhua went on to say: "Legitimate opposition to foreigners" can also be found in Western and other countries. As for the assertion that Chinese anti-foreign "measures are sometimes uncivilized," this was caused by those foreigners who "cling to their vested interests and refuse to make any concessions."[6]

Of course, the role of the revolutionaries was by no means confined to verbal declarations but, more importantly, was expressed in the actual struggle. It could be said that the revolutionaries participated in every struggle in the country, and with the passage of time they played an increasingly prominent role. After its founding in 1905, the Tongmenghui organized branches successively in all provinces of the country. Each branch recruited a considerable number of distinguished local personalities, including such enlightened gentry, businessmen, and prominent educators as Xie Ronglu in Shanxi, Zhou Shubiao in Shandong, Wen Fei in Hunan, Zhu Zhihong in Sichuan, Guo Xiren in Shaanxi, Yang Yuanmao in Henan, Chu Fucheng in Zhejiang, and Lei Zaihan in Guangxi.

Almost all of them were activists in the movement to recover economic rights. Since they could not fully express their patriotic fervor, they turned to revolution. They joined the Tongmenghui, thus greatly augmenting its strength in the patriotic movement.

The local organizations of the Tongmenghui took a very active part in the rights recovery movement. Since the Fujian branch "failed to obtain results" by inciting the secret societies (*huidang*), from 1906 onward, it "began to turn its attention to society." It established open organizations like the Qiaonan Public Welfare Society which contacted various circles, and because of its extensive support it gave a powerful impetus to the anti-imperialist, patriotic struggle. "The most well-known cases are those to abolish the mining contracts concluded with France by the prefectures of Yanping, Jianou, and Shaowu; to recover the ancient relics of Songfeng Hall; to resist foreign occupation of the public land in the Cangqianshan area; and to support merchants, workers, and peasants in rejecting heavier taxation. Thus the people placed full confidence in the Qiaonan Public Welfare Society."[7] The Nanning branch of the Tongmenghui in Guangxi initiated and led the fight against French designs on the Nanning-Beihai railway rights. On the initiative of Branch Secretary Lei Zaihan and others, a provisional office of the Nanning Bureau of the Nanning-Beihai railway was organized, a mass meeting was held, and contributions collected for building the railway. This bureau then became a secret organization of the revolutionaries.[8] Throughout the struggle to regain mining rights in seven prefectures of Yunnan, Tongmenghui members were in the vanguard. Li Bodong, Xu Lian, and others organized the Dare-to-Die Society, pledging that "foreigners will have to go over the dead bodies of all the Yunnan people in order to engage in mining here." They held many meetings and made speeches to arouse the masses to fight the French attempt to secure the right to mine, and to build the Yunnan-Vietnam railway. They even declared that they were "breaking off relations" with the Qing court.[9]

In addition, Chen Gan, Zhou Shubiao, and other members of the Shandong Tongmenghui branch contacted people from all walks of life to form the Society for the Preservation of Mines, in which most of the members were "graduates from various schools." They were resolutely opposed to Germany's forcible seizure of mining rights along the Tianjin-Pukou railway and in Maoshan and four other places. They solemnly declared that if the treaty was not abolished, they would impose "restrictions on mining and boycott German goods in order to support our struggle."[10] In Shanxi, Jing Dingcheng, Wang Yongbin, Xie Ronglu, and Jing Yaoyue as well as constitutionalists like Liang Shanji made every effort to reach people in all social strata. They played a major role in the recovery of the Shanxi mines. All members of the Tongmenghui in provinces like Zhejiang, Jiangsu, Henan, Hunan, Hubei, and Anhui were in varying degrees involved in the provincial struggles.

In their attitude to the rights recovery movement, the Tongmenghui members were more radical than the constitutionalists, for they were "well aware of the fact that nothing can be accomplished in negotiations with foreigners unless drastic action is taken with the backing of the people."[11] Therefore, they were distinguished for their initiative in mobilizing young students and masses of the lower strata, and their call for strikes, boycott of classes, and other drastic measures. On the other hand, the constitutionalists were often too timid and hesitant to take any such actions. For instance, in the midst of the struggle to recover mining rights seized by the Fortune Company in Henan in 1909, the Qing government even permitted the company to sell the coal locally, thus dealing a blow to the mines operated by the national capitalists. This news caused an uproar in Kaifeng. The Mining Research Society, controlled by the constitutionalists, called a meeting of representatives from various circles at the palace mansion to discuss ways to deal with the situation. At the meeting, student representatives made highly emotional speeches, which caused the presiding speaker to call off the meeting hurriedly and perfunctorily. This disappointed and puzzled the participating students and Tongmenghui members.

Yang Yuanmao, one of the leaders of the Tongmenghui, took up the matter and canvassed support to call another meeting, which was attended by 8,000 people, mostly students from various schools.[12] At the meeting, the representatives of students and teachers made "impassioned, forceful, sincere and touching" speeches amidst a "solemn atmosphere of righteous indignation."[13] After the meeting, the Miners' Trade Union of Henan Province was established by representatives of various groups who elected Yang Yuanmao as president. While sending representatives to the capital to submit a statement of the people's will to the higher authorities, the union sent out students as "propagandists" to various counties and prefectures north of the Yellow River to "campaign against the purchase of coal from the Fortune Company,"[14] and, in effect, to boycott the firm. As a result, several thousand colliery owners and miners in Jiaozuo area "gathered in great strength to challenge the company."[15]

The case of Hunan was even more illustrative. Wen Fei, secretary of the Tongmenghui Hunan branch, was supervisor of the Changsha Railway Institute. With the initiation of the Movement for the Preservation of Railway Rights in 1911, the Tongmenghui Hunan branch worked hard in cooperation with the constitutionalists to form the Hunan Association to Support Railways. They called meetings of thousands of people at which they made speeches denouncing the crimes of the Qing dynasty. The constitutionalists advocated presenting petititons to the court, while Wen Fei and Zou Daifan called for strikes, boycott of classes, and refusal to pay taxes. The radical views of the League members were in sharp contrast to the moderate and cautious tone of the constitutionalists. Yang Wending, governor of Hunan, sent troops to suppress the movement. "However, Wu Zuolin, Wen Jingwei, Wang You, and Yi Zongxi, executive officers of the association, remained firm."[16] Their attitude greatly inspired the people, "adding momentum to the revolution."[17]

The above examples show that the bourgeois revolutionaries played the role of radicals and gave tremendous impetus to the intensive development of the movement. They maintained a delicate relationship with the constitutionalists. When the movement was confined to making representations, stating views or sending letters, and telegraphing petitions, cooperation was the main aspect of the relationship between the two sides, while their contradictions were not noticeable. Though conflicts sometimes occurred, they were of a local and temporary nature. The constitutionalists always charged the League members with being "too radical and reckless."[18] But the League members stood firm. Under the mounting pressure of the imperialist powers and officials of the Qing government, the constitutionalists had to maintain their relations with the League members, for they had no other popular support except that from the Tongmenghui and young students. However, when the movement deepened and developed into a political confrontation with the Qing government, serious differences between them surfaced. The root cause for the differences lay naturally in the profound divergence of their political purposes.

In domestic affairs the constitutionalists stood for constitutionalism, and in foreign affairs they advocated the recovery of economic rights. Though they deeply resented the Qing government's sale of railways and mines to foreigners, they were reluctant to make a decisive break with the government. Therefore, they always tried hard to confine the rights recovery movement within the limits acceptable to the government, and even used the movement as a means to stifle the revolution. But most League members held the view that the struggle for the recovery of economic rights "did not constitute a fundamental revolution," and that national salvation eventually called for the overthrow of the traitorous Qing government. They argued that "in order to attain our goal of recovering our rights, there is no alternative to an anti-Manchu revolution."[19] Their views were undoubtedly correct, because ever since the signing of the Boxer Protocol in 1901 the Qing government had been reduced to an imperialist tool to enslave the Chinese people. Therefore, while condemning imperialist aggression, the revolutionaries invariably and relentlessly lashed out at the traitorous behavior of the Qing government and "secretly agitated for revolution."[20]

An important characteristic distinguishing the revolutionaries from the constitutionalists was that in the rights recovery movement the revolutionaries cherished no illusions about the traitorous Qing government. While waging the struggle unyieldingly, they prepared to turn it into an anti-Qing uprising. That is also the reason why they are called radicals. However, the transformation of the rights recovery movement into an anti-Qing uprising could be accomplished only with the emergence of a revolutionary situation. In the absence of such a situation, it would be impossible to attain the anticipated goal. The activities of the revolutionaries during the struggle to preserve railway rights in Jiangsu and Zhejiang can illuminate this point.

The rights recovery movement culminated in the struggle of the people of Jiangsu and Zhejiang against the British seizure of the Suzhou-Hangzhou-Ningbo Railway rights. The struggle started in 1905. And in October 1907, the Qing government, under British pressure, issued an imperial decree alleging that, because the Jiangsu and Zhejiang railway companies were short of funds, it had to borrow money from the British to construct the Suzhou-Hangzhou-Ningbo Railway. The decree enraged the people of the two provinces, and a vigorous loan resistance movement quickly developed. Zhang Binglin, in charge of the Tongmenghui in Japan, and others sponsored a meeting to discuss the question of the Suzhou-Hangzhou-Ningbo Railway. The meeting was held at Kinkikan (Hall of Brightness) in Tokyo on November 3, 1907. Over 800 people participated in the meeting, including the members of the League from Zhejiang and Jiangsu as well as people from other provinces. Zhang Binglin made the opening speech, declaring that the right to build the Suzhou-Hangzhou-Ningbo Railway could not be recovered by mere verbal protests and petitions, and that the only alternative was to send representatives back to China to agitate for a general strike, and "then to occupy the telecommunications bureau, demolish the governor's office," and proclaim the "independence of Jiangsu and Zhejiang."[21] His speech was followed by those of Liu Shipei and Zhang Ji who expressed their support for his opinion that only strikes by the workers and shopkeepers "could serve the purpose."[22] This proposal, however, provoked a controversy among the Chinese students in Japan.

Consequently, the Railway and Mine Association of Henan, Shanxi, Shaanxi, and Gansu sponsored another meeting of Chinese students in Japan on November 17, attracting over 4,000 people within and outside the meeting hall. Zhang Binglin once again put forward his proposal. Some people shouted at the meeting that "China's railways and mines could be saved only by resorting to assassination."[23] Emotions ran high. However, throughout the debate the majority of the participants did not agree to resort to extreme measures. In order to support the struggle waged by the people of Jiangsu and Zhejiang, they favored forming a society for rejecting foreign loans as a prelude to establishing a nationwide society for rejecting foreign loans[24] and mobilizing resistance on a national scale. Zhang Binglin and others adhered to their own opinion and, after the meeting, sent Gu Naibin, vice-president of the Zhejiang Tongmenghui branch 2,000 copies of leaflets calling for "refusal to pay the grain and other taxes, and demanding independence for Jiangsu and Zheijiang provinces." On November 25, representatives of the societies for rejecting foreign loans from various parts of Zhejiang held a meeting in Hangzhou, during which Gu Naibin distributed the leaflets and advocated the independence of Jiangsu and Zhejiang. But the meeting was controlled by the constitutionalist gentry, who vehemently objected to the proposal for strikes and revolts. In the end, nothing came of that meeting.

In objective terms, the reason for the failure of the revolutionaries in their attempt to turn the struggle for railway rights waged by the Jiangsu and Zhejiang people into an anti-Qing uprising was the obstruction and sabotage carried out by the constitutionalists. Nevertheless, the incident fully revealed the weakness of the revolutionaries in this movement. They evidently failed to perceive the thrust of the movement's development and to correctly evaluate the subjective and objective conditions needed for reorienting the struggle.

The rights recovery movement was essentially a legal struggle. Though the movement produced some drastic action which the feudal rulers would not tolerate, they were not directly intended to oppose the rule of the Qing government. The movement could not be reoriented until the subjective and objective conditions had changed. As far as the railway struggle in Jiangsu and Zhejiang was concerned, the conditions for such a reorientation were not yet ripe. In terms of objective conditions, the strong resentment of the lower social strata was not directly anti-Qing in nature, and the policies of the Qing government had not yet driven the constitutionalists and the people under their influence to despair. On the side of the revolutionaries, all League members in Jiangsu and Zhejiang naturally took part in the activities of the Society for Rejecting Foreign Loans. For example, Xia Chao and Gu Naibin were involved in drawing up a plan to burn down Sheng Xuanhuai's manor. And Hang Xinzhai initiated an inaugural meeting of the Society for Rejecting Foreign Loans in Haining, at which "he made a passionate speech on the vital importance of railways and moved the audience to tears."²⁵ Consequently, he was elected chairman of the society.

In Zhejiang as a whole, however, the Tongmenghui did not achieve notable success in the struggle, for it did not have its own program of action, nor did it secure the leadership of the Society for Rejecting Foreign Loans in the province. Though they spoke for the lower strata of the population and expressed radical views, they failed to carry out large-scale activities which could have united the broad masses of the people under their banner. In such circumstances, an abrupt call for an uprising to turn the constitutionalist-controlled conference on rejecting foreign loans into a meeting similar to that held in Independence Hall during the American revolution simply could not succeed. Instead, it would only result in their isolation. This was borne out by subsequent developments. The constitutionalists were supported by the gentry, merchants, and students in categorically rejecting the idea of an uprising while insisting on the struggle to reject foreign loans. When the high tide of the 1911 Revolution came, Tang Shouqian, leader of the constitutionalists and president of the Zhejiang Railway Company, easily obtained the governorship of Zhejiang by capitalizing on his part in the railway struggle.

The putschist acts of the revolutionaries in Zhejiang were, of course, in complete accord with the guiding principles laid down by the top leaders of the Tongmenghui. In insisting upon armed struggle to overthrow the Qing dynasty, these Tongmenghui leaders were wiser than the constitutionalists. But in the whole process of revolution, they were not adept at using legal forms of struggle to mobilize and organize the masses. They did not persist in improving the masses' understanding of imperialism and the Qing government. Nor did they win over the masses who had fallen under the influence of the constitutionalists. Thus they could not form a broad revolutionary front. In the rights recovery movement this weakness was manifested in two tendencies: though they reacted indifferently to the movement, they acted rashly in trying to convert the movement into armed uprising. Therefore, in the country as a whole, despite their radical role in promoting the rights recovery movement, the revolutionaries in various provinces failed to obtain the leadership of the movement. It was not until the initiation of the Sichuan railway movement that this situation changed to some extent.

The railway protection movement, which began in 1911, was the prelude to the 1911 Revolution. This movement broke out when the Qing government, under the pretext of "railway nationalization," negotiated the sale of the Guangdong-Hankou and Sichuan-Hankou railways to imperialist powers. It was a mighty storm that swept through Sichuan, Hubei, Hunan, and Guangdong. It was most vigorous and sustained in Sichuan and soon headed toward revolution. There were many reasons why this movement in Sichuan took such a turn. One reason was that people of various social strata owned shares in the railways, and their economic interests were directly and seriously impaired by the Qing government's action. Among other causes, the impetus given by the revolutionaries was undoubtedly the most crucial. The strategy and tactics of the revolutionaries in Sichuan were on a much higher level than those pursued in the railway struggles by the Jiangsu and Zhejiang revolutionaries. Most of the Sichuan revolutionaries were soberly aware of the fact that the constitutionalists dared not challenge the reactionary rule of the Qing dynasty. Therefore, besides joining the constitutionalists in the legal struggle, they pursued an independent policy of secretly gathering revolutionary forces.[26]

As in other provinces, the struggle for the preservation of railway rights in Sichuan was launched by the constitutionalists through two legitimate agencies: the Advisory Board and the Railway Shareholders' Association. There were a small number of revolutionaries in both these agencies: some twenty in the Shareholders' Association and less in the Advisory Board. Among them, Zhu Zhihong, Long Mingjian, Wang Ziyi, Cheng Yingdu, and Zhang Zhijing were well-known figures. Though small in number, these revolutionaries were very active and exerted great influence on the people. Since they enjoyed a legal status as the people's spokesmen, they emerged as a conspicuous force at the outset of the struggle. Previously, the Tongmenghui in Sichuan had been loosely organized with little contact between its members in Chongqing and Chengdu. When the railway protection movement erupted, they had to change this situation. In early June 1911,

Zhu Zhihong went to Chengdu to attend the conference of all Sichuan railway shareholders as a representative of the railway shareholders in Chongqing. He was asked to seek instructions from Yang Shukan and Zhang Peijiao, leaders of the Tongmenghui's Chongqing branch, and to establish contacts with the revolutionaries in Chengdu in order to strengthen the revolutionary forces.[27]

When Zhu Zhihong arrived in Chengdu, Pu Dianjun, Luo Lun, and other constitutionalists were considering the forming of a society of comrades for the protection of railways. Zhu Zhihong held many secret meetings and discussions with Tongmenghui members Cao Du, Zhu Guochen, Xiao Shen, Zhang Yi, Liu Yuguang, Zeng Zhaolu, Wang Dianyang, Yang Boqian, Fang Chaozhen, and Long Mingjian, and with members who were in the New Army. They all agreed to join the Society for the Protection of Railways so as to "arouse the people and lead them to revolution."[28] They also decided that after joining the society, they would refrain from talking openly about revolution. Thus, while organizing the masses, they would not give local officials any pretext for suppressing them. Consequently, many Tongmenghui members joined the society and a number of them assumed leadership roles. For example, Liu Yang became head of the Youyang branch of the society; Zhu Zhihong and Liu Zuying were leading members of the Chongqing Association for the Preservation of Railway Rights; Luo Futian was head of the Leshan branch of the Society;[29] and Cheng Yingdu became chief of the Public Speaking Department of the Chengdu head office. (The head office had four departments: general affairs, documents and correspondence, negotiations, and public speaking.) The Public Speaking Department was in charge of propaganda and agitation. Its main task was to dispatch members to other parts of the country to make speeches. It also published *The Report by the Sichuan Society of Comrades for the Protection of Railways* and other periodicals which disseminated news about the railways in order to arouse popular resistance. Thus, the Society for the Protection of Railways became a large association of patriotic political groups, including constitutionalists, the Revolutionary League, and Gelaohui (Society of Brothers and Elders). Although the constitutionalists constituted the majority, the League, too, held an important position because the Gelaohui was under its influence.

By taking advantage of the two legitimate organizations, the Society for the Protection of Railways and the Shareholders' Association, the revolutionaries mercilessly exposed imperialist aggression and the Qing government's action in selling the railways, thus further raising the revolutionary consciousness of the masses and pressing the constitutionalists to move forward. On August 8, 1911, for example, the shareholders' special conference discussed the question of how to deal with the nationalization of railways. In order to keep an eye on things, Zhao Erfeng and the railway officials also attended the conference. Constitutionalists like Deng Xiaoke took the view that if the Qing government would reimburse the shareholders for the full value of their shares, the railway struggle could be called off. Zhao Erfeng was about to speak up in support of this view when Zhu Zhihong seized the floor. He insisted on the principle that the railways in Sichuan should be commercialized and vigorously attacked the Qing government's policy of using foreign loans to take over the railways. The conference adopted Zhu's proposal and appealed to Zhao Erfeng to forward a petition to the emperor on its behalf. "Although Erfeng abhorred it, he promised to do so, and the conference was adjourned."[30] Zhu Zhihong's action showed that in the railway protection struggle the revolutionaries were an unyielding force and played a pivotal role.

After the establishment of the General Association for the Protection of Railways, a significant step was taken whereby people were sent to various prefectures and counties on special missions to enlarge and reorganize the shareholders' associations into branches (or chapters) of the General Association in order to enlist more support to oppose the Qing government. Since only shareholders belonged to the shareholders' associations, membership naturally consisted mainly of landlords and gentry, but the Society for the Protection of Railways absorbed many peasants and lower-strata urban residents into the struggle. The peasantry constituted the largest democratic revolutionary force and by far surpassed the bourgeoisie in its anti-imperialist and anti-feudal zeal. Without the participation of the peasants, the democratic revolution could not have won complete victory. The involvement of peasantry in the struggle to protect the railways had a great impact on the subsequent development of the movement. It was a step which was undoubtedly very conducive to tightening the links between the revolutionaries and the masses and expanding their strength in the movement.

After the founding of the Society for the Protection of Railways, the movement underwent a change, and the struggle spread like a raging fire. On August 24, 1911, the shareholders' conference was held, and a meeting on the preservation of railway rights also took place with over 10,000 participants. As a result, a unanimous resolution was adopted, calling for strikes by shopkeepers and a boycott of classes. Then, Zhu Zhihong, Wang Ziyi, and others seized the opportunity to push the movement forward: they not only supported strikes by shopkeepers and students, but proposed that workers and peasants also go on strike. This change in mood, from requesting a petition to be forwarded to the emperor to a call for strikes, reflected the Sichuan people's increasing disillusionment with, and despair of, the Qing government. It was already felt that "petitioning was no solution" and that peaceful means were of no avail. Therefore, the revolutionaries were absolutely right to lead the masses in the direction of revolution. The students' boycott of classes and the shopkeepers' strikes, coupled with their refusal to pay taxes in Chengdu, were widely echoed in the prefectures, counties, townships, and rural areas. In the vast areas of the countryside, the peasants, acting on their own accord, also refused to surrender grain. In effect, the peasants and workers were already on strike. It was indeed something close to an actual uprising.

As the parliamentary petition movement organized by the constitutionalists met with repeated failures, they could not continue to stress their own political propositions. They were now compelled to show radical inclinations. On the one hand, they voiced support for the shopkeepers and students in an attempt to exploit mass strength to force the Qing government to "appease popular feelings and temporarily commercialize the railways";[31] on the other hand, they demanded insistently that the masses maintain "order,"[32] for fear that the movement would incite people to rebellion and thus jeopardize their own interests. The vacillation of the constitutionalists gradually deprived them of their ability to manipulate the movement. At this critical juncture, the great majority of the revolutionaries were prepared to oppose the Qing government's despotic measures with violence, although a few of them did not make a clear break with the constitutionalists but merely echoed their proposals.

It is necessary to point out that the struggle of the people in Sichuan was not isolated but was closely linked with the revolutionary situation throughout the country. On the one hand, their struggle gave a strong impetus to the revolution in other parts of the country, sweeping away the oppressive atmosphere resulting from the defeat of the Huanghuagang uprising in Guangzhou. It was generally felt that the revolution was approaching its high tide, and people immediately began to make responsive preparations. On the other hand, the revolutionaries in other parts of the country also rendered massive support to Sichuan. In July, when the movement for preserving railway rights was in full swing, the Tongmenghui set up its central China general office in Shanghai, with Song Jiaoren as its executive secretary. This office was made responsible for promoting the revolution in various provinces in the Yangzi River valley. Plans were also made for Sichuan.[33] Moreover, Wu Yuzhang and Zhang Maolong were sent to Sichuan to "agitate among the soliders and contact people in the lower reaches of the Yangzi." The support given to Sichuan by the media was all the more pronounced.

The newspapers run by the revolutionaries in other provinces, such as *Dajiang bao* of Wuhan, *Pingmin ribao* of Guangdong, and *Jianyan bao* of Fujian carried articles that castigated the Qing government for its traitorous act, reported news on the protection of railways, and called on the people to rise up in resistance. In this respect, *Minli bao* of Shanghai was particularly outstanding. It carried more than ten inflammatory articles by Song Jiaoren alone. In an article entitled "On the Recent Reactionary Acts of the Government," he pointed out that the program to nationalize the railways was "a subversive policy that impedes the people's enterprises" and "tramples underfoot rights that the people have already obtained. It is not any different from murdering someone in order to seize his property."[34] When the shopkeepers and students went on strike in Sichuan, he further urged the people of Sichuan to take active measures to carry the struggle to the end. He called on the people of Hunan, Hubei, Guangdong, and other provinces to "rise up simultaneously in great numbers and fight for a common cause together with the people of Sichuan." He said, "I think that the evils of despotism which have plagued this vast East Asian land for several thousand years may this time be swept away altogether."[35] This was a call for an all-out revolution, reflecting the ardent hopes that the revolutionaries of the whole country placed in the struggle in Sichuan.

When the shopkeepers and students went on strike, the entire country was on the verge of insurrection. In view of the rising revolutionary fervor on the part of the masses, and the lesson drawn from the Chengdu uprising of 1907, which failed when victory was already in sight, most revolutionaries in Sichuan considered it easier to first start the uprising in prefectures and counties. In early August, Long Mingjian and the titular leader of the Gelaohui, Qin Zaigeng, agreed that Gelaohui leaders from different parts of the country should meet at Luoquanjing, in Zizhou. An invitation was sent out in Qin Zaigeng's name. The meeting was attended by Wang Tianjie, Chen Kongbo, and other revolutionaries, most of whom were also Gelaohui leaders. They discussed the strategy for the uprising and decided to organize a railway protection army based on the Society for the Protection of Railways. It was also decided to start a revolution against the Qing government, and leaders were nominated for the uprising, which was to be launched at different places. This meeting was a concrete step taken by the revolutionaries to break the constitutionalists' control of the railway protection movement and pushed the movement in the direction of an anti-Qing revolution.[36] However, before the people had time to arm themselves, Zhao Erfeng struck first. On September 7, Pu Dianjun, Luo Lun, and others were lured into a trap and arrested; dozens of petitioners were shot in the streets, resulting in a tragic, bloody incident. The crack of guns was immediately turned into a signal for a popular uprising. Though the city was under a curfew, the revolutionaries seized the opportune moment and used the river to send out "water telegrams" calling on people to rise in revolt. The revolutionaries rushed in great numbers to different prefectures and counties to mobilize the peasants and secret societies and organized an army for protecting the railways. Thus revolution surged through the entire province of Sichuan. The revolutionaries actively sought support for the revolution from the lower strata of the masses, which was something the constitutionalist gentry did not dare to do.

This time, armed struggles in different places, though conducted in the name of the Tongzhijun (Army of Comrades), were actually under the leadership and influence of the revolutionaries. It was recorded that in the various counties in southwestern Sichuan, "the revolutionaries intermingled with" people's armies, "both acting under the banner of the Army of Comrades," and that rebels "rose all at once, numbering several hundred and as many as several thousand."[37] On September 25, Wang Tianjie and Wu Yuzhang gathered a "people's army" totaling over a thousand men and declared independence in Rongxian county. This sent shock-waves everywhere and was repeated successively in Pengshan, Meishan, Qingshen, and a dozen other prefectures and counties. The main goal was to carry out an anti-Qing revolution, and this was clearly manifested in the actual struggle. But as the forces of revolution in Sichuan were too dispersed to form a powerful, province-wide unified leadership, the uprising aimed at seizing local political power was unable to move quickly to the point where a democratic republic could be established.

Nevertheless, the struggle in Sichuan for the protection of railways was a revolutionary storm of unprecedented magnitude which unequivocally expressed the masses' long-held demand for the recovery of their rights. Although the Qing government hurriedly dispatched troops from Hubei to Sichuan in an effort to suppress the revolt, anti-imperialist, patriotic fervor had by that time already built itself into a growing anti-Qing revolution, and revolutionary developments could no longer be checked. Hence the beginning of the 1911 Revolution.

To summarize the above, it was the bourgeoisie who stirred up the surging waves of the rights recovery movement in the first decade of the twentieth century. Yet in all these revolutionary storms, the revolutionaries, whose role differed from time to time, always constituted a steadfast and vigorous force and occupied an important position. They always called upon people to strive for higher goals, assuming as they did the role of radicals. Under semi-colonial and semi-feudal social conditions, the struggle for national independence was a revolutionary factor, independent of human will. The constitutionalists, who occupied a leading position in the anti-imperialist front, tried hard to prevent the revolutionary tide from rising, but the harsh reality of the patriotic struggle repeatedly laid bare the traitorous and despotic features of the Qing government, thus helping to arouse a great number of patriots to a higher revolutionary consciousness. Inevitably, this quickly led them to support the revolution. And yet, it was under the impetus and leadership of the revolutionaries that the mass struggle against the imperialist powers' plunder developed into a struggle against the Qing government's betrayal of the country and ended in the overthrow of a government bitterly denounced as "the imperial court of Westerners." Such was the 1911 Revolution.

## Notes

1. "On the Recent Reactionary Acts of the Government," *Minli bao*, 19 June 1911.
2. Lei Chou (Jing Dingcheng), "The Qing Government Is Determined to Sell China's Mineral Products," *Min bao*, no. 4.
3. Hanmin (Hu Hanmin), "Zhang Zhidong Sells Mines"; Taiyan (Zhang Taiyan), "China's Senior Captain Kawakita—Yuan Shuxun," *Min bao*, nos. 2 and 24.
4. Hanmin, "The Question of Commercializing the Guangdong-Hankou Railway Remains Unsolved," *Min bao*, no. 6.
5. "Postscript Attached to the Note Written by Chen Xingtai on the Eve of His Suicide," *Min bao*, no. 2.
6. *Min bao*, no. 4.
7. Liu Tong, "Summary of the Recovery of Fujian Province," *Documents on the 50th Anniversary of the Founding of Republic of China* (Taibei, 1962), vol. 2, part 4, p.309.
8. Lei Peihong, "Recollections on the 1911 Revolution," in *The 1911 Revolution in Guangxi* (1961), vol. I, pp. 32–33.
9. Selections from *Journal of Yunnan*, p. 355
10. Academia Sinica, ed., *Archives of Mining* (Taibei, 1960), p. 1201
11. Zhang Runsan, "The Henan People's Negotiations with and Struggle Against the Fortune Company," unpublished article, deposited with the Political Consultative Conference of Henan Province.
12. Yang Yuanmao (Mianzhai), *jinshi* of 1904, became supervisor of the School of Politics and Law and president of the Institute of Education in Henan.
13. Zhang, "The Henan People's Negotiations."
14. Wang Jingfang, "A Brief Account of Mining Controversies Involving the Fortune Company," deposited with the Archives of Henan Province.
15. "A Summary of Recent Events Outside the Capital," *Dongfang zazhi* (The Eastern Miscellany), vol. 6, no. 5.
16. "A Record of the Actual Events in the Liberation of Hunan," *Qiangguo gongbao*, Hankou, 3 May 1912. Wu Zuolin and others were members of the Tongmenghui.
17. Liu Yuezhen, "Biographical Extracts of Revolutionary Figures in Liling," in *Collected Documents of Hunan* (Hunan, 1948), vol. 1, p. 195.
18. Zhang, "The Henan People's Negotiations."

19. Hanmin, "Opposing Foreigners and International Law," *Min bao*, no. 4.
20. Jing Dingcheng, "Details of Criminal Cases," p. 56.
21. *Zhongxing ribao*, 20 Feb. 1908.
22. *Shenzhou ribao*, 24 Nov. and 4 Dec. 1907.
23. Ibid.
24. Ibid.
25. Mo Bei, *The Railway Struggle in Jiangsu and Zhejiang*, vol. 2, Dec. 1907.
26. Wu Yuzhang, *The 1911 Revolution* (Beijing, 1961), p. 121.
27. Xiang Chu, *Ba County Gazetteer*, vol. 22, 1939.
28. Huang Shou, "Record of the Railway Struggle Waged by the Society for the Protection of Railways and the Tongmenghui of Sichuan in 1911" (draft manuscript), p. 19; and Xiong Kewu et al., *A Draft History of the Party in Sichuan; Selected Writings on the History of the 1911 Revolution* (Beijing, 1980), vol. 2, p. 168.
29. Huang Rong, *Leshan County Gazetteer*, vol. 12, 1934.
30. Huang, "Record of the Railway Struggle," p. 30.
31. Chinese Historical Association, ed., *The 1911 Revolution* (Shanghai, 1957), vol. 4, p. 458.
32. "Notice by the Gentry of Sichuan to Admonish the Inhabitants of Chengdu to Use Civilized Means to Recover Railways," *Historical Materials on the Movement in Sichuan to Protect Railways* (Beijing, 1959), p. 312.
33. Luo Jialun, ed., *Correspondence and Calligraphy of Huang Xing* (Taibei, 1956), p. 39.
34. *Minli bao*, 17 and 19 June 1911.
35. *Minli bao*, 14 and 21 Sept. 1911.
36. Tang Zongyao and Hu Gongxian, "The Meeting Held in Luoquanjing, Zizhou, and the Organization of the Army of Comrades," in *Memoirs of the 1911 Revolution* (Beijing, 1962), vol. 3, p. 143.
37. Zou Lu, *A Draft History of the Chinese Guomindang* (Chongqing, 1944), pp. 965–66.

# The Chinese National Association and the 1911 Revolution

Kojima Yoshio

The 1911 Revolution was a nationalist, democratic revolution. It opposed the imperialist invasion, overthrew the Qing dynasty which had become subservient to imperialism, and replaced the absolute monarchy with a republican system of government. The revolutionary efforts in the early twentieth century developed into a popular movement to overthrow the "foreign court," a movement motivated by powerful nationalist sentiments seeking to save the nation. Patriotism permeated China's social fabric and gave rise to the mass uprising to "remove the Qing and destroy the foreigners," the "resist France" and "resist Russia" anti-imperialist struggles, and various nationalist movements such as "restore rights" and "boycott American goods" and "boycott Japanese goods."

Established in Tokyo in 1905, the Chinese League (Zhongguo tongmenghui) sent its members home to propagandize and enlighten the Chinese people. The League also organized a series of armed uprisings in cooperation with secret societies and officers of the New Army. The Guangzhou uprising of 27 April 1911 (March 29 according to the lunar calendar), which was the last and most important of these uprisings, ended in a crushing defeat with many casualties, including the famous 72 martyrs. Nevertheless, this valiant attempt struck terror in the hearts of Qing officials and inspired the Chinese people. While preparing for this uprising, the general headquarters of the Chinese League, based in Tokyo, established the Chinese National Association (Zhongguo guominhui), led by three dominant figures: Liu Kuiyi and Li Zhaofu, who represented the Chinese League, and Xiong Yueshan, who had been sent to Tokyo to help lay the groundwork for the uprising.

During this period, the imperialist nations concluded a number of treaties, e.g., the Franco-Japanese and Russo-Japanese agreements and Anglo-Russian Entente, all in 1907, and the second Russo-Japanese Agreement in 1910. These treaties allocated spheres of interest and terms of cooperation for the nations that had invaded China and provided the powers with springboards for further incursions into China.

In 1911 Great Britain sent an army into the Pianma area in Yunnan. France reinforced its army on the Vietnam-China border in order to claim mining rights in seven prefectures of Yunnan. Following the example of Japan, which in 1909 had "taken independent action to improve and re-route the An-Feng Railway, tsarist Russia, in February 1911, requested the amendment of the Second Yili Treaty of 1881. In response to major political changes in 1910, such as Japan's absorption of Korea and increased Japanese and Russian incursions into the Dongbei district, Chinese, both at home and abroad, demanded preparations for resistance. Although the Chinese National Association stated that its specific raison d'être was to resist the British, French, and Russian invasions, it did not overlook minor, concurrent invasions by other imperialist nations. Ostensibly, the primary role of the Chinese National Association was to build up its own, largely civilian, militia which would be strong enough to resist the imperialist invasion. On the other hand, its secret purpose was to develop military power to overthrow the Qing dynasty, which had been gradually causing the ruin of the nation by signing away state concessions one after another. In his *The Draft History of the Guomindang*, Zou Lu wrote that in 1911 Chinese students in Japan suggested that they felt the need for a Chinese National Association and established the general headquarters in Shanghai and a local branch in each province. With this they hoped to muster people under their banner and prepare for a majori uprisng.[1] As is written here, the real purpose for the formation of the Chinese National Association was to expand and reinforce the revolutionary movement by sending as many revolutionaries as possible to China.

## The Establishment of the Chinese National Association

On November 13, 1910 Sun Yat-sen held a conference with Huang Xing, Hu Hanmin, Zhao Sheng, and others and decided to carry out another uprising in Guangzhou. According to their plan, after seizing the Guangzhou area, one army would move from Hunan to Hubei and the other advance into Jiangxi and capture Nanjing. Then both armies were to concentrate on the subjugation of the north. In January 1911, an overall planning department was established in Hong Kong. Huang Xing was general director and Zhao Sheng, vice-director. Tan Renfeng went to the Yangzi valley to prepare the groundwork for the revolution, and Xiong Yueshan was assigned to Tokyo.[2]

On February 26, 1911, Xiong,[3] who was appointed chief secretary of the general assembly of Chinese students in Japan, Liu Kuiyi (chief director of general affairs), representative of the Tokyo headquarters of the Chinese League, and Li Zhaofu, secretary of the secretariat, convened a general meeting of Chinese students. The assembly decided that student volunteers should return to China and organize a national army in each province in order to resist the British, Russian, and French invasions. Xiong Yueshan opened the meeting with an analysis of the situation and was followed by Liu Kuiyi, Liu Jiyan, Chen Ce, He Wei, and Xia Zhongmin. It was also decided to organize the Chinese National Association. Liu Jiyan proposed that after the meeting they turn to the Chinese Minister to Japan for financial help, and that by forming a national army they would show the Japanese people that Chinese students could still work in unity. The suggestion was approved unanimously, and the students, headed by Liu Jiyan, conducted a well-organized demonstrative parade.[4] And on March 5, five representatives from each province gathered at the Foreign Students Hall in Japan and presented various opinions about the National Association and its future strategy. They agreed unanimously on using force to save their country, and after the discussion, four members were elected to draft the regulations of the National Association. The four, Li Zhaofu, Fu Menghao, Chen Ce, and Yuan Lingc, were all members of the Chinese League.[5] That same day, Chinese women students held a Women's General

Assembly on the initiative of Tang Qunying, Lin Yancun, Zhu Guangfeng, and a student named Liu. Around one hundred women attended, and it was suggested that they also form an organization and cooperate to save the nation. Tang Qunying, a member of the Chinese League, was elected president, and Lin Yancun, secretary of general affairs. It was also suggested, though not decided at the time, that they publish a magazine to stir up their women compatriots in China. The magazine, *Chinese Women Students' Society Journal,* was subsequently established.[6]

Immediately after the meeting on 26 February, the Chinese National Association sent a telegram to the press in China accusing the government of having disgraced the nation and lost power, and they demanded that various groups form a national army to save the nation.[7] The association also requested the press to telegraph every provincial assembly demanding that they hold provisional meetings to organize a national army.[8] The association prepared various articles concerning the national crisis which were published in the mainland press, and student provincial organizations sent an appeal, "A Letter of Warning," to their respective provinces.[9]

The official name of the association in Japan was the Chinese National Association Established in Japan. Its central organ was the Board of Directors, headed by Li Zhaofu, who served in the Tokyo headquarters of the Chinese League.[10] Its avowed purpose was to "inspire a militant spirit, to cultivate the attributes of a militant people, and also to study the general principles of politics, education, and business." Specifically, it aimed "to establish a militia, a gymnasium, a society for the preservation of national skills, a society for military research, and a merchant group," and "to emphasize military drill and calisthenics in every school." Though the association was organized under the guidance of the revolutionary faction, on returning to China its representatives were subject to the restriction that "they could not incite people to revolution."[11] The reason for this was that the association ostensibly represented a multiracial group with diversified opinions but sharing a common patriotic objective. Furthermore, in order to function on the mainland, they had to conform to the law.

## The General Assembly of the Chinese People and Merchant Groups in Shanghai

At the same time that the association was formed in Tokyo, the Chinese Society for the Protection of Territory was organized under the leadership of the Yunnan Provincial Assembly. Merchants initiated a proposal to boycott British goods.[12] The Shanxi Provincial Assembly sent telegrams to the other provincial assemblies calling for joint action to cope with the crisis.[13] Since public opposition to British, French, and Russian aggression gradually became more serious and clamorous, the formation of the association in Japan was in accord with the mood of Chinese public opinion. The resolution of the association's council in Japan called for the establishment of branches in every province. It was also decided to send telegrams to all provinces via the provincial assemblies of Yunnan and the Three Eastern Provinces (Manchuria), calling for coordination through a headquarters in Shanghai.

The first group that went from Tokyo to China consisted of two members of the Chinese League from Yunnan, Wang Jiuling and Yang Dazhu.[14] They landed at Shanghai on March 5 and met the revolutionary leader Song Jiaoren. Soon afterward, Song wrote an editorial, "The Heart-breaking Affair of the Yunnan Border," in *Minli bao*. Wang Jiuling explained the situation in Yunnan at the general meeting of the Chinese Society for the Protection of Territory held in Shanghai on March 11. Around one thousand people of various backgrounds—gentry, merchants, students, and journalists—attended the meeting. Two members of the Chinese League living in Shanghai, Zhu Shaoping and Shen Manyun spoke at this meeting.[15]

As a result of the appeals of the Chinese National Association in Japan and the influence of the representatives of the Yunnan students in Japan, various groups in Shanghai gradually became more active. On March 12, the National Federation of Commercial Associations (president, Li Pingshu; vice-presidents, Shen Manyun and Ye Huijun) was established in Shanghai.[16] The formation of the Chinese Dare-to-Die Corps was also reported on March 18.[17] In April, the Chinese Students' Federation, with Zhu Shaoping as head, was organized.[18] All these groups had the common aim of saving the nation by force in concert with the national army proposed by the Chinese National Association.[19]

Six representatives of the association in Japan left Tokyo on April 16. Of the four who were Chinese League members, two went to Shanghai to prepare for the revolution, and two to Yunnan. The other two went to Manchuria. The group reached Shanghai on April 23.[20] With the help of Chinese League members, the two organizers assigned to Shanghai, Fu Menghao and Jiang Xifan, succeeded in rallying gentry, merchant, and student elements to the cause of revolution.

As a result, on May 7, a general meeting was held at Zhangyuan in Shanghai to welcome the representatives of the Chinese National Association.[21] The association established an office on May 11 and organized a provisional secretariat.[22] On May 7 the Shanghai Journalists' Federation, the Fujian Students' Association, the National Commerce Association, the Yunnan-Guizhou Society of Fellow-Provincials in Shanghai, the National Academic Association, the Hubei Society of Fellow-Provincials in Shanghai, and various other groups organized a welcoming party. These groups also sent representatives who constituted the association's provisional secretariat. Shen Zhongli was elected president but resigned and was subsequently succeeded by the vice-president, Shen Manyun. On June 2, Zhang Zi (Muliang), a member of the Chinese League, was sent to Shanghai from Tokyo to help Fu Menghao and Jiang Xifan in their revolutionary activities.[23] On June 12, after a two-month preparatory period, the inaugural meeting of the association's headquarters was held at Zhangyuan in Shanghai. Almost 4000 people, including gentry, merchants, students, and journalists, attended. At this meeting, the name of the headquarters was changed to the General Assembly of the Chinese People, and Shen Manyun was elected president; Ma Xiangbo, vice-president; and Ye Huijun was elected resident director.[24] Others were elected as follows:[25]

General Affairs Department: Zhu Shaoping, Lu Hanchang, Shi Jialin, Fu Menghao;

Accounts Department: Wang Shilin, Zhang Muliang;

Secretariat: Yang Qianli, Li Huaishuang, Cheng Wenqing, Jiang Xifan;

Advisory Department: Tong Bichen, Xi Yanggao, Zhang

Huchen, Zhang Peiyi, Nong Jingsun, Wang Yongqin, Liu Chenglie, Xiao Xingtai, You Jiyun, Xu Jiqing, Cai Gang, Pan Xunchu, Lin Jiqing;

Investigation Department: Chen Yingshi, Xu Yaoyuan, Wang Quyu, Wang Hanliang, Gao Jinzhou, Ming Shaozhen, Xu Rongpu, Yu Zuomin;

Editorial Department: Qu Shaoyi, Fang Xieyin, Qin Tieshan, Zhu Bowei, Sang Dansheng, Dai Boxing, Wu Shuzhen, Zheng Zhongjing. The General Assembly was a broadly based organization composed of provincial and student associations.

The second article of the declaration issued by the General Assembly defined its role: "The purpose of this assembly is to promote a militant spirit and the formation of militias, and to exhort the people to do their utmost to carry out their duties."[26] To the revolutionaries, "carrying out duties" meant overthrowing the Qing dynasty and saving the nation. For this purpose, unity and the cultivation of a militant spirit were deemed essential. On June 17, the General Assembly decided to form a model gymnastic group, consisting of about one hundred members, which aimed at cultivating a militant spirit. On August 13, the first practice ceremony was performed by the model gymnastic group led by Nong Zhu (Jingsun), who was also head of the Chinese Gymnastic Association for the Cultivation of Spirit and Force.[27]

In Japan, the *Chinese Women Students' Society Journal* began publication, and women in mainland China also organized a Women's National Association in Shanghai in early August. There were six organizers: Zhang Zaimin, Zhang Weihua, Wang Xiong, Yin Ruizhi, Yin Weijun, and Wu Zhongqiu. Their aims were said to be the same as those of the men's association. But as this was a women's organization, they stressed particularly the following points: to reform the custom of restricting women to household chores and to develop tasks suitable for women of militant spirit. The Women's National Association in China established an office in Shanghai which was built in cooperation with the Yin sisters, Ruizhi and Weijun.[28]

Meanwhile, merchants in Shanghai formed groups that would be under the aegis of the National Federation of Commercial Associations. These included the Association of Book Sellers (April 29), the Association of Dealers in Beans and Rice (May 28), the

Association of Ginseng Merchants (May 30), and the Association of Muslim Merchants (June 25).[29] The main motive of all these organizations was to save the nation from destruction. In July, the Association of South Shanghai Merchants opened an institute to encourage people to practice military arts.[30] Public entertainers, among them Pan Yueqiao and Xia Yueshan, took the initiative, and Shen Manyun, a member of the Chinese League was elected director of the institution. The influential members and leaders of the National Federation of Commercial Associations, the Assembly of Chinese People, and the Students' Federation acted concurrently as members or directors of other groups.[31] They all participated in the Shanghai revolt carried out on November 3 after the Wuchang Uprising and contributed greatly to achieving the independence of Shanghai.

## The Chinese National Association Outside of Shanghai

The objectives of the Chinese National Association in Japan were to establish its headquarters in Shanghai and branches in each province, and to form a people's army (*guominjun*) on the basis of civilian and gymnastic circles. At the time of its foundation, the National Assembly of the Chinese People issued proclamations in each prefecture and province urging people to establish branches.[32] The activities were promoted by representatives of the organization in Japan.

Yunnan was particularly ripe for nationalist agitation because of the French seizure of mining rights in seven prefectures and the British aggression in Pianma district. Thus the association sent a number of agents there. The first group consisted of Yang Dazhu and Wang Jiuling, and the second included Huang Jialiang and Xiao Deming. All four were members of the Chinese League. Later, Chen Yanjie and Li Risheng were sent.[33] Yang Dazhu and Wang Jiuling were said to have convened a national mass meeting on the issue of mining rights. Yang and the others, helped by the head of the provincial assembly and in coordination with the governor-general, Li Jingxi, succeeded in establishing the national assembly in Kunming. However, the establishment of this assembly faced many obstacles.[34]

Prior to the activities of the Chinese National Association's representatives, the Yunnan Provincial Assembly had already established the Society for the Protection of Territory and had appealed to the Qing government and provincial assemblies to recapture Pianma. At the same time, merchants took the lead in conducting a boycott against British goods. Yet, despite these favorable social conditions, the association's representatives were hampered in their open activities by pressures from the central government and the cautious self-protective policy of Governor-general Li Jingxi. The authorities ordered the disbandment of the patriotic rally initiated by Yang Dazhu, Wang Jiuling, and others because radical ideas were expressed.[35] The gymnastic institute established under the leadership of Li Xiehe, who was an army officer, became virtually ineffective because he was transferred to another province.[36]

In addition, according to reports in *Minli bao*, attempts by Xiao Deming, Huang Jialiang, Li Risheng, and Wang Jiuling to activate the provincial assembly did not achieve immediate success because of the assembly's hesitation.[37] However, this is understandable since these activities were obviously subversive and motivated by the real purpose of "overthrowing the Yunnan government and carrying out the revolution by gathering people of all provinces in a unified body."[38] The point is that the revolution did proceed under a cloak of secrecy.

As for Manchuria, Wang Baozhen of Hebei and Jin Dingxun of Jilin arrived in Mukden in April and tried to contact the various bodies, including the provincial assembly.[39] They elicited support from people in the Normal School and other educational institutions, but it was difficult to establish a nationalist organization in Jilin.[40] It was only in September that the National Association succeeded in holding a general meeting. The group selected one representative of the Han and Mongol races as chairman and vice chairman, respectively.[41] In Haerbin (Heilongjiang), two students who had studied in Japan approached various people and obtained their agreement to establish a people's army. In June, it was reported that gentry and merchants held a meeting.[42] In August, people in Yingkou (Liaoning) who obtained several documents, including "Regulations of the National Association," from the Shanghai and Jilin general assemblies of the Chinese people, held a meeting with the participation of gentry and student leaders. A subcommittee was later set up.⁴³ Although these activities indicate that national associations were formed in each of the Manchurian provinces, specific details on subsequent moves are not available.

The Fujian students in Japan sent home seven representatives, including three League members, Song Yuanyuan, Zhu Tengfang, and Chen Jingsong. They arrived in Shanghai on May 3 and were welcomed by members of the Fujian Students' Association, which was a revolutionary body, and by the Association of Fujian Fellow-Provincials in Shanghai. After the meeting, it was agreed that Zheng Quan, as representaive of the Fujian Student's Association; Wang Qi, representing both the League and the Association of the Fellow-Provincials; and Zeng Zemin, who represented two Fujian prefectures, would accompany the seven students.⁴⁴ In Fuzhou, they were assisted by Zheng Zuyin, director of the Fujian branch of the Chinese League and also a member of the provincial assembly. On May 16, the entire group visited the provincial assembly and obtained the support of the vice-chairman, Chen Zhilin, and others.⁴⁵ On May 23, the representatives of five bodies—the Provincial Assembly, the Educational Association, the Merchants' Association, the Peasants' Association, and the Industrial Association—discussed ways of establishing a militia. Signed by 49 people, representing the five groups, their recommendation was publicized, and on July 2 the Fujian Society for Establishing a Militia was founded.⁴⁶ Aside from these movements led by leaders of the various quarters, gymnastic associations were established in schools in Fujian.⁴⁷ The Fujian Preservation Association was also established by gentry and student leaders.⁴⁸ A press report that Fujian, which faced Taiwan, might fall under Japanese control together with Manchuria, deepened the sense of crisis.⁴⁹ It was mainly because of this sense of crisis that promotion of the association's activities in Fujian became relatively easy. Furthermore, the large number of martyrs in the Guangdong uprising of April 27 aroused support for the revolution in the neighboring province of Fujian. This point should not be ignored. It should be also noted that a suicide squad, comprised mainly of students in the gymnastic association, played a major role in securing the independence of Fujian during the revolution.⁵⁰

On June 2, Ding Weifen and Yan Zhongwen, representatives of

the Chinese National Association in Japan, arrived in Jinan, Shandong.[51] A party member since the inauguration of the Chinese League, Ding Weifen was regarded as a leader of the Shangdong branch of the League.[52]

In referring to the activities of the association's representatives in China, Zou Lu wrote that "Jiang Yansheng (Xifan) was already named chief representative and Ding Weifen returned to Shandong and organized subcommittees."[53] It was stated clearly that the two leaders' activities were not limited to establishing the association's branches. In the first series of the *Biographies of Revolutionary Personalities,* a section on Ding Weifen records: "In the spring of 1911, I returned with orders to form a clandestine organization."[54] This shows that he was engaged in revolutionary activities apart from the ensuing public activities.

Back in Jinan, Ding Weifen called on the gentry and students, and after meetings with the provincial assembly on June 11 and the Educational Association on June 30, it was decided to establish the National Association in Shandong. Zhang Zhuofu was named chairman and Zhou Jianlong, vicechairman.[55] Using the association's office as a foothold, Ding Weifen devoted himself to the revolutionary movement. Jiang Xifan, who was assigned to operations in Shanghai after the Wuchang revolt, returned to Jinan with other comrades and pressed the provincial governor, Sun Baoqi, to declare independence.[56]

In Zhejiang, branch parties were established not only in the provincial capital, Hangzhou, but also in Jiaxing, Huzhou, Ningbo, Taizhou, and in various districts. The Zhejiang Students' Association in Japan dispatched six representatives, who reached Shanghai on June 2.[57] On their way to Hangzhou, they received a warm welcome in Jiaxing, where they established a provisional branch.[58] On arrival in Hangzhou, they were accorded a warm reception by Chu Fucheng, a member of the provincial assembly and a prorevolutionary, who played an active role as an intermediary with various institutions, including the provincial assembly.[59] Chu was the general manager of the Merchants' Association in Jiaxing. Making full use of his membership in the provincial assembly, he contributed greatly to the establishment of the association in Zhejiang.

In Zhejiang, the readiness of the provincial governor, Zeng

Yun, to support the major objectives of the association[60] assisted its relatively smooth progress. On June 30, students representing the association in Japan, Xu Banhou, superintendent of a normal school, and members of the provincial assembly took the initiative in convening a meeting to establish the association in Zhejiang.[61] Its name was changed to National Militant Association; and Xu Banhou was elected chairman and Chu Fucheng, vicechairman. Subsequently, representatives visited various cities in the province and established branches.[62] Especially important among these cities was Jiaxing, Chu Fucheng's home town.[63] With the cooperation of Yin Ruizhi, who was pro-revolutionary, a Women's National Association was also established in Jiaxing.[64]

Branches were founded in Yangzhou and Changzhou in Jiangsu. It was also reported that a member of the Self-government Association proposed to organize a merchants' group, which would be later replaced by a national army, in the two districts of Dantu and Danyan.[65] In Jiangxi, it was reported that a national army was set up on the initiative of various elements in Jiujiang.[66] In Guangxi, Chen Guohua, superintendent of the Guilin School of Law and Government, proposed forming a national army. Though preparations were made to name him leader of the army, the project was abandoned due to pressure from the Foreign Ministry.[67]

## Conclusion

The Chinese National Association was established with the principal aim of saving the country. The association succeeded in stirring up revolutionary sentiment through the establishment of branches, gymnastic associations, and militias as well as a national army, not only in the Shanghai headquarters, but also in such areas as Yunnan, Manchuria, Fujian, Shandong, Zhejiang, Jiangsu, Jiangxi, and Guangxi. But it was frequently hampered by the Qing government which pursued a policy of restricting the formation of a national association and the organization of a national army. This was done on the advice of the Chinese minister to Tokyo who opposed the return of Chinese students from Japan who promoted the movement. He informed his home government that the revolutionary campaign was closely connected with the National

Association.[68] Acting upon this information, countermeasures aimed at preventing the formation of a national army were taken in advance in many provinces, impeding the establishment of local branches by the National Association. In areas where the Chinese National Association did not exist, merchant groups, militias, and gymnastic associations that aimed at saving the nation assumed their revolutionary roles and went into action when independence movements rose in the provinces following the Wuchang Uprising. For example, public groups in Ningbo and merchant groups in Wuxi rose up, to say nothing of the merchant groups and gymnastic associations in Shanghai.[69]

From the report by the Chinese minister to Japan, it can be easily seen that the Chinese National Association was established as an affiliate of the Chinese League.[70] This affiliation resulted from the Guangzhou uprising of April 27, 1911. Emphasizing the necessity of the Guangzhou revolt, Sun Yat-sen said: "Since the conclusion of the Russo-Japanese treaty, the situation has become so critical that we cannot afford to delay." He stressed the danger to China in the wake of the second Russo-Japanese treaty. This treaty and the danger of new British, Russian, and French incursions of China's borders spurred the Chinese students to action. Xiong Yuehan, secretary-general of the Association of Chinese Students in Japan, who was sent from the Hong Kong headquarters in anticipation of the Guangzhou uprising, utilized to the full his position in order to mobilize Chinese students in Japan to form the Chinese National Association. The pamphlet "A Warning on China's Critical Situation," which the Chinese National Association edited and produced, was handed over by him to the representatives of Chinese students in Japan.[71]

Among the representatives sent home by the association in Japan were a number of students who can be easily identified as members of the League, such as Yang Dazhu, Wang Jiuling, Fu Menghao, Jiang Xifan, Huang Jialiang, Xiao Demin, Zhang Zi, Ding Weifen, and Song Yuanyuan. Moreover, a large number of Chinese students returned to China without being noticed and started underground activities. They included Lin Wen (Shishuang) as well as Liu Kuiyi who went to Fujian to mobilize comrades in support of Guangzhou. Liu Kuiyi himself went to Shanghai and discussed formation of a militia to move in concert with the Guangzhou uprising.[72]

In this context, it should be pointed out that the Chinese National Association was an organization set up prior to the Guangzhou uprising and was intended to rise in coordination with the revolt. Although the revolt ended in failure on April 28, the activities aimed at saving the homeland and enlightening the people increased support for revolution and contributed greatly to the independence movements in the various provinces following the Wuchang revolt. The Chinese National Association was established at the initiative of the Chinese League whose activities were not sufficient to lead to concerted action in support of the Guangzhou uprising. It can be assumed that some members were ordered to use the cover of the association to join the uprising and that the attempted uprising served to increase the membership of the association.

[Translated by Okui Yaeko]

## Notes

1. Zou Lu, "Shandong juyi" [Shandong uprising], in *Zhongguo Guomindang shigao* [The draft history of the Guomindang], part 3, revolution 2.
2. Liu Kuiyi, "Huang Xing zhuanji" [The biography of Huang Xing], in *Xinhai Geming*, vol. 4 (Shanghai).
3. *Gaimushō genson kiroku* (Ministry of Foreign Affairs Archives) Otsu Hi [Category 2, confidential], no. 907, 13 March 1911, "Chūgoku kibōkeikokusho ni kansuru ken" [On the letter of warning of the Chinese national crisis].
4. "Dongjing liuxuesheng dahui [General meeting of Chinese students in Japan]. *Shi bao*, 11 March 1911.
5. "Liuxuesheng aiguo dahui" [Patriotic general meeting of Chinese students in Japan], *Minli bao*, 13 March 1911.
6. "Liuxuesheng aiguo dahui ji" [Report from a patriotic general meeting of Chinese students in Japan], *Minli bao*, 14 March 1911; "Liuxuejie fandui Zhong-E wenti zhi jieguo" [The consequence of antipathy toward the Sino-Russian problem among Chinese students in Japan], *Shen bao*, 24 March 1911.
7. *Minli bao, Shi bao*, 28 Feb. 1911.
8. *Minli bao, Shi bao*, 1 March 1911.
9. "Zhongguo weiwang jinggao shu" [A warning of the Chinese national crisis], *Shi bao*, 18–26 March 1911; "Liu Ri Zhongguo Guominhui aigao shu" [Appeal from the Chinese National Association in Japan], *Minli bao*, 7–8 April 1911; "Liu-Ri Zhongguo Guominhui pinyibu jueyian" [The draft of the council of the Chinese National Association in Japan], "Zhongguo Guominhui zhangcheng" [The regulations of the Chinese National Association], *Minli bao*, 24 April 1911; "Guominhui jinxing celüe" [The Policy of the Chinese National Association], *Minli bao*, 30 April–2 May 1911;

## THE CHINESE NATIONAL ASSOCIATION

"Yunnan weiwang jinggao shu" [A warning of the Yunnan Crisis], *Minli bao*, 2 April 1911; "Jilin liu Ri xuesheng qigao xiangren shu" [Appeal to Home Provincials from Jilin Students in Japan], *Minli bao*, 28–29 April 1911; "Liu Ri Fujian Tongxianghui jinggao Husheng tongbao shu" [The Association of Fujian Fellow-Provincials in Japan warns Fujian Provincials in Shanghai], *Minli bao*, 31 May 1911; "Wei Guominhui shi jinggao quanguo fulao xiongdi" [Guangdong National Association in Japan appeals to the activities of the Chinese National Association to all the people), *Minli bao*, 15–16 May 1911; "Liu-Ri Jiangsu Tongxianghui zhi Jiangsu Ziyiju han" [Letter to the Jiangsu Provincial Assembly from the Association of Jiangsu Fellow-Provincials in Japan], *Minli bao*, 28 May 1911; "Jinggao quan-Zhe tongbao shu" [Appeals to all Zhejiang people), *Minli bao*, 9 June 1911.

10. *Gaimushō genson kiroku*, Otsu Hi no. 1448 "Shinkoku Kakumeitōin ni kansuru ken" [On Chinese revolutionaries].

11. *Minli bao*, 24 April 1911.

12. "Yunnan zhuandian" [Special Report from Yunnan], *Shi bao*, 28 Feb. 1911; "Yunnan Baojiehui xuanyan" [Proclamation of the Yunnan Society for the Protection of Territory), *Minli bao*, 2 March 1911.

13. "Xian Gongdian" [Official telegram from Xian], *Shi bao*, 6 March 1911; editorial, "Lun Ying-E jiaoshe zhi yingxiang" [The impact of the Anglo-Russian negotiation), *Shi bao*, 15 March 1911.

14. "Yunnan daibiao dao-Hu ji" [The Yunnan representative arrives at Shanghai], *Minli bao*, 6 March 1911; editorial (written by Song Jiaoren), "Yunnan bianshi shiangxin tan" [The heart-breaking affair on the Yunnan border], *Minli bao*, 7–8 March 1911.

15. "Zhangyuan zhi Baojie Dahui" [The general meeting of the Chinese Society for the Protection of Territory at Zhangyuan], *Minli bao*, 12 March 1911; "Zhongguo Baojie Dahui jishi" [Report of the Society for the Protection of Chinese Territory], *Shi bao*, 12 March 1911.

16. "Quanguo shangtuan lianhehui ji" [Report of the National Federation of Merchant Associations], *Shi Bao*, 13 March 1911; Kojima Yoshio, "Shingai Kakumei ni okeru Shanhai dokuritsu to shinshōsō" [The merchant class and Shanghai's independence during the 1911 Revolution), in *Chūgoku kindaika no shakai kōzō* [The social structure of Chinese modernization]; Chen Weibin and Yang Liqiang, "Shanghai shangtuan yu Xinhai Geming" [Shanghai merchants and the 1911 Revolution), *Lishi Yanjiu*, 1980, no. 3.

17. "Zhongguo Gansidui chuxian" [The organization of the Chinese "Dare-to Die" corps], *Shi bao*, 18 March 1911.

18. "Quanguo Xuejie Lianhehui shi" [Report of the National Federation of Chinese Students], *Minli bao*, 24 April 1911; "Xuejie Lianhe dahui ji" [Report of the National Federation of Chinese Students], *Shi bao*, 24 April 1911; "Xuejie Lianhehui jinshi" [Recent activities of the National Federation of Chinese Students], *Minli bao*, 2 May 1911.

19. "Zhongguo Xuejie Lianhehui zhangcheng" [Regulations of the National Federation of Chinese Students], *Minli bao*, 15 June 1911; "Xuejie Lianhehui jishi" [Report of the National Federation of Chinese Students], *Minli bao*, 19 June 1911.

20. "Liudong xuesheng zhi Guominhui" [Chinese Students in Japan and the Chinese National Association], *Shi bao*, 21 April 1911; "Guominhui daibiao guiguo" [Representatives of the Chinese National Association return home], *Minli bao*, 24 April 1911.

21. "Huanying Guominhui daibiao ji" [Reception of the representatives of the Chinese National Association], *Minli bao*, 8 May 1911.

22. "Guominhui jinxing zhongzhong" [Some activities of the Chinese National Association], *Minli bao*, 12 May 1911.

23. "Zonghui zhi daibiao xuzhi" [Representatives of the general meeting continue to arrive], *Minli bao*, 3 June 1911.

24. "Zhangyuan zhi fengyun dahui" [The epoch-making general meeting at Zhangyuan], *Minli bao*, 12 June 1911.

25. "Guomin Zonghui kaichuang ji" [The first general meeting of the Chinese National Association], *Minli bao*, 14 June 1911.

26. "Guomin Zonghui xuanyan shu" [Declaration of the general meeting of the Chinese National Association], *Minli bao*, 15 June 1911.

27. "Guominhui zhi mofantuan kaicao ji" [The model gymnastic group demonstrates their maneuvers], *Shi bao*, 18 June 1911.

28. "Zhongguo Nuzi Guominhui jianzhang" [Brief regulations of the Chinese Women's Association], *Shi bao*, 5 Aug. 1911; Gong Yixing, "Guangfujun zhi" [History of the restoration army], in *Xinhai Geming*, vol. 1.

29. "Shuye Shangtuan zhi tonggao" [Notice from the Association of Booksellers], *Minli bao*, 28 April 1911; "Shuye Shangtuan zhi shengkuang" [Vigorous activities of the Association of Booksellers], ibid., 20 May 1911; "Zhabei Shangtuan Chenglihui" [The founding meeting of the Merchants' Association of Zhabei district], ibid., 27 May 1911; "Dou-Miye Shangtuan chengli" [The Organization of the Association of Soybean and Rice Dealers], ibid., 30 May 1911; "Huijiao Shangtuan zhi dahui" [The founding meeting of the Association of Muslim Merchants]," ibid., 26 June 1911; "Zhuyu Shangtuan" [The Association of Pearl Dealers], *Shi bao*, 26 June 1911; "Shuiguo Shangtuan" [The Association of Fruit Dealers], ibid., 11 July 1911.

30. "Zhenwu xuexiao jiang chengli" [Military school about to be organized], *Minli bao*, 18 July 1911; "Hunan Shangtuan Zhenwu xuexiao zhiyuan biao" [The list of employees of the military school attached with the Association of South Shanghai Merchants], ibid., 25 July 1911.

31. "Xuejie lianhehui jinshi" [Recent activities of the National Federation of Chinese Students], *Minli bao*, 22 May 1911.

32. "Guominhui bugao quanguo" [The Chinese National Association appeals to the whole country], *Minli bao*, 16 June 1911.

33. "Guominhui jinkuang" [Recent activities of the Chinese National Association], *Shi bao*, 3 June 1911.

34. Zhang Dayi, "Tongmenghui Yunnan fenbu zhi chengli ji qi huodong" [Organization and activities of the Yunnan branch of the Chinese League], in *Zhonghua Minguo kaiguo wenxian* [Historical documents on the establishment of the Chinese Republic], part 1, vol. 12 (Taibei).

35. "Diandu buxu kaihui ji" (Yunnan governor-general prohibits meetings], *Minli bao*, 29-30 June 1911.

36. Ibid.

37. "Wu daibiao ku Dian" [Five representatives appeal against the miserable plight in Yunnan], *Minli bao*, 24 Aug. 1911.

38. Zhang, "Tongmenghui Yunnan fenbu."

39. "Guominhui daibialo Ru-Man ji" [Representatives of the Chinese National Association visit Manchuria], *Minli bao*, 30 April 1911.

40. "Shangwu jingshen ru Manzhou" [Militant atmosphere pervades Manchuria], *Minli bao*, 20 May 1911.

41. "Guomin Dahui kaihui ji" [First meeting of the Chinese National Association in Manchuria], *Minli bao*, 18 Sept. 1911.

42. "Tichang Guominjun" [Call for the organization of a People's Army], *Minli bao*, 15 June 1911.

43. "Guomin fenhui kaihui ji" [First meeting of Yinkou branch of the Chinese National Association], *Minli bao*, 3 Sept. 1911; "Yinfu zhi beiguan" [Pathetic situation in Yinkou], ibid., 9 Oct. 1911.

44. "Fujian daibiao you dong dao-Hu" [Fujian representatives arrive in Shanghai from Japan], *Shi bao*, 5 May 1911; "Min daibiao lianmei nangui" [Fujian representatives all return to the home province at once], *Minli bao*, 22 July 1911.

45. "Quanbian tuanlian daibiaotuan hui-Min" [Call for sending the Fujian Militia

representatives back to their home province], *Shi bao*, 24 May 1911.

46. "Fujian Zantang zhi huiyi" [Meeting at Zantang], *Shi bao*, 31 May 1911; "Minsheng tuanlian qichenghui chengli" [Setting up the Fujian Society for Establishing a Militia], ibid., 9 July 1911.

47. "Minren duiwai zhi fengyun" [Anti-foreign sentiments of Fujian peoples heighten], *Minli bao*, 23 April 1911; "Junguomin zhi hongtian zhendi" (Marvelous activities of gymnastic associations), ibid., 7 July 1911.

48. "Baocun guohuo gonghui ji" [The Provincial Association of Encouragement for the Use of Home Products], *Minli bao*, 18 July 1911; "Minsheng baocun guohuo dahui zhi shengkuang" [Victorious meeting of the Provincial Association of Encouragement for the Use of Home Products].

49. "Liu Ri Fujian Tongxianghui jinggao Minsheng tongbao shu" [Letter to the Fujian people from the Association of Fujian Fellow-Provincials in Japan], *Shi bao*, 31 May 1911.

50. Zheng Quan, "Fujian guangfu shilue" [Brief history of the independence of Fujian], in *Zhonghua Minguo kaiguo wushinian wenxian*, part 2, vol 4.

51. "Guomin fenhui zhi fengyun" [Activities of the Shandong branch of the Chinese National Association], *Minli bao*, 1 July 1911.

52. Wang Linge, "Xinhaiqian zhi geming yundong" [The revolutionary movement before 1911], in *Shandong jindaishi ziliao* [Documents of Shandong modern history], Zhongguo Shixuehui Jinan fenhui [The Jinan Branch of the Historical Society of China], ed., vol. 2 (Jinan).

53. Zou, "Shandong juyi."

54. "Ding Weifen," in *Geming renwu zhi* [The biographies of revolutionary personalities], Zhongguo Guomindang dangshi shiliao bianzuan weiyuanhui [Committee for Compiling Documents for the Guomindang History], ed., vol. 1 (Taibei).

55. "Guomin fenhui chengli ji" [Organization of the Shandong branch of the Chinese National Association], *Minli bao*, 7 July 1911; "Shandong zhi Guomin fenhui ji" [The Shandong branch of the Chinese National Association], *Shi bao*, 23 July 1911.

56. "Jiang Yansheng," in *Geming renwu zhi*, vol. 11.

57. "Zhe-Dian ren zhi relei" [Ardent appeal from Zhejiang and Yunnan people], *Minli bao*, 3 June 1911.

58. "Huanying Guominhui daibiao" [Welcome to the representatives of the Chinese National Association], *Minli bao*, 11 June 1911.

59. "Guominhui daibiao dao-Hang" [Representatives of the Chinese National Association arrive at Hangzhou], *Minli bao*, 17 June 1911.

60. "Zengfu zangchen guominhui" [Provincial governor Zeng Yun supports the Chinese National Association], *Minli bao*, 23 June 1911.

61. "Guomin Shangwu chengli dahui guanggao" [Announcement for the founding meeting of the National Militant Society], *Minli bao*, 28 June 1911; "Guomin Shangwu dahui ji" [Founding meeting of the National Militant Society], ibid., 6 July 1911.

62. From Shaoxing, "Guomin fenhui jinxing ji" [Recent activities of the branch of the Chinese National Association], *Minli bao*, 9 July 1911; from Ningbo, "Guomin Shangwu dahui ji" [Meeting of the National Militant Society], ibid., 16 July 1911; from Yanzhou, "Guominhui daibiao zhi fengyun" [Vigorous activities of the Representatives of the Chinese National Association], ibid., 16 July 1911; from Huzhou, "Shangwu fenhui chengli dahui" [Organization of the branch of the National Militant Association], ibid., 17 July 1911; from Jiaxing, "Guomin shangwu dahui ji" [Meeting of the National Militant Association], ibid., 18 July 1911; from Taizhou, "Guomin shangwu fenhui chengli ji" [Organization of the branch of the National Militant Association], ibid., 31 July 1911; from Quzhou, "Guomin shangwu fenhui" [The branch of the National Militant Association], ibid., 2 Aug. 1911; from Chuzhou, "Huanying daibiao dahui" [Welcome to the Representatives of the National Militant Association], ibid., 6 Aug. 1911.

63. From Jiashan, "Guomin fenhui zhi fengyun" [Vigorous activities of the branch of the Chinese National Association], *Minli bao*, 21 July 1911; from Shimen, "Shangwuhui zhi fengyun" [Vigorous activities of the National Militant Association], ibid., 3 Aug. 1911; from Tongxiang, "Guominhui chengli ji" [Organization of the branch of the Chinese National Association], ibid., 29 Aug. 1911.

64. From Jiaxing, "Zhuangzai Nüzi Guominhui" [The splendid Chinese Women's National Association], *Minli bao*, 10 Sept. 1911.

65. From Yangzhou, "Zancheng Guominhui zhi zhishi duo" [Ardent supporters of the Chinese National Association increase), *Shi bao*, 21 July 1911; from Zhenjiang, "Xingban shangtuan zhi tiyi" [Appeal to organize a merchants' association], ibid., 8 Aug. 1911; from Zhenjiang "Xiaoliangong yaoban shangtuan" [Local officials also insist on the organization of a merchants' association], *Minli bao*, 22 Aug. 1911; from Changzhou, "Guomin fenhui chengli ji" [Organization of the branch of the Chinese Association], ibid., 10 Sept. 1911.

66. From Jiujiang, "Guominjun chuxian" [Organization of the People's Army], *Minli bao*, 16 April 1911.

67. From Guilin, "Guominjun" [The People's Army], *Minli bao*, 8 May 1911; from Guilin, "Guominjun jiesanyi" [The People's Army Disbanded], ibid., 10 May 1911.

68. From Hubei, "Ruidu chijin zuzhi Guominjun" [Governor-general Rui Cheng prohibits the organization of the People's Army], *Shi bao*, 10 March 1911; from Hunan, "You jinzhi xuesheng faqi Guominjun" [Students prohibited again from organizing the People's Army]," ibid., 10 April 1911; "Zhengfu jinmin aiguodian" [The government prohibits the sending of patriotic telegrams], ibid., 12 April 1911.

69. Lin Duanfu, "Ningbo guangfu qinli ji" [My experience during the restoration of Ningbo], in *Xinhai Geming Huiyilu*, vol. 4; Qin Yuliu, "Wuxi Qianye Shangtuan zuzhi guangfu dui Yuanqi" [The story of the organization of the Restoration Corps by the Association of Wuxi Primitive Bankers], in *Guangfudui jishi* [The history of the Restoration Corps].

70. Shen Yunsun, "Zhongguo Guomin Zonghui cailiao xuanji" [Selected documents of the general meeting of the Chinese National Association], in *Jindaishi ziliao* [Documents of Chinese modern history], vol. 25; "Guomin Zonghui tonggao" [Announcement of the general meeting of the Chinese National Association], *Minli bao*, 1 Dec. 1912.

71. Gaimushō genson kiroku, "Chūgoku kibōkeikokusho."

72. Liu, "Huang Xing zhuanji."

# The 1911 Revolution in Hunan and the Popular Movement

Shimizu Minoru

China's 1911 Revolution brought to an end two thousand years of despotic dynastic rule and culminated in the emergence of Asia's first republican government. Above all, it was a political revolution that could not have come about without the active participation of the peasantry led by bourgeois and petty bourgeois revolutionaries. But its effects were short-lived, for a mere six months later Yuan Shikai wrested back political control from the revolutionary forces with the institution of his warlord government.

The purpose of this paper is to shed more light upon the reasons why the revolution failed, by examining a driving force behind the 1911 uprising in Hunan province, the *huidang* (secret societies), whose members came largely from the lowest classes. While scholars have given the *huidang* some attention, the consensus is that they were shortsighted, disunified, and fractious groups. I will focus more heavily on the vigorous activities of the *huidang* in the hope of according these societies a measure of the recognition that I believe they deserve. Thus it is necessary to look in some detail at the constitutionalists who oppressed the *huidang* and finally succeeded in undoing the results of the revolution. By depicting those groups who fought the constitutionalists, I hope to bring out the counterrevolutionary, oppressive character of the latter. I have chosen to concentrate upon the *huidang* and constitutionalists because I believe that an analysis of their relationship has significant bearing on the true nature of the 1911 Revolution.

## The Popular Movement in Hunan

Under the 1901 treaty which settled the Boxer Rebellion, China was reduced to a semi-colonial status. As it grew increasingly submissive to foreign powers, the Qing dynasty recognized the need to effect, at least superficially, a new constitutional government to maintain domestic control. At the same time, it greatly increased the tax burden on the masses to cover revenues and reparations payments. Coinciding with a succession of natural disasters and famines, the new taxes brought utter impoverishment to the masses. The fundamental social contradictions under the Qing dynasty and the popular movements that rose in opposition to it are characteristic features of this period. The late Qing popular constitutional movement quickly gained momentum, reaching peaks in 1902, 1906, and 1910.

Let us now look at the popular movement as it unfolded in Hunan. In July 1900, 20,000 local people attacked Italian, British, and French churches in Hengzhou, killing and injuring a number of foreigners. In August, in Chenzhou more than 2,000 people besieged a British church. The following month, more than 10,000, including members of the secret society Gelaohui, beggars, drifters, and peasants, chiefly from Shaoyang, Hengzhou, Xiangxiang, and Xinning, organized the "Restore the Han, destroy the West" army under the leadership of He Jinsheng and assaulted churches, government offices, officials, and the *xiangshen* (gentry). In November of 1904, the Hunan revolutionary organization Huaxinghui, and Tongchouhui, a federation of Gelaohui branches, staged an unsuccessful revolt in Changsha. In December 1906, the Hongjianghui, which was an alliance of *huidang*, with members of the Hunan branch of the Tongmenghui assembled several tens of thousands and rose in rebellion in Pingxiang, Liuyang, and Liling, placing under their control an area bordering Hunan and Jiangxi. In April 1910, more than 10,000 starving people staged a large-scale rice riot in Changsha, the capital of Hunan, demanding a reduction in commodity prices and the release of government rice. They destroyed a provincial government office, churches, foreign trading companies, and schools, as well as the shops of rice wholesalers and dealers.

At first glance these might seem to be unrelated incidents; they had, however, two important characteristics in common. First, they all involved mainly lumpenproletariat and semi-proletariat— poor laborers and peasants, drifters, and starving people—whose plight was a direct result of the collapse of the rural economy and the penetration of imperialism. These people were largely organized into *huidang*. Second, in each case the *huidang* joined forces with the leadership of the revolutionaries. In the following sections we will focus attention upon those two points. First I will examine the actions of the popular movement under the leadership of the *huidang* and consider the kind of solidarity that made it possible for them to become the center of the movement. Next I will analyze the policies and moves of prominent *huidang* and local Gemingdang (revolutionary party) leaders, and consider how they were able to effect the dynamic alliance that produced Hunan's revolution of 1911.

The behavior patterns of the popular movement had three major characteristics. Responding to the appeal "Down with the rich, help save the poor," rioters assaulted the government officials, *xiangshen*, and wealthy merchants who controlled and exploited them and distributed the looted food and money among the poor. Rarely were ordinary villagers or travelers molested, showing clearly that the movement was basically a class struggle. At the same time it was a struggle between rural communities and the cities, which were the stronghold of the exploiting groups as well as symbols of regional authority. The masses' rage was also directed at the products of the new constitutional government: schools, the local government apparatus, industries, and police and military training schools. Obviously the masses believed that the fruits of modernization had been obtained at their expense.

The second characteristic of the movement was its anti-Christian and anti-foreign nature expressed in the slogan "Take revenge on religion, expel foreigners." Churches and missionaries were attacked at Chenzhou, Hengzhou, and Shaoyang. In addition, during the rice riot in Changsha, American, British, German, and Japanese trading companies, factories, warehouses, ships, and other outposts of imperialism were the targets of fierce assaults.

Third, the movement was strongly anti-Qing, an inevitable consequence in view of the Qing support for the wealthy, the *xiangshen,* and Westerners. What is more, they controlled the bureaucracy, traditionally despised for its corruption; hence the slogan *"guanbi minbian"* (officials oppress, the people rebel). The tradition of opposition to corrupt officials was promoted by the *huidang* by another rally call, "Oppose the Qing, restore the Ming" and by the revolutionaries, "Oppose the Qing, support a republic."

These patterns of behavior did not always occur with the consistency they required to function as an organically unified force. In addition, the popular movement during the 1911 Revolution had other characteristics that heightened its complexity.

Contradictions in the implementation of the new constitutional government, resulting from a series of modernization policies designed to preserve the dynasty's despotic control, gradually increased popular antagonism toward *xiangshen,* merchants, and the wealthy—the promoters of reform. Still fettered by a feudal mode of production, the peasants' lot only grew more desperate as "modernization" policies were implemented. Anti-Christian outbreaks were still common between 1900 and 1903, but toward 1911, with the opening of the port of Changsha, anti-foreign resistance was more often directed against the proliferating capitalist and imperialist establishments, notably Western factories and trading companies.

A factor that worked to the disadvantage of the revolution was the tendency to separate class struggle and anti-foreignism from opposition to the Qing dynasty. The revolutionaries, who were only dimly aware of imperialism, were adamant in their opposition to the Qing dynasty but de-emphasized the other aspects of the revolution, especially anti-foreignism. Still, the revolutionaries, calling on the people to "Drive out the Manchu dynasty, restore the Middle Kingdom and establish a republic and for equal rights to land," lived up to their name in their uncompromising attitude toward attempts at bourgeois reform by the Qing and the constitutionalists. It was the revolutionaries who clearly confronted the masses with the questions of nationalism, race, and revolution.

Another limiting factor was the basic policy of *huidang*-centered groups to attack cities from mountain village bases. Attacks were launched daily from mountain hamlets, which were safe from government attack. This sort of resistance did not take the form of landlord-tenant confrontation within the local community. Instead, the *huidang*, coalescing in a new fictitious community that was freed from traditional communal relations and united in the spirit of chivalry and secrecy, pitted itself against the traditional community. Such solidified groups of the poor, whose base lay outside the traditional framework of the village community, were able to put up strong resistance against the *xiangshen*, merchants, churches, and foreigners. But ultimately they were unable to bring about reform within rural communities, since theirs were not indigenous movements and could not be sustained.

## The Huidang and Their Response to the Revolutionaries

Hunan was known for its large number of secret societies, which had maintained a broad rural base in the province since the mid-nineteenth century. The Gelaohui was originally a mutual aid society that spread in the mountainous farming villages of Sichuan, Guizhou, and Hunan during the Qianlong and Jiaqing eras (1736–1820). During the turbulent Taiping Rebellion it expanded to the Yangzi and its tributaries to urban areas, and in the 1890s it became the largest secret society in central China. In the early twentieth century, the Hunan Gelaohui, under guidance from the revolutionaries, played a crucial role as the core of the organized peasantry, thus setting the stage for the 1911 Revolution.

The Gelaohui was composed mainly of unemployed peasants and drifters. The emergence of such groups was partly the result of the shift in the centers of trade with the opening of new ports and the dissolution of the Zeng Guofan army, which had helped to suppress the Taiping Rebellion. Another important factor, however, was the appearance of a large group of landless peasants. Chronic natural disasters and famine were partly responsible for the straits they were in, but political and economic changes following the Opium War were also to blame. One new factor was the rapid inflow of foreign goods, induced by the inequitable exchange rate, which disrupted the traditional Chinese mode of production. Another was increased oppression by the government and foreign powers during the first and second westernization movements; eventually it caused the rural economy to collapse. To survive, most displaced peasants looked to the Gelaohui, since modern industry was still not developed enough to provide an alternative. Urging the people to "Share happiness, share sufferings," the Gelaohui absorbed these people and provided havens in remote mountain villages, like the one depicted in the Chinese novel *The Water Margin*. They established operation bases in urban areas and even constructed roads when necessary. In these areas the Gelaohui was not only safe from the hands of government authorities, but it also enjoyed widespread public support.

Members of *huidang*, being alienated from the established order, were the target of government enmity, and thus the organizations remained secretive. In protest against social inequality, they rallied behind such slogans as "Destroy the rich, help the poor" and "Oppose the Qing, restore the Ming." At times their members' actions did not live up to their ideals: some engaged in gambling and dealt in opium. Historical records that sometimes characterize the *huidang* as groups of gamblers and ruffians merely reflect the government line. Members of the Gelaohui were not altogether estranged from the rural community; on the contrary, they had close contacts with it, as reports from local Qing officials indicate: "When soldiers come, the bandit groups (Gelaohui) disband and behave as ordinary folk; when soldiers leave, they form again." "The secret societies, soldiers, civilians, merchants, and officials hereabouts are all bandits." Actually, members of the Gelaohui operated under strict humanitarian rules that forbade murder, the disruption of commercial markets, or the terrorizing of travelers. They would not rape and would steal only rice, money, or cloth. It is easy to understand why the villagers sympathized with them.

The assortment of members of the Gelaohui possessed a high degree of solidarity based on their common problems of poverty and oppression rather than on blood ties. They formed an egalitarian society in which each member was treated alike, regardless of rank or class. Whether they were acquainted or not, members called one another "brother." Moreover, they shared a religious solemnity and chivalrous spirit that stressed humanism, loyalty, and bravery. It was the freedom and freshness of this egalitarian communal group, and its transcendence of the traditional framework of ruler and ruled and of limits imposed by blood ties that allowed the Gelaohui to become the core of the revolutionary force.

In the early twentieth century, the Gelaohui in Hunan province joined the vanguard in popular struggles by allying with the revolutionaries. Besides the Gelaohui and the revolutionaries, there were at that time no other politically influential groups capable of organizing the masses effectively. The terms of the alliance were worked out by enlightened leaders of the secret societies and local members of the Gemingdang who were close to them. The result was the formation of *huidang* federations with some revolutionaries included. These were the Tongchouhui, the Hongjianghui, and the Gongjinhui. Through these organizations and their organizers, local members of the Gemingdang and *huidang* leaders, people of the lowest class, whom the *huidang* represented, were brought together with the bourgeois revolutionaries, who were represented by the Huaxinghui and the Tongmenghui. Their relationships are illustrated in the following chart.

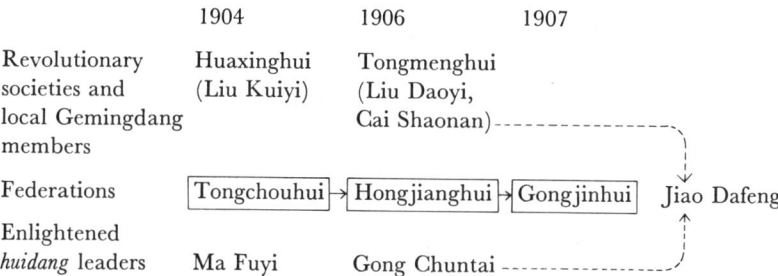

Noting the revolutionary potential of the *huidang*, the revolutionaries in Hunan decided to make use of them. To this end, they sent men, including Liu Kuiyi, Liu Daoyi, Cai Shaonan, and Jiao Dafeng, back to their native villages, where they knew the local situation and could win the *huidang* to their cause. A number of influential *huidang* leaders soon accepted the advice and guidance of the revolutionaries and were committed to overthrowing the Qing dynasty. The more authority the *huidang* leaders had, the greater the unity achieved between groups.

The primary goal of the federations of *huidang* and revolutionaries, expressed by the battle cry "Oppose the Qing, win a republic," went beyond that of the *huidang*, who had hoped to restore the Ming. Both the Hongjianghui manifesto of 1906 and the Gongjinhui declaration of 1907 called for the destruction of the Manchu dynasty, and for freedom, equality, equal human rights, and equalization of land rights. Although they could not really expect to achieve all their goals, the idea of egalitarianism struck a responsive chord among *huidang* members and peasants, who flocked behind the banners of the federations. That the alliance of Gelaohui and revolutionaries made the revolution possible is evident in the exuberant shout of *huidang* members in Hengzhou the day they achieved victory: "From today we Gelaohui are our own masters!"

The relationship of the *huidang* and revolutionaries was a symbiotic one. By cooperating with the revolutionaries, the *huidang* were able to become strong enough to destory the Qing dynasty and thereby liberate their members from oppression and exploitation. Likewise, by organizing the *huidang* and funneling their energy into the revolution, the revolutionaries were able to realize their goal of establishing a republic. It is difficult to overstate the significance of the alliance of local Gemingdang members and *huidang* leaders in bringing about the revolution. But because the revolutionaries relied on the *huidang* leaders, the course of the revolution itself was influenced by their thinking and actions.

## Victory Gained and Victory Lost

The success of the revolution in Wuchang, the capital of Hubei province, gave tremendous encouragement to groups struggling elsewhere. Overjoyed at the victory at Wuchang, a revolutionary army, composed mainly of *huidang* members and a newly organized group of soldiers from the revolutionary secret society Gongjinhui liberated Changsha, the provincial capital of Hunan. They then set up a military government, appointing the army leaders Jiao Dafeng and Chen Zuoxin military governor and vice-governor, respectively. The revolutionary army's nucleus was, of course, soldiers and *huidang* members belonging to the Gongjinhui, but as total victory in the revolution grew near, army ranks swelled from an estimated 4,000 to perhaps 50,000 or 60,000 as the influx of poor people continued. That is why the regime could raise an army to aid the revolutionary regime in Hubei. Many *huidang* leaders and soldiers of the new army were appointed officials. Because of its composition, the army directly reflected the feelings of the masses, and Jiao, then 25 years old, came up with a revolutionary, though not thoroughgoing, program of reform.

Once the revolutionary regime was in place, Jiao shifted the emphasis to social stability, urging stores, companies, schools, and other organizations to return to normalcy. At the same time, the Jiao regime was not anti-imperialistic and sought to avoid friction with foreign powers. It even accepted members of the old ruling class, including bureaucrats and gentry, as long as they agreed to oppose the Qing and support the revolution. In the early stages, Jiao was able to rally support from many classes, including merchants, urban and rural gentry, and the constitutionalists.

The revolutionary army rejected the constitutionalists' plan for assuming power by having "a cultural revolution and Tan Yankai as military governor." Counter-revolutionary elements were executed. Less than ten days after the start of the revolution, the strategic rural areas of Yuezhou, Hengzhou, Baoqing, Changde, and elsewhere were liberated by troops dispatched from Changsha. This victory in turn encouraged groups in nearby villages. In the countryside, the revolution escalated beyond a political, nationalist upheaval to become a class struggle against bureaucrats and gentry.

Dazed at first, the constitutionalists and feudal ruling class soon regrouped to organize resistance to the revolution. In installing a new system of control, they made strategic use of the revolutionary regime's policy of keeping social order and of opportunities to voice their opinions through channels inside the revolutionary regime. In such ways they worked to defeat the revolution from within. On October 23, such prominent constitutionalists as Tan Yankai and Chen Bingyu persuaded Jiao to approve the establishment of a provincial senate that would represent the popular will. Parliamentary approval was necessary to implement orders of the governor-general. The following day the constitutionalists demanded and achieved a bifurcated governmental structure consisting of military and civilian administrations. The important posts within both sections were filled by constitutionalists who belonged to the senate. The constitutionalists' reforms appeared democratic, but actually they were designed to protect the interests of the propertied classes, mainly wealthy merchants and gentry, and to circumscribe Jiao's power.

Jiao found that the constitutionalists' efforts to label him a "bandit" and "enemy of order" were drawing the people and his revolutionary army further and further away from him. On October 26, when Jiao appointed different men to the posts of Xilu zhaofushi and Nanlu anfushi without prior approval of the parliament, the senate demanded his resignation. This action generated a sharp confrontation between the revolutionaries and the military regime on the one hand, and the constitutionalists and the senate on the other. The latter camp began to plot the overthrow of the revolutionary regime. Getting wind of the plot, Jiao quickly called together representatives of the various groups and proposed further reform of the political system. With overwhelming support from revolutionary soldiers and *huidang*, he decided to abolish the senate and the bifurcated governmental structure, and concentrate all power in the position of governor-general. The Hunan regime was busy at the time organizing an army to join the revolutionary front in Wuhan, and the 49th Regiment, made up of career revolutionary soldiers who constituted the driving force behind the liberation of Changsha, had already left for Hubei the same month on the 28th. Two days later it was decided to send the 50th Regiment to help the Hubei army. While the army busied itself with preparations, the Changsha regime was left defenseless. On the last day of the month, an army commander, Mei Xin, seized the chance and carried out a coup d'état. He had been in collusion with the constitutionalists and was accompanied by the remnants of troops under Huang Zhonghao, commander of the Patrol and Defense Forces who was killed by the revolutionaries. Military governor Jiao and vice-governor Chen Zuoxin were both killed, and Tan Yankai was installed. The coup d'état effectively placed power, both in name and reality, in the hands of the constitutionalists and the old ruling class. All this took place a mere ten days after the liberation of Changsha.

## The Tan Yankai Regime and the Popular Movement

Tan Yankai's assumption of the post of military governor represented a victory for the constitutionalists and the other counter-revolutionaries. It is pertinent at this point to sketch briefly just how the constitutionalists came into being, and the means by which they managed to regain power.

Originally the constitutionalists were gentry entrenched in the Qing dynasty ruling structure. Alarmed by the growth of popular movements in the early twentieth century, they demanded that the Qing make certain concessions, including greater local autonomy and the promotion of industry. With a series of reforms starting in 1906, the gentry class increased its political power through influential constitutional institutions, the Ziyiju (Provincial Assembly) and the Zizhengyuan (National Assembly). Economically, it grew stronger by playing a leading role in the promotion of industry. The main organizations that were politically and socially active on the eve of the revolution were the Hunan General Chamber of Commerce, the General Industrial Association, the General Agricultural Affairs Association, and the Office for Self-government; politically, the Provincial Assembly in Hunan, and the Hunan branches of the Xianyouhui (Friends of the Constitution Association) and the 1911 Club were the most active. When the Qing dynasty strengthened its anti-bourgeois, centralized, despotic control, the gentry decided to press for the early establishment of a national parliament and the private construction of railroads. They also worked to prevent the central government from taking over the existing private lines. Then when revolution seemed imminent, they adopted an anti-Manchu posture. Finally, when they learned of the rebellion in Wuchang, the constitutionalists in Hunan turned to support the revolutionary forces, offering them funds and frequently meeting with the revolutionaries. In this way they became part of the revolution. Most constitutionalists did not resist the revolutionary regime, and for this reason were invited to participate in the new government. Eventually, as we have seen, they were able to seize power. They could do so because as landholding bourgeoisie they had accumulated political and economic influence before and after the revolution, which gave them a strong voice in the management of the government.

Also of importance in the revival of the constitutionalists was the policy of right-wing revolutionaries like Song Jiaoren. Song and others did nothing to oppose the October 31 coup, content that the new regime led by Tan Yankai would not align itself with the Qing dynasty. Not only did they fail to grasp the constitutionalists' true intentions, but readily compromised with them, choosing parliamentary government over armed struggles. Some took part in the new "republican" government as bureaucrats and assembly members, joining the ranks of the oppressors. Indeed, the military regime carried out a skillful counter-revolution. They suppressed internal dissent in the name of order, and when Yuan Shikai assumed the presidency, they supported him.

The masses had only the briefest flirtation with revolution and wound up at a greater disadvantage than before, forced to begin all over again. Let us now examine the popular struggles carried on in Hunan during the time Tan Yankai was in power, from 1911 through October of 1913. The struggles of this period can be divided into three categories according to their participants: those of the *huidang*, those of ex-soldiers, and those of rank-and-file members of the Gemingdang. These do not, of course, account for all the confrontations of the time, but a brief description of these three types may provide insight into the results of the revolution and the people and tactics responsible for subverting the will of the masses.

## Huidang Uprisings

Even after the failure of the revolution, a large number of *huidang*, including the Hongjianghui, Gedihui, Hongdenghui, and Dadaohui, controlled areas not under effective government control, especially district and provincial borders and urban areas. The *Minli bao* reported almost daily on *huidang* riots, which they called "bandit riots." Their number defied counting. Many escalated into large-scale rebellions involving the poor and starving. Many of these people had played central roles in the struggle that toppled the Qing dynasty and established Jiao's military government. But as the old order under the ruling class led by Tan Yankai was revived, not only constitutionalists and gentry but right-wing revolutionaries as well rejected the *huidang* as obstacles to "cultural revolution." The post-revolution *huidang* resistance movements, gathering behind slogans of "Destroy the rich, help the poor" and "Expel foreign elements," were committed to opposing the groups that exploited and oppressed them, especially the Tan Yankai regime and its revolutionary pretenses.

Right-wing revolutionary leaders in Hunan not only brushed aside the struggles of *huidang* but sided with the old rulers in their desire for a more orderly revolution. Tan Renfeng, for instance, published an article in which he demanded that *huidang* members become more open and flexible. He argued that since the Manchu dynasty had been brought down and a republic was established, it was against the interests of the people for the *huidang* to build halls, issue cloth bandages to new members, and incite riots in villages. The Hunan revolutionaries regarded the *huidang* as ignorant people who did not understand the great cause of republicanism. They opposed the *huidang* uprisings and helped the new regime destroy "bandits" in rural areas.

## Uprisings by Discharged Soldiers

Jiao Dafeng's army of *huidang* members and poor peasants performed splendidly in the battle of Wuhan. However, for financial reasons, the Tan Yankai regime reduced their numbers and their wages. After the collapse of the Qing dynasty in February 1912, some 30,000 soldiers were discharged, many of whom returned to their home provinces and districts. There, using the names of military officials, they issued false calls to arms, rioted, and caused destruction.

The decision to discharge soldiers was based partly on economic considerations, but another very important reason was that hopes for an egalitarian society after the revolution had spread among the ranks. Fearing the effect this might have on the social order, Tan Yankai dissolved the corps that had played the central part in the revolution, in the hope that this would dispel the army's revolutionary atmosphere. Therefore the massive discharge of soldiers was one of the immediate factors in the confrontation between revolutionary and counter-revolutionary elements within the military government.

## Uprisings by Lower-Class Members of the Gemingdang

The Guomindang (National party) was formed from various political parties and organizations and factions in August 1912 by Huang Xing, Song Jiaoren, and others, with the objective of setting up a party cabinet. The revolutionary organization Tongmenghui was dissolved. A Guomindang branch was organized in Hunan in late September, and military governor Tan Yankai was made its head. Opportunists, including constitutionalists, the old bureaucracy, and military officers, entered the party in large numbers. Hunan, Hubei, and Jiangxi became important spheres of influence for the Guomindang. Song Jiaoren and other right-wing revolutionaries severed relations with the *huidang*, soldiers, and peasantry, and instead, turned their attention to parliamentary struggles, indiscriminately compromising with the old ruling class. Many lower-class members of the Gemingdang, however, refused to abandon the revolutionary movement. Cooperating with discharged soldiers, *huidang* members, and the poor, they pressed for the overthrow of the military government and political reforms. They became even more active after the establishment of the Guomindang. In Hunan, a number of new organizations, including the Revolutionary Party, the Political Reform Party, and the Association for the Improvement of Hunan Politics, were set up by Gemingdang members who were once followers of Jiao Dafeng and Chen Zuoxin. Mainly, they sought to extend their influence in the Changsha area, at the same time working toward the dissolution of the office of military governor and the establishment of a republic. They spread rumors all over Hunan to the effect that they would soon go on the offensive and remove the military governor. This triggered uprisings and terrorism, but in the end they, too, were suppressed by the military government in the name of order.

The goal of defeating the Manchus and establishing a republic was achieved in the 1911 Revolution, but the basic pattern of feudal exploitation remained almost untouched. When the revolutionary fervor died down and the new government, determined to preserve the old order, was firmly in place, the ruling class was once again free to exploit and oppress the masses. While the pre-revolutionary struggles of the *huidang* echelon, along with the later efforts of discharged soldiers and lower-class members of the Gemingdang, were the result of peculiar historical conditions, these post-revolutionary struggles were an attempt by the masses to free themselves from renewed oppression. The former took place at a time of rural crisis during the late Qing dynasty, the latter after the achievements of the revolution had been swept away. In the latter case, as we can see in their slogans demanding the overthrow of the military government, the masses saw clearly that the revolution's fruits had been snatched away from them. The Tan Yankai regime represented both the newly revived, established ruling class, concealed behind a thin revolutionary veneer and right-wing revolutionaries who had turned their backs on the masses. The masses perceived the true character of the Tan regime far more clearly than Song Jiaoren and the other right-wing revolutionaries.

## Conclusion

By focusing upon the *huidang* and the constitutionalists, I have described how the 1911 Revolution was first won and then lost in Hunan. My point, once again, is that the 1911 Revolution was a bourgeois democratic revolution in response to the semi-colonization of China by imperialists. The fundamental force behind the revolution was based on peasants and other segments of the masses, who in general opposed the semi-feudal, semi-colonial government. It was neither a revolution of the gentry nor a revolution through which the Qing passed power over to the constitutionalists. Likewise, there were no fundamental contradictions between the Han ruling class and the Manchu dynasty and military clique. The revolution succeeded and then failed because the peasants could not create the political force necessary to give direction to the revolution; they had no choice but to rely on the bourgeois revolutionaries and the Tongmenghui or on the *huidang*. Even after they were deprived of power, many revolutionaries were elated by the victory over the Manchus and willingly turned their backs on the peasant masses in the name of social order. Tied closely to the constitutionalists and the old ruling class, they helped usher in control by the warlords. The *huidang*, on the other hand, who represented the oppressed masses and played a pivotal role in overthrowing the despotic dynasty, failed to confront and tackle the basic contradictions within rural society, the foundation of despotic rule. In the end, they were unable to gain control of the local means of production, namely the land. Plunged once again into the dark world of pre-revolution days, the people had no choice but to start anew their struggle for liberation.

[Translated by Takechi Manabu]

References

Shimizu Minoru. "Chōsa kome sōdō to minshū" [Changsha rice riots and the masses], *Nagoya Daigaku Tōyō-shi kenkyū hōkoku* 1.

——. "Hyō, Ryū, Rei ni okeru kakumei hōki ni tsuite" [On rebellions in P'ing, Liu, and Li districts], *Tōyō-shi kenkyū* 29–4.

——. "Konan ni okeru Shingai Kakumei no ichidanmen ni tsuite" [One aspect of the 1911 Revolution in Hunan], *Tōhōgaku* 47.

——. "Konan Rikkenha no keisei katei ni tsuite" [On the formative process of the constitutionalists in Hunan], *Nagoya Daigaku Tōyō-shi kenkyū hōkoku* 6.

——. "Kyōshinkai oboegaki" [Notes on the Gongjinhui], *Nagoya Daigaku insei ronshū* 1.

——. "Shingai Kakumei kenkyū ni kansuru oboegaki" [Notes on studies of the 1911 Revolution], *Nagoya Daigaku Tōyō-shi kenkyū hōkoku* 2.

——. "Shingai Kakumei zen no Konan ni okeru kakumei undō" [Revolutionary movements in Hunan province before the 1911 Revolution], *Rekishi no riron to kyōiku* 38.

# Sun Yat-sen and the Founding of the Provisional Nanjing Government

## Chen Xiqi

The 1911 Revolution was the first great revolution in modern China, and Sun Yat-sen's leadership of the revolution was the most important achievement in his life. The revolution marked the end of 2000 years of feudal autocracy in China and established a republic founded and led by Sun Yat-sen. The overthrow of the Qing dynasty conformed to the trend of the times and to popular demand, and was the most progressive cause of that time in China and in all of Asia. Sun Yat-sen's activities before and after the founding of the republican provisional government in Nanjing epitomize his leadership of the revolutionary movement and his devotion to the cause.[1]

The Wuchang Uprising broke out on October 10, 1911. Sun Yat-sen gave consistent leadership to this great bourgeois revolutionary movement from the founding of the Xingzhonghui (Society to Restore China's Prosperity) to the outbreak of the uprising itself. He was fully confident of the eventual overthrow of the Qing government. Prior to the uprising, he had already predicted that "the revolutionary tide is soaring, unprecedented in history."[2] Although he knew that Hubei revolutionaries were planning an uprising, he hoped for better preparations in advance and did not expect the uprising so soon. That is why he once said: "The success of the Wuchang Uprising is unexpected."[3] He considered the timing "a little early."[4] It is a mistake to conclude from this comment that Sun Yat-sen had done nothing for the uprising.

The success of the uprising brought about the real possibility of overthrowing the monarchy and establishing a republic. Sun Yat-sen immediately set about realizing this change. He was then living abroad, not because he wanted to be away from the motherland—"I will be very glad all my life to participate in the fighting personally"—but because he thought his duty lay elsewhere. At the time he believed he ought to "dedicate his efforts to diplomatic affairs."[5] In the forty days following the uprising, he visited the United States, Great Britain, and France.

At that time, Sun Yat-sen thought that "domestically, success is only a question of time. What I fear is outside interference."[6] He never abandoned the struggle at home. He worked out a plan for the period after the Wuchang Uprising on his way from Chicago to New York and sent another leader of the 1911 Revolution, Huang Xing, to Hankou to lead the revolutionary army against the Qing troops. He declared explicitly: "The present uprising in central China is under my command."[7] On learning that Huang Xing had "already arrived safely in Hankou," he expressed satisfaction that the struggle at home had good leadership: "The situation has improved greatly."[8] In light of the overall conditions and his own situation, he thought that he could make a greater contribution to the establishment of the republic through diplomatic activities. A modern revolution is not merely an internal affair; international support and recognition are of major importance. It should be noted that Sun Yat-sen was somewhat naive about international affairs and entertained illusions about imperialist intentions, but this does not negate the value of the diplomatic activities he carried on during this period.

At that time, the revolutionary party thought that in order to overthrow the Qing government quickly and establish the republic smoothly, it was necessary to stop foreign support of the Qing. If some countries could not be brought to support the revolution, at least they might be persuaded to remain "neutral." The goal was a worthy one. To this end, Sun Yat-sen issued from abroad the "Letter to Every Country," in which he reaffirmed the Tongmenghui's (Chinese Revolutionary League) consistent policy in foreign affairs and recognized the validity of all international treaties the Qing government had signed as well as all outstanding loans. Yet, he also declared: "Any country will be considered an enemy if it helps the Qing government against our troops."[9]

Sun Yat-sen tried to win not only diplomatic recognition and financial assistance but he also tried to gain sympathy and support of public opinion. While these activities did not yield nearly what he had hoped for, neither were they completely fruitless. Sun Yat-sen's analysis of the major imperialist countries showed clearly that Britain had the most powerful forces and the largest sphere of influence in China. Therefore, Britain was the main focus of his diplomatic activities. This was just on the eve of World War I. Contradictions between the major imperialist countries were becoming extremely acute, and China was one of the areas in which their interests conflicted. It was not, therefore, unreasonable to take advantage of these contradictions in order to prevent a united imperialist front against the Chinese revolution.

In foreign affairs, Sun Yat-sen paid much attention to getting the public in foreign countries to influence governmental policies toward China. He worked very hard to obtain Japanese support of the Chinese revolution. Before the Wuchang Uprising, Sun Yat-sen frequently wrote his Japanese friends in the hope that they could persuade their government to allow him to return to Japan and openly lead the Chinese revolution. After the Wuchang Uprising, while in the United States, he once again asked Miyazaki Tōten and others to persuade the Japanese government to allow him to return home via Japan as a "Chinese leader," in order to dispel the belief, then prevalent in foreign countries, that the Japanese government was covertly protecting the Beijing government, and to "raise the morale of the revolutionary army."[10] In Britain, he won over Archibald R. Colquhoun, a well-known British railway prospector and author, who had once doubted whether republicanism could be carried out in China, as a warm supporter and propagandist for the Chinese revolution. Colquhoun declared in London newspapers: "Sun Yat-sen's programme for the establishment of the Republic of China is carefully considered, well prepared, and will be carried out very soon." He called on "every good friend who is sympathetic to China to wish the Chinese revolution success." Even "all the foreign-language newspapers in the East" gave "good reports" of what Colquhoun had said.[11] Many Britishers who sympathized with the Chinese revolution wrote to the British government calling for support of Sun Yat-sen's revolution.[12] Sun also lodged a three-point demand with the British government through the assistance of the head of Vickers, the arms manufacturers: 1) to abrogate all the loans to the Qing court; 2) to help stop Japan from supporting the Qing court; and 3) to order the governments of British colonies to lift the ban of exile on Sun Yat-sen so as to facilitate his return home.[13] The British government agreed. Though its motives were not sincere, objectively it did something that helped advance the Chinese revolution. At that time, a number of imperialist powers, under the guise of "neutrality," were seeking new proxies through which they could control China. But the stopping of foreign loans was a heavy blow, financially and politically, to the Qing government.

The moment Sun Yat-sen learned of the successful Wuchang Uprising, he turned his thoughts to the establishment of the new republican government. While Sun Yat-sen was still abroad, a complicated situation had emerged in China. While various provinces declared independence one after another, and with growing popular support for a republic, a number of old officials and constitutional monarchists also expressed support for the revolution. It became difficult to tell who was sincere and who was not. The revolutionaries failed to bring the situation under their control, and internal conflicts grew. It was extremely difficult under these circumstances to establish a unified central government.

In November, when Sun Yat-sen learned that the political situation was "entirely in chaos," and that "China seemed about to be divided into many republics," he was keenly aware of his historic responsibility and declared indignantly: "The responsibility for defending China's future should be held by me."[14] Fearing that "the great cause of revolution would be lost," in late November he decided to "abandon his diplomatic endeavors abroad and hurry home so as to save the country from danger."[15]

On his route home, Sun Yat-sen gave more practical consideration to the problem of establishing the republic. His talk with Hu Hanmin in Hong Kong provides an important clue to his thoughts and activities before and after the founding of the Provisional Government in Nanjing. Hu Hanmin suggested that, for the moment, Sun Yat-sen should stay in Guangzhou, train troops, gather strength, and then set out for the reunification of north and south. Declining Hu's suggestion, Sun said that "with regard to the overall situation, the Shanghai-Nanjing area is the front. If I am not there at the front but stay back in Guangzhou to engage in war work, it means that I am taking the easy way. Comrades are looking to me. If I do as you say, what won't they say about me?" He felt that he could not abandon his responsibilities and said, "If I do not go to Shanghai and Nanjing, there will be no one to take charge of internal and external affairs."[16] "The major problem today," he said, "is anarchy. If we are able to set up our government, the Qing regime is bound to fall."[17] He decided to go to Shanghai and Nanjing immediately in order to establish a republican government.

Taking the overall situation into consideration, Sun decided that the main thing was to establish a republican government and that he should see to it personally. This was not only required by developments in the revolutionary situation but was demanded by the Chinese people. Sun Yat-sen returned as a highly esteemed leader of the entire nation, and all obstacles to the establishment of a provisional government were swept aside. On the second day of his return, he was nominated for the presidency of the republic at a conference of senior members of the Chinese Revolutionary League. Three days later, on December 29, he was officially elected the Provisional President of the Republic of China by representatives from 17 provinces. On New Year's Day, 1912, Sun Yat-sen left Shanghai for Nanjing for his inauguration. On January 3, the Provisional Government of the Republic of China was set up in Nanjing.

When the provisional government was being organized, Sun Yat-sen played an extremely important role. The Chinese Revolutionary League had discussed the organic program of the provisional government when deciding who was to be the president, and Sun Yat-sen had insisted on the presidential system, pointing out that the cabinet system in which "the head of state is placed outside of politics" was definitely unfeasible during extraordinary times. Too many checks would "frustrate the great cause of revolution," he said.[18] Sun Yat-sen had always detested rivalry for power and gain and had always been reluctant to accept personal power and position. But at that early period of the republic—crucial for both internal and external affairs—he wanted to be able to play the role for which he was suited. Not for personal gain or power but courageously to assume revolutionary responsibilities: this was Sun Yat-sen's consistent thought and behavioral style.

The establishment of the provisional government in Nanjing determined that China's political future could only be in republicanism. Prior to Sun Yat-sen's return from abroad, representatives to the north-south negotiations had proposed convening a national conference to discuss which system of government should be adopted. But after Sun Yat-sen was elected provisional president, the conference of provincial representatives telegraphed the Qing negotiator that the election of the provisional president had clearly demonstrated majority support for the republic. "There is no need to reconvene a national conference," the telegram said.[19]

In his inaugural address, Sun Yat-sen solemnly declared: "The Provisional Government is a government of the revolutionary era." Its task was to "clear away all remnants of autocratic monarchy, to install the republican system, and to realize the goals of the revolution."[20] The Nanjing Provisional Government of the Republic of China was established in accordance with Sun Yat-sen's revolutionary principles. After the establishment of the government, Sun Yat-sen continued to make unremitting efforts and to wage a dauntless struggle for safeguarding the revolutionary and democratic character of the new-born republic.

Sun Yat-sen tried hard to ensure that the members of the revolutionary party played leading roles in the new-born republic. In organizing the provisional government, Sun Yat-sen insisted that members of the revolutionary party be the nucleus. He appointed members of the revolutionary party or those most willing to implement the revolutionary party's principles to the most important posts, such as minister of defense, foreign minister, finance minister, and general secretary of the provisional government. As for the other cabinet posts, where he had to appoint members of the old bureaucracy or constitutionalists, he employed the tactic of "giving nominal power to the minister and actual power to the vice-minister" so as to ensure that the revolutionaries would be in firm control. He also appointed many young revolutionaries to posts in the various government departments. Wu Yuzhang, who once worked in the provisional government, recalled: "This provisional government was composed of constitutional monarchists, bureaucrats, warlords, and revolutionaries, with the latter predominating. This was a government in which the bourgeoisie constituted the main body."[21] The Nanjing provisional government was unlike any government in Chinese history. Sun Yat-sen was the president, but he acted as a public servant. He was against building magnificent government offices. "If there are no houses to accommodate the new government, what is wrong with sheds and similar shelters?"[22] Sun Yat-sen and other revolutionaries who held important posts worked strenuously to fulfill their duties, but they lived very simply. The clear-cut revolutionary nature of the provisional government stemmed from the fact that revolutionarires, with Sun Yat-sen as leader, held all the key positions.

Sun Yat-sen also attempted to build the new republic according to the revolutionary party's program. In March 1912 he signed the "Provisional Constitution of the Republic of China" which was by nature a constitution of a bourgeois republic. This constitution declared, for the first time in Chinese history, that sovereignty was vested in the people and that all the people were equal and enjoyed democratic rights.

Of course, for various reasons, many of the provisions written into the constitution were never realized or implemented by the provisional government. And because the provisional government did not last very long, it was not possible to implement various laws which were of a quite democratic character. One after another, they were later rescinded by Yuan Shikai. However, the progressive significance of the revolutionary spirit which Sun Yat-sen injected into the republic's legislation should not be underestimated.

At the same time, as he scrupulously implemented the revolutionary program and put members of the revolutionary party in the government to provide guidance and leadership, Sun Yat-sen strove to win over all those who expressed support for the republic and all patriots willing to work for the common good. He did his best to smooth out contradictions among members of the revolutionary party, stressing that the establishment of the republic required the "coordinated effects of all working together for a common cause, and that no wall of suspicion should be allowed to come between them."²³ Even people like Zhang Taiyan, whose political convictions were far apart from those held by Sun Yat-sen, were "not to be confused with those who are against the republic,"²⁴ and Sun invited Zhang to become confidential advisor to the provisional Nanjing government. But at the same time Sun adamantly refused to allow opponents of the republic to join the government. On the other hand, he welcomed those well-known people who supported the republic, or at least did not oppose it, and invited some of them to take up posts in the provisional government.²⁵ Sun Yat-sen's drawback was that he could not always clearly identify those who merely pretended to support the republic. Still, one must admire Sun's magnanimity and his efforts at uniting with all who favored the republic so that they could contribute to the effort to establish a new nation. Moreover, Sun ordered that former officials should not be arbitrarily suspected,²⁶ and he proscribed the vindictive killing of members of the Protect the Emperor Society. He also declared that no one should be retroactively charged and condemned.²⁷ All this showed that Sun, in order to build the republic, did his utmost to win over those who had opposed the revolution and who were no longer engaged in any destructive activities.

China at that time was a semi-colonial, semi-feudal country, and the forces of reaction were quite powerful. Therefore, if the revolution were to triumph sooner, and if the country were to be built up as quickly as possible and become strong and united, every effort had to be made to bring together all those who supported or who did not oppose the republic. In this respect, Sun Yat-sen's example is still a valid lesson for us today.

Sun Yat-sen also repeatedly propagated the idea of uniting all the nationalities within China to build up a new state, and this was of enormous significance and value during the 1911 Revolution. Sun said clearly: "The republic must unite the five big nationalities—Han, Manchu, Mongolian, Hui, and Tibetan—in the common cause of prosperity and happiness."²⁸ In 1912, Sun Yat-sen sent a telegram to the Mongol nobles and chieftains living in Beijing, urging them not to harbor any apprehensions about the revolution because the aim of the revolution was "not to take revenge on the Manchus, but to unite the people to eliminate tyranny, to bring together the whole nation, making no distinction between Han, Manchu, Mongol, Hui, and Tibetan, so that all could enjoy equally the freedom that belongs to mankind." He warned the Mongol chiefs to beware of tsarist Russian aggression and expressed the hope that they "make this known to their compatriots and work together harmoniously for the great, common cause."[29] In placing the interests of the nation and country first, Sun Yat-sen acted as the most progressive representative of the emergent bourgeoisie. He did not serve narrow class interests but the highest interest of the nation.

After he was elected provisional president, Sun Yat-sen faced two formidable tasks. One was to overthrow the Qing government and eliminate the imperial system, and the other was to consolidate the republic. To accomplish these goals he had to have dealings with Yuan Shikai.

A compromise with Yuan had already been reached before Sun's return to China. On November 9, Huang Xing had written to Yuan urging him to leave the Qing government and join the revolutionaries and become the Napoleon or the Washington of China. A conference of provincial delegates held in Hankou on December 3 decided that if Yuan changed sides, he was to be made president. On December 20, Huang Xing sent Gu Zhongchen to negotiate with Liao Yuchun and had agreed to let "whoever overthrows the Qing government first become president." On the whole, Sun and his comrades agreed with this proposal to use Yuan to overthrow the Qing government. Sun had raised no objections to allowing Yuan to become president. In November 1911 Sun had cabled his agreement from abroad in this manner: "People are saying Yuan will be nominated; all right, if it is appropriate. Carry on if appropriate but seek early consolidation of the nation."[30] In December, speaking to Hu Hanmin in Hong Kong, Sun expressed strong fears of foreign intervention if the revolution were delayed too long. He believed that using Yuan Shikai to overthrow the Qing government was "virtually worth an army of a hundred thousand." After Sun Yat-sen was elected provisional president, he cabled Yuan Shikai that he was "waiting expectantly" for Yuan to take over the presidency and urged him to "decide soon."[31] Sun himself chaired the negotiations with Yuan.

Sun Yat-sen could not alter the revolutionaries' decision to offer the presidency to Yuan, nor was he able to discern Yuan's real nature at that time. But throughout the negotiations, Sun Yat-sen held to the principle of "overthrowing the Manchu dictatorship and consolidating the Republic of China," and he resolutely countered all Yuan Shikai's plots against these two principles. During the negotiations, Sun Yat-sen refused to give up preparations for armed struggle, although at that time he encountered many difficulties in trying to equip, organize, and pay the revolutionary forces. Sun Yat-sen maintained that "whatever the outcome of the peace negotiations, preparations for the Northern Expedition must not be slackened."[32] He personally worked out the six-pronged advance for the Northern Expedition. He had the backing of the revolutionary armed forces during the peace talks, and he prepared for the Northern Expedition if negotiations broke down.

During the talks, Sun Yat-sen closely linked the overthrow of the monarchy with the consolidation of the republic. He maintained that the abdication of the Qing emperor must be an important condition for peace negotiations and firmly opposed any proposal which in any way resembled monarchism. He announced that "no solution is possible without the immediate abdication of the Qing emperor and the promulgation of a republic."[33] Even when he resigned office, he continued to exhort the Nanjing provisional senate: "We must consolidate the foundations of the Republic of China. This is our bounden duty."[34]

During the ensuing talks, Yuan Shikai constantly maneuvered and created side issues in an attempt to use the talks not only to force the emperor's abdication but also to eliminate the Nanjing provisional government so he could form his own government in Tianjin. Sun Yat-sen fought back resolutely and exposed Yuan Shikai's plots. He also wired all foreign legations in China, pointing out that Yuan "wants to order the immediate dissolution of the Nanjing provisional government. It is utterly impossible for the Republic of China to comply. Even if the nation does give way, it will be for the sake of the republic but not for the sake of Yuan."[35] Sun Yat-sen also telegraphed Wu Tingfang, the southern representative in the negotiations, and ordered him to make public criminal charges against Yuan Shikai, and he warned Yuan that "if he instigated armed rebellion again, he would be held fully responsible."[36] Thus, Yuan Shikai was compelled to abandon his plot to set up another government. He announced his approval of the republic and forced the Qing emperor to abdicate on February 12. However, he inserted the following statement into the abdication speech: "Yuan Shikai has full powers to organize the provisional government of the republic and to consult with the people and the army on ways of unification."[37] He tried to give the impression that he was being appointed by the Qing emperor as he continued to try to set up another government and abolish the government of the Republic of China. Earlier, Sun Yat-sen had stressed that "the abdication of the Qing emperor automatically cancelled the political power of the throne, and that the emperor had no power to appoint anyone." Sun Yat-sen immediately denounced Yuan Shikai's plot to get rid of the Qing court and assume office himself, and he pointed out that "the government of the republic cannot be formed through appointment by the Qing emperor."[38] Sun Yat-sen's statement, which commanded respect because it was indisputably just, terrified Yuan Shikai, and he was forced to send a telegram admitting that "President Sun's telegram . . . is quite correct. . . . No further mention will be made about appointment by the Qing emperor."[39] To ensure that Yuan Shikai's election to the presidency after Sun's resignation would not damage the future of the republic, Sun Yat-sen submitted three conditions before his resignation: the site of the provisional government must be Nanjing; following the new president's investiture in Nanjing, the former president and all members of various departments must resign; and the new president must abide by all the laws promulgated by the departing president. Although these precautionary measures taken by Sun Yat-sen did not prevent Yuan Shikai from endangering the Republic of China, Sun's painstaking efforts to uphold the republic were laudable.

Throughout the peace talks, Sun Yat-sen's efforts to uphold the republic were attacked by the imperialists and reactionary forces. Some people in the revolutionary party were incapable of understanding Sun Yat-sen's painstaking efforts and some accused him of being "enamored with the position of president." One person even said that he wanted to use a pistol to tame Sun.[40] Much pressure was brought to bear on him. But Sun Yat-sen maintained that "personal fame and position are not to be sought. The future of the republic must not be given up lightly."[41] During the entire course of his negotiations with Yuan Shikai, Sun's behavior was imbued with this lofty revolutionary spirit of not contending for personal fame and position but striving to safeguard the future of the republic.

Owing to the unfavorable balance of class forces and the internal weakness of the revolutionary party, and despite Sun Yat-sen's unremitting struggle against Yuan Shikai during the peace talks, the result was that Yuan Shikai, the running dog of imperialism and the representative of the large landlords and the comprador class, seized the fruits of the revolution. On the whole, Sun Yat-sen was defeated. But he did not lose completely. He had his successes. In the peace talks he did manage to use Yuan to unseat the Qing emperor. The Qing dynasty, which had ruled China for over 260 years, collapsed. The feudal monarchical system which had lasted over 2000 years in China was terminated with the emperor's abdication. This was the major achievement of the 1911 Revolution. Although a huge price was paid for this achievement, Sun Yat-sen said: "The Qing emperor has abdicated; the monarchy is no more, ended in name and in fact."[42] Because of Sun Yat-sen's struggle, Yuan Shikai was forced to admit publicly that "a republic is the best state system." He announced that he would "never let monarchical government be restored in China."[43] He solemnly vowed that "the spirit of the republic would be given full play, the filth of autocracy would be washed away, and the constitution would be strictly enforced."[44] Although these words were uttered hypocritically by Yuan Shikai and later did not stop him from trying to become emperor, these statements, which he was forced to make under pressure from Sun Yat-sen, put Yuan Shikai in a vulnerable political position. Therefore, the republic became China's only legitimate political system, and whoever was against the republic and wanted to restore the monarchy would inevitably arouse widespread popular opposition and could expect to be stripped of honor and strongly denounced.

During the peace talks, Sun Yat-sen compromised and struggled. But struggle predominated. Of course, he also had shortcomings and made mistakes. But, under the objective conditions, he carried on a sustained struggle in a lofty and heroic spirit. The great achievements he made for the revolution and the republic had far-reaching significance for the development of Chinese history.

During these months before and after the establishment of the Nanjing provisional government, Sun Yat-sen was intensely active. He worked vigorously on the diplomatic front in order to establish the Republic of China; he personally established and led the first bourgeois, republican government in Chinese history and upheld the revolutionary and democratic character of the government; he overthrew the Manchu government and abolished, once and for all, the imperial system in China, and he forced Yuan Shikai to admit that the republic was the only legitimate and sensible political system for the country. The victories won by Sun Yat-sen were the result of the efforts of the numerous members of the revolutionary party and people whom Sun Yat-sen had led over many years. From Sun Yat-sen's activities centering on the establishment of the provisional government in Nanjing, we can see that he was really a "great historic figure standing in the forefront, directing the trend of the times."[45] He persisted in upholding the principles of revolution and democracy and carried out unremitting struggle. He played a peerless role in advancing the 1911 Revolution. "His magnificent contributions in leading the people to overthrow the imperial system and in establishing the republic"[46] during the 1911 Revolution will be forever remembered and extolled by the Chinese people.

## Notes

1. See also Chen Xiqi, "Sun Zhongshan yu Xinhai Geming" [Sun Yat-sen and the 1911 Revolution], *Zhongshan Daxue Xuebao* [Journal of Zhongshan University], (1979) no. 4; idem, "Sun Zhongshan wei chuangjian gongheguo er douzheng de weida gongxun" [Sun Yat-sen's great meritorious service in the struggle to establish the republic], *Zhongshan Daxue Xuebao* (1981), no. 3.
2. Fu Munekata Kotarō han [Letter in reply to Munekata Kotarō], *Sun Zhongshan quanji* [Complete works of Sun Yat-sen] (Beijing: Zhonghua shuju, 1981), vol. I, pp. 523–24.
3. "Jianguo fanglüe" [Program for national reconstruction], *Sun Zhongshan xuanji* [Selected works of Sun Yat-sen] (Beijing: Renmin chubashe, 1981), p. 208.
4. "Wo de huiyi" [My reminiscences], *Sun Zhongshan quanji*, vol. 1, p. 557.
5. "Jianguo fanglüe," vol. 1, p. 209.
6. "Zai Yungaohua huaqiao huanyinghui de yanshuo" [Speech at the welcoming

gathering of the overseas Chinese of Yungaohua], *Sun Zhongshan quanji*, vol. 1, p. 511.

7. Yu Tsuruoka Eitarō de tanhua [Conversation with Tsuruoka Eitarō), *Sun Zhongshan quanji*, vol. 1, p. 543.

8. Zhi Xianmali dian [Telegram to Homer Lea], *Sun Zhongshan quanji*, vol. 1, p. 546.

9. Ibid., p. 545.

10. Ibid., p. 543.

11. "Jianguo fanglüe," pp. 170–71.

12. H. Z. Schiffrin, "The Enigma of Sun Yat-sen," in *China in Revolution: The First Phase, 1900–1913*, ed. M.C. Wright (New Haven: Yale Univerity Press, 1968), p. 468.

13. "Jianguo fanglüe," p. 210.

14. "Yu Kang-de-li de tanhua" [Conversation with Sir James Cantlie], *Sun Zhongshan quanji*, vol. 1, p. 559.

15. "Banian shiyue shiri" [The eighth anniversary of October 10], *Guofu quanji* [Collected works of Sun Yat-sen], ed. Guomindang (Taibei: Zhongguo Guomindang zhongyangweiyuanhui dangshiweiyuanhui, rev. ed., 1957), vol. 6, p. 285.

16. *Hu Hanmin Zizhuan* [Autobiography of Hu Hanmin], *Geming wenxian* [Documents on the revolution], ed. Guomindang (Taibei: Guomindang dangshi shiliao bianzhuanweiyuanhui, 1953), vol. 3, pp. 55–56.

17. Yu Hu Hanmin, Liao Zhongkai de tanhua [Conversation with Hu Hanmin and Liao Zhongkai], *Sun Zhongshan quanji*, vol. 1, p. 570.

18. *Hu Hanmin Zizhuan*, vol. 3., p. 56.

19. "Xinghai ge-sheng daibiao huiyi rizhi" [Daily records of the provincial representative assemblies in 1911], *Xinghai geming huiyilu* [Reminiscences of the 1911 Revolution] (Beijing: Zhonghua shuju, 1963), vol. 6, p. 253.

20. "Zhonghua minguo linshi dazongtong xuanyanshu" [Declaration of the provisional president of the Chinese Republic], *Sun Zhongshan xuanji*, vol. 1, p. 90.

21. Wu Yuzhang, *Xinhai geming* [The 1911 Revolution] (Beijing: Renmin chubanshe, 1961), p. 154.

22. Yu Shangha *Dalu bao* jizhe de tanhua [Conversation with the correspondent of the Shanghai newspaper *The Continent*], *Sun Zhongshan quanji*, vol. 1, p. 581.

23. *Xinhai geming ziliao* [Materials on the 1911 Revolution] (Beijing: Zhonghua shuju, 1961), p. 7.

24. Sun Zhongshan fu Cai Yuanpei han [Sun Yat-sen's letter in reply to Cai Yuanpei], original manuscript deposited in the Chinese Second Historical Archives, quoted from *Lishi Yanjiu* [Historical research] (1980), no. 6.

25. Ibid.

26. *Guofu dangxuan linshi dazongtong shilu* [The true record of Sun Yat-sen's election to the provisional presidency] (Taibei, 1967), vol. I, p. 217.

27. *Xinhai geming ziliao*, p. 7.

28. Ibid., p. 70.

29. Ibid., p. 30.

30. Zhi Minguo Junzhengfu dian [Telegram to the republican military government], *Sun Zhongshan quanji*, vol. 1, p. 547.

31. Zhi Yuan Shikai dian [Telegram to Yuan Shikai], *Sun Zhongshan quanji*, vol. 1, p. 576.

32. Zhi Chen Jiongming dian [Telegram to Chen Jiongming], *Guofu quanji*, vol. 3, p. 169.

33. *Xinhai geming ziliao*, p. 29.

34. Huang Jilu, et al., *Yanjiu Zhongshan xiansheng de shiliao yu shixue* [Study of the historical materials and historiography on Sun Yat-sen] (Taibei, 1965), p. 369.

35. *Minli bao*, 29 Jan. 1912.

36. *Guofu quanji*, vol. 3, pp. 188–89.

37. *Guofu dangxuan linshi dazongtong shilu*, vol. II, p. 241.

38. Ibid., p. 286.
39. Ibid., p. 302.
40. Lo Hui-min, ed., *The Correspondence of G.E. Morrison, I, 1895–1912* (Cambridge: Cambridge University Press, 1976), p. 705.
41. Fu Wu Tingfang jieshi madian-suochen zhi gexiang banfa dian [Telegram in reply to Wu Tingfang urging that he immediately telegraph methods for carrying out provisions that were submitted], *Guofu quanji*, vol. 3, p. 182.
42. Zhi Wu Tingfang zhuangao Tang Shaoyi yi minguo keju Yuan Shikai wei shi ren dazongtong dian [Telegram to Wu Tingfang urging him to communicate to Tang Shaoyi that Yuan Shikai could be elected President of the Republic], *Guofu quanji*, vol. 3, p. 176.
43. *Guofu dangxuan linshi dazongtong shilu*, vol. II, p. 285.
44. Ibid., p. 317.
45. "Jinian Sun Zhongshan xiansheng" [In commemoration of Dr. Sun Yat-sen], *Mao Zedong xuanji* [Selected Works of Mao Zedong] (Beijing: Renmin chubanshe, 1977), vol. 5, pp. 311–12.
46. Ibid.

# The Foreign Powers

# International Financial Relations Behind the 1911 Revolution: The Fall in the Value of Silver and Reform of the Monetary system

## Hamashita Takeshi

The external economic relations of China at the time of the 1911 Revolution have been analyzed in terms of the competitive extension of credits by the powers which were encroaching on China in search of economic and territorial gains. This period has also been studied from the point of view of the formation of new domestic Chinese enterprises. On the other hand, the measures taken by the powers in this period to reorganize monetary relations between the West and Asian countries in order to cope with the fall in the value of silver should be carefully examined from the following considerations:

1) The external economic relations of China should be studied not only by analyzing the process of political negotiations over foreign credits, but also by investigating the historical motive force that governed the powers' economic behavior.

2) Domestic economic relations have to be examined in terms of the general historical formation and circulation of capital during this period in addition to the analysis of individual enterprises and capital in China.

3) Both internal and external economic relations must be studied in terms of the reciprocal relationship between the two.

At the beginning of the twentieth century, the value of silver fell rapidly, and the powers felt pressured to reform the monetary systems of those Asian countries then on silver systems. Their objective was to achieve monetary unification with their respective Asian settlements. As a consequence, the value of silver in China (which did not have a legal silver tender) fluctuated in a different relationship to the value of silver in the international market. The purchasing power of silver in the open market and open ports fluctuated according to commodity price changes, affecting the relationship between the silver dollar (*yuan*) and silver tael (*liang*), since in the internal market and taxation system of China, the value of silver was pegged in terms of copper cash. The fluctuations in the value of Chinese silver were thus significantly affected by both the external and internal economies through their reciprocal relations, and may be seen as a basic factor determining the direction and content of economic activity generally.

An understanding of the circumstances surrounding the changing value of silver will require elucidation of the financial motive force determining the relations between foreign and domestic capital, the powers and the Chinese central government, central and local finance, the open ports and internal markets, and so on. In this paper, these relations for the period in question will be summarized.

## The Fall in the Value of Silver and Asia's Gold Exchange Standard

### The Fall in the Value of Silver in Europe

The fall in the value of silver (its value in terms of gold) began in the 1870s as a result of the increase in the production of silver and the adoption of a gold monetary system by the European countries. In order to cope with this depreciation, the states of the Latin Union (which operated on a bimetallic standard), the United States (which produced silver in quantity), and England (with its trade interests in Asian countries) pushed for an international bimetallic system.[1] However, after the Fourth International Monetary Conference at Brussels in 1892, the policy of securing the value of silver through international agreements on bimetallism ceased, and the value of silver entered a second period of rapid decline, as shown in Table 1. The powers then undertook to fix the relationship of gold and silver in their Asian colonies in order to stabilize the international value of silver and thus secure their trading profits. At the same time they attempted a financial reorganization to absorb surplus silver by coining new silver currencies. Thus a gold exchange standard was introduced, and China could not stay unaffected by this move.

Table 1. Silver Depreciation and Rates of Exchange in Shanghai

| | Bar silver in London (d. per oz.) | | Exchange in Shanghai (Bank T.T. on London, d. per Haikwan tael) | |
|---|---|---|---|---|
| | Highest | Lowest | Highest | Lowest |
| 1895 | 31 5/16 | 27 3/16 | 3 0 7/8 | 2 8 3/8 |
| 1896 | 31 9/16 | 29 3/4 | 3 1 1/8 | 2 10 5/8 |
| 1897 | 29 13/16 | 23 5/8 | 2 11 1/8 | 2 3 1/4 |
| 1898 | 28 3/8 | 25 | 2 8 7/8 | 2 5 3/8 |
| 1899 | 29 | 26 5/8 | 2 9 1/8 | 2 7 |
| 1900 | 30 1/8 | 27 | 2 11 1/8 | 2 8 |
| 1901 | 29 9/16 | 25 | 2 10 1/2 | 2 5 1/8 |
| 1902 | 26 | 21 11/16 | 2 6 1/2 | 2 1 3/4 |
| 1903 | 28 1/2 | 21 11/16 | 2 7 3/8 | 2 1 5/8 |
| 1904 | 28 9/16 | 24 7/16 | 2 9 1/8 | 2 3 7/8 |
| 1905 | 30 5/16 | 25 7/16 | 2 11 1/4 | 2 6 1/4 |
| 1906 | 33 1/8 | 29 | 3 1 7/8 | 2 9 5/8 |
| 1907 | 32 7/16 | 24 3/16 | 3 1 | 2 4 5/8 |
| 1908 | 27 1/16 | 22 | 2 7 | 2 2 3/8 |
| 1909 | 24 7/8 | 23 1/16 | 2 5 1/4 | 2 3 1/4 |
| 1910 | 26 1/4 | 23 3/16 | 2 6 11/16 | 2 3 1/2 |
| 1911 | 26 1/8 | 23 11/16 | 2 5 7/8 | 2 4 1/4 |
| 1912 | 29 11/16 | 25 1/8 | 2 10 13/16 | 2 5 7/8 |
| 1913 | 29 3/8 | 25 15/16 | 2 10 3/4 | 2 6 13/16 |
| 1914 | 27 1/4 | 22 1/8 | 2 7 11/16 | 2 1 15/16 |
| 1915 | 27 3/4 | 22 5/16 | 2 7 13/16 | 2 2 3/4 |
| 1916 | 37 1/8 | 26 1/4 | 3 6 9/16 | 2 6 11/16 |

Source: China, Maritime Customs, *Decennial Report, 1912-21*, (Shanghai: The Statistical Department of the Inspectorate General of Customs, 1924), Appendix.

## Effects of the Drop in the Value of Silver

The effects of the decline in the value of silver may be summarized in the following four points:

1) The financial burdens of nations with a silver standard increased vastly, due to the rise in real terms of their repayments to the gold standard countries.

2) Exports to countries on the silver standard from countries on the gold standard were impeded, due to the rise in the relative prices of Western goods; at the same time, the West's imports greatly increased.

3) In silver-producing countries such as the United States, where profits of silver production were directly influenced, silver producers joined in pushing their governments to adopt an open-door policy toward Asian countries.

4) The increase in real terms in the silver value of holdings led to a growth in direct long-term investment by Western nations in countries on the silver standard.

## Adoption of the Gold Monetary System in India and Japan

In India, prior to the introduction of a gold standard, the government ended the free coining of silver in 1893 in order to avoid increases in the financial burden involved in remitting monies to the mother country, Great Britain. In 1899, a gold monetary system was introduced which stabilized the value of silver at one rupee to 1 s. 4d.[2]

Japan deposited its war reparations from the Sino-Japanese War in London as reserve, and in 1898 adopted a gold standard with a gold-silver ratio of 1:32, and the yen equivalent to 2 shillings. By this measure, the Japanese government intended to decrease its expenditures on goods imported from the silver standard countries and decrease imports themselves from gold standard nations. However, neither the gold standard of India nor of Japan involved an actual gold currency. In the case of Japan, the new monetary system was based on the gold reserves of the government and central bank and its foreign exchange value supported by capital imports.[3]

## The Gold Exchange System of the Philippines and the Straits Settlements

After the Spanish-American War of 1898 and American occupation of the Philippines, currency reform was immediately initiated. Three proposals were considered: (1) maintenance of the silver standard; (2) introduction of the American currency system; and (3) introduction of a gold standard linked to the American dollar. In 1903, the third proposal was adopted at a gold-silver ratio of 1:32, with one peso equivalent to 50 American cents. Gold exchange reserves, Filipino payments for American bonds, the profits from dollar-peso coinage, and trade surpluses were deposited in New York.[4]

In 1906, after much trial and error, a gold exchange system was introduced in the Straits Settlements (Singapore, Malacca, and Penang, where British colonial currency reforms are said to have been most successful). To cope with the decline and instability of

Table 2. Rates for Bank Bills Drawn on London from the Straits Settlements (four months sight bills)

| Year | Highest s. d. | Lowest s. d. | Average s. d. | Range Percent |
|---|---|---|---|---|
| 1891 | 3 6 1/4 | 3 1 3/8 | 3 3 | 11 1/2 |
| 1892 | 3 1 3/8 | 2 9 1/8 | 2 10 5/8 | 11 3/8 |
| 1893 | 2 9 5/8 | 2 4 1/2 | 2 7 3/8 | 15 1/4 |
| 1894 | 2 3 7/8 | 2 0 1/8 | 2 1 3/4 | 13 7/16 |
| 1895 | 2 3 1/16 | 1 11 1/2 | 2 1 1/2 | 7 3/8 |
| 1896 | 2 3 | 2 1 | 2 2 1/8 | 16 1/2 |
| 1897 | 2 1 13/16 | 1 9 9/16 | 1 11 15/16 | 7 1/2 |
| 1898 | 2 0 | 1 10 3/16 | 1 11 5/16 | 2 3/4 |
| 1899 | 2 0 5/16 | 1 11 3/8 | 1 11 15/16 | 3 15/16 |
| 1900 | 2 2 3/16 | 1 11 3/4 | 2 0 1/2 | 9 5/16 |
| 1901 | 2 1 5/8 | 1 9 7/8 | 1 11 11/16 | 14 5/8 |
| (1891–1901) | 3 6 1/4 | 1 9 7/8 | 2 3 3/8 | 39 5/8 |
| 1902 | 1 10 11/16 | 1 6 5/8 | | |
| 1903 | 2 1/16 | 1 7 1/8 | | |
| 1904 | 1 11 13/16 | 1 9 7/8 | | |
| 1905 | 2 4 15/16 | 1 7 11/16 | | |

Source: E.W. Kemmerer, *Modern Currency Reforms*, p. 398.

the foreign exchange of the Straits Settlements dollar (see Table 2), the Straits dollar was pegged at 28 pence, and bonds to secure the currency issue were placed in London. The Straits Settlements Currency Commission was given the right to sell exchange certificates in London and Singapore.[5] In Thailand, the free coining of silver was stopped in 1902, and a gold exchange standard (at the rate of 20 baht to the pound) was introduced in 1908.[6]

### The Dutch East Indies and French Indo-China

In 1877, following currency reform in the Netherlands, the Dutch East Indies adopted a gold standard, with the 10-guilder gold piece introduced as the standard coin of the colony. The Bank of Java, acting as the central bank, controlled silver circulation, the gold reserve, and gold held abroad in order to secure the stability of the gold-silver relationship.[7]

In French Indo-China, the silver piastre was adopted as legal tender in 1878, but when the value of silver continued to depreciate, free coining of silver was stopped in 1902 and the import and export of gold terminated in 1905. Thus the currency system was effectively divorced from the international silver market.[8]

### Results of the Adoption of the Gold Exchange Standard

The powers fixed the relationship between gold and silver and linked the value of the silver currencies in their settlements with their own systems. These were the results:

1) While the rate of depreciation in the value of silver slowed, it began, simultaneously, to fluctuate according to the demand for silver coin in the settlements.

2) Trade between Asia and the gold standard countries increased. That is, imports of industrial products from Western countries and exports of raw materials and foodstuffs from the Asian countries expanded. One typical example can be seen in the relation between the Philippines and the United States after 1902 (see Table 3).

Table 3. Foreign Trade in the Philippines (in units of $1,000,000)

| | | | Exports | | | |
|---|---|---|---|---|---|---|
| Year | United States | United Kingdom | Certain Other European Countries | Hong Kong and China | Other Countries | Total |
| 1900 | 2.96 | 8.10 | 4.23 | 4.11 | 3.59 | 22.99 |
| 1901 | 4.55 | 11.13 | 2.67 | 3.04 | 3.12 | 24.50 |
| 1902 | 11.48 | 8.02 | 3.16 | 3.68 | 2.34 | 28.67 |
| 1903 | 13.07 | 9.46 | 4.26 | 2.29 | 3.30 | 32.40 |

| | | | | Imports | | | |
|---|---|---|---|---|---|---|---|
| Year | United States | United Kingdom | Certain Other European Countries | Hong Kong and China | British East Indies | French East Indies | Other Countries | Total |
| 1900 | 2.15 | 5.58 | 4.60 | 7.74 | 1.74 | 0.76 | 2.29 | 24.86 |
| 1901 | 3.53 | 5.69 | 6.05 | 5.05 | 3.38 | 2.36 | 4.09 | 30.16 |
| 1902 | 4.15 | 5.64 | 6.38 | 6.47 | 1.67 | 5.57 | 3.45 | 33.34 |
| 1903 | 3.84 | 4.62 | 5.10 | 5.14 | 2.72 | 8.17 | 4.23 | 33.81 |

Source: E.W. Kemmerer, *Modern Currency Reforms*, p. 291.

3) Asian bullion markets, such as the one in Shanghai, grew with the increasing exchange of gold and silver. This occurred because (a) the general demand for silver increased in connection with the coinage of silver currencies under the gold exchange standard, and (b) the internal value of silver, being higher than its exchange value, created speculation. This benefited the Western countries,

Table 4. China's Export and Import of Gold and Silver in 1907 (Haikwan taels)

| Export | | | | | | |
|---|---|---|---|---|---|---|
| | Gold | | | Silver | | |
| | Bars, Dust, etc. | Coin | Total | Bars and Sycee | Coin | Total |
| Europe | 4,740,121 | | 4,740,121 | 2,618,086 | 409,096 | 3,027,182 |
| United States | | | | 135 | | 135 |
| India and Burma | | 21,200 | 21,200 | 10,294,735 | 184,466 | 10,479,201 |
| Straits Settlements | | | | 64,632 | 154,996 | 219,628 |
| Saigon and Tonkin | | | | | 36,710 | 36,710 |
| Hong Kong and Macao | 282,104 | 16,429 | 298,533 | 453,704 | 23,410,757 | 23,863,461 |
| Siam | | | | | 84,894 | 84,894 |
| Manila | | | | | 7,067 | 7,067 |
| Japan and Taiwan | 328,127 | 288,393 | 616,520 | | 473,247 | 473,247 |
| Korea | | 140,000 | 140,000 | 44,200 | 23,895 | 68,095 |
| Vladivostok | | 7,400 | 7,400 | | 18,130 | 18,130 |
| | 5,350,352 | 473,422 | 5,823,774 | 13,474,492 | 24,803,258 | 38,277,750 |

| Import | | | | | | |
|---|---|---|---|---|---|---|
| | Gold | | | Silver | | |
| | Bars, Dust, etc. | Coin | Total | Bars and Sycee | Coin | Total |
| Europe | 1,143,905 | | 1,143,905 | 176,000 | 215,555 | 391,555 |
| United States | | 78,800 | 78,800 | 157,261 | | 157,261 |
| India and Burma | | | | 33,498 | | 33,498 |
| Straits Settlements | | | | 924 | 24,834 | 25,758 |
| Saigon and Tonkin | | | | | 9,960 | 9,960 |
| Hong Kong and Macao | 24,793 | 18,000 | 42,793 | 66,129 | 5,923,083 | 5,989,212 |
| Siam | | | | | 5,820 | 5,820 |
| Manila | | | | | | |
| Japan and Taiwan | | 6,801,674 | 6,801,674 | | 258,345 | 258,345 |
| Korea | 4,075 | 185,984 | 190,059 | 11,638 | 181,373 | 193,011 |
| Vladivostok | | 16,790 | 16,790 | | 5,200 | 5,200 |
| | 1,172,737 | 7,101,248 | 8,274,021 | 445,450 | 6,624,170 | 7,069,620 |

Source: China, The Imperial Maritime Customs, Trade Report of 1907, *Returns of Trade* (1908), p. 48.

which hoped to absorb gold from Asia on a large scale for their gold reserves. Table 4 shows this in the case of China. Similarly, Japan, in aiming to absorb gold, favored a silver standard in Taiwan and Korea.[9]

Thus the pressure of the falling value of silver forced the powers into financial reorganizations in their settlements in order to maintain the international gold standard in its golden age.

## Influences of the Fall in the Value of Silver on China

### The Increase in China's Financial Burden
Following the Sino-Japanese War, Qing China was rapidly drawn into debt-finance, becoming heavily dependent on foreign loans to cover its war expenditures, reparations payments, and development costs. The reparations stemming from the Boxer Uprising tightened the powers' economic hold on China, with the allied nations attempting to compensate for the declining value of money debts owed them by the Qing government.[10] This decline resulted from the depreciation in the value of silver.

### The Influence of Trade
In general, the depreciation in the value of silver made trade more profitable to the silver standard countries. To take the example of cotton goods (the largest item of export to China), the American consul in Amoy reported the following reasons for the reduction in the piece goods trade: 1) the chief problem lay in the big shifts in exchange rates; Chinese wholesale merchants hesitated to buy import goods since they could not predict movements in the rates; 2) the silver-copper cash ratio did not relate directly to the changing parity of silver and gold in the international market, hence the price of cotton goods fluctuated, greatly weakening their competitive position in the Chinese internal market.[11] The fluctuation in the value of silver reflected fluctuations in China's import balance (see Table 5).

An English merchant suggested that the reason for the 1908 slump in the cotton trade lay in the fall in the value of both copper cash and silver, and the rise in the price of rice as well as in the accumulation of stock due to the excessive issuing of credits by the native-style banks of Shanghai.[12] Thus these observations indicated that fluctuations in the value of silver and its exchange rate acted to hinder imports.

The stagnation of English and American cotton exports did not, however, necessarily work in favor of the producers of native cotton cloth in China, but rather gave India and Japan an oppor-

Table 5. General Imports and Exports of China (Haikwan taels in units of 1,000,000)

| Year | Import | Export | Import Balance |
| --- | --- | --- | --- |
| 1895 | 171 | 143 | 28 |
| 1896 | 202 | 131 | 71 |
| 1897 | 203 | 164 | 39 |
| 1898 | 210 | 159 | 51 |
| 1899 | 265 | 196 | 69 |
| 1900 | 211 | 159 | 52 |
| 1901 | 268 | 170 | 98 |
| 1902 | 315 | 214 | 101 |
| 1903 | 327 | 214 | 113 |
| 1904 | 344 | 239 | 105 |
| 1905 | 447 | 228 | 219 |
| 1906 | 410 | 236 | 174 |
| 1907 | 416 | 264 | 152 |
| 1908 | 395 | 277 | 118 |
| 1909 | 418 | 339 | 79 |
| 1910 | 463 | 381 | 82 |
| 1911 | 471 | 377 | 94 |
| 1912 | 473 | 371 | 102 |
| 1913 | 570 | 403 | 167 |
| 1914 | 569 | 356 | 113 |
| 1915 | 454 | 418 | 36 |
| 1916 | 516 | 481 | 35 |
| 1917 | 549 | 463 | 86 |

Source: Hsiao Liang-lin, *China's Foreign Trade Statistics 1864–1949* (Cambridge, Mass.: East Asian Research Center, Harvard University, 1974), p. 23.

tunity to increase their exports of cotton yarn since they were in a position to settle accounts in silver with other Asian countries. Thus international competition for the Chinese market was strongly influenced by general monetary conditions.

At the beginning of the twentieth century, China's trade in major export products was also declining in the face of international competition. From the 1880s on, with the intensification of international competition, the price of China's tea and raw silk was decided less and less by Chinese production costs and more and more by international market prices. That is, Chinese prices of these goods began to be determined by the price of tea in Ceylon, and of raw silk in Italy and France. At the same time, soybean exports grew rapidly until it became one of China's main export products, helping to compensate for the cost of imports from abroad (see Table 6).

Table 6. Prices of Principal Foreign Imports and Chinese Exports (Haikwan taels)

| Year | Grey Shirtings (per piece) | Cotton Yarn Indian (per picul) | Cotton Yarn Japanese (per picul) | Tea Black (per picul) | Silk Yellow, Sichuan (per picul) | Beans Niuzhuang (per picul) | Rice Shanghai (per picul) |
|---|---|---|---|---|---|---|---|
| 1895 | 1.28 | 18.37 | 19.98 | 20.56 | 174.40 | 1.20 | 2.50 |
| 1896 | 1.29 | 19.58 | 19.82 | 21.75 | 187.98 | 1.46 | 2.10 |
| 1897 | 1.39 | 21.52 | 22.58 | 22.41 | 227.53 | 1.78 | 2.60 |
| 1898 | 1.34 | 19.17 | 21.40 | 22.95 | 204.50 | 2.04 | 2.40 |
| 1899 | 1.32 | 19.08 | 21.68 | 23.33 | 227.00 | 1.85 | 2.40 |
| 1900 | 1.62 | 19.49 | 21.30 | 20.38 | 207.33 | 1.59 | 2.00 |
| 1901 | 1.61 | 20.93 | 21.68 | 17.14 | 240.00 | 2.20 | 2.00 |
| 1902 | 1.68 | 21.75 | 23.14 | 17.62 | 256.25 | 1.91 | 2.70 |
| 1903 | 1.49 | 24.20 | 24.97 | 17.53 | 289.50 | 2.00 | 2.70 |
| 1904 | 1.70 | 26.04 | 25.01 | 22.12 | 321.00 | 2.44 | 2.10 |
| 1905 | 1.60 | 25.75 | 26.11 | 21.31 | 362.00 | 3.12 | 2.55 |
| 1906 | 1.50 | 25.05 | 25.44 | 20.90 | 325.00 | 2.14 | 2.32 |
| 1907 | 1.48 | 24.64 | 25.12 | 21.79 | 310.00 | 2.50 | 2.91 |
| 1908 | 1.79 | 24.35 | 25.41 | 22.24 | 284.30 | 2.35 | 3.00 |
| 1909 | 1.55 | 25.45 | 24.66 | 25.30 | 326.60 | 2.80 | 2.50 |
| 1910 | 1.85 | 27.96 | 25.03 | 28.25 | 323.10 | 3.14 | 3.00 |
| 1911 | 1.89 | 27.41 | 25.13 | 29.15 | 344.30 | 3.14 | 4.00 |
| 1912 | 1.69 | 27.60 | 25.01 | 24.36 | 280.06 | 3.48 | 3.78 |
| 1913 | 1.70 | 27.35 | 25.02 | 26.42 | 254.71 | 3.23 | 2.90 |
| 1914 | 1.77 | 26.06 | 25.06 | 26.42 | 255.12 | 5.25 | 2.96 |
| 1915 | 1.77 | 24.41 | 25.09 | 35.79 | 273.69 | 2.66 | 3.50 |
| 1916 | 1.90 | 24.00 | 25.18 | 29.27 | 283.61 | 2.21 | 3.65 |
| 1917 | 1.72 | 31.97 | 27.30 | 26.25 | 309.09 | 2.98 | 3.37 |

Source: China, The Maritime Customs, *Decennial Reports, 1912–21*, Appendix.

## The Increase in Investment

The fall in the exchange value of silver in Shanghai was, of course, directly related to the fall in the value of silver in London, but the purchasing power of silver in China was not necessarily related to changes on the London market; in fact, the internal market value of the silver *yuan* (expressed in terms of Shanghai taels and copper cash) was not the same as its value in the international market, but was somewhat higher. This difference encouraged investment.

In the late 1890s, growing investment in China took the form of purchases of stock within the foreign settlements and was connected with the new right, stipulated in the Treaty of Shimonoseki, permitting the establishment of industrial enterprises. Following the establishment of the Shanghai Stockholders' Association in 1891, a Shanghai stock exchange was established in 1905

Table 7. Early Growth of the Shanghai Stock Exchange

|  | Number of Companies | |
| --- | --- | --- |
|  | Dec. 1894 | Dec. 1912 |
| Banks | 3 | 2 |
| Trust | — | 1 |
| Insurance | 9 | 6 |
| Shipping | 7 | 4 |
| Docks and Wharves | 8 | 6 |
| Mining | 4 | 4 |
| Lands | 2 | 6 |
| Plantations (Rubber and Tobacco) | — | 40 |
| Cottons, etc. | — | 6 |
| Industrial | 9 | 13 |
| Stores | — | 7 |
| Hotels | — | 1 |
| Miscellaneous | 5 | 5 |

Source: *The North-China Herald*, 15 Dec. 1894 and 23 Dec. 1912.

in order to absorb Chinese as well as foreign capital. The primary forms of investment were bonds issued by the Foreign Settlement Industrial Bureau, debentures, stocks, and mortgages. As shown in Table 7, shortly after the Sino-Japanese War, about half of the enterprises attracting investment were businesses related to foreign trade, but by the second decade of the twentieth century, investment in manufacturing, mining, services, and raw materials (rubber) industries had also grown. During the same period, remittances from overseas Chinese also grew, and their investment in Chinese enterprises increased.[13]

The continuing growth of imports during this period was closely connected with the increase in capital. The second most important object of investment was silver and gold. For example, gold coins were imported into Shanghai and recast into ingots for export. One major source of gold coins was the foreign banks in Japan, which bought Japanese gold in order to make a further profit on their remittances.[14] Silver was also imported through the Shanghai silver market which functioned as an intermediary according to the demand of Asian settlements on a gold exchange standard for silver coin.

**The Relationship of Native and Foreign Banks in Shanghai**
After the central government adopted the new policy of assigning quotas for payments against foreign loans and indemnities to

individual units of the Maritime Customs, a new pattern of capital circulation took shape with Shanghai as its focus. This new pattern may be summarized as follows: 1) The quota payments of the various Customs units were remitted to Shanghai, where the Shanghai *daotai*, representing the Chinese government, would make the repayments to the foreign banks; 2) the *daotai* temporarily deposited the accumulating funds in the Shanghai native banks which could then use them for investment purposes; 3) the foreign banks (as creditors) could exchange the silver drafts from the *daotai* for gold to remit to the home country; they could take payment in silver itself from the native banks; or they could treat the funds as investment loans to the native banks in the Shanghai market.[15] Thus, the Maritime Customs taxes, which were formally under the control of the central financial organs, flowed into the Shanghai finance market and were ultimately concentrated in foreign banks. This new pattern, handled within the system of

Table 8. Yang-li and Yin-chai of Shanghai

| Year | Yang-li; tael (Yearly average) | Yin-chai; tael (Yearly average) |
| --- | --- | --- |
| 1895 | 0.754438 | 0.06 |
| 1896 | 0.735139 | 0.22 |
| 1897 | 0.744188 | 0.24 |
| 1898 | 0.746148 | 0.21 |
| 1899 | 0.743564 | 0.16 |
| 1900 | 0.744042 | 0.17 |
| 1901 | 0.737518 | 0.08 |
| 1902 | 0.744191 | 0.18 |
| 1903 | 0.749310 | 0.29 |
| 1904 | 0.738727 | 0.20 |
| 1905 | 0.728984 | 0.23 |
| 1906 | 0.737586 | 0.13 |
| 1907 | 0.737738 | 0.21 |
| 1908 | 0.736821 | 0.19 |
| 1909 | 0.742848 | 0.17 |
| 1910 | 0.742935 | 0.21 |
| 1911 | 0.757161 | 0.12 |
| 1912 | 0.750850 | 0.04 |
| 1913 | 0.738355 | 0.05 |
| 1914 | 0.725395 | 0.07 |
| 1915 | 0.727561 | 0.04 |

Source: China People's Bank, Shanghai Branch, comp., *Shanghai qianzhuang shiliao* [Historical materials of the native banks in Shanghai] (Shanghai: Shanghai renmin chupanshe, 1960, 1979), pp. 609, 628–29.

Table 9. Silver Reserves of Foreign and Chinese Banks in Shanghai
(in units of 1,000)

| Year | Foreign Banks (Shanghai tael) | (Yuan) | Chinese Banks and Native Banks (Shanghai tael) | (Yuan) |
|---|---|---|---|---|
| | Bar and Sycee | Dollar | Bar and Sycee | Dollar |
| 1905 | 5,190 | 3,850 | 310 | 1,130 |
| 1906 | 8,510 | 3,370 | 210 | 950 |
| 1907 | 9,108 | 2,730 | 240 | 900 |
| 1908 | 15,616 | 6,080 | 1,470 | 1,100 |
| 1909 | 17,276 | 3,020 | 350 | 1,470 |
| 1910 | 14,061 | 3,100 | 3,200 | 2,050 |
| 1911 | 21,453 | 3,070 | 4,080 | 5,340 |
| 1912 | 17,955 | 5,380 | 3,880 | 4,450 |
| 1913 | 37,595 | 9,530 | 5,920 | 3,970 |
| 1914 | 57,558 | 13,950 | 1,990 | 5,660 |
| 1915 | 32,680 | 9,010 | 6,440 | 10,950 |
| 1916 | 15,680 | 8,050 | 1,120 | 4,780 |
| 1917 | 19,325 | 7,120 | 2,280 | 6,060 |

Source: Tanaka Yoshinori, *Chūgoku heisei kaikaku mondai ippan* [A Survey of Chinese monetary reform] (Tokyo: Yokohama Shōkin Ginkō, 1920), pp. 62–63.

trade financing, was nominally only a method of repayment, but as it worked to raise the price of gold exchange bills, exporters found it more and more difficult to remit monies to their home countries. In the triangular relationship between the central financial organs (via the *daotai*) and the native and foreign banks, the former two were doomed to be eternally in a debtor position. In consequence, foreign banks came to control both the external exchange market and the price of silver on the Shanghai market.[16] Under these circumstances, then, foreign banks greatly influenced the interest rate of the Shanghai market by managing the accumulation of silver according to the fluctuating need for purposes of remittance (see Table 8 on yang-li, the value of a silver dollar expressed in terms of tael, and yin-chai, the interest charged on interbank loans among native bank *qianzhuang*, and also Table 9).

As we have seen, fluctuation in the gold-silver ratio caused by fluctuations in the value of silver influenced even central finance, and thus stabilization of the value of silver externally was desirable for both trade and investment reasons. Hence currency reform became an important issue for China. The point which needs to be stressed here is that, in the development of the entire relationship, the foreign banks played an increasingly dominant role.

## The Problem of a Gold Exchange Standard for China

### The Anglo-Chinese Commercial Treaty of 1902

In the Anglo-Chinese Commercial Treaty of 1902 (and the similar Sino-American and Sino-Japanese treaties of 1903), only one clause dealt with the fall in the value of silver. The major points of this treaty were: 1) abolition of the inland tax (*likin*) and the increase of tax in the open ports, facilitating entry of foreign merchants into the inland market while also increasing the revenues of the central government;[17] 2) the opening of new ports in China's northeastern provinces—the first following Yingkou's opening in 1860—which brought an increase in soybean exports and the development of new trade relations between China and Japan and Europe (Japan was to actively push forward in this area after the Russo-Japanese War);[18] 3) protection by law of investments in foreign enterprises by Chinese and in Chinese enterprises by foreigners, and reduction of exemption from import tariffs and consumer taxes on raw materials required by foreign enterprises;[19] and 4) unification of the Chinese currency system by the Qing government.[20]

In these clauses, the interests of the powers in the Chinese inland economy were clearly set forth, and hence the treaties provided at least one answer to the reasons adduced by the aforementioned British merchant for the 1908 cotton trade slump. But we should not forget that during the negotiations, the Hunan-Hubei governor-general, Zhang Zhidong, and the Jiangxi-Jiangsu governor-general, Liu Kunyi, opposed the Chinese negotiators Sheng Xuanhuai and Lü Haihuan on the grounds that currency reform was an internal matter and thus should not be included in treaties.[21] This criticism by Zhang Zhidong represented an attempt to protect the financial and currency interests at the provincial level and presaged the later difficulties in getting agreement from the local level when the powers proposed various concrete currency reform plans to the Qing government.

## The Commission on International Exchange

In order to carry out the obligation of currency reform placed on it by the treaties, the Qing government ordered its chargé d'affaires ad interim in Washington, Shen Tong, to ask Secretary of State Hay to render assistance in China's currency reform.[22] In his letter to Hay, Shen carefully noted that it was not his government's intent to strengthen only the Sino-American relationship. But Rockhill, the American minister to Beijing, had pledged, before promising remission of half the Boxer indemnity, not to increase indemnity repayments to offset the fall in the value of silver. This had inspired the Chinese government to make its appeal.[23] Hay at once organized an exchange commission, composed of J. Jenks, H. Hanna, and C. Conant, all three of whom had been involved in Philippine monetary reform. The commission first visited England, France, Germany, Holland, Russia, and Japan, in the hope that international cooperation might be secured for the proposed monetary reform. For their part, these other countries to which China was indebted organized their own exchange commissions to conduct discussions with the American representatives. Characteristic of the composition of these commissions was the inclusion of representatives of their respective central banks and their colonial banks in Asia. The latter included the Hongkong and Shanghai Banking Corporation, the Banque d'Indochine, the Deutsch-Asiatischen Bank, the Russo-Chinese Bank, and Japan's Yokohama Specie, First, and Mitsui banks.[24] The American commissioners stressed that the position of foreign banks with intimate interests in currency fluctuation would be taken into consideration and the projected reforms advanced step by step. We can conclude from this that foreign banks did in fact have intimate interests in the currency systems of the colonies in Asia and would inevitably play a major role in China's currency reform— something which might have been surmised from the description of their various banking functions described earlier.

The American representatives made the following proposals to the various national commissions: 1) that a gold exchange standard be adopted for the silver-using countries on the basis of a silver coin of unlimited legal tender; 2) that a national currency for the Chinese empire, consisting of silver coins which should be full legal tender throughout the empire, was urgently desirable;

and 3) that stability in the price of silver bullion should be promoted through reasonable regularity in the purchase of silver required by each government for actual coinage purposes.[25]

These three points reveal both the common interests of the gold standard countries coping with the depreciation of silver, and the particular American interest (as a silver producer) in applying the experience derived from Philippine monetary reform and stabilizing the silver price.

The major points made in response to the American proposals were as follows: Great Britain insisted that a gold standard rather than just a gold exchange standard be adopted; this was in line with its currency policy in the Straits Settlements.[26] France insisted on the right to act independently and criticized the American propositions on the grounds that they took Britain's position in China too lightly. France further insisted that the American proposals could be realized only on the basis of certain conditions, namely, that the use of foreign currency in China be abolished, that the government be the sole minter of silver coin, and that maintenance of gold reserves be guaranteed by a favorable trade balance. (It should be recalled here that at approximately the same time, France broke the linkage between the piastre used in French Indo-China and silver in the international market.) Holland replied that, in the absence of agreement on an international bimetallic standard, it would agree to the American proposals. The Germans maintained that as they only used Reichsmarks, except in their East African colonies and Jiaozhou, they had only a limited demand for silver, but had no disagreement with the American plan. Russia suggested that if the American proposals could be reworked to include the establishment of a fixed parity with gold as soon as practicable, it would give its complete assent. Russia intended to protect and consolidate the use of the ruble in China's northeastern provinces. As for Japan, it insisted on the adoption of a gold standard if at all possible.[27]

Even though these responses (with the exception of that of France) show that there was general agreement on the need for adoption of a gold (exchange) standard by China, each country was concerned that the system in China be in line with that in its own colonies. Furthermore, Japan was intent on securing full compatibility with its own standard. Thus international agreement could not be reached on concrete steps to reform.

## The Gold Exchange Standard Proposal by Jenks

After the discussions with the various national commissions, the American commissioner Jenks sent a memorandum to the Chinese government in October 1903, which included the following points: 1) The Chinese imperial government should promptly take effective steps, satisfactory to a majority of the indemnity treaty powers, to establish a general monetary system consisting chiefly of silver coins with a fixed gold value; 2) China would be asked to invite and employ foreign assistance, and particularly to appoint a foreign controller of currency; 3) the Chinese government should adopt a standard unit of value consisting of a certain number of grains of gold, and a gold-silver ratio of 1:32 should be maintained; free minting of subsidiary silver coins should be allowed; 4) the Chinese government should open credit accounts in London and other places for the maintenance of the parity of the silver coin and should also seek loans for this purpose; 5) when gold exchange funds became insufficient, the currency controller might adjust the exchange rate in order to attract gold; and 6) the controller and the representatives of the powers should be authorized to recommend economic reforms to the imperial government.[28]

From these points we can see that Jenks was proposing adoption of a gold standard under foreign supervision, and also that loans be sought to build up foreign exchange funds abroad. This was in keeping with the treaty obligations outlined previously. Comparing this proposal with those of the other creditor nations, we can see that it incorporated features of the monetary system in the Asian colonies of both Great Britain and the United States.

## The Response of China and the Foreign Banks

### Various Responses to the Jenks Proposals

Let us now consider, from a Chinese perspective, the process of currency reform which began at that time and was only consummated in 1935. For their part, British merchants in China complained of the delay in the Qing government's implementation of its treaty obligations. The chambers of commerce of Hong Kong, Shanghai, Tianjin, and Hankou jointly petitioned the diplomatic corps in Beijing and the British home government to push the Chinese side into accelerating the reform process.[29] But among the foreigners in China there were also doubts about the chances for success of Jenks's plan and criticism of its lack of attention to internal conditions.[30]

On the Chinese side, even before Jenks's proposal was received, some domestic proposals had been put forward for adoption of a gold standard to counter increases in the foreign debt stemming from the depreciation of silver; but these proposals were not supported by concrete measures.[31] In 1904, Zhang Zhidong strongly criticized not only the 1:32 gold-silver ratio in Jenks's proposal as being much higher than the actual ratio prevailing in the market (in fact, the real ratio was closer to 1:42 at the time), but also the idea of the monetary system being controlled by foreigners. He insisted on a silver rather than a gold standard and on the unification of the internal currency on the basis of the silver tael. Since he was on the verge of minting one-tael silver pieces in Hubei, it is hardly suprising that he promoted the idea of unifying the internal silver currency through increasing the circulation of such coins. At the same time, he warned against ignoring the copper cash used by the common people, pointing out that if the government minted only silver and gold pieces, the livelihood of the people would be destroyed.[32] On the whole, however, his advice was put forward with a view to protecting important local financial resources, in this case the minting of silver taels in order to offset the growing burdens on local government.

**The Controversy over Monetary Reform**

In 1905, an imperial edict calling for monetary unification based on the one-tael silver coin met with resistance from some provincial governors who were already circulating silver dollars (with a weight of 0.72 taels) within their jurisdiction. Subsequently, in 1907 another edict ordered the switch to the silver dollar system.[33] Thereafter, the Chinese controversy over monetary reform often simply ignored Jenks's proposal to concentrate on the unification of the internal currency. Still, the range of proposals was broad enough to include the idea of a gold coin standard (suggested by Minister to Britain, Wang Daxie), a gold standard (Ministry of Finance), and a silver standard (Tang Shaoyi), even if none of them were implemented. In 1909, the Chinese government formally founded a Currency Study Bureau, and regulations concerning the currency system were issued the next year.[34] These regulations stipulated that the currency system was to be unified on the basis of the silver dollar and the value of the currency maintained by reserve funds abroad; that silver would be accumulated as reserve backing for a paper currency; and that only after these measures were successful would the ratio between gold and silver be made public. In order to realize these ideas, negotiations for a loan were initiated with a four-power consortium. In 1911, Vissering, president of the Bank of Java, who had been invited to act as adviser on monetary reform to the Qing government, proposed gradual adoption of a gold exchange standard.[35] The difference between his proposal and that of Jenks was that it anticipated that the various steps involved would be carried out sequentially in three distinct periods and that attention would center on the role of the central bank.

After the Qing monarchy was superseded by the Republic, the new government intended to establish a special bureau for monetary reform similar to that set up by the Qing government, but this plan was rejected by parliament. Despite this setback, the government continued its studies of various monetary reform plans and in October 1912 organized a monetary commission with the aid of Vissering and Roest. In December it decided to adopt a gold exchange standard.[36] However, a second monetary commission, appointed by Yuan Shikai in February 1913, was soon bogged down again in controversy over the standards and proved unable to reach any decision. It need only be noted here that during the deliberations, strong criticism was made of the idea of accumulating large exchange reserve funds abroad. In February 1914, a National Currency Act and regulations for its implementation were promulgated.[37] After the so-called Second Revolution, monetary reform was restricted to regional improvements such as the issuing of new silver dollars, the redemption of provincial notes, the imposition of controls on silver and copper bonds, and the establishment of local currency bureaus. In 1918, the minister of finance and concurrent chief of the Monetary Bureau, Cao Rulin, proposed the issuing of gold notes in preparation for implementing a gold standard system. Prompting him to make this proposal was the fact that gold account outlays were running at almost one-third of total expenditures.[38] The method he intended to employ was to secure loans from Japan and deposit the funds in the

Bank of Japan as gold reserves (the method was set forth in the "Gold Note Regulations"), but the anti-Japan boycott prevented realization of his plan. With the rise in the price of silver owing to the First World War, the controversy over monetary reform reached a new turning point.

**A Scheme for Sweeping Monetary Reform by Sun Yat-sen**
A brief description of Sun Yat-sen's approach to monetary reform is in order. Sun advocated total monetary reform as a precondition for reorganization of China's financial system. The chief points of his plan were as follows:

1) Unification of the internal currency would not be on the basis of gold or silver coin, but of paper currency.

2) Tax revenues would be managed by the Tax Bureau, which would both issue paper currency against guaranteed bonds and also collect it (demonetize it).

3) The Currency Issue Bureau would issue paper currency in exchange for bullion in order to meet the needs of general circulation. The government would buy and sell commodities using the paper currency via a system of public warehouses, and the currency collected through sales would be burned.

4) As the paper currency would circulate readily and yet be strictly controlled, there could not be the slightest danger of financial panic.[39]

Sun's scheme belongs to the internal monetary unification persuasion, but his insistence on issuing paper currency alone would have inevitably necessitated a powerful, unified central government. It is of interest that the advice of Sakatani Yoshirō (appointed financial adviser by Sun himself) concerning establishment of a gold standard and a central bank, was ignored.[40]

Two fundamental obstacles prevented the execution of any of the above monetary reform proposals. Firstly, if stabilization of the external value of silver through adoption of a gold (exchange) system was to be the objective in a reform program, China would be entirely reliant on foreign loans for its exchange fund since it could not obtain it either from positive export balance or minting profits. As foreign exchange was monopolized by foreign banks, the management of the exchange fund itself would of necessity be dependent on those banks. Secondly, if unification of the internal currency through the adoption of a silver standard became the aim, it would be thwarted by the virtual impossibility of centralizing the rights of issue and minting due to opposition from provincial governments like those led by Zhang Zhidong. These governments could not agree to the loss of issue rights and minting at a time when they were facing increases in repayment quotas on foreign loans and military expenditure. After the 1911 Revolution, as the provincial separatist tendencies accelerated, the chances of centralizing financial control were further weakened. Thus we can see that monetary reform—whether before or after 1911—was prevented by growing needs and interests at the local level.

**Gold Reserves of Foreign Banks in China**
As seen above, the characteristic feature of the external financial relations of China was the merging of trade settlement, debt servicing, and capital investment within the exchange settlement relationships controlled solely by foreign banks. This meant that the problem of a gold exchange standard in China related directly to the foreign banks' primary exchange business and to their major interest in deriving continued profits from a stabilized exchange. The powers needed to regulate gold-silver relations to prevent losses from exchange fluctuations even if Chinese monetary reform could not immediately go ahead. However, they could not regulate these relations through a centralized financial administration inside China as they could in their full-fledged Asian colonies, but had to achieve their policy goals through the foreign banks. Consequently, in order to stabilize the silver price, foreign banks unilaterally adopted a form of "gold exchange standard" in their financial relations with China. This meant that the international stabilization of the Chinese monetary system came to depend more and more upon the business of the foreign banks.

From the business reports of the Hongkong and Shanghai Banking Corporation we can confirm that the sterling reserve funds, current account gold, and deposits fixed in gold increased yearly, as did holdings in sterling bonds in London (See Table 10). In April 1891, when silver-based and gold-based accounts were separated, the Hongkong and Shanghai Bank used its gold funds to compensate for the fluctuating price of silver. Thus

Table 10. Abstract of Assets and Liabilities of the Hongkong and Shanghai Banking Corporation (in units of 1,000)

|  | Dec. 1897 | Dec. 1902 | Dec. 1907 | Dec. 1912 |
|---|---|---|---|---|
| Liabilities (Hong Kong $) | | | | |
| Paid-up Capital | 10,000 | 10,000 | 15,000 | 15,000 |
| Reserve Fund | | | | |
| (sterling) | 7,000* | 10,000 | 15,000 | 15,000 |
| (silver) | | 4,750 | 13,000 | 17,000 |
| Insurance | 250 | 250 | 250 | 250 |
| Notes in Circulation | 9,888 | 16,575 | 15,711 | 24,826 |
| Current Accounts | | | | |
| (silver) | 44,141 | 86,727 | 79,411 | 121,122 |
| (gold) | 18,728 | 33,051 | 47,546 | 54,838 |
| Fixed Deposits (silver) | 31,731 | 46,112 | 50,679 | 70,409 |
| (sterling) | 26,447 | 54,803 | 46,441 | 42,075 |
| Bills Payable | 18,751 | 14,397 | 11,476 | 6,011 |
| Profit and Loss Accounts | 2,430 | 4,222 | 4,943 | 5,031 |
| Assets (Hong Kong $) | | | | |
| Cash | 17,584 | 35,254 | 40,509 | 41,980 |
| Coins lodged with Hong Kong govt. | | 8,600 | 10,000 | 16,000 |
| Bullion in hand and in transit | 7,106 | 8,419 | 4,132 | 5,170 |
| Indian and Colonial Securities | 5,045 | 11,602 | 8,418 | 12,509 |
| Sterling Reserve Fund Investments | 7,453 | 10,000 | 15,000 | 15,000 |
| Bills discounted, loans and credits | 61,259 | 98,812 | 101,598 | 139,870 |
| Bills Receivable | 69,846 | 107,638 | 118,007 | 135,675 |
| Bank Premises | 972 | 829 | 1,792 | 5,360 |

Source: *The North-China Herald.*
* Reserve fund for 1897 was not divided into sterling and silver.

these gold items played a role equivalent to that of a gold exchange fund.

Meanwhile, in order to rectify the unfavorable exchange situation stemming from an excess of imports, the bank actively entered new fields of trade, such as soybeans, rubber, rice, and sugar.[41] Obviously, foreign banks were acting much like a Chinese central bank would have acted to balance external and internal business. What is more, foreign banks were issuing bank notes, loaning their silver stock on native banks, and controlling the exchange rate between the silver dollar and silver tael. This "stabilization" by foreign banks did not, of course, mean a reduction in China's foreign debt. On the contrary, it created favorable circumstances for investment and spurred the penetration by other foreign banks (such as the International Bank) into China.[42] Hence foreign debt increased steadily in administrative, industrial, communications, and other spheres.

## Conclusion: Monetary Reform and Local Finance

Although the international conditions were conducive to Chinese monetary reform, the problem became locked in controversy over the problem of standards and methods of implementation. The ultimate reason lay in opposition from those local governments that had the most to gain from fluctuations in the silver-copper ratio. Zhang Zhidong's arguments, referred to earlier, reflected the growing competition between central and local governments, a competition in which the various provincial governments attempted to protect their new sources of revenue, particularly the minting of copper coins.

The prohibition on the minting of copper cash at the end of the nineteenth century, intended to prevent debasement, had resulted in the minting of new copper coins with face values from 2 to 200 cash.[43] The minting of ten-cash copper coins had commenced in Guangdong and Fujian in 1900, and after an edict legalizing minting was issued the following year, twenty-two mints (including the one in Tibet) began to produce various kinds of copper coins as shown in Table 11. Despite a new prohibition on such minting in 1908, it continued in Sichuan, Jiangsu, Hunan, Hubei, Fujian, Zhejiang, Henan, Tianjin, Guangdong, and the northeastern provinces, on the understanding that minting would cease when existing stocks of copper ingot were consumed. After the advent of the republic, production of copper coins increased substantially. As seen in the case of Chengdu mint (Tables 12 and 13), the tendency was to mint copper coins of high nominal value together with one-dollar silver coins. Four results of this large-scale minting of copper coins may be noted:

1) The exchange rate of copper cash fell and commodity prices rose (see Table 14). We can find evidence of this tendency in the

Table 11. Copper and Brass Coins Produced by Chinese Provincial Mints to 1913 (pieces)

| | 100 Cash | 50 Cash | 20 Cash | 10 Cash | 5 Cash | 2 Cash | One Cash |
|---|---|---|---|---|---|---|---|
| Tianjin | | | 77,218,494 | 1,273,757,545 | 1,170,122 | 13,353,877 | 92,126,149 |
| Hubei | | | 267,500 | 6,805,736,254 | 27,763,600 | | 46,382,000 |
| Sichuan | 447,253 | 2,653,548 | 131,839,884 | | 85,491 | | |
| Fengtian | | | 55,369,787 | 15,884,528 | | | |
| Yunnan | | | 645,475 | 16,661,002 | | | |
| Fujian | | | 117,681 | 692,991,868 | 1,082,819 | 3,438,054 | 12,560,000 |
| Jilin | | | 1,784,790 | 13,763,990 | | 978,500 | |
| Jiangsu | | | 4,991,661 | 874,259,634 | | | |
| Anhui | | | 44,806 | 519,268,192 | 7,060 | | |
| Zhejiang | | | 2,506,319 | 973,798,614 | 7,833,860 | 8,162,910 | |
| Guangdong | | | | 1,154,726,357 | | | |
| Jiangnan | | | | 2,932,985,850 | | | 25,450,000 |
| Hunan | | | | 10,095,303,625 | | | |
| Honan | | | | 910,702,894 | | | 9,419,512 |
| Qingjiangpu | | | | 74,005,585 | | | |
| Shangdong | | | | 285,851,290 | | 2,116,330 | |
| Jiangxi | | | | 379,722,467 | | | |

Source: Tōa Dōbun-kai, *Saikin Chūgoku Bōeki* [Present condition of China's foreign trade] (Tokyo: Tōa Dōbun-kai, 1918), pp. 619–20.

Table 12. Copper and Brass Coins Produced by Chengdu Mint (pieces)

| Year | 200 Cash | 100 Cash | 50 Cash | 20 Cash | 10 Cash |
|---|---|---|---|---|---|
| 1903–1904 | | | | 8,037,671 | 17,235,067 |
| 1905 | | | | 17,282,484 | 78,725,587 |
| 1906 | | | | 16,278,652 | 96,310,653 |
| 1907 | | | | 14,144,820 | 114,154,542 |
| 1908 | | | | 20,606,498 | 127,284,424 |
| 1909 | | | | 19,074,490 | 131,617,208 |
| 1910 | | | | 9,193,444 | 74,857,036 |
| 1911 | | | | 5,147,928 | 25,456,183 |
| 1912 | | | 9,354,084 | 12,476,661 | 60,550,205 |
| 1913 | 1,956,103 | 9,639,602 | 30,337,353 | 9,614,403 | 21,977,500 |
| 1914 | 13,788 | 680,821 | 51,468,510 | 8,309,706 | |
| 1915 | | | 47,751,491 | 16,090,730 | 389,935 |
| 1916 | 738,572 | 3,754,007 | 37,584,443 | 7,299,032 | 285,570 |
| 1917 | 4,179,640 | 11,333,030 | 39,989,000 | | |
| 1918 | 8,045,956 | 13,718,401 | 40,734,082 | 59,818 | 914,780 |

Source: E. Kann, *The History of Minting in China* (Shanghai: The Numismatic Society, n.d.), p. 37.

Table 13. Silver Coins Produced by Chengdu Mint

| Year | One-Dollar Pieces | 50-Cent Pieces | 20-Cent Pieces | 10-Cent Pieces | 5-Cent Pieces |
|---|---|---|---|---|---|
| 1901–1902 | 1,404,737 | 62,885 | 108,180 | 392,397 | 300,920 |
| 1903 | 781,609 | 135,116 | 116,686 | 70,644 | 173,728 |
| 1904 | 323,523 | 6,490 | 15,500 | | 28,480 |
| 1905 | 226,411 | 104,027 | 303,666 | 474,674 | |
| 1906 | 1,080,538 | 71,912 | 209,072 | 66,500 | 65,560 |
| 1907 | 1,493,162 | 18,090 | 39,840 | 81,700 | 46,000 |
| 1908 | 1,180,823 | 78,876 | 107,226 | 191,880 | 59,269 |
| 1909 | 1,792,768 | 12,100 | 19,920 | 134,267 | |
| 1910 | 738,107 | 12,534 | | 112,820 | 566,100 |
| 1911 | 316,730 | 13,730 | 21,285 | 32,050 | |
| 1912 | 2,866,988 | 146,916 | 95,950 | 370,541 | |
| 1913 | 3,815,291 | 62,900 | | | |
| 1914 | 6,926,211 | 26,200 | | | |
| 1915 | 6,786,100 | 69,100 | | | |
| 1916 | 5,426,750 | 150,000 | | | |

Source: E. Kann, *The History of Minting in China*, p. 36.

trade reports of customs commissioners in the various ports. The effect of this depreciation on farming and handicraft production differed from area to area; in the northeastern provinces, which were developing rapidly due to expanding soybean production, the effect was not great, while in the lower Yangzi basin, where tea and silk exports were in decline, the damage was considerable.

Table 14. Depreciation of Value of Copper Coins in Yinxian (per tael)

| Year | Copper Cash | Copper Dollar |
|---|---|---|
| 1902 | 900–950 | |
| 1903 | 840–870 | |
| 1904 | 860–870 | |
| 1905 | 810–955 | |
| 1906 | 890–980 | 104–117 |
| 1907 | 960–980 | 103–109 |
| 1908 | 900–950 | 106–126 |
| 1909 | 900–950 | 125–136 |
| 1910 | | 125–130 |
| 1911 | | 120–130 |
| 1912 | | 124–134 |
| 1913 | | 130–132 |
| 1914 | | 130–137 |
| 1915 | | 134–140 |
| 1916 | | 115–134 |

Source: Cai Zhiqing, ed., *Yinxian tongzhi* [General gazetteer of Yinxian], vol. 5 (Hangzhou: Zhejiang shengli tushuguan, 1937), 228b-31a.

2) The copper-rice exchange ratio employed for taxation purposes underwent a change disadvantageous to the farmer.[44]

3) The profits of enterprises seriously declined.[45]

4) The pace of wage increases did not keep up with that of commodity price inflation.

It is noteworthy that the impact of these factors was most serious around the time of the 1911 Revolution. Hence the controversy over Chinese monetary reform should have been extended to include stabilization of the problematic fluctuation in copper value. The realization of monetary reform would have required the resolution of the financial relationship between central and local governments and improvement of private financial institutions to keep pace with a developing commerce and industry.

In point of fact, in the period immediately following the Revolution, we do find growth in such financial institutions under the supervision of the central government, such as the Bank of China and Bank of Communications, and sudden growth in local banks managed by local governments and in those native banks maintaining close relations with foreign banks.

[Translated by Shinomiya Ayako]

## Notes

1. H. B. Russell, *International Monetary Conferences* (New York and London: Harper, 1898), chap. 6. Yoshioka Akihiko, "Igirisu mengyō shihon to hon'isei ronsō" [The cotton industry's capital in England and controversies on monetary standard] in *Kindai kakumei no kenkyū* [Study of modern revolution], Okada Tomoyoshi, ed., vol. 2 (Tokyo: University of Tokyo Press, 1973).
2. British Parliamentary Papers (BPP), "Report of Herschell Committee, 1893." "Report of Fowler Committee, 1899."
3. Count Matsukata Masayoshi, *Report on the Adoption of the Gold Standard in Japan* (The Government Press, 1899), chap. 11.
4. E. W. Kemmerer, *Modern Currency Reforms: A History and Discussion of Recent Currency Reforms in India, Porto Rico, Philippine Islands, Straits Settlements and Mexico* (New York: MacMillan, 1916), part III.
5. Ibid., part IV.
6. J. Ingram, *Economic Change in Thailand 1850–1970* (Stanford: Stanford University Press, 1971), chap. 7.
7. G. Vissering, "Netherlands India," in *On Chinese Currency* (Amsterdam: De Bussay, 1914), vol. 1, pp. 114–32.
8. André Touzet, *Le régime monétaire indochinois* (Paris: Giard et Brière, 1939), chap. 1.
9. Murakami Katsuhiko, "Shokuminchi sankin kyūshū to Nihon sangyō kakumei" [Absorption of gold produced in colonies and the Japanese industrial revolution], *Keizaigaku ronshū*, vol. 16, Dec. 1973. See also *Nihon sangyō kakumei no kenkyū* [Studies on the Japanese industrial revolution], Ōishi Kaichirō, ed. (Tokyo: University of Tokyo Press, 1975), chap. 10.
10. Wang Shuhuai, *Genzi peikuan* [The Boxer indemnity] (Taibei: Shangwu yinshu guan, 1974), chap. 3, section 1.
11. Consular Report of Amoy, by G. Anderson, 2 May 1905, *Monthly Consular and Trade Reports*, March 1906, no. 306 (Washington, D.C.: Government Printing Office).
12. *The North-China Herald*, 20 July 1908.
13. Lin Jinzhi, "Jindai huaqiao touzi guonei qiye de jige wenti" [Several issues on overseas Chinese investments in domestic industry in modern times], *Jindaishi yanjiu*, no. 1, 1980, pp. 199–230.
14. Kojima Hitoshi, *Nihon no kinhon'isei jidai 1897–1917* [Era of gold standard in Japan 1897–1917] (Tokyo: Nihon Keizai Hyōronsha, 1981), chap. 3.
15. H. B. Morse, "Report on Foreign Trade," *Trade Returns for the Year 1904* (Shanghai: China, The Imperial Maritime Customs, The Statistical Department of the Inspectorate General of Customs, 1905), pp. xx–xxi.
16. H. B. Morse, "Report on Foreign Trade," *Trade Returns for the Year 1903* (Shanghai: China, The Imperial Maritime Customs, The Statistical Department of the Inspectorate General of Customs, 1904), pp. xiv–xv.
17. Commercial Treaty, 1902, article VIII, section 1 (China, The Maritime Customs, *Treaties, Conventions, etc., between China and Foreign States,* vol. I [Shanghai, The Statistical Department of the Inspectorate General of Customs, 1917], p. 548).
18. Commercial Treaty Between United States and China, 1903, article XII; Commercial Treaty Between Japan and China, 1903, article X (China, The Maritime Customs, *Treaties, Conventions, etc.*, vol. I, p. 754; vol. II, p. 622).
19. Commercial Treaty, 1902, article IV (China, The Maritime Customs, *Treaties, Conventions, etc.*, p. 545).
20. Ibid., article II: China agrees to take the necessary steps to provide for a uniform national coinage which shall be legal tender in payment of all duties, taxes and other obligations throughout the Empire by British as well as Chinese subjects (p. 544).

21. *Qingji waijiao shiliao* [Compiled sources on foreign relations of the Qing period], vol. 153, pp. 27, 29.
22. Shen to Hay, 19 Jan. 1903, The Commission on International Exchange, *Stability of International Exchange: Report on the Introduction of the Gold-Exchange Standard into China and Other Silver-Using Countries* (Washington, D.C.: Government Printing Office, 1903), pp. 42–46.
23. Paul A. Varg, *Open Door Diplomat: The Life of W. W. Rockhill* (Urbana: University of Illinois Press, 1952), p. 48.
24. Sir Ewen Cameron of the Hongkong and Shanghai Bank; Stanislas Simon, director of Banque de l'Indo-Chine; Frang Urbig, Vorstandsmitglied der Deutsch Asiatischen Bank; Dimitry de Pokotiloff, director of the Russo-Chinese Bank; Soeda Juichi, managing director of Nippon Kōgyō Bank; Sōma Nagatane, managing director of Yokohama Shōkin Bank; Shibusawa Eiichi, president of Daiichi Bank; Hayakawa Senkichirō, executive director of Mitsui Bank, participated in the respective national commissions (Commission on International Exchange, *Stability of International Exchange*, p. 139).
25. Papers Presented by the United States Commission to the British, French and Russian Commission, 1903 (Commission on International Exchange, *Stability of International Exchange*, pp. 47–97).
26. In the Straits Settlements, a gold-exchange standard was actually implemented in 1906 (Kemmerer, *Modern Currency Reforms*, p. 450).
27. "Resolutions and Reports on the Foreign Commissions," Commission on International Exchange, *Stability of International Exchange*, pp. 141–73.
28. Jeremiah W. Jenks, "Commissioner in China, Memoranda on a New Monetary System for China, 1904" in Commission on International Exchange, *Gold Standard in International Trade: Report on the Introduction of the Gold-Exchange Standard into China, the Philippine Islands, Panama, and Other Silver-Using Countries and on the Stability of Exchange* (Washington, D.C.: Government Printing Office, 1904), pp. 80–81.
29. "Resolutions of the Chamber of Commerce of Hongkong, Shanghai, and Tientsin" (April 1903) (*Stability of International Exchange*, pp. 247–53).
30. J. W. Jamieson, commercial attaché to His Majesty's legation in Beijing, Report on the Foreign Trade of China for the Year 1903, BPP, *Diplomatic and Consular Reports*, Annual Series no. 3280, 1904.
31. Chen Du, ed., *Zhongguo jindai bizhi wenti huibian* [Collected essays on the problem of the modern Chinese monetary system] (Shanghai, 1932), part I, pp. 22–24.
32. Ibid., 104–8.
33. Ibid., part III, pp. 27–28.
34. Ibid., part I, pp. 214–20.
35. G. Vissering, "Currency Reform," in *On Chinese Currency*, part I.
36. Chen Du, *Zhongguo jindai bizhi wenti huibian*, part I, pp. 464–75.
37. Ibid., pp. 490–500.
38. Ibid., part II, pp. 711–13.
39. Ibid., pp. 592–94.
40. Ko Sakatani Shishaku Kinen Jigyō-kai, "Chūgoku heisei kaikaku" [Chinese monetary revolution] in *Sakatani Yoshirō-den* [Personal History of Sakatani Yoshirō] (Tokyo: Sakatani Shishaku Kinen Jigyō-kai, 1951), chap. 13.
41. Maurice Collis, "Branch Offices," in *Wayfoong: The Hongkong and Shanghai Banking Corporation* (London: Faber and Faber, 1965), chap. 4.
42. For example, in 1898, British and Chinese Corporation; in 1891, Banque de l'Indo-Chine; in 1902, International Banking Corporation and Banque Belge pour l'Etranger; and in 1903, Netherland Trading Society were established.
43. Zhang Zhenkun, "Qingmo shinianjian de bizhi wenti" [The currency problem in the last ten years of the Qing dynasty], *Jindaishi yanjiu*, no. 1, 1979, pp. 249–87.

44. From 1900 to 1910, the rate of land tax collection per *tan* rose from 3852 to 7552 copper in Chuanshating, Jiangsu (Yeh-chien Wang, *Land Taxation in Imperial China, 1750–1911* [Cambridge, Mass.: Harvard University Press, 1973], pp. 118–19).

45. China, Maritime Customs, *Decennial Report, 1912–21*, Shanghai, vol. II, pp. 12–13.

# The 1911 Revolution and United States East Asian Policy

## Marius B. Jansen

It is the theme of this paper that the Chinese Revolution of 1911 brought official and private responses that signalled important and long-range shifts in American East Asian policy. The Revolution of 1911 was not the only element involved; United States policymakers had shown indications of such a shift a few years earlier, and Japan helped to confirm that shift by its actions in 1915 and after. Before long the political instability that followed the revolution in China threatened to shake American faith in that revolution's leadership. One might consequently be tempted to dismiss American gratification with the revolution as a footnote to history that had little long-range consequence. Yet that would be an error. The shift of government from faltering monarchy to faltering republic was central to a shift in American attitudes and policies toward China. That shift was the more marked because change in China coincided with political change in the United States as the Taft administration was succeeded by that of Woodrow Wilson. It was a shift with important consequences for East Asian policies in future decades.

Twentieth-century U.S. East Asian policy was predominantly pro-Chinese until 1945. It was a stance anticipated by the Open Door notes of 1900, which came to signify a stand of protection and sponsorship for Chinese aspirations. Japan's victory over Russia in 1905 established it as the foremost imperialist power in northeastern Asia; and consequently the chief threat to Chinese aspirations and sovereignty. From that point on, it becomes appropriate to refer to Akira Iriye's "rival expansionisms" of Japan and the

United States.[1] The Russo-Japanese War was followed by the first sharp conflict about immigration problems between Japan and the United States, and in 1907 the United States Navy prepared its first contingency plan for possible war with Japan.[2] The U.S.-Japan relationship became competitive, while the U.S.-China relationship became protective in rhetoric. America's instinctive initial response to the revolution served to illustrate and to strengthen these attitudes.

So long as China was under Qing rule, it was difficult to arouse much sense of companionship between the American and Chinese policies. The image held of the Qing government was dominanted by assumptions of corruption, weakness, and inefficiency; the dynasty was also tarnished by resentment of the Boxer paroxysm against missionary activity. In contrast, Japan's constitutional order and rapid modernization had created a more appealing image of reform and change. The 1911 Revolution, however, for a period, at least, changed China's image from one of superannuation and ineffectiveness to one of idealism and youth, while Japan's image changed from promising youth to threatening bully. More important still, many Americans, including a new president, regarded the Revolution of 1911 as a response to American and Christian influence.

The Revolution of 1911 came during the waning days of the Republican administration of William Howard Taft. Taft had had the sobering discipline of imperial administration in the Philippines. He had also worked out a modus vivendi with imperial Japan in the Taft-Katsura agreement that the Japanese interpreted as condoning their acquisition of Korea. The "dollar diplomacy" of his years put the United States in line with other powers through cooperative consortia of banks for development in China. These loans, it should be noted, helped spark resistance to railroad centralization under central government initiatives and thus helped bring on the revolution. Huntington Wilson, Taft's assistant secretary of state, expected the continuation of such policies from the new administration of Woodrow Wilson and believed them conducive, as he put it, to the "protection of China's integrity and sovereignty, the uplift of the Chinese people, morally, materially, and governmentally, the development of China's resources, and the maintenance of our traditional policy of the 'open door.'" When Wilson's new administration ruled out

American participation in the Reorganization Loan in March 1913 as inimical to "the administrative independence of China," Huntington Wilson advanced a resignation he had already submitted.[3] In contrast to Taft's "realistic" dollar diplomacy, Woodrow Wilson showed a more idealistic and even visionary approach that was informed by his missionary friends. In the months after the revolution, Wilson's stand would come to rest on his interpretation of the Revolution of 1911 in the larger stream of modern Chinese history.

Wilson's views on China were importantly influenced by missionaries, some of them former students, who wrote him frequently to give their views of conditions and events. Eugene Trani summarizes Wilson's views as follows: "By the time of his election to the presidency [Wilson] had come to the belief that the United States had a peculiar role in China; spread democratic ideals, teach Christian morals, help the Chinese in the quest for stability and progress."[4]

The missionary opinion that influenced Wilson was overwhelmingly enthusiastic, indeed euphoric, about the Revolution of 1911. Many early hopes centered on the person of Sun Yat-sen, as an apparently Western-oriented Christian convert "who appeared to epitomize what the missionary endeavor was trying to accomplish."[5] Although initial optimism about Sun Yat-sen was moderated by doubts about his second marriage and his ties with Japan,[6] his magnanimous resignation of the provisional presidency gave the impression of a selfless patriot. The revolution seemed to augur well for the evangelization of China. Missionaries reported that the United States was immensely popular in China, that revolutionary leadership was in the hands of the young and Western-educated, and that political events "indicated not only political unrest but also a moral awakening when new ideas triumphed over the old."[7] These views were at considerable variance from those held by many journalists and by the United States minister to China, Calhoun, a Taft appointee, who believed in cooperative diplomacy and much preferred stability to uncertain change. Calhoun reported that Sun Yat-sen was alienated from the rural interior of China and warned that he seemed tinged with radicalism and anti-foreign sentiments.[8] In the larger swell of American opinion, however, the missionary endorsement was probably more important than official doubts. Optimism and enthusiasm for republicanism in China far outweighed official preference for the "stability" of the old order. In any case, Wilson soon sided with the missionaries.

The first clear expression of this came in the text of his "Statement on the Pending Chinese [Reorganization] Loan of March 18, 1913." After announcing that the United States would not participate, Wilson went on to say that "the awakening of the people of China to a consciousness of their possibilities under free government is the most significant, if not the most momentous, event of our generation. With this movement and aspiration the American people are in profound sympathy."[9] Charles E. Scott, a former Princeton student who was secretary of the American Presbyterian Mission in Qingdao, wrote the new president on May 31 to congratulate him on his step. The Chinese, he assured Wilson, "are gratified beyond measure that your administration has broken with the 'dollar diplomacy' which the Chinese look upon as brutal and iniquitous. Since we have pulled out of the deal America and Americans have gone up above par with the Chinese. They feel that Americans are their only friends. . . ."[10] Although it has since become clear that American bankers were far from eager to participate in the loans and would have required active government encouragement, Wilson himself clearly shared Scott's view of the matter. Josephus Daniels's diary account of a cabinet discussion on March 28, 1913 quotes Wilson's sentiment:

> I [Wilson] feel so keenly the desire to help China that I prefer to err in the line of helping that country than otherwise. If we had entered into the loan with other powers we would have got nothing but more influence in China and lost the proud position which America secured when Secretary Hay stood for the open door in China after the Boxer Uprising. He declared he believed that our position would be stronger not to be in partnership with other countries but to stand ready to aid China and to be able to say to Russia "what are your designs on Manchuria," and to Japan, "what are your wishes on this part of China," and to England, Germany, or any other country, "what are your designs," and being free, this country could help China and restore the relationship which this country occupied toward

that country and the world when Mr. Hay was Secretary of State."[11]

A second product of Wilson's determination to strike an individual and moral course for United States policy in China was shown in his determination to "recognize China on the great day in its history when the Parliament or Congress of this new Republic will meet, and ask other countries to do likewise, and that he did not wish this country's action to be at all dependent upon them."[12] In this case remonstrance came from the Russians, who suggested that the United States would think poorly of similar Russian unilateral action in South America. Wilson quite properly brushed this aside.

Unfortunately, the bright hopes that had been held for a parliamentary system under Yuan Shikai faded with the assassination of Song Jiaoren in March 1913. On April 8, the day the constituent assembly was to meet, Daniels's cabinet meeting notes recorded that the president and cabinet "devoutly hope that everything will go well in China today"; three days later Wilson's replies to questions addressed to him at a news conference showed confusion as to why the constituent assembly had adjourned without electing officers.[13] But on April 18, Daniels's notes showed how responsive the new administration could be to religious sentiment and optimism. Secretary of State Bryan began by reading from the *Washington Post* a clipping to the effect that the new Chinese government had made a formal appeal to all Christian churches in China to set aside April 27 as a "day of prayer that China may be guided to a wise solution of the critical problems besetting her. This act of the government is regarded here as striking evidence of the extraordinary changes which have taken place in the nation since the revolution. Prayer had been requested for the 'national assembly, for the new government, for the president of the republic, not yet elected, for the constitution of the republic, for the recognition of the republic by the powers, for the maintenance of peace and for election of strong and virtuous men to office.' " Bryan held forth on the significance of such requests from a nation that had so recently barred Christian missionaries, and "the President said that he did not know when he had been so stirred and cheered as when he read that message in the paper this morning." Some doubts about the sincerity of the message were expressed, but "this did not appeal to the President." This led directly to the discussion of recognition, and "Secretary Bryan was requested to wire China and get all the facts. . . . The opinion was expressed by the President and others, particularly Mr. Bryan, in favor of recognizing China and that by Tuesday we would get enough information to recognize China by April 17, on which date the churches would all offer prayers for the republic of that country."[14] By May 2 the White House was in receipt of a message from Yuan Shikai expressing gratitude for recognition and vowing that "the sole aim of the government which [the Chinese people] have established is and will be to preserve this form of [republican] government and to perfect its workings."[15] In these steps Wilson again had the enthusiastic support of American missionaries in China.

A third expression of Wilson's conviction that the American and missionary course were ultimately one was to be found in the efforts he made to secure a Christian layman as minister to the new China. He was anxious "that our representatives in China and Japan should be of the best quality the country affords. I believe that there is probably nothing more nearly touches the future development of the world than what will happen in the East and it ought to happen, so far as our influence extends, under the best possible guidance."[16] His first choice for China was President Eliot of Harvard, who declined. Once Bryan was chosen as secretary of state the requirements were narrowed further, for the orthodox Bryan even had misgivings about Eliot, who was a Unitarian. John R. Mott, the foreign secretary of the International Committee of the Y.M.C.A., seemed a perfect choice. "The Christian influence, direct or indirect, is very prominently at the front [in China]," Wilson wrote Bryan, "and I need not say, ought to be kept there." When Mott cited the importance of his work and commitments as reasons for declining, Wilson assured him that he could take time off to continue that, because he was "eager to unite what you represent with what this government means to try to represent."[17] When Mott nevertheless declined, Wilson's friend and advisor Cleveland Dodge wrote Wilson that "the mere fact of your wishing to have Mott in China has made a great impression both here and abroad, and has announced to the world, more definitely than anything else could have done, the kind of policy which you intend to adopt in your dealings with China."[18] The search for a suitable candidate continued. When Norman Hapgood indicated interest, Colonel House interviewed him on April 4 and "asked about his religious views. He did not seem to have any worthwhile. I told him I had talked to the President, and I was sure he would offer him China provided he was an orthodox Christian. I explained that Mr. Bryan felt very strongly upon this point, and that it was necessary for the President to recognize it. Bryan merely desires it in the case of China where the uplift is being brought about by the missionaries, the Y.M.C.A., and like forces."[19] Hapgood evidently failed to pass the test, and consideration was given to several other candidates before the choice went to Paul Reinsch, a political scientist at the University of Wisconsin and son of a Lutheran clergyman, in July of 1913.

This brief excursion into the early days of the Wilson administration suggests several points of importance for future U.S.-East Asian relations.

First was the conviction that missionary influence had been central to the emergence of a "new" China whose members were certain to emerge in positions of leadership. That conviction made it logical to try to identify with that group, if necessary in a unilateral course, by avoiding contacts with the "old diplomacy." In the long run, such a policy would bring the United States the friendship of a "new China" that was going to be of incalculable importance on the future world stage.

Second was the conviction that this course was truly anti-imperialist and unselfish. This created a setting from which the policies of other powers, especially Japan, invited moral condemnation. From Japan's initial hesitation about intervention against the revolution, to its confusion over the issue of recognition, followed by its seizure of German holdings in Shandong and then its efforts to consolidate Japanese advantage in the Twenty-one Demands of 1915, the imperial government seemed to display itself as polar opposite to Wilson's new diplomatic morality. This had ominous significance for future U.S.-Japanese relations.

The story does not, of course, end there. Wilson's early and naive enthusiasm for the revolution was soon tempered by political considerations of stability that found American policy supporting Yuan Shikai against the revolutionaries. Secretary of State Bryan opined that if the revolutionaries won their second attempt, disorder in China would have been so great that foreign intervention would almost certainly follow, and when Huang Xing came to the United States in 1914 after the failure of the "Second Revolution," Yuan Shikai was assured that the president would not see him. General Yamagata's misgivings about revolution in China were not very different, and Sun Yat-sen fared no better in Japan than Huang did in America. Official American sympathy supported Yuan Shikai even during his abortive monarchical attempt, and after 1916 the Wilson administration was (vainly) encouraging bankers to cooperate in a reorganization loan to forestall the Japanese.[20] Such efforts, justified in Wilson's eyes by the desirability of forestalling Japanese moves, did not, in Japanese eyes, seem very different frcm their own attempts to win and maintain political primacy in the turbulent setting of Chinese republicanism.

Yet if Wilson was naive in detail, he was also wise in general, for by his rhetoric and stance he anticipated and helped stimulate the attitudes and expectations of much of "young China." His desire to abandon the old course of secret agreement and special privilege resonated with trends that were bringing empire to an end in China, Russia, Turkey, Austria-Hungary, and Germany. He was right to see in the collapse of the Qing empire one of the momentous events in modern world history, and wrong only in his optimism about the outlook for cultural and political influence in the setting that followed. His errors, centering on euphoric expectations of a democratic order in China, were to characterize American policy again in future years.

Such rhetoric also proved to have its domestic cost. The disappointment of Wilson's hopes for China, combined with his reluctant agreement to Japan's position on Shandong at Versailles, left him vulnerable to charges of hypocrisy and betrayal from new-found "friends of China" who used Wilson's rhetoric to contest his leadership. Conservative "Asia firsters" remained an important force in American politics into the 1950s. As a result the Revolution of 1911, by changing American images of China and by introducing idealistic rhetoric of benevolence for young Chinese revolutionary leaders, introduced a cast of characters and ideas that was not played out until Stanley Hornbeck, a disciple of Paul Reinsch, completed his assignment in the Division of Far Eastern Affairs in the Department of State in the 1940s.

## Notes

1. Akira Iriye, *Pacific Estrangement: Japanese and American Expansion, 1897–1911* (Cambridge, Mass.: Harvard University Press, 1972).
2. Richard D. Challener, *Admirals, Generals, and American Foreign Policy, 1898–1914* (Princeton: Princeton University Press, 1973).
3. Arthur S. Link, ed., *The Papers of Woodrow Wilson* (Princeton: Princeton University Press, 1978), vol. 27, pp. 195–97.
4. Eugene P. Trani, "Woodrow Wilson, China, and the Missionaries 1913–1921," *Journal of Presbyterian History*, vol. 49, no. 4 (Winter 1971), p. 332.
5. Michael V. Metallo, "American Missionaries, Sun Yat-sen, and the Chinese Revolution," *Pacific Historical Review* XLVII, no. 2 (May 1978), p. 266.
6. See Marius B. Jansen, *The Japanese and Sun Yat-sen* (Cambridge, Mass.: Harvard University Press, 1954), and Etō S. and M.B. Jansen, tr., *My Thirty-three Years' Dream: The Autobiography of Miyazaki Tōten* (Princeton: Princeton University Press, 1982).
7. Metallo, "American Missionaries," p. 265.
8. It should be noted that in Japan, too, popular opinion was considerably more enthusiastic about the revolution than official opinion.
9. *Wilson Papers*, vol. 27, p. 193.
10. Ibid., p. 488.
11. Ibid., p. 237. Daniels wrote that Wilson went on to say that "the Japanese ambassador had called after his statement on the Reorganization Loan, "and it developed then that the United States had asked Japan to take part of the proposed loan to China and Japan had acceded to this in the Taft administration. 'It seems,' said the President, 'in speaking of this matter that the United States had invited Japan to dinner, then absented itself when dinner was served and Japan did not understand it.' Of course he laughed. Mr. Bryan and I [Daniels] both feel . . . we ought to have informed the other governments of our actions, but he did not believe any serious result would follow." In 1970 terms, this would have been called a "Wilson Shock" in Tokyo.
12. Ibid., p. 249, Daniels's diary.
13. Ibid., p. 285.
14. Ibid., pp. 327–29.
15. Ibid., pp. 381–82.
16. Wilson to Eilot, ibid., p. 65. January 20, 1913, thus before taking office.
17. Ibid., p. 202.
18. Ibid., p. 247.
19. Ibid., p. 262. Li Tien-yi, *Woodrow Wilson's China Policy, 1913–1921* (1952; reprint, New York: Octagon Books, 1969), p. 83, adds that others considered and not named were Henry Morgenthau, not a Christian, who was posted to Turkey, instead, and William T. Ellis, who was rejected as lacking diplomatic skills although he was a Christian.
20. Li, *Wilson's China Policy*, pp. 143ff.

# The Issue of Imperialism and the 1911 Revolution

Marie-Claire Bergère

Although the best specialists have for many years called attention to the need to bridge the gap between the study of modern Chinese history and the analysis of international relations,[1] a significant dialogue has not yet sufficiently developed between historians of China and analysts of international politics. This may be the reason why, in spite of many studies dealing with the 1911 Revolution and the foreign powers, some questions still remain unclear. In this paper I will address myself to one of them: why was it that the issue of imperialism around which Chinese opponents of the Qing dynasty had united and upon which Sun Yat-sen had so much capitalized, more or less faded away after the outbreak of the revolution and the collapse of the dynasty?

The Chinese revolutionary movement developed during the first decade of the twentieth century as a response to foreign imperialist aggression. Its goal was to put China back in the position of a powerful nation, to restore the country's international stature, and to recover railway and mining rights. The Qing dynasty was criticized and opposed for its inability to prevent foreign encroachments: it thus became a target for Chinese nationalists.

The fall of the Qing, however, did not lead to the return of Chinese sovereign rights but to a further deterioration of the country's international position. Why did not Chinese revolutionaries try to use popular anti-imperialist currents (that the dynasty had been unwilling or unable to mobilize) to further a national restoration? A widely accepted answer is that the responsibility for this failure is to be laid upon the foreign powers.

Confronted with the revolutionary outbreak, foreign powers had three courses open to them: (1) They could support the revolution and help China to establish a truly independent government which eventually would threaten their privileges. (2) They could support the dynasty. This would mean accepting the continuation of the previous system which associated collective forms of economic and financial exploitation with the existence of specific spheres of influence. They would ensure the survival of a central government which guaranteed that treaties would be respected and the indemnities paid. (3) They could choose caution, refrain from aiding either side, and wait for ulterior developments.

Each of these courses of action was in time considered by one or another power.[2] But a common China policy prevailed which opted in a first phase for the adhesion to neutrality. Because of its predominant interests in China and because it was Japan's ally, Britain played a decisive role in the formulation and the working out of this common policy.[3] Other powers aligned themselves. Some, such as Japan and Russia, were hesitant and quite reluctant.[4] Others, such as France and the United States, did so willingly.[5]

The scholars who have studied the diplomatic history of the period believe that international relations in Asia must be viewed in the larger context of world politics (i.e., at that time, of European politics). In China, a precarious balance of power had been established after the Boxer Expedition and the Russo-Japanese War. Any local upheaval could lead to a serious disruption of international order. At a time of growing tensions in Europe, neither Britain nor France wanted their Japanese or Russian allies to get actively involved in Chinese affairs. Such an involvement would have been difficult to control and, eventually, to contain. It would have diverted attention and forces toward what was considered a secondary scene.

When, in December 1911, it became clear that the old Chinese political system could not be saved, the foreign powers decided to support Yuan Shikai who from the start was their favorite (although not Japan's). This choice reflected their desire to see a strong government that would keep the door open.

The 1911 Revolution did lead to an increased foreign influence in the country. It provided the powers with new opportunities to expand their role. In 1912, fearing that revolutionary leaders in the provinces would withold the customs revenues which were pledged to the service of foreign loans, the powers instituted an International Commission of Bankers to superintend the repayment of these loans. They also entrusted the Inspector General and his commissioners with the collection of the customs receipts and their deposit in foreign banks, and with the responsibility for making loan payments as they fell due and reserving the surplus for the legitimate Chinese government.[6] Henceforth the foreigners assumed the right to decide which government was legitimate and to finance it with customs revenue surplus. Moreover, Yuan Shikai had to sign the Reorganization Loan (April 1913) as a price for recognition. This loan, which provided Yuan with the funds he needed to crush his opponents, enhanced foreign control over Chinese finance and administration. In the wake of the 1911 Revolution, the Chinese government had also to give up its control over several border regions: Outer Mongolia, where Russian influence became predominant, and Tibet, which fell under British influence.

There was no attempt, however, at a new division of China. But this restraint was not derived from any consideration for China's sovereignty: it was the consequence of relations among the foreign powers and system of alliances.

Very briefly put, this is the classical account of foreign attitudes and policy during the 1911 Revolution. The relations between China and the foreign powers are approached as the "China problem," a problem to be taken up by Western and Japanese policymakers. China is studied as the object of their common concern. And emphasis is laid upon relations among the foreign powers.

In relation with this analysis, a widely accepted interpretation of the declining violence of the anti-imperialist campaign is that once in power revolutionaries were compelled to operate within the same old international framework as the previous Qing regime. They had to bear the same constraints or worse constraints, and the range of policy alternatives available to them was strictly limited. So the responsibility for the failure of the revolutionary goal of national restoration is laid upon the oppressive policy conducted by the foreign powers.

Exact in a very general way, this statement has to be qualified.

What we need here is to assess more precisely the interaction between the emergence of Chinese nationalism and the international context within which Japanese and Western policymakers operated. In this respect I would present three suggestions or hypotheses.

(1) I would first suggest that Chinese revolutionaries did not fail: they did not even try to apply their anti-imperialist program. It has been said that revolutionary leaders had been as much shocked by the traumatic experience of the Boxer war as the Qing officials. They were determined to eschew any action that might promote another foreign invasion. From the start, they acted very cautiously. As soon as the Wuchang Uprising broke out, General Li Yuanhong gave assurance to the British consul general in Hankou that treaty rights and foreign lives and properties would be respected. As a consequence, the revolutionary struggle was exclusively fought against the Qing dynasty. Resistance to the Qing became equivalent to opposition to foreign imperialism. If we go a step further, we could say that anti-Qing opposition became a substitute for anti-imperialist action. This substitution has been rationalized by presenting the Qing government and officials as supporting foreign interests: this is a controversial issue. From another angle we could consider this substitution as self-imposed and unconscious, a deviation similar to what psychoanalysts call a transfer. Although foreign imperialists were identified as the most dangerous enemies, the Manchus were the ones who were attacked because they represented an easier target. Anti-Manchu struggle could thus been seen as an escape, a non-rational solution to the fundamental contradiction between violent anti-imperialist feelings and an impossible anti-imperialist struggle (given the overwhelming superiority of foreign economic and military forces).

(2) As a second hypothesis, I would suggest that Yuan Shikai's rise to power should not be retained as an important factor to explain the decline of the anti-imperialist current. Although modern nationalism in China had developed as a response to foreign aggression, anti-imperialism was not its only content. From the start, economic modernization was one of its fundamental components. Apart from a few leaders who consider it easier for developing countries to rely on their own forces to re-invent the steam

engine, the general opinion is that economic modernization cannot proceed without some forms of foreign contact. Sun's nationalism did not exclude cooperation with foreign economic interests. Written during the post-revolutionary decade, "The International Development of China" makes this point very clear. The problem was, of course, how to obtain economic and financial cooperation and at the same time resist foreign control, a difficult problem that Yuan Shikai failed to solve. Judging from his attitude in the Hanyeping case, Sun's performance, had he remained in a power position, may have been no better.

(3) Finally I would suggest that the reaction of the foreign powers to the 1911 Revolution was not totally negative and repressive. The foreign powers selected Yuan as their man because they thought he would be more conservative and hopefully more manageable. But they also considered him as more experienced and more competent to lead China on the path to economic modernization. (At that time Sun's ability as a statesman had not been tested.) The goal of the foreign powers was not to hinder Chinese economic development but to take part in it and as far as possible to benefit from it and to control it.

With the establishment of the international consortium, the imperialist system started to evolve toward new forms of economic aid and control, which after two world wars came to dominate the relations between the industrial and the developing countries. Although some foreign countries considered it just a scheme for perpetuating old practices, the international consortium may well be considered one of the earliest manifestations of what was to become known many years later as neo-imperialism. In this sense, the 1911 Revolution elicited a specific response from the foreign powers. The premises of neo-imperialist ideology and policy appeared in the wake of the 1911 Revolution as a result of interaction between the emergent Chinese nationalism and the collective forms of foreign domination prevalent in China at that time.

## Notes

1. Akira Iriye, "Public Opinion and Foreign Policy: The Case of Late Qing China," in *Approaches to Modern Chinese History*, Albert Feuerwerker, Rhoads Murphey, and Mary Wright, eds. (Berkeley: University of California Press, 1967). For an example of such a gap, cf. Roberta Dayer, *Bankers and Diplomats in China, 1917–1925: The Anglo-American Relationship* (London: Frank Cass, 1981).

2. Cf. John Reid, *The Manchu Abdication and the Powers, 1908–1912: An Episode in Pre-War Diplomacy* (Berkeley: University of California Press, 1935).

3. Cf. Peter Lowe, *Great Britain and Japan 1911–1915: A Study of Far-Eastern Policy* (London: Macmillan, 1969).

4. Masaru Ikei, "Japan's Response to the Chinese Revolution of 1911," *The Journal of Asian Studies* XXV, no. 2 (Feb. 1966), pp. 213–27.

5. Marianne Bastid, "La diplomatie française et la révolution chinoise de 1911," *Revue d'Histoire Moderne* (1969).

6. Albert Feuerwerker, *The Foreign Establishment in China in the Early Twentieth Century* (Ann Arbor: Center for Chinese Studies, 1967).

# The Foreign Powers and the 1911 Revolution: A Harmonious Interval During a Period of Discord

Harold Z. Schiffrin

The decade preceding the outbreak of the First World War (1904–14) has been aptly described as "The International Anarchy."[1] Ambitions, fears, and jealousies fed imperialist rivalries throughout the world. While professing peaceful intentions, and sometimes even hoping for peace, the major European powers expected war and prepared for war. International relations were little more than a cynical search for aggrandizement, and it was never certain that the lure of aggrandizement would not dissolve and reverse so-called friendships and alliances. Yet, by 1911 the opposing alignments were fairly fixed: the Triple Entente (France, Russia, and Britain) faced the Triple Alliance (Germany, Austria-Hungary, and an Italy of uncertain allegiance).

On July 1, 1911, tension had been heightening to such an extent that the mere visit of a German gunboat to the Moroccan port of Agadir touched off a Franco-German crisis that immediately involved their respective allies.[2] Though this "Second Moroccan Crisis"[3] was settled peacefully—France got a protectorate over Morocco and Germany was compensated with part of the French Congo—the whole affair was a frightening and ominous reminder of the perilous and senseless state of international relations: millions of Europeans had almost been condemned to death because two governments could not agree as to how they should divide a piece of Africa to which neither had any right except that of armed robbery. Italy's war with Turkey over Tripoli that same year was a lesser crisis of the same genre. More were to follow. And the resolution of each crisis brought only temporary respite and left a residue of fear, frustration, and enmity that was to fuel the great conflagration in 1914.

Given this explosive state of international relations, at first glance it seems surprising that the major event in the Far East at this time, the Chinese Revolution of 1911, did not immediately provoke a similar international crisis, since all the major powers, including Japan and the United States, claimed to have serious and often conflicting interests in the area. On the contrary, with respect to China, the behavior of the powers during this period of international discord was characterized by a unique display of conformity. It is the purpose of this paper to try to explain why the powers, at loggerheads in other parts of the world, agreed on a policy of neutrality toward the Chinese Revolution.

The first, and most obvious, answer is that European imperialism did not attach prime importance to China and East Asia in general. (Japan, naturally, did give the highest priority to East Asia; why, in determining its China policy at this time, it nevertheless followed Europe's lead will be discussed later.) Compared to the major foci of European rivalry—the Balkans, Africa, and the Middle East, including Afghanistan—contention over China was a sideshow. This contrast was the result of strategic considerations, dictated by geographic proximity and ethnic and religious issues, as well as historical sentiments and economic interests. China did not arouse most of these considerations at all; and those that it did, such as economic ambitions, did not match the appeal exerted by these other regions. The anticipated break-up of the Turkish Empire, for example, released deep-rooted and passionate feelings which a projected break-up of the Chinese Empire could never provoke.

Profits from trade and investments—ostensibly the most important motivation for Western penetration of China—never lived up to expectations. The pessimistic conclusions of the Mitchell Report, drawn up in 1852, were essentially still valid in 1911: the self-sufficient nature of the Chinese economy would not allow for a massive consumption of British (or other European) goods.[4] By 1911, Western imperialism concentrated more on industrial investments than trade, which had proved disappointing. But despite all the activity in financing and railways building, the total export of foreign capital, while not insignificant, was only a fraction of what was invested in other regions. Though foreign investment in China had doubled since 1900, by 1914 it totaled only U.S. $1610 million. Yet about this same time—1913—foreign investments in Africa totaled U.S. $4700 million and worldwide foreign investments were U.S. $44,000 million. Furthermore, during this "Golden Age" of international investment, in which Britain was the leader, regions like Canada, the United States, Australia—"regions of recent development"—were the major targets of investment. Other regions, like Africa, afforded colonial-type development in which imperialist powers invested in primary production for export to the industrial countries.[5]

China, of course, was not another Canada or Australia. Nor, however, was China a colony: the foreign powers had to negotiate with the Chinese government for investment rights which, even under the faltering Manchu dynasty, were not easily obtained. Why, then, was not China, like India, conquered by a single imperialist power, or, like Africa, divided among several European powers?

The last time that the prospect of dismembering China had been contemplated was near the close of the century when the foreign powers were scrambling for concessions and spheres of influence. The Boxer Uprising, however, had seriously dampened the notion. Despite the disaster which the Boxers brought upon China, they gave the entire world a taste of what would be involved if a total conquest of China were to be attempted. In reading foreign diplomatic correspondence during the 1911 Revolution, especially the British material, which is most voluminous, one is increasingly impressed with the fear that the Boxers had previously spread.[6] After the summer of 1900 a resurgence of "Boxerism," as it was called, was a perennial foreign nightmare. This undoubtedly served as a brake upon imperialist, expansionist ambitions. And if any hopes of dismembering China still lingered, the 1911 Revolution obliterated them: it was clear to foreigners that, among other motivating factors, there was a definite anti-imperialist impulse behind the revolutionary movement.

The revolution proved that anti-imperialist, but not necessarily anti-foreign, sentiments had struck strong roots among the Chinese people. British diplomats now realized that "patriotism" was not a strange concept to the Chinese.[7] This realization has been succinctly recorded by a British official, whose report caused both apprehension and regret in London. "The idea of 'China for the Chinese,'" he wrote in 1913, "would seem to be gaining ground. Students returning from Japan, America, and England all share the ardent desire to control the settlements and concessions in China and abolish extra-territoriality. They complain of the treatment of Chinese by foreigners at Shanghai and other treaty ports, and wish to keep in their own control the finances, railways, and other enterprises of China."[8]

In other words, the nationalist component of the 1911 Revolution was an important additional reason for discouraging foreign intervention. Though the prevailing opinion among foreigners was that some sort of monarchy, but not a republic, would be the most suitable form of government for China, as early as November when the revolutionaries captured Shanghai and held most of the southern provinces, it was clear that they were a force to contend with and could not be easily dismissed. In general, foreigners, who usually tended to make a mockery of Chinese fighting qualities, were impressed with the absence of the "comic element" in the battles between revolutionary and imperial forces.[9] The revolution made them take the Chinese people more seriously.

At the same time, the revolutionaries were scrupulous in avoiding threats or injury to foreign lives and property.[10] They even promised to maintain existing treaty rights, though they warned that a republican regime would not honor new commitments made by the Manchu dynasty. Thus the foreigners had no palpable reason for intervening. They could keep what they already had without taking any overt action. They were not willing to pay the high cost of further incursions upon Chinese sovereignty. Furthermore, it would have been difficult for them to agree on how to divide the China "spoils," despite the confident assertion of Russia's ambassador to Beijing that "in China there is room for us all."[11]

The important point is that the foreign stranglehold on Chinese finances ensured that any new Chinese government would be beholden to foreigners. First of all, previous commitments had already enabled foreigners to control a large portion of Chinese tax receipts. Secondly, concurrent with the outbreak of the revolution—and one of its causes—was the centrifugal pull of the provinces which deprived both the revolutionaries and the imperial forces of much-needed income. This meant that any central government would immediately require foreign loans to avoid bankruptcy. Awareness of this dependency undoubtedly served to restrain the revolutionaries both in their behavior toward the foreign powers, and in their readiness to compromise with Yuan Shikai, which is what the British and other foreigners wanted. In addition, as already mentioned, the revolutionaries feared giving foreigners any pretext for intervention, as in the case of the Taiping Rebellion. This points up one of the ironies of the 1911 Revolution: mutual fear influenced the policies of both Chinese and foreigners, and induced mutual restraint.

To return now to the Japanese, the only foreigners for whom continental Asia constituted the centerpiece of foreign policy considerations. Although some Japanese contemplated intervention for different purposes—to partition China, to help the Manchus, or to help the revolutionaries—there was no clear-cut consensus as to what kind of China would be best for Japan. Most important, however, was the Japanese reluctance to go it alone. At this time Japan felt obligated to coordinate policies with its British ally who, as it turned out, did not reciprocate. Without consulting the Japanese, Britain acted to secure the cease-fire in December 1911 and backed Yuan Shikai in the ultimate settlement. Japan, moreover, had only recently swallowed Korea with the acquiescence of its ally, Britain, and its erstwhile enemy, Russia. For the time being, Japanese imperialism was sated, and there was no urgent need to risk offending the other powers by taking an independent, interventionist course in China. Probably, too, Japan had insufficient investment capital to undertake independent financial ventures in China. So Japan went along with the others, who followed Britain's lead in maintaining neutrality and in pressing for an early end to the fighting. Though admitted to the four-power financial consortium (Britain, France, Germany, and the United States) along with Russia in June 1912, Japan scored no real gains from the 1911 Revolution. However, Russia and Britain did, which added to Japan's frustration and feeling of having been betrayed.[12]

The Boxer episode had showed that if foreign armies intervened in China, Russia would be the big winner. During the 1911

Revolution, the British Foreign Office took into consideration the fact that Russia had more forces in East Asia than any other power.[13] And this was another consideration in Britain's decision to opt for neutrality and avoid armed intervention. Russia itself was undoubtedly the most cynical and brazenly imperialist of all the foreign powers involved with China. During the revolution, Russia's foreign minister, Sazonov, wrote that "Russia and Japan must use the present favorable moment to fortify their position in China." "Our political interests," he went on, "are directly opposed to the maintenance of China's territorial integrity."[14] Yet Russia, weakened by internal turbulence since the 1905 Revolution, the year it was humbled by Japan, and now concerned with omens of war in Europe, could not undertake independent intervention in China. What it did gain were concessions in Manchuria and Mongolia, but only with the agreement of Britain which, in return, obtained Russian acceptance of British predominance in Tibet.

Thus, as a result of the 1911 Revolution, the imperialist powers held on to their previous gains and scored some additional ones on the periphery of the now broken Manchu Empire—Mongolia, Manchuria, and Tibet. But this marked the high tide of imperialism. No further gains could be expected without paying an exorbitant price that was beyond the means of the European powers, who had higher priorities elsewhere. And the Japanese, who in 1915 would begin their solo attempt to realize imperialist ambitions in China, would eventually find that the cost was disastrously high.

## Notes

1. G. Lowes Dickinson, *The International Anarchy, 1884–1914* (London: Allen & Unwin, 1926).
2. Ibid., chap. VII.
3. The "First Moroccan Crisis," provoked by the visit of the German emperor to Tangier in March 1905, lasted until April 1906.
4. On the Mitchell Report, see Nathan A. Pelcovits, *Old China Hands and the Foreign Office* (New York: King's Crown Press, 1948), pp. 15–17.
5. See Chi-ming Hou, *Foreign Investments and Economic Development in China 1840–1937* (Cambridge, Mass.: Harvard University Press, 1965), pp. 17, 120–24, 251n60. Hou also quotes another source which gives a higher total for foreign investments in China—U.S. $2257 million. But this is not a significant difference. See p. 235n17.

6. My impressions of British reactions to the 1911 Revolution are based upon a reading of diplomatic dispatches now available in the Public Record Office, London (FO 371).
7. Wilkinson to Grey, 29 Nov. 1911, FO 371/1310, no. 2055.
8. Jordan to Grey, 6 May 1912, FO 371/1318, no. 22592.
9. Wilkinson to Grey, 29 Nov. 1911, FO 371/1310, no. 2055.
10. See Harold Z. Schiffrin, *Sun Yat-sen: Reluctant Revolutionary* (Boston: Little, Brown, 1980), pp. 154–55.
11. Quoted in Dickinson, *International Anarchy*, p. 285.
12. On Japanese policy during the revolution, see Masaru Ikei, "Japan's Response to the Chinese Revolution of 1911," *The Journal of Asian Studies* XXV, No. 2 (Feb. 1966): 213–27; and Marius B. Jansen, *Japan and China: From War to Peace, 1894–1972* (Chicago: Rand McNally College Pub., 1975), pp. 202–6.
13. Jordan to Grey, 15 Dec. 1911, FO 371/1310, no. 151.
14. Quoted in Dickinson, *International Anarchy*, p. 300.

# The 1911 Revolution and the Foreign Powers

S. L. Tikhvinski

The alliance of the Manchu-Chinese rulers and the Western colonialists, born as a result of the Qing struggle against the peasant war of the Taipings from 1860 to 1864, became apparent in 1900 and 1901 when the troops of eight powers suppressed the popular anti-imperialist and anti-feudal Yihetuan (Boxer) uprising. Since 1860, during its last 50 years of rule, the Qing monarchy managed to survive in China thanks to the active support from abroad; the foreign powers were interested in its preservation.

By the end of the first decade of the twentieth century, one hundred cities, ports, and wharves of the Qing empire had been opened to foreign capitalists for free trade. In only ten years, from 1901 to 1910, the Qing government opened for foreign trade 37 cities in 12 provinces of the country. The imperialist powers maintained their armed forces in China on a permanent basis. In March 1911, in northern China alone there were 1042 French, 1882 British, 494 Japanese, 151 German, 238 Italian, 160 American, 42 Austro-Hungarian officers and men, as well as 31 from tsarist Russia. (Not included are the large foreign naval forces which were stationed in the eastern and other regions of China.) Furthermore, the alliance of the Manchu-Chinese feudal reactionaries with colonial-comprador elements, personified by the Qing regime, suited the foreign powers very well. It ensured the powers unrestrained control of the country and colonial oppression of the peoples of the Qing empire.

The emergence in the political arena of the young Chinese bourgeoisie and new bourgeois-like landowners resulted in frequent patriotic anti-colonial uprisings in various regions of the country, especially in the Yangzi basin. They were directed against the continued penetration of foreign capital, which was obstructing the commercial and industrial activities of the young bourgeoisie. The Manchu government was an obedient tool in the hands of the imperialist powers. Its policy caused indignation on the part of the Chinese bourgeoisie, which was in need of capitalist enterprises uninhibited by feudal chains and free from the oppression of the financial capital and the pressure of the major foreign powers.

On May 3, 1911, the Qing government took a decision to nationalize the railways (both those in operation and those under construction). This act served as a plausible excuse for the Qing government to hand the railways in Sichuan, Hubei, Hunan, and Guangdong provinces over to the imperialist bank consortium. The local bourgeoisie and liberal landlords were consequently deprived of a profitable sphere of application of their capital. The decision provoked anti-government disturbances that took the shape of a popular uprising in Sichuan in the autumn of 1911. To suppress this uprising, the Qing government mobilized large armed forces, and troops from neighboring provinces were sent to Sichuan.

By the autumn of 1911 a revolutionary situation emerged in the country: broad masses of the Chinese people did not want to live as they had before. The Manchu Qing government displayed its total inability to rule the country. It sank into a state of corruption and court intrigues, and by its repeated concessions to the solicitations of foreign powers it turned itself against those Chinese feudals who at the turn of the century had been their staunch supporters.

Representatives of the main factions of the anti-Manchu struggle clearly realized and criticized the Qing policy of capitulation to foreign capital and their betrayal of the national interests. The treacherous policy of the Qing contributed to a large extent to the development of the revolutionary situation in 1911.

The overthrow of Manchu rule became possible as a result of the merging of the four main groups in the struggle against the Qing:

1) the national-liberation movement, headed by the Chinese

League which was set up by Sun Yat-sen and bourgeois-landlord revolutionary organizations affiliated with the League;

2) the constitutional monarchy movement of the Chinese bourgeoisie and landlords;

3) the spontaneous uprisings by peasants and the urban lower strata, under the leadership of secret societies; and

4) the liberation struggle of the non-Chinese peoples forcibly included into the empire by the Qing government.

Let us briefly analyze the attitude of each of these groups toward foreign powers.

In spite of the progressive and democratic nature of the program of the Chinese League, it had some serious shortcomings. Sun Yat-sen and his supporters failed to realize, in particular, the true class character of modern social contradictions, anti-feudal and anti-imperialist tasks of the imminent revolution. They narrowed down the essence of the contradictions to a purely national conflict between the Chinese (Han) and the Manchus.

Broad circles of liberal landlords and representatives of the young national bourgeoisie, which had taken part in the movement for the reforms of 1895 to 1898 and then in the constitutional monarchist movement of 1905 to 1911, could not but show their attitude to the Manchu court as well as to the imperialist powers. However, unlike the toiling masses and revolutionary democrats grouping around Sun Yat-sen, these reformists took a less resolute, inconsistent position, showing readiness for conciliation and compromise with the feudal bureaucracy. The imperialist powers had close links with the leaders of the constitutionalists.

Despite this, the leaders of the constitutional monarchist opposition protested the policy of continuous concessions to foreign countries that infringed on the economic interests of the bourgeoisie. They suggested that the movement in defense of railroads and mines from foreign capital, which spread to some provinces of eastern and southern China, should be utilized in seizing political and economic positions in the country. The Chinese bourgeoisie, however, did not even make an attempt to stir the whole country to the struggle against foreign capital.

Introduction of racial elements into the slogans of the struggle against oppression by forcign countries was characteristic of bourgeois reformers, supporters of constitutional monarchy. They considered foreign colonial expansion as expansion of the White race against the Yellow race and called for "the protection of the race." The ulterior motive of the great-power nationalism which they advocated was their exploitation of non-Han peoples who had been forcibly annexed to the Qing empire.

During the years prior to the overthrow of the Qing monarchy, spontaneous anti-government and anti-feudal uprisings of the peasantry and the lower strata of the urban population had intensified. As a rule, such protests took place under the leadership of traditional secret societies, such as Gelaohui, Hongbang, Qingbang, and Santianhui. These protests were of distinctly antidynastic character and were caused by the increase in taxes. They opposed paying off a "Boxers' indemnity" to foreign states, the high cost of living, speculation by the local authorities and merchants, the despotism of bureaucrats, the military and police, deterioration of traditional handicrafts and occupations, penetration of foreign industrial goods, and modern means of transport which furthered the decline of the handicrafts and traditional means of transport.

In 1910 alone, according to preliminary data in China, more than 80 revolts by starving masses and more than 30 uprisings by peasants and the urban poor took place to protest high taxes and extortion. Rice riots took place in Changsha, and violent peasants' riots took place in Shandong. These spontaneous uprisings, which were not led by the most progressive social forces—the bourgeoisie and the proletariat, who were small in number, the latter being economically and politically weak and immature as a class—were objectively aimed against the Manchu monarchy, the oppression of feudal lords, and imperialist aggression. After the bloody suppression of the Boxer Rebellion by the imperialists in 1901, local uprisings continuously took place, increasing in number on the eve of the 1911 Revolution.

The weakening of the Qing Empire stimulated the upsurge of the liberation movements of non-Chinese ethnic minorities. Under the influence of the 1911 Revolution, the peoples of Mongolia, Tibet, and Xinjiang, who had been subjected to oppression and discrimination by the Manchu government, which treated them as colonial peoples, waged struggles for their independence. It should be noted that the imperialist powers, Russia and Great

Britain in particular, supported separatist movements in China's borderlands (acting, of course, in their own self-interests). Russia promoted the formation of an autonomous Mongolia, and it was an important step toward the restoration of the Mongolian state system and objectively a progressive phenomenon in the history of the Mongolian people.

In the course of the preparation and realization of the 1911 Revolution, the Chinese bourgeoisie did not put forward any clear-cut anti-imperialist demands. It did not raise such demands as the withdrawal of foreign troops, which were stationed in the country after the suppression of the uprising led by Yihetuan, the turning over to the Chinese government of custom duties controlled by foreigners, or the elimination of foreign settlements and the humiliating terms of the "Final (Boxer) Protocol" of 1901.

In the foreign policy program of the Chinese League, which did not undergo any significant change after the 1911 Revolution, the revolutionaries tried to persuade foreign powers to observe neutrality toward the civil war in China and tried at any cost to prevent their intervention on the side of the Manchu government as well as their financing of counterrevolutionary forces. Spontaneous anti-imperialist sentiments of the first group of the Chinese people's national liberation movement were not reflected in the the program of the Chinese League, but some League members in the provinces took part in anti-imperialist boycotts of foreign goods and companies.

In the documents from before and during the revolution, we find repeated calls by the revolutionaries not to fight against foreigners; they also appealed to the foreign powers, pledging to observe all treaties and agreements concluded earlier by the Qing government, provided the powers refrained from rendering assistance to the Qing. Sun Yat-sen tried at all costs to prevent the powers from taking concerted actions on the side of the Qing, bearing in mind that it was only foreign help that saved the Manchu regime in 1860 and 1900. Between 1895 and 1911, Sun Yat-sen and the Chinese League were also limited to a certain extent in their anti-imperialist actions by the support of certain political circles in Japan, France, and England, which tried to use the Chinese revolutionaries in the interests of the internecine struggle of various imperialist groups in China. No resolute anti-imperialist actions were even provoked by the powers' undisguised interference in the talks between the north and the south in 1911 on the side of Yuan Shikai (the most popular leader of the Chinese feudals and compradors, who was given the post of the commander-in-chief of the imperial army by the Manchu rulers) and by the refusal of the Chinese maritime custom houses controlled by foreigners to transfer a part of the customs duties collected in central and eastern China to the provisional Nanjing government.

Documents and publications of the representatives of the various revolutionary democratic and, in particular, constitutional monarchist groups on the eve of the revolution sharply criticized the predatory policy of foreign states in China and the policy of depriving the people of their sovereign right to exploit their natural resources, to build railroads, etc. But it was ultimately the Qing government that was responsible for its own lack of desire or inability to oppose foreign penetration.

Sun Yat-sen and his comrades-in-arms failed to realize the real nature of the alliance between imperialist states and the reactionary Manchu regime. They relied on the possibility of non-interference by foreign states in the anti-Manchu revolution by making different kinds of promises.

The counterrevolutionary camp included Manchu court nobility, military leaders, landlords and servicemen of the so-called eight-banner troops, feudal bureaucratic and military strata, who loyally served the Qing regime, as well as Chinese feudals and compradors. It was inspired and guided by the imperialist states which rendered political, military, and financial support. The interference of imperialist states on the side of the Chinese feudal comprador reaction contributed largely to the defeat of the revolution.

Evident bankruptcy of the Manchu regime, nationwide revolutionary upsurge in China in summer and fall of 1911, the inability of the Qing government to meet the rising revolution, and the sharpening of differences between the major imperialist states on the eve of World War I—all this determined the wait-and-see tactics of the foreign powers during the first days of the Wuchang Uprising. The imperialist powers followed closely the revolutionary events, refraining from an active joint military support for the Qing government, though their preference and sympathies rested most certainly with the latter. The attitude of the powers during this stage of the uprising was affected to a certain degree by the foreign policy of Sun Yat-sen and the Chinese League, both before and during the revolution. But the events that followed showed that the hopes for a long-term effect of such a policy were illusory.

Although the rivalry between major imperialist powers prevented the staging of a joint intervention, political interference by the powers could not be averted. Japan actively supported the Qing monarchy, trying to persuade Russia to intervene jointly in order to restore the power of the Chinese emperor. Great Britain, France, the United States, and Germany did not consider it feasible to support the Qing and put their stakes on Yuan Shikai who deserted the Qing because of its failure to avert the revolution. They also established contacts with constitutional monarchy circles among the bourgeoisie and landlords.

The four-power bank consortium financed the government of Yuan Shikai (later Russia and Japan joined and the United States withdrew). The bank consortium pledged to grant Yuan Shikai a loan of six million pounds to finance the struggle against the revolutionary movement.

From the beginning of the 1911 Revolution onward, the imperialist powers recognized the Qing government and transferred to it the money collected by the foreign-controlled customs in the revolutionary provinces (thus depriving the revolutionary authorities of their main source of income). They amassed a large military and naval force in China (comprising 51 naval ships manned by 19,000 people), which impeded the activities of the revolutionary troops.

On November 30, a cease-fire between the Qing troops and the revolutionary army, mediated by the British consul, was concluded in Wuchang. On December 8, 1911, Tang Shaoyi, a Yuan Shikai emissary, arrived from Beijing to negotiate with the revolutionaries. He was to persuade them to agree to the establishment of a constitutional monarchy. Not trusting Li Yuanhong, commander of the revolutionary troops in Wuchang, representatives of the revolutionary provinces insisted on moving the peace talks to Shanghai. On December 20, 1911, the imperialist powers impudently intervened by sending a joint note through their consuls general in Shanghai. Addressed to the delegates of the north and the south at the peace conference, the note demanded an end to the conflict. In view of the blunt interference of the imperialist powers, who sided with the reactionary feudal and comprador forces rallying behind General Yuan Shikai, premier of the Qing government and troops commander, and due to the speedy retreat by liberal Chinese bourgeoisie and landlords, frightened by the mounting popular revolutionary activity, Sun Yat-sen had to relinquish his provisional presidency to Yuan who forced the Manchu court to decree the emperor's abdication and promised to introduce a republican administration in exchange for the action.

Having settled its disputes with Great Britain and Japan before the revolution in China got underway and preoccupied with European affairs, imperialist Russia did not interfere in China's domestic problems to the extent Great Britain, France, Germany, and the United States did. Noteworthy is the account A. Voznesensky, secretary of the Russian consulate to Hankou, made describing his talk with General Huang Xing, south China viceregent. Pointing out that for the survival of the Chinese republic Russia constituted no more danger than any other foreign power, Huang stressed that Russian influence on Chinese affairs was both favorable and desirable. "The activities of your consuls on the Yangzi during the revolution were sympathetic to the republican cause rather than not. We appreciate your assistance, and Russian tradesmen and tea merchants can take into account this friendly public attitude toward Russia."[1]

The bourgeois revolutionaries, who represented the more industrially developed provinces of east, south, and central China, compared to those in the north, expected to secure the majority of seats in the future parliament elected on the basis of the provisional Nanjing constitution and thus limit the power of Yuan Shikai and the feudal-landed and comprador-bureaucratic forces supporting him. But the attempt to limit the power of the reactionary forces by parliamentary means, without getting the broad masses involved in the struggle, came to naught. Having received a large loan from imperialist powers to suppress the revolution, Yuan Shikai launched an offensive: he dealt with the activists of the Nationalist party (Guomindang), created on August 25, 1912 after the dissolution of the Chinese League, and drowned in blood isolated revolutionary outbreaks of petty bourgeoisie, soldiers, and peasants from June to September 1913. This went down in the history of China as the "Second Revolution." The military dictatorship of Yuan Shikai, leader of the feudal landlords and comprador-bureaucratic forces of northern China and a group of the Beiyang (northern) clique nurtured by Yuan Shikai under the Qing regime, was firmly established in the country. Sun Yat-sen and other activists of the revolutionary wing of Chinese bourgeoisie were forced to emigrate.

As a result of the 1911 Revolution, the monarchist regime and the Manchu rule were overthrown, and the Chinese Republic was proclaimed. A provisional revolutionary government in Nanjing headed by Sun Yat-sen was established, and a provisional constitution drawn up. It was a bourgeois constitution which was progressive under the historical conditions of the time. The leaders of the revolution for a number of reasons did not set themselves the direct goal of anti-imperialist struggle but brought instead to the foreground the anti-Manchu slogan of national liberation. The bourgeoisie sought to destroy the Manchu feudal monarchy and to clear the path for a capitalist development in order to free the country from the imperialist yoke and make it an independent, sovereign state.

Thus it may be contended that the 1911 Revolution objectively was of both anti-feudal and anti-imperialist character. In the article "The Struggle of Parties in China," published in 1913, V. I. Lenin pointed out that the main weakness of the revolutionary party of Sun Yat-sen was that it failed to sufficiently involve broad masses of the Chinese people in the revolution.[2]

## Notes

1. *The 1911 Revolution: Collection of Documents and Materials* (in Russian) (Moscow: 1968), pp. 264–65.
2. V. I. Lenin, *The Complete Works* (in Russian), vol. 23, p. 139.

# Glossary

## People

| Pinyin | Wade-Giles | Chinese | Alternate name(s) |
|---|---|---|---|
| Ai Shi Ke | Ai-shih-kê | 哀時客 | Liang Qichao |
| Cai Gang | Ts'ai Kang | 蔡綱 | |
| Cai Jun | Ts'ai Chün | 蔡鈞 | |
| Cai Shaonan | Ts'ai Shao-nan | 蔡紹南 | |
| Cai Yuanpei | Ts'ai Yuan-p'ei | 蔡元培 | |
| Cao Du | Ts'ao Tu | 曹篤 | |
| Cao Rulin | Ts'ao Ju-lin | 曹汝霖 | |
| Chen Bingyu | Ch'ên Ping-yü | 陳炳燠 | |
| Chen Ce | Ch'ên Ts'ê | 陳策 | |
| Chen Chi | Ch'ên Ch'ih | 陳熾 | |
| Chen Du | Ch'ên Tu | 陳度 | |
| Chen Duxiu | Ch'ên Tu-hsiu | 陳獨秀 | |
| Chen Gan | Ch'ên Kan | 陳干 | |
| Chen Gaodi | Ch'ên Kao-ti | 陳高第 | |
| Chen Guohua | Ch'ên Kuo-hua | 陳國華 | |
| Chen Jingsong | Ch'ên Ching-sung | 陳景松 | |
| Chen Jiongming | Ch'ên Chiung-ming | 陳炯明 | |
| Chen Kongbo | Ch'ên K'ung-po | 陳孔伯 | |
| Chen Qimei | Ch'ên Ch'i-mei | 陳其美 | Chen Yingshi |
| Chen Qizhang | Ch'ên Ch'i-chang | 陳其璋 | |
| Chen Tianhua | Ch'ên T'ien-hua | 陳天華 ⎤ | |
| Chen Xingtai | Ch'ên Hsing-t'ai | 陳星台 ⎦ | |
| Chen Xulu | Ch'ên Hsü-lu | 陳旭麓 | |
| Chen Yanjie | Ch'ên Yen-chieh | 陳延階 | |
| Chen Yingshi | Ch'ên Ying-shih | 陳英士 | Chen Qimei |
| Chen Zhilin | Ch'ên Chih-lin | 陳之麟 | |

291

# GLOSSARY

| Pinyin | Wade-Giles | Chinese | Alternate name(s) |
|---|---|---|---|
| Chen Zuoxin | Ch'ên Tso-hsin | 陳作新 | |
| Cheng Dequan | Ch'êng Tê-ch'üan | 程德全 | |
| Cheng Jiasheng | Ch'êng Chia-shêng | 程家檉 | |
| Cheng Wenqing | Ch'êng Wên-ch'ing | 程文卿 | |
| Cheng Yingdu | Ch'êng Ying-tu | 程瑩度 | |
| Chu Fucheng | Ch'u Fu-ch'êng | 褚輔成 | |
| Cixi | Tz'ŭ-hsi | 慈禧 | |
| Dai Boxing | Tai Po-hsing | 載伯行 | |
| Deng Jingya | Têng Ching-ya | 鄧警亞 | |
| Deng Xiaoke | Têng Hsiao-k'ê | 鄧孝可 | |
| Ding Weifen | Ting Wei-fên | 丁惟汾 | |
| Ding Wenjiang | Ting Wên-chiang | 丁文江 | |
| Dong Hongyi | Tung Hung-i | 董鴻禕 | |
| Dong Xunshi | Tung Hsün-shih | 董恂士 | |
| Du Tou | Tu T'ou | 獨頭 | |
| Duan Qirui | Tuan Ch'i-jui | 段祺瑞 | |
| Fang Chaozhen | Fang Ch'ao-chên | 方潮珍 | |
| Fang Xieyin | Fang Hsieh-yin | 方燮尹 | |
| Fei Sheng | Fei Shêng | 飛生 | |
| Feng Weiying | Fêng Wei-ying | 馮爲瑩 | |
| Feng Ziyou | Fêng Tsu-yu | 馮自由 | |
| Fu Menghao | Fu Mêng-hao | 傅夢豪 | |
| Gao Jinzhou | Kao Chin-chou | 高錦舟 | |
| Gong Baoquan | Kung Pao-ch'üan | 龔寶銓 | |
| Gong Chuntai | Kung Ch'un-t'ai | 龔春台 | |
| Gong Ming | Kung Ming | 公明 | |
| Gong Yixing | Kung I-hsing | 龔翼星 | |
| Gu Jingzhai | Ku Ching-chai | 顧敬齋 | |
| Gu Naibin | Ku Nai-pin | 顧乃斌 | |
| Gu Zhongchen | Ku Chung-ch'ên | 顧忠琛 | |
| Guangxu | Kuang-hsü | 光緒 | |
| Guo Xiren | Kuo Hsi-jên | 郭希仁 | |
| Han Dengju | Han Têng-chü | 韓登舉 | |
| Hang Xinzhai | Hang Hsin-chai | 杭辛齋 | |
| He Haiqiao | Hê Hai-ch'iao | 何海樵 | |
| He Jinsheng | Hê Chin-shêng | 賀金聲 | |
| He Wei | Hê Wei | 何畏 | |
| Hong Ruchong | Hung Ju-ch'ung | 洪汝冲 | |
| Hu Gongxian | Hu Kung-hsien | 胡恭先 | |

# PEOPLE

| Pinyin | Wade-Giles | Chinese | Alternate name(s) |
|---|---|---|---|
| Hu Hanmin | Hu Han-min | 胡漢民 | |
| Hu Shengwu | Hu Shêng-wu | 胡繩武 | |
| Hu Sijing | Hu Ssǔ-ching | 胡思敬 | |
| Huang Dezhao | Huang Tê-chao | 黃德昭 | |
| Huang Di | Huang Ti | 黃帝 | |
| Huang Jialiang | Huang Chia-liang | 黃嘉梁 | |
| Huang Jilu | Huang Chi-lu | 黃季陸 | |
| Huang Jinshen | Huang Chin-shên | 黃晉紳 | |
| Huang Keqiang | Huang K'ê-ch'iang | 黃克強 | Huang Xing |
| Huang Rong | Huang Jung | 黃鎔 | |
| Huang Shou | Huang Shou | 黃綬 | |
| Huang Xing | Huang Hsing | 黃興 | Huang Keqiang |
| Huang Zhenya | Huang Chên-ya | 黃振亞 | |
| Huang Zhonghao | Huang Chung-hao | 黃忠浩 | |
| Huang Zongxian | Huang Tsung-hsien | 黃宗憲 | |
| Jiang Guilin | Chiang Kui-lin | 蔣貴麟 | |
| Jiang Xifan | Chiang Hsi-fan | 蔣洗凡 | |
| Jiang Yansheng | Chiang Yen-shêng | 蔣衍升 | |
| Jiao Dafeng | Chiao Ta-fêng | 焦達峯 | |
| Jin Chongji | Chin Ch'ung-chi | 金冲及 | |
| Jin Dingxun | Chin Ting-hsün | 金鼎勛 | |
| Jin Tianhe | Chin T'ien-hê | 金天翮 | |
| Jin Yi | Chin I | 金一 | |
| Jing Chang | Ching Ch'ang | 兢廠 | |
| Jing Dingcheng | Ching Ting-ch'êng | 景定成 | Lei Chou |
| Jing Meijiu | Ching Mei-chiu | 景梅九 | |
| Jing Yaoyue | Ching Yao-yüeh | 景耀月 | |
| Kang Nanhai | K'ang Nan-hai | 康南海 | |
| Kang Youwei | K'ang Yu-Wei | 康有爲 | |
| Lei Chou | Lei Ch'ou | 壘仇 | Jing Dingcheng |
| Lei Peihong | Lei Pei-hung | 雷沛鴻 | |
| Lei Zaihan | Lei Tsai-han | 雷在漢 | |
| Li Bodong | Li Po-tung | 李伯東 | |
| Li Hongzhang | Li Hung-chang | 李鴻章 | |
| Li Huaishuang | Li Huai-shuang | 李懷霜 | |
| Li Jingxi | Li Ching-hsi | 李經羲 | |
| Li Pingshu | Li P'ing-shu | 李平書 | |

| Pinyin | Wade-Giles | Chinese | Alternate name(s) |
|---|---|---|---|
| Li Risheng | Li Jih-shêng | 李日生 | |
| Li Shaoling | Li Shao-ling | 李少陵 | |
| Li Shengduo | Li Shêng-to | 李盛鐸 | |
| Li Shiyue | Li Shih-yüeh | 李時岳 | |
| Li Xiehe | Li Hsieh-hê | 李協和 | |
| Li Xin | Li Hsin | 李新 | |
| Li Yuanhong | Li Yüan-hung | 黎元洪 | |
| Li Zhaofu | Li Chao-fu | 李肇甫 | |
| Liang Qichao | Liang Ch'ih-ch'ao | 梁啓超 | Ai Shi Ke |
| Liang Renjiang | Liang Jên-chiang | 梁任江 | Reng Gong |
| Liang Shanji | Liang Shan-chi | 梁善濟 | |
| Liao Shoufeng | Liao Shou-fêng | 廖壽豐 | |
| Liao Yuchun | Liao Yü-ch'un | 廖宇春 | |
| Liao Zhongkai | Liao Chung-k'ai | 廖仲愷 | |
| Lin Duanfu | Lin Tuan-fu | 林端輔 | |
| Lin Jinzhi | Lin Chin-chih | 林金枝 | |
| Lin Jiqing | Lin Chi-ch'ing | 林濟青 | |
| Lin Shishuang | Lin Shih-shuang | 林時塽 | |
| Lin Wen | Lin Wên | 林文 | |
| Lin Yancun | Lin Yen-ts'un | 林演存 | |
| Liu Chenglie | Liu Ch'êng-lieh | 柳成烈 | |
| Liu Chengyu | Liu Ch'êng-yü | 劉成禺 | |
| Liu Daoyi | Liu Tao-i | 劉道一 | |
| Liu Jiyan | Liu Chi-yen | 劉基炎 | |
| Liu Kuiyi | Liu K'ui-i | 劉揆一 | |
| Liu Kunyi | Liu K'un-i | 劉坤一 | |
| Liu Shipei | Liu Shih-p'ei | 劉師培 | |
| Liu Tong | Liu T'ung | 劉通 | |
| Liu Yang | Liu Yang | 劉揚 | |
| Liu Yuezhen | Liu Yüeh-chen | 劉約眞 | |
| Liu Yuguang | Liu Yü-kuang | 劉裕光 | |
| Liu Zuyin | Liu Tsu-yin | 劉祖蔭 | |
| Long Jiguang | Lung Chi-kuang | 龍濟光 | |
| Long Mingjian | Lung Ming-chiên | 龍鳴劍 | |
| Lu Hanchang | Lu Han-ch'ang | 蘆韓昌 | |
| Lu Xun | Lu Hsün | 魯迅 | Zhou Shuren |
| Lu Yafa | Lu Ya-fa | 陸亞發 | |
| Luo Futian | Lo Fu-t'ien | 羅福田 | |
| Luo Jialun | Lo Chia-lun | 羅家倫 | |

# PEOPLE

| Pinyin | Wade-Giles | Chinese | Alternate name(s) |
|---|---|---|---|
| Luo Lun | Lo Lun | 羅倫 | |
| Luo Runzhang | Lo Jun-chang | 羅潤璋 | |
| Luo Zhenyu | Lo Chên-yu | 羅振玉 | |
| Lu Haihuan | Lü Hai-huan | 呂海寰 | |
| Lu Hesheng | Lü Hê-shêng | 呂和聲 | |
| Ma Fuyi | Ma Fu-i | 馬福益 | |
| Ma Junwu | Ma Chün-wu | 馬君武 | |
| Ma Xiangbo | Ma Hsiang-po | 馬湘伯 | |
| Mai Menghua | Mai Mêng-hua | 麥夢華 | Shangxinren |
| Mao Zedong | Mao Tsê-tung | 毛澤東 | |
| Mei Xin | Mei Hsin | 梅馨 | |
| Ming Shaozhen | Ming Shao-chên | 明少貞 | |
| Mo Bei | Mo Pei | 墨悲 | |
| Ning Wu | Ning Wu | 寧武 | |
| Niu Yongjian | Niu Yung-chien | 鈕永建 | |
| Nong Jingsun | Nung Ching-sun | 農勁蓀 | |
| Nong Zhu | Nung Chu | 農竹 | |
| Ou Jujia | Ou Chü-chia | 歐榘甲 | |
| Pan Peizhu | P'an P'ei-chu | 潘佩珠 | Phan Bôi Châu (Vietnamese) |
| Pan Xunchu | P'an Hsün-ch'u | 潘訓初 | |
| Pan Yueqiao | P'an Yüeh-ch'iao | 潘月樵 | |
| Pan Zuyi | P'an Tsu-i | 潘祖彝 | |
| Pu Dianjun | P'u Tien-chün | 蒲殿俊 | |
| Qin Tieshan | Ch'in T'ieh-shan | 秦鐵珊 | |
| Qin Yuliu | Ch'in Yü-liu | 秦毓鎏 | |
| Qin Zaigeng | Ch'in Tsai-kêng | 秦載賡 | |
| Qiu Jin | Ch'iu Chin | 秋瑾 | |
| Qu Fangmei | Ch'ü Fang-mei | 瞿方梅 | |
| Qu Shaoyi | Ch'ü Shao-i | 瞿紹伊 | |
| Ren Gong | Jên Kung | 任公 | Liang Qichao |
| Sanduo | San-to | 三多 | |
| Sang Dansheng | Sang Tan-shêng | 桑丹生 | |
| Sanhuyimin | San-hu-i-min | 三戶遺民 | Yang Yulin |
| Shangwusheng | Shang-wu-shêng | 尚武生 | |
| Shangxinren | Shang-hsin-jên | 傷心人 | Mai Menghua |
| Shen Lianfang | Shên Lien-fang | 沈蓮芳 | |
| Shen Manyun | Shên Man-yün | 沈縵雲 | |

| Pinyin | Wade-Giles | Chinese | Alternate name(s) |
|---|---|---|---|
| Shen Tong | Shên T'ung | 沈桐 | |
| Shen Weibin | Shên Wei-pin | 沈渭濱 | |
| Shen Yunsun | Shên Yün-sun | 沈雲蓀 | |
| Shen Zhongli | Shên Chung-li | 沈仲禮 | |
| Shen Zuxian | Shên Tsu-hsien | 沈祖憲 | |
| Sheng Xuanhuai | Shêng Hsüan-huai | 盛宣懷 | |
| Shi Jialin | Shih Chia-lin | 史家麟 | |
| Song Bolu | Sung Po-lu | 宋伯魯 | |
| Song Jiaoren | Sung Chiao-jên | 宋敎仁 | Yufu |
| Song Yuanyuan | Sung Yüan-yüan | 宋淵源 | |
| Song Zhenlü | Sung Chên-lü | 宋振呂 | |
| Su Peng | Su P'êng | 蘇鵬 | |
| Su Shaolou | Su Shao-lou | 蘇少樓 | |
| Sun Anren | Sun An-jên | 孫安仁 | |
| Sun Baoqi | Sun Pao-ch'i | 孫寶琦 | |
| Sun Sibai | Sun Ssŭ-pai | 孫思白 | |
| Sun Wen | Sun Wên | 孫文 | |
| Sun Yixian | Sun I-hsien | 孫逸仙 | Sun Yat-sen |
| Sun Zhongshan | Sun Chung-shan | 孫中山 | |
| Tan Bian | T'an Pi-an | 譚彼岸 | |
| Tan Renfeng | T'an Jên-fêng | 譚人鳳 | |
| Tan Yankai | T'an Yen-k'ai | 譚延闓 | |
| Tang Caichang | T'ang Ts'ai-ch'ang | 唐才常 | |
| Tang Jiaodun | T'ang Chiao-tun | 湯覺頓 | |
| Tang Qunying | T'ang Ch'ün-ying | 唐群英 | |
| Tang Shaoyi | T'ang Shao-i | 唐紹儀 | |
| Tang Shouqian | T'ang Shou-ch'ien | 湯壽潛 | |
| Tang Zhijun | T'ang Chih-chün | 湯志鈞 | |
| Tang Zongyao | T'ang Tsung-yao | 唐宗堯 | |
| Tao Chengzhang | T'ao Ch'êng-chang | 陶成章 | |
| Tong Bichen | T'ung Pi-ch'ên | 童弼臣 | |
| Wang Baozhen | Wang Pao-chên | 王葆眞 | |
| Wang Daxie | Wang Ta-hsieh | 汪大燮 | |
| Wang Dianyang | Wang Tien-yang | 王殿颺 | |
| Wang Hanliang | Wang Han-liang | 王漢良 | |
| Wang Jiaju | Wang Chia-chü | 王嘉榘 | Wang Weiren |
| Wang Jingfang | Wang Ching-fang | 王景芳 | |
| Wang Jingfang | Wang Ching-fang | 王敬芳 | |
| Wang Jingwei | Wang Ching-wei | 汪精衛 | |

# PEOPLE

| Pinyin | Wade-Giles | Chinese | Alternate name(s) |
|---|---|---|---|
| Wang Jiuling | Wang Chiu-ling | 王九齡 | |
| Wang Ming | Wang Ming | 王明 | |
| Wang Qi | Wang Ch'i | 王起 | |
| Wang Quyu | Wang Ch'ü-yü | 王渠玉 | |
| Wang Shilin | Wang Shih-lin | 王石麟 | |
| Wang Shuhuai | Wang Shu-huai | 王樹槐 | |
| Wang Tianjie | Wang T'ien-chieh | 王天傑 | |
| Wang Weiren | Wang Wei-jên | 王偉人 | Wang Jiaju |
| Wang Xiong | Wang Hsiung | 王雄 | |
| Wang Yangming | Wang Yang-ming | 王陽明 | |
| Wang Yongbin | Wang Yung-pin | 王用賓 | |
| Wang Yongqin | Wang Yung-ch'in | 王詠琴 | |
| Wang You | Wang Yu | 王猷 | |
| Wang Ziyi | Wang Tsu-i | 汪子宜 | |
| Wen Fei | Wên Fei | 文斐 | |
| Wen Jingwei | Wên Ching-wei | 文經緯 | |
| Wen Ti | Wên T'i | 文悌 | |
| Weng Tonghe | Wêng T'ung-hê | 翁同龢 | |
| Wu Juting | Wu Chü-t'ing | 吳菊庭 | |
| Wu Shuzhen | Wu Shu-chên | 吳書箴 | |
| Wu Tingfang | Wu T'ing-fang | 伍廷芳 | |
| Wu Xiangxiang | Wu Hsiang-hsiang | 吳相湘 | |
| Wu Yuzhang | Wu Yü-chang | 吳玉章 | |
| Wu Zhongqiu | Wu Chung-ch'iu | 吳鐘秋 | |
| Wu Zuolin | Wu Tso-lin | 吳作霖 | |
| Xi Yanggao | Hsi Yang-kao | 席仰高 | |
| Xia Chao | Hsia Ch'ao | 夏超 | |
| Xia Yueshan | Hsia Yüeh-shan | 夏月珊 | |
| Xia Zhongmin | Hsia Chung-min | 夏重民 | |
| Xiang Chu | Hsiang Ch'u | 向楚 | |
| Xiao Can | Hsiao Ts'an | 蕭參 | |
| Xiao Deming | Hsiao Tê-ming | 蕭德明 | |
| Xiao Focheng | Hsiao Fo-ch'êng | 蕭佛成 | |
| Xiao Xingtai | Hsiao Hsing-t'ai | 逍星台 | |
| Xie Ronglu | Hsieh Jung-lu | 解榮路 | |
| Xie Yingbo | Hsieh Ying-po | 謝英伯 | |
| Xiong Kewu | Hsiung K'ê-wu | 熊克武 | |
| Xiong Yueshan | Hsiung Yüeh-shan | 熊越山 | |
| Xu Banhou | Hsü Pan-hou | 徐班侯 | |

| Pinyin | Wade-Giles | Chinese | Alternate name(s) |
|---|---|---|---|
| Xu Jiqing | Hsü Chi-ch'ing | 徐際青 | |
| Xu Lian | Hsü Lien | 徐濂 | |
| Xu Qin | Hsü Ch'in | 徐懃 | |
| Xu Rongpu | Hsü Jung-p'u | 徐榕圃 | |
| Xu Yaoyuan | Hsü Yao-yüan | 徐耀遠 | |
| Yan Fu | Yen Fu | 嚴復 | |
| Yan Zhongwen | Yen Chung-wên | 顏仲文 | |
| Yang Boqian | Yang Po-ch'ien | 楊伯謙 | |
| Yang Dazhu | Yang Ta-chu | 楊大鑄 | |
| Yang Du | Yang Tu | 楊度 | |
| Yang Dusheng | Yang Tu-shêng | 楊篤生 | |
| Yang Liqiang | Yang Li-ch'iang | 楊立強 | |
| Yang Mianzhai | Yang Mien-chai | 楊勉齋 | Yang Yuan-mao |
| Yang Pusheng | Yang P'u-shêng | 楊譜笙 | |
| Yang Qianli | Yang Ch'ien-li | 楊千里 | |
| Yang Shenxiu | Yang Shên-hsiu | 楊深秀 | |
| Yang Shukan | Yang Shu-k'an | 楊庶堪 | |
| Yang Wending | Yang Wên-ting | 楊文鼎 | |
| Yang Xinzhi | Yang Hsin-chih | 楊信之 | |
| Yang Yuanmao | Yang Yüan-mao | 楊源懋 | Yang Mianzhai |
| Yang Yulin | Yang Yü-lin | 楊毓麟 | Sanhuyimin |
| Yang Zhenhong | Yang Chên-hung | 楊振鴻 | |
| Yang Zhongshi | Yang Chung-shih | 楊仲笹 | |
| Ye Huijun | Yeh Hui-chün | 葉惠鈞 | |
| Yi Zongxi | I Tsung-hsi | 易宗羲 | |
| Yin Chengxian | Yin Ch'êng-hsien | 殷承瓛 | |
| Yin Ruizhi | Yin Jui-chih | 尹銳志 | |
| Yin Weijun | Yin Wei-chün | 尹維俊 | |
| You Jiyun | Yu Chi-yün | 由霽雲 | |
| Yu Zuomin | Yü Tso-min | 餘作民 | |
| Yuan Linge | Yüan Lin-kê | 袁麟閣 | |
| Yuan Shikai | Yüan Shih-k'ai | 袁世凱 | |
| Yuan Shuxun | Yüan Shu-hsün | 袁樹勳 | |
| Yufu | Yü-fu | 漁父 | Song Jiaoren |
| Zeng Guofan | Tsêng Kuo-fan | 曾國藩 | |
| Zeng Yun | Tsêng Yün | 增韞 | |
| Zeng Zemin | Tsêng Tsê-min | 曾澤民 | |

# PEOPLE

| Pinyin | Wade-Giles | Chinese | Alternate name(s) |
|---|---|---|---|
| Zeng Zhaolu | Tsêng Chao-lu | 曾昭魯 | |
| Zhang Binglin | Chang ping-lin | 章炳麟 | Zhang Taiyuan |
| Zhang Dayi | Chang Ta-i | 張大義 | |
| Zhang Huchen | Chang Hu-ch'ên | 張虎臣 | |
| Zhang Ji | Chang Chi | 張繼 | |
| Zhang Maolong | Chang Mao-lung | 張懋隆 | |
| Zhang Muliang | Chang Mu-liang | 張木良 | Zhang Zi |
| Zhang Peijue | Chang Pei-chüe | 張培爵 | |
| Zhang Peiyi | Chang P'ei-i | 章佩乙 | |
| Zhang Pengyuan | Chang P'êng-yuan | 張朋園 | |
| Zhang Runsan | Chang Jun-san | 張潤三 | |
| Zhang Taiyan | Chang T'ai-yen | 章太炎 | Zhang Binglin |
| Zhang Weihua | Chang Wei-hua | 張維華 | |
| Zhang Xun | Chang Hsün | 張勳 | |
| Zhang Yi | Chang I | 張頤 | |
| Zhang Zaimin | Chang Tsai-min | 章在民 | |
| Zhang Zhenkun | Chang Chên-k'un | 張振鵾 | |
| Zhang Zhidong | Chang Chih-tung | 張之洞 | |
| Zhang Zhijing | Chang Chih-ching | 張知竟 | |
| Zhang Zhuofu | Chang Cho-fu | 張卓甫 | |
| Zhang Zi | Chang Tzu | 章梓 | Zhang Muliang |
| Zhao Erfeng | Chao Êrh-fêng | 趙爾豐 | |
| Zhao Shen | Chao Shên | 趙伸 | |
| Zhao Sheng | Chao Shêng | 趙聲 | |
| Zheng Guanying | Chêng Kuan-ying | 鄭觀應 | |
| Zheng Quan | Chêng Ch'üan | 鄭權 | |
| Zheng Zhongjing | Chêng Chung-ching | 鄭仲敬 | |
| Zheng Zuyin | Chêng Tsu-yin | 鄉祖蔭 | |
| Zhou Enlai | Chou Ên-lai | 周恩來 | |
| Zhou Jianlong | Chou Chien-lung | 周建龍 | |
| Zhou Laisu | Chou Lai-su | 周來蘇 | |
| Zhou Shubiao | Chou Shu-piao | 周樹標 | |
| Zhou Shuren | Chou Shu-jên | 周樹人 | Lu Xun |
| Zhu Bowei | Chu Po-wei | 朱伯爲 | |
| Zhu Guangfeng | Chu Kuang-fêng | 朱光鳳 | |
| Zhu Guochen | Chu Kuo-ch'ên | 朱國琛 | |
| Zhu Shaoping | Chu Shao-p'ing | 朱少屏 | |

| Pinyin | Wade-Giles | Chinese |
|---|---|---|
| Zhu Tengfang | Chu T'êng-fang | 朱騰芳 |
| Zhu Yuanzhang | Chu Yüan-chang | 朱元璋 |
| Zhu Zhihong | Chu Chih-hung | 朱之洪 |
| Zou Daifan | Tsou Tai-fan | 鄒代藩 |
| Zou Lu | Tsou Lu | 鄒魯 |
| Zou Rong | Tsou Jung | 鄒容 |

## Places

| | | |
|---|---|---|
| Anhui | Anhui (Anhwei) | 安徽 |
| Baoqing | Paoch'ing | 寶慶 |
| Baxian | Pahsien | 巴縣 |
| Beihai | Peihai | 北海 |
| Beijing | Peiching (Peking) | 北京 |
| Cangqianshan | Ts'angch'ienshan | 倉前山 |
| Changde | Ch'angtê | 常德 |
| Changsha | Ch'angsha | 長沙 |
| Changzhou | Ch'angchou | 常州 |
| Chengdu | Ch'êngtu | 成都 |
| Chenzhou | Ch'ênchou | 辰州 |
| Chongqing | Ch'ungch'ing | 重慶 |
| Chuanshating | Ch'uanshat'ing | 川沙廳 |
| Chuzhou | Ch'uchou | 處州 |
| Dalian | Talien | 大連 |
| Damalu | Tamalu | 大馬路 |
| Dantu | Tant'u | 丹徒 |
| Danyang | Tanyang | 丹陽 |
| Dongbei | Tungpei | 東北 |
| Dongwan | Tungwan | 東莞 |
| Eluosi | Êlossŭ | 俄羅斯 |
| Fujian | Fuchien (Fukien) | 福建 |
| Fuzhou | Fuchou (Foochow) | 福州 |
| Gansu | Kansu | 甘肅 |
| Guangdong | Kuangtung (Kwangtung) | 廣東 |
| Guangxi | Kuanghsi (Kwangsi) | 廣西 |
| Guangzhou | Kuangchou (Canton) | 廣州 |
| Guilin | Kuilin (Kweilin) | 桂林 |
| Guizhou | Kuichou (Kweichow) | 貴州 |
| Haerbin | Haêrpin (Harbin) | 哈爾濱 |

## PLACES

| Pinyin | Wade-Giles | Chinese |
|---|---|---|
| Haining | Haining | 海寧 |
| Hangzhou | Hangchou (Hangchow) | 杭州 |
| Hankou | Hank'ou (Hankow) | 漢口 |
| Hebei | Hêpei (Hopei) | 河北 |
| Heilongjiang | Heilungchiang | 黑龍江 |
| Henan | Hênan | 河南 |
| Hengzhou | Hêngchou | 衡州 |
| Hu | Hu | 滬 |
| Huanghuagang | Huanghuakang | 黃花崗 |
| Hubei | Hupei | 湖北 |
| Hunan | Hunan | 湖南 |
| Huzhou | Huchou | 湖州 |
| Jiading | Chiating | 嘉定 |
| Jiandao | Chientao | 間島 |
| Jiangsu | Chiangsu (Kiangsu) | 江蘇 |
| Jiangxi | Chianghsi (Kiangsi) | 江西 |
| Jiangyin | Chiangyin | 江陰 |
| Jianou | Chienou | 建甌 |
| Jiaozhou | Chiaochou (Kiaochow) | 膠州 |
| Jiaozuo | Chiaotso | 焦作 |
| Jiashan | Chiashan | 嘉善 |
| Jiaxing | Chiahsing | 嘉興 |
| Jilin | Chilin (Kirin) | 吉林 |
| Jintan | Chint'an | 金壇 |
| Jiujiang | Chiuchiang (Kiukiang) | 九江 |
| Kaifeng | K'aifêng | 開封 |
| Kunming | K'unming | 昆明 |
| Leshan | Leshan | 樂山 |
| Liangshanpo | Liangshanp'o | 梁山泊 |
| Liaodong | Liaotung | 遼東 |
| Liaoning | Liaoning | 遼寧 |
| Liling | Liling | 醴陵 |
| Liuyang | Liuyang | 瀏陽 |
| Liyang | Liyang | 溧陽 |
| Luoquanjing | Loch'üanching | 羅泉井 |
| Maoshan | Maoshan | 茅山 |
| Meishan | Meishan | 眉山 |
| Menggu | Mêngku | 蒙古 |
| Nanjing | Nanching (Nanking) | 南京 |
| Nanning | Nanning | 南寧 |

| Pinyin | Wade-Giles | Chinese |
|---|---|---|
| Nicheng | Nich'êng | 泥成 |
| Ningbo | Ningpo (Ningpoo) | 寧波 |
| Pengshan | P'êngshan | 彭山 |
| Pianma | P'ienma | 片馬 |
| Pingxiang | P'inghsiang | 萍鄉 |
| Puguo | P'ukuo | 普國 |
| Pukou | P'uk'ou | 浦口 |
| Qiaonan | Ch'iaonan | 橋南 |
| Qingshen | Ch'ingshên | 青神 |
| Quzhou | Ch'üchou | 衢州 |
| Rongxian | Junghsien | 榮縣 |
| Shaanxi | Shenhsi | 陝西 |
| Shahe | Shahê | 沙河 |
| Shandong | Shantung | 山東 |
| Shanghai | Shanghai | 上海 |
| Shanxi | Shanhsi | 山西 |
| Shaowu | Shaowu | 邵武 |
| Shaoxing | Shaohsing | 紹興 |
| Shaoyang | Shaoyang | 邵陽 |
| Shengxian | Shênghsien | 嵊縣 |
| Shimen | Shihmen | 石門 |
| Sichuan | Ssŭch'uan (Szechuan) | 四川 |
| Songfeng | Sungfêng | 松風 |
| Suzhou | Suchou | 蘇州 |
| Taibei | T'aipei | 台北 |
| Taizhou | T'aichou | 台州 |
| Taoyuan | T'aoyuan | 桃源 |
| Tianjin | T'ienchin (Tientsin) | 天津 |
| Tongxiang | T'unghsiang | 桐鄉 |
| Weihaiwei | Weihaiwei | 威海衛 |
| Wuchang | Wuch'ang | 武昌 |
| Wuxi | Wuhsi | 無錫 |
| Xianggang | Hsiangkang (Hong Kong) | 香港 |
| Xiangxiang | Hsianghsiang | 湘鄉 |
| Xiaoshan | Hsiaoshan | 蕭山 |
| Xinchang | Hsinch'ang | 新昌 |
| Xinjiang | Hsinchiang (Sinkiang) | 新疆 |
| Xinning | Hsinning | 新寧 |
| Yangzhou | Yangchou | 揚州 |
| Yangzi | Yangtzu | 揚子 |

| Pinyin | Wade-Giles | Chinese |
|---|---|---|
| Yanping | Yenp'ing | 延平 |
| Yanzhou | Yenchou | 嚴州 |
| Yili | Ili | 伊犁 |
| Yingkou | Yingk'ou (Yingkow) | 營口 |
| Yixing | Yihsing | 宜興 |
| Youyang | Yoyang | 酉陽 |
| Yue | Yüeh | 粵 |
| Yuenan | Yüehnan | 越南 |
| Yuezhou | Yüehchou | 岳州 |
| Yunnan | Yünnan | 雲南 |
| Zhabei | Chapei | 閘北 |
| Zhangyuan | Changyüan | 張園 |
| Zhejiang | Chêchiang (Chekiang) | 浙江 |
| Zhenjiang | Chênchiang | 鎮江 |
| Zhongguo | Chungkuo | 中國 |
| Zhuji | Chuchi | 諸暨 |
| Zizhou | Tzuchou | 資州 |

## Organizations

| | | |
|---|---|---|
| Baoguohui | Paokuohui | 保國會 |
| Changlun sichang | Changlun ssŭch'ang | 長綸絲廠 |
| Dadaohui | Tataohui | 大刀會 |
| Gedihui | Kêtihui | 哥弟會 |
| Gelaohui | Kêlaohui | 哥老會 |
| Gemingdang | Kêmingtang | 革命黨 |
| Gemingjun | Kêmingchün | 革命軍 |
| Gongheyong sichang | Kunghêyüng ssŭch'ang | 公和永絲廠 |
| Gongjinhui | Kungchinhui | 共進會 |
| Gongping yanghang | Kungp'ing yanghang | 公平洋行 |
| Guanbaoju | Kuanpaochü | 官報局 |
| Guangfuhui | Kuangfuhui | 光復會 |
| Guojiadanganju | Kuochiatanganchü | 國家檔案局 |
| Guomindang | Kuomintang | 國民黨 |
| Guominjun | Kuominchün | 國民軍 |
| Guozijian | Kuotzuchien | 國子監 |
| Hongbang | Hungpang | 紅幫 |

# GLOSSARY

| Pinyin | Wade-Giles | Chinese |
|---|---|---|
| Hongdenghui | Hungtênghui | 紅燈會 |
| Hongjianghui | Hungchianghui | 洪江會 |
| Huaxinghui | Huahsinghui | 華興會 |
| huidang | huitang | 會黨 |
| Hujun dudufu | Huchün tutufu | 滬軍都督府 |
| Jinchang sichang | Chinch'ang ssŭch'ang | 晉昌糸廠 |
| Jinhua sichang | Chinhua ssŭch'ang | 錦華糸廠 |
| Ju-E yiyongdui | Chu-Ê iyungtui | 拒俄義勇隊 |
| Junguomin jiaoyuhui | Chünkuomin chiaoyühui | 軍國民教育會 |
| Minyidang | Minitang | 民意黨 |
| Qichang yanghang | Ch'ich'ang yanghang | 旗昌洋行 |
| Qingbang | Ch'ingpang | 青幫 |
| Qingnianhui | Ch'ingnienhui | 青年會 |
| Renmin chubanshe | Jênmin ch'upanshê | 人民出版社 |
| Santianhui | Sant'ienhui | 三天會 |
| Sijianye gongsuo | Ssŭchienyeh kungso | 糸繭業公所 |
| Siye huiguan | Ssŭyeh huikuan | 糸業會館 |
| Taixingxiang | T'aihsinghsiang | 泰興祥 |
| Tongchouhui | T'ungch'ouhui | 同仇會 |
| Tongkangtai sichang | T'ungk'angt'ai ssŭch'ang | 同康泰糸廠 |
| Tongmenghui | T'ungmênghui | 同盟會 |
| Tongrengonghui | T'ungjênkunghui | 同仁公會 |
| Tongzhijun | T'ungchihchün | 同志軍 |
| Weixinhui | Weihsinhui | 維新會 |
| Wenputong zhongxuetang | Wênput'ung chunghsüehtang | 文普通中學堂 |
| Xianyouhui | Hsienyuhui | 憲友會 |
| Xiehe sichang | Hsiehê ssŭch'ang | 協和糸廠 |
| Xin Yuenan gongxianhui | Hsin Yüehnan kunghsienhui | 新越南公憲會 |
| Xinchangheng sichang | Hsinch'anghêng ssŭch'ang | 信昌恒糸廠 |
| Xingzhonghui | Hsingchunghui | 興中會 |
| Xueshengjun | Hsüehshêngchün | 學生軍 |
| Xuwudang | Hsüwutang | 虛無黨 |
| Yanhengchang | Yenhêngch'ang | 延恒昌糸廠 |

| Pinyin | Wade-Giles | Chinese |
|---|---|---|
| sichang | ssǔch'ang | |
| Yazhou heqinhui | Yachou hêch'inhui | 亞州和親會 |
| Yihe yanghang | Ihê yanghang | 怡和洋行 |
| Yihetuan | Ihêtuan | 義和團 |
| Yishuju | Ishuchü | 譯書局 |
| Zhangjiang shuyuan | Changchiang shuyüan | 漳江書院 |
| Zhenhuaxingyahui | Chênhuahsingyahui | 振華興亞會 |
| Zhongguoguominhui | Chungkuokuominhui | 中國國民會 |
| Zhongguoshixuehui | Chungkuoshihhsüehhui | 中國史學會 |
| Zhonghua shuju | Chunghua shuchü | 中華書局 |
| Zhonghuaminguogongdang | Chunghuaminkuokungtang | 中華民國工黨 |
| Ziyiju | Tzuichü | 諮議局 |
| Zizhengyuan | Tzuchêngyüan | 資政院 |

## Publications

| | | |
|---|---|---|
| *Anhui suhuabao* | *Anhui suhuapao* | 安徽俗話報 |
| *Dajiang bao* | *Tachiang pao* | 大江報 |
| *Dalu zazhi* | *Talu tsachih* | 大陸雜誌 |
| *Dongfang zazhi* | *Tungfang tsachih* | 東方雜誌 |
| *Guomin bao* | *Kuomin pao* | 國民報 |
| *Guowen bao* | *Kuowen pao* | 國聞報 |
| *Hansheng* | *Hanshêng* | 漢聲 |
| *Huaxian xinbao* | *Huahsien hsinpao* | 華暹新報 |
| *Hubei xueshengjie* | *Hupei hsüehshêng chieh* | 湖北學生界 |
| *Jianyan bao* | *Chienyen pao* | 建言報 |
| *Jincheng* | *Chinch'êng* | 晉乘 |
| *Jingzhong ribao* | *Chingchung jihpao* | 警鐘日報 |
| *Kaizhi lu* | *K'aichih lu* | 開智錄 |
| *Lishi yanjiu* | *Lishih yenchiu* | 歷史研究 |
| *Min bao* | *Min pao* | 民報 |
| *Minli bao* | *Minli pao* | 民立報 |
| *Pingmin ribao* | *P'ingmin jihpao* | 平民日報 |
| *Qiangguo gongbao* | *Ch'iangkuo kungpao* | 強國公報 |
| *Qingyi bao* | *Ch'ingi pao* | 清議報 |

| Pinyin | Wade-Giles | Chinese |
|---|---|---|
| *Shang bao* | *Shang pao* | 商報 |
| *Shanghai dalubao* | *Shanghai talupao* | 上海大陸報 |
| *Shenzhou ribao* | *Shênchou jihpao* | 神州日報 |
| *Shiwu bao* | *Shihwu pao* | 時務報 |
| *Su bao* | *Su pao* | 蘇報 |
| *Tianyi bao* | *T'ieni pao* | 天義報 |
| *Wanguo gongbao* | *Wankuo kungpao* | 萬國公報 |
| *Xinmin congbao* | *Hsinmin ts'ungpao* | 新民叢報 |
| *Youxue yibian* | *Yuhsüeh ipien* | 遊學譯編 |
| *Yunnan zazhi* | *Yünnan tsachih* | 雲南雜誌 |
| *Zhejiang chao* | *Chêchiang ch'ao* | 浙江潮 |
| *Zhixin bao* | *Chihhsin pao* | 知新報 |
| *Zhongguo baihuabao* | *Chungkuo paihuapao* | 中國白話報 |
| *Zhongguo ribao* | *Chungkuo jihpao* | 中國日報 |
| *Zhongxing ribao* | *Chunghsing jihpao* | 中興日報 |

## Others

| Pinyin | Wade-Giles | Chinese |
|---|---|---|
| Bairi weixin | Paijih weihsin | 百日維新 |
| Beiyang | Peiyang | 北洋 |
| Dingyou | Tingyu | 丁酉 |
| fen | fên | 分 |
| guanbi minbian | kuanpi minpien | 官逼民變 |
| guandu shangban | kuantu shangpan | 官督商辦 |
| Guisi | Kuissŭ | 癸巳 |
| Han | Han | 漢 |
| hebang | hêpang | 合邦 |
| Hui | Hui | 回 |
| jianhang | chienhang | 繭行 |
| jianjuan | chienchüan | 繭捐 |
| jiao | chiao | 角 |
| jiaoding | chiaoting | 校定 |
| Jiaqing | Chiaching | 嘉慶 |
| jinshi | chinshih | 進士 |
| Kulun banshi dachen | K'ulun panshih tach'ên | 庫倫辦事大臣 |
| lianbang | lienpang | 連邦 |
| lianhe | lienhê | 連合 |

| Pinyin | Wade-Giles | Chinese |
|---|---|---|
| Man | Man | 滿 |
| mincui zhuyi | mints'ui chui | 民粹主義 |
| Ming | Ming | 明 |
| minzu zhuyi | mintsu chui | 民族主義 |
| Nanlu anfushi | Nanlu anfushih | 南路安撫使 |
| Qianlong | Ch'ienlung | 乾隆 |
| Qing | Ch'ing | 清 |
| Ruan | Juan | 阮 |
| saosi nügong | saossŭ nükung | 繅絲女工 |
| shang | shang | 商 |
| shi | shih | 士 |
| shixing yuan | shihhsing yüan | 實行員 |
| sichang | ssŭch'ang | 絲廠 |
| sihang | ssŭhang | 絲行 |
| sihao | ssŭhao | 絲號 |
| sijuan | ssŭchüan | 絲捐 |
| sizhan | ssŭchan | 絲棧 |
| Taidong | T'aitung | 泰東 |
| Taiping | T'aip'ing | 太平 |
| Tang | T'ang | 唐 |
| Tongzhi | T'ungchih | 同治 |
| Wuxu | Wuhsü | 戊戌 |
| wuzhengfu zhuyi | wuchêngfu chui | 無政府主義 |
| xiangshen | hsiangshên | 鄉紳 |
| Xilu zhaofushi | Hsilu chaofushih | 西路招撫使 |
| xinfa | hsinfa | 新法 |
| Xinhai | Hsinhai | 辛亥 |
| xinyi | hsini | 新義 |
| xiucai | hsiuts'ai | 秀才 |
| yamen | yamên | 衙門 |
| yanghang | yanghang | 洋行 |
| yangli | yangli | 洋厘 |
| Yuan (yuan) | Yüan (yüan) | 元 dynasty (currency) |
| yujianshang | yüchienshang | 餘繭商 |
| Zang | Tsang | 藏 |
| zhangcheng | changch'êng | 章程 |
| zongli | tsungli | 總理 |
| zulei | tsulei | 族類 |

# Index

anarchism, 95
An-Feng Railway, 176
Anglo-Chinese Commercial Treaty, 240
Anglo-Russian Entente, 134, 176
anti-feudalism, 45-46
anti-imperialism, 9-10, 19-20, 22-23; and anti-foreign sentiments, 275-76; as revolutionary cause, 3, 43-45, 61, 267, 270, 275
anti-Manchuism: xii, 3, 8, 9, 11, 21-22, 108, 161; and anti-imperialism, 43-44; publications on, 37-38, 41; as revolutionary slogan, 33-34, 35, 36, 45, 195-96
anti-Qing movement. *See* anti-Manchuism
Arao Sei, 91
Army of Comrades, 171
army: national, 176, 177, 178, 180, 186, 187; New Army, 76, 166, 175; people's (*guominjun*), 182; Student Army, 99-100
Arrow War, xi
Asian Solidarity Association, 125, 126
Assembly of Chinese People, 182
Association for the Improvement of Hunan Politics, 206
Association of Fujian Fellow-Provincials in Shanghai, 184
Association of South Shanghai Merchants, 182

Bank of Java, 231, 245
banks, 237-40; foreign, 241, 247-49
Beiyang Army, xii, 289
Bogdo Khân government. *See* Mongolia
Boxer (Yihetuan) Movement, xii, 19, 20, 22, 39-40, 77, 260, 268, 277, 281, 284, 285
Boxer Protocol, 36, 161, 194, 285
Bryan, William Jennings, 261-62, 263, 264

Cai Gang, 181
Cai Jun, 100
Cai Shaonan, 199
Cai Yuanpei, 102

Calhoun, W.J., 259
Cao Du, 166
Cao Rulin, 245
Changsha Railway Institute, 160
Chen Bingyu, 201
Chen Ce, 177
Chen Chi, 89
Chen Gan, 158
Chen Gaodi, 86
Chen Guohua, 186
Chen Jingsong, 184
Chen Kongbo, 170
Chen Qimei, 57, 117, 126. *See also* Chen Yingshi
Chen Qizhang, 89
Chen Tianhua 21, 63, 65, 71-72, 101, 157
Chen Yanjie, 182
Chen Yingshi, 181. *See also* Chen Qimei
Chen Zhilin, 184
Chen Zuoxin, 200, 202, 206
Cheng Dequan, 56
Cheng Jiacheng, 101
Cheng Wenqing, 180
Cheng Yingdu, 165
Chengdu uprising, 170
China, Republic of: recognition, 269
China: alliance with foreign nations advocated, 86, 87, 88, 89, 90, 90-91; and concept of Middle Kingdom, 146-48; on Russian mediation over Mongolia, 139, 140-41
Chinese Communist party, xiii, xiv, 15
Chinese Gymnastic Association for the Cultivation of Spirit and Force, 181
Chinese League. *See* Tongmenghui
Chinese National Association (Zhongguo guominhui), 175, 176, 180; establishment of, 177; local organizations, 182-86; objectives, 178, 186-88
Chinese Revolutionary League. *See* Tongmenghui
Chinese Society for the Protection of Territory, 179, 183

309

# 310 INDEX

Chinese students, in Japan, 11-12, 71, 100-101, 105, 106, 107-10, 184, 185, 186, 187
Chinese Students Federation, 179
Chu Fucheng, 157, 185, 186
Cixi, Empress, xii
classes, role of in revolution, 25
Colquhoun, Archibald R., 211
comprador-merchants, 50
Conant, C., 241
constitutionalists, 5, 194; on constitutional monarchy, 21, 24-25; counterrevolution by, 201-2; economic policy of, 283; economic rights movement, 159, 160, 164-67, 170, 171-72; on masses, 25-26; in provisional government, 214, 215; role in revolution, 26-27, 203-4; and secret societies, 193; and Tongmenghui, 160-61; vs. revolutionaries, 30
currency reform, in China, 240-43, 244-47, 249, 251-52

Da Hunan-bei tongmenghui, 97
Dadaohui, 204
*Dadong hebang xinyiu*, 86, 87-88, 90, 91
Dadong yishuju, 86
Dai Boxing, 181
Daitō confederation 84-85, 86, 88, 92
*Daitō gappō ron*, 84, 91. See also *Dadong hebang xinyiu*
Daniels, Josephus, 260, 261
Dare-to-Die Society, 158, 179
Deng Jingya, 26
Deng Xiaoke, 167
Ding Weifen, 185, 187
Dodge, Cleveland, 262
Dong Hongyi, 99, 101
Dong Xunshi, 99, 101
Dongya Tongmenghui, 125
Dongyou Fengchao. See Phong Trao Dong Du
Du Fu, xiii
Duan Qirui, 16
Dutch East Indies, currency reforms, 231
Dutou, 99
Duy Tan Hoi, 115; as constitutional monarchist party, 124, 125; decline of, 116, 120; disbandment of, 118, 126; members in Japan, 121, 122, 125; objectives, 119

East Asian League, 125
Eastern Socialist Party (Japan), 84
Eastern Study Movement, 115, 123
economic rights movement, 153-55, 157. *See also* mining rights movement; railway rights movement
economy, rural, collapse of 197

1898 Reform Movement, 19, 24, 30, 38, 86

Fang Chaozhen, 166
Fang Xieyin, 181
Feng Ziyou, 98, 101, 122, 125
financial consortium, four-power, 271, 277, 282, 287
financial relations, international, 227
foreign firms, silk-weaving industry, 49-50, 51-52
Foreign Settlement Industrial Bureau, 237
foreigners: antagonism against, 194, 195, 196
France: interests in China, 156, 158, 176, 182, 277, 281, 285, 288; movements to resist, 20; supports Yuan Shikai, 287
Franco-Japanese treaty, 116, 118, 176
French Indo-China, currency reforms, 231, 242
Fu Menghao, 177, 180, 188
Fujian, revolutionary activities in, 184
Fujian Preservation Association, 184
Fujian Society for Establishing a Militia, 184
Fujian Students' Association, 180, 184

Gao Jinzhou, 181
Gedihui, 204
Gelaohui (Society of Brothers and Elders), 101, 166, 170, 194, 284; emergence of, 197-200
Gemingdang, 195, 199, 200, 204, 206, 207
General Guild of the Jiangsu-Zhejiang Silk-Reeling and Cocoon Industry, 53
gentry, 179, 194, 195, 196, 203
Gen'yōsha, 84
Germany: interests in China, 5, 88, 89, 158-59, 263, 277, 281, 288; supports Yuan Shikai, 287
gold standard, 228, 230; in China, proposed, 243-47; effects of adoption, 232
Gong Baoquan, 101
Gong Chuntai, 199
Gongjinhui (Progressive Association), 103, 199, 200
Great Britain: currency reform, 228, 230; interests in China, 145, 162, 176, 182, 277-78, 281, 284, 285, 288; supports Sun Yat-sen, 211-12; supports Yuan Shikai, 287
Great Unity Translation and Publishing Company, 86
Greater Hunan Hubei League, 97
Grigor'ev, A.M., 61-62, 63
Gu Jingzhai, 53
Gu Naibin, 163

# INDEX

Gu Zhongchen, 217
Guangdong uprising, 184
Guangfuhui (Restoration Society), 95, 102, 103, 124
Guangxu, Emperor, xii
Guangzhou uprising, 175, 187, 188
Guilin School of Law and Government, 186
Guo Xiren, 157
*Guomin bao*, 11
Guomindang, xiii, xiv, 206-7
*guominjun*, 182
Guozijian, 122

Han Chinese, in Mongolia, 130-31
Han nationalism, 34, 47, 66, 146-48, 283-84; Han-Manchu antagonism, 5, 21, 283
Hang Xinzhai, 163-64
Hanna, H., 241
Hanyeping case, 271
Hapgood, Norman, 263
Hay, John, 241, 260, 261
He Jinsheng, 194
He Wei, 177
Hongbang, 284
Hongkong and Shanghai Banking Corporation, 241, 247
Hong Ruchong, 90, 91
Hongdenghui, 204
Hongjianghui, 194, 199, 200, 204
Hornbeck, Stanley, 265
Hu Hanmin, 126, 157, 177, 212, 217
Hu Yaobang, xiv
Huang Jialiang, 182, 183, 187
Huang Jinshen, 53, 56
Huang Xing, 46, 63, 64, 65, 69, 101, 103, 125, 126, 177, 206, 210, 217, 264, 288
Huang Zhonghao, 202
Huang Zongxian, 50
Huanghuagang uprising, 169
Huaxinghui (Society for China's Revival), 63, 64, 70, 76, 77, 95, 101, 103, 194, 199
Hubei, military government, 14
Hubei Society of Fellow-Provincials in Shanghai, 180
*huidang*. *See* secret societies
Hunan, popular movement in, 194-97; railway rights movement, 160

imperialist powers: interests in China, xi-xii, 5, 20, 74, 75, 182, 187, 274-75, 281; and Republic, 276-77; and revolution, 15, 27, 268, 271, 286-87
India, currency reforms, 230
intellectuals, as revolutionaries, 26, 33, 35
International Commission of Bankers, 269

Inukai Tsuyoshi, 123
investments, and silver standard, 236-37
Invigorate China, Revive Asia Society, 126
Iriye, Akira, 257
Italy, forces in China, 281
Itō Hirobumi, 108
Iverson and Co., 49, 50

Japan: Chinese revolutionaries in, 102, 121, 162, 175, 177; Chinese students in, 11-12, 71, 100-101, 105, 106, 107, 184, 185, 186, 187; currency reforms, 230; emperor, 106, 108; government, 107, 108; interests in China, 73, 74-75, 176, 274, 277, 281, 287; interests in Mongolia, 138, 139; nationalism in, 67; recognition of the Republic, 263; and revolution, 285, 287; supports Sun Yat-sen, 211; Vietnamese in, 115, 116-17
Jardine, Matheson and Co., 49, 50
Jebzundamba Khutukhta, 132, 133, 136
Jenks, J., 241, 243
Jiandao, 68, 70, 73, 74
Jiang Xifan, 180, 185, 187
Jiang Yansheng, 180, 185, 187
Jiang-Zhe sijianye gongsuo, 53
Jiangsu, 50, 51, 52, 53, 161, 162
Jiao Dafeng, 199, 200-202, 204, 205, 206
Jiaozhou, German occupation of, 88, 89
Jin Chongji, 99
Jin Dingxun, 183
Jin Tianhe, 97
Jin Yi, 97
Jing Dingcheng, 159
Jing Meijiu, 125
Jiyūtō, 107
Ju-E yiyongdui (Resist Russia Military Corps), 99-100
Junguomin jiaoyuhui. *See* Militant People's Educational Association

Kaishintō, 107
*Kaizhi lu*, 9, 37
Kang Youwei, 86; on alliance with foreign powers, 88, 89, 89, 91; influence of, 62, 107, 122; reformism of, xii, 5, 19, 21, 24, 25
Kemuyama Sentarō, 95, 102; influence on anarchism publications, 97-98
Khalkha Mongolia. *See* Mongolia
Kiakhta Agreement, 145
Kinsei Museifushugi, 95, 96
Kishida Ginko, 81
Korostovets, I.Y., 137
Kōtoku Shūsui, 95

Ky Ngoai Hau Cuong De, 116

Lamaism, 132
land rights, equalization of, 29, 31, 200
landlords, in nationalist movement, 27, 33, 35
language, unity in, 41-43
Lei Zaihan, 157, 158
Lenin, V. I., xiii, 40-41, 42, 47, 104
Li Bo, Xiii
Li Bodong, 158
Li Hongzhang, 89
Li Huaishuang, 180
Li Jingxi, 182, 183
Li Pingshu, 179
Li Risheng, 182, 183
Li Xiehe, 183
Li Yuanhong, 270, 287
Li Zhaofu, 175, 177, 178
Liang Qichao, 86, 90, 106, 107; and Phan Boi Chau, 121, 122, 125; revolutionary thought of, 4, 20-21, 24, 26, 29-30
Liang Shanji, 159
Liao Shoufeng, 51
Liao Yuchun, 217
Liaodong peninsula, 88
*likin*. *See* taxes
Lin Shishuang, 187
Lin Wen, 187
Lin Yancun, 178
Liu Chenglie, 181
Liu Chengyu, 37, 38
Liu Daoyi, 199
Liu Jiyan, 177
Liu Kuiyi, 175, 177, 187, 199
Liu Kunyi, 51, 89, 240
Liu Shipei, 162
Liu Yang, 166
Liu Yuguang, 166
Long Jiguang, 126
Long Mingjian, 165, 166, 170
Lu Haihuan, 240
Lu Hesheng, 55
Lu Xun, xiii, 104
Lu Yafa, 70
Luo Futian, 166

Ma Fuyi, 199
Ma Junwu, 38
Ma Xiangbo, 180
Manchuria, 72, 73; revolutionary activities in, 183-84
Mao Zedong, xiv
masses: distrusted, 22, 25-26, 61, 77; as revolutionary force, 64, 65, 71, 73, 195
Mei Xin, 202

Meiji Restoration, 105, 106, 108, 120
merchants, revolutionary organizations of, 181-82
Militant People's Educational Association (Junguomin jiaoyuhui), 95, 99-102, 103
military, revolutionary potential of, 64, 65
*Min bao*, 12, 14, 61, 156, 157
Ming dynasty, movement to restore, 35, 36, 41
Ming Shaozhen, 181
mining rights movement, 19-20, 156, 158-60
*Minli bao*, 169
Minyidang. *See* Narodnaya Volya
missionaries: influence on U.S. China policy, 259, 260-61, 263; struggles against, 35, 195
Mitchell Report, 274
Miyazaki Tōten, 211
*Modern Anarchism* (Kinsei Museifushugi), 95-96
Mongolia: anti-Qing movement, 131, 132; delegation to Russia, 132-34; Han Chinese in, 130-31; independence, 129, 136, 269, 284, 285; Japanese interests in, 138, 139; and Qing, 130-31; Russo-Chinese negotiations on, 139-44; Sun Yat-sen and, 216-17
Morimoto Tōkichi. *See* Tarui Tōkichi
Mott, John R., 262

Nanjing provisional government, 14, 46; and customs duties, 286; established, xi, 213-14; cabinet posts, 214-15
Narodnaya Volya, 95, 98, 101, 102, 103, 104
Narodniks, Russian, 95, 96, 97, 98-99, 104
National Academic Association, 180
National College, 122
National Commerce Association, 180
National Cultural Society, 43
National Federation of Commercial Organizations, 179, 181, 182
National Militant Association, 186
nationalist movement, 3, 34-36, 38-40
nationalities relations, 34, 47, 284-85
New Vietnam Public Offering Society, 116
Nguyen dynasty, 119, 120, 121
Nguyen imperial family, 116
1911 Revolution, impact on Asian people, 115, 116, 117, 118, 119
Niu Yongjian, 100
Nong Jingsun, 181
Nong Zhu, 181
Northern Expedition, 218

Ōi Kentarō, 84
Onogawa Hidemi, 97
Opium War, xi, 4, 34, 35, 197
Ou Jujia, 65

pan-Asianism, 83, 84-85, 87, 88, 92
Pan Xunchu, 181
Pan Yueqiao, 182
peasantry, as revolutionary force, 26, 33, 35, 167-68, 170, 193, 195, 207; uprisings, 284
Perovskaya, Sofia, 104
Phan Ba Ngoc, 117
Phan Boi Chau, 115, 122; in Guangzhou, 119; on international relations, 118; and Japan, 116-17, 120,121, 125; publications, 116, 118; and Sun Yat-sen, 123-24; in Thailand, 117
Philippines, currency reforms, 230, 242
Phong Trao Dong Du, 115, 123
Pianma, 176, 182
Ping-Liu-Li uprising, 70
Political Reform party (Hunan), 206
Progressive Association. *See* Gongjinhui
Protect the Emperor Society, 216
Pu Dianjun, 166, 170

Qiaonan Public Welfare Society, 158
Qin Tieshan, 181
Qin Yuliu, 100
Qin Zaigeng, 170
Qing government: industry under, 30; Mongolia policy of, 131-32; overthrow of, 217, 218; relations with foreign powers, 12, 20-21. *See also* anti-Manchuism
Qingbang, 284
Qingnianhui, 99, 100
Qiu Jin, 104
Qu Shaoyi, 181
Quoc-tu-gian, 122

Railway and Mine Association 162
railway rights movement, 19-20, 154, 164-68; Guandong-Hankou, 156, 165; Hunan, 160; Jiangsu and Zhejiang, 161-63, 165; Nanning-Beihai, 158; Sichuan, 169-71; Sichuan-Hankou, 165; Suzhou-Hangzhou-Ningbo, 162; Yunnan-Vietnam, 156, 158
railways: building of, 31; nationalization of, 282
Reformation Society. *See* Duy Tan Hoi
Reinsch, Paul, 263, 265
Reorganization Loan, 259, 269
Resist Russia Military Corp, 99-100
Restoration Society. *See* Guangfuhui

revolutionaries: and constitutionalists compared, 30; and economic rights movement, 153, 155-58; goals of, 22, 25; in Japan, 102, 121, 162, 175, 177; on masses,22, 26; publications by, 155-58, 169; and secret societies, 199-200; weakness of, 14, 26, 34, 46
revolutionary forces, 282-83
Revolutionary League, 166
Revolutionary party (Hunan), 206
Richard, Timothy, 91
Rockhill, W.W., 241
Roset, W.A., 245
Russell and Co., 49, 50, 53
Russia: interests in China, xi, 11, 90, 176, 277-78, 281, 287, 288; on Chinese-Mongol relations, 137; mediates China-Mongol relations, 135-36, 138-44; Mongolia policy of, 134-35, 284-85; Mongolian delegation to, 132-34; movements to resist, 11, 20; position on revolution, 287; relations with China, 75; relations with Japan, 138, 139; as threat to China, 88, 89
Russo-Chinese Declaration, 144
Russo-Japanese Agreement, 134, 176, 187
Russo-Japanese Entente, 139, 141
Russo-Japanese War, 115, 120, 121, 134, 240, 268
Russo-Mongol Agreement, 144

Saigō Takamori, 108
Sakatani Yoshirō, 246
Sang Dansheng, 181
Sanhuyimin, 97-98. *See also* Yang Yulin
Santianhui, 284
Sazonov, S., 137, 278
Scalapino, R.A., 95
Scott, Charles E., 260
Second Revolution, 245, 264, 288-89
secret societies, 26, 76, 157, 193; alliance of, 194; alliance with revolutionaries, 199-200; composition of, 197, 198; and Huaxinghui plot, 64; in Hunan, 197; revolutionary potential of, 64, 65, 68, 195, 196, 207-8; role of in revolution, 22, 25; uprisings by, 70, 204-5, 285
Self-government Association, 186
Shanghai, revolutionary activities in, 180-82
Shanghai Female Silk Filature Workers Mutual Benevolent Association, 57
Shanghai Journalists' Federation, 180
Shanghai saosi nugong tongrengonghui, 57
Shanghai Stockholders' Association, 236

Shaoxing, 53
Shen Congwen, xiii
Shen Lianfang, 56
Shen Manyun, 179, 180, 182
Shen Zhongli, 180
Sheng Xuanhuai, 163, 240
Shi Jialin, 180
Shimonoseki, Treaty of, 236
Sichuan, 165, 169; uprising, 282
Sijianye gongsuo, 55, 56, 57
silk-reeling industry (Shanghai), 49, 50-52; cocoons, 52-53, 54-55; and foreign capital 52, 54; workers, 55
silver, value of, 227-28, 232; effects of decline 229-30, 234-40
Simla Conference, 145
Sino-French War, xi, 21
Sino-Japanese war, xi, 3, 4, 21, 51, 52, 92, 237
Society for China's Revival. *See* Huaxinghui
Society for Rejecting Foreign Loans, 163-64
Society for the Preservation of Mines, 158
Society of Brothers and Elders. *See* Gelaohui
Society to Restore China's Prosperity (Xingzhonghui), 4-5, 36, 41, 103, 124, 209
soldiers, discharged, uprisings by, 205
Song Bolu, 91
Song Jiaoren, 46, 179, 204, 206, 207, 261; on anti-imperialism, 72-73; anti-Manchu sentiments, 62-63; background, 62-63; on China's weakness, 65-66, 72, 75; on diplomacy and international law, 73, 74; exile in Japan, 65-66, 67; and Huaxinghui plot, 64-65; on leadership, 71, 72, 75; in Manchuria, 68-69, 72; on mobilization of masses, 64, 65, 71, 73; revolutionary strategy of, 76-77
Song Yuanyuan, 184, 187
*sonnō-jōi* movement, 106
Straits Settlements, currency reforms, 230-31, 242
strikes 159, 168, 169, 170
Student Army, 99-100
Students' Federation, 182
*Su bao*, 99, 100
Su Peng, 102
Su Shaolou, 126
Sun Baoqi, 185
Sun Yat-sen, 69, 283; on anti-imperialism, 267; on democracy, 23-24; on economy, 46, 246; foreign policy, 210, 285-87; landownership, 29, 31, 103; on Manchus, 37, 45; and Mongolia, 216; and Phan Boi Chau, 123-24; and preparations for revolution, 177, 209, 210; and provisional government, xii, 212-14, 215-16, 219-21, 288; recognition of, 27, 211, 259, 264, 271; on revolution, 3, 13, 15-16, 25, 28-29, 187; and Society to Restore China's Prosperity, 4-5, 103; and support for revolution, 21-22; Three People's Principles, 19, 28, 29, 31, 61; and Yuan Shikai, 217-20

Taft, William Howard, 257, 258, 259
Taft-Katsura Agreement, 258
Taiping Heavenly Kingdom, xi, 36, 197, 281
Tan Bian, 95, 97
Tan Renfeng, 205
Tan Yankai, 201, 202, 203-4, 205, 206, 207
Tang Caichang, 89
Tang Jiaodun, 125
Tang Qunying, 178
Tang Shouqian, 164
Tao Chengzhang, 102
Tao Qian, xiii
Tarui Tōkichi: background, 83; Daitō confederation ideals, 84-85, 86
taxes: *likin*, 240; Maritime Customs, 238, 286; on raw silk and cocoon, 51, 56
terrorism, assassinations, 101, 108
Thailand, currency reforms, 231
Three People's Principles, 19, 61, 103; Principle of Democracy, 23, 31; Principle of Livelihood, 28, 29, 31; Principle of Nationalism, 19, 22, 31
Tianjin treaty, 121
Tibet, 129, 145, 269, 284
Tōa Dōmeikai, 125
Tong Bichen, 180
Tongchouhui, 194, 199
Tongmenghui (Chinese League, Chinese Revolutionary League), 19, 22, 61, 76, 77, 103, 104, 116, 123, 153, 175, 194, 199, 206, 210, 282, 285, 287; and constitutionalists, 160-61; and economic rights movement, 155, 156-61, 162-68; in Japan, 162; local organizations of, 157-59, 165-66
Tongzhi Restoration, 4
Tongzhijun, 171
Tōyama Mitsuru, 84
Tōyō Shakaitō (Eastern Socialist Party), 84
trade, and silver standard, 234-35
Trani, Eugene, 259

INDEX 315

Twenty-One Demands, 15

United States: East Asia policy, 257; interests in China, 277, 281, 287, 288; recognition of the Republic, 262; and silver value, 228, 229; supports Sun Yat-sen, 211; supports Yuan Shikai, 287
uprisings, 70, 169, 170, 175, 184, 187, 188, 204-7, 282, 284
urban labor, revolutionary potential of, 64, 65

Vietnam, anti-French movement, 116, 119-20, 121
Viet-Nam Cong Hien Hoi, 116
Viet-Nam Quang Phuc Hoi, 116, 118, 119, 126, 127
Vietnam Restoration Society. *See* Viet-Nam Quang Phuc Hoi
Vietnamese revolution: and Yunnan and Guangxi, 123
Vietnamese revolutionaries, and Japan, 115, 120, 121, 122
Vietnamese students, in Japan, 119, 123, 125
Vissering, G., 245
Voznesensky, A., 288

wage struggle, silk-reeling industry, 55-57
Wang Baozhen, 183
Wang Daxie, 244
Wang Dianyang, 166
Wang Hanliang, 181
Wang Jiaju, 99, 100, 101, 102
Wang Jingfang, 100
Wang Jiuling, 179, 182, 183, 187
Wang Tianjie, 170, 171
Wang Weiren. *See* Wang Jiaju
Wang Xiong, 181
Wang Yangming, 72
Wang Yongbin, 159
Wang Yongqin, 181
Wang You, 160
Wang Ziyi, 165, 168
Waseda University, 96, 99
Weixinhui. *See* Duy Tan Hoi
Wen Fei, 157, 160
Wen Jingwei, 160
Wen Ti, 89
Weng Tonghe, 89
westernization movements, xii, 197
White Lotus Rebellion, xi
Wilson, Huntington, 258, 259
Wilson, Woodrow, 257, 259, 260; China policy of, 258-59, 261, 262-63; missionary influence on, 259, 260, 263

Women's National Association in China, 181
women: revolutionary groups, 177-78, 181, 186; workers, 57
Wu Tingfang, 218
Wu Yuzhang, 169, 171, 214
Wu Zuolin, 160
Wuchang New Army, 101
Wuchang Uprising, xi, 26, 136, 182, 187, 188, 200, 209, 210, 211, 212, 270
Wuxi, 50, 51, 52, 53

Xi Yanggao, 180
Xia Chao, 163
Xia Yueshan, 182
Xia Zhongmin, 177
*xiangshen*. *See* gentry
Xiangyouhui, 203
Xiao Deming, 182, 183, 187
Xiao Focheng, 118
Xiao Shen, 166
Xiao Xingtai, 181
Xie Ronglu, 157, 159
Xie Yingbo, 117
Xin Yunan gongxianhui, 116
Xingzhonghui. *See* Society to Restore China's Prosperity
*Xinmin congbao*, 12, 14, 24
Xiong Yueshan, 176, 177
Xu Banhou, 186
Xu Jiqing, 181
Xu Lian, 158
Xu Qin, 122
Xu Rongpu, 181
Xu Yaoyuan, 181
Xuesheng Jun, 99-100

Yamagata Aritomo, 264
Yan Fu, 63
Yan Zhongwen, 185
Yang Boqian, 166
Yang Dazhu, 179, 182, 183, 187
Yang Du, 106
Yang Dusheng, 65
Yang Shenxiu, 89, 91
Yang Shukan, 166
Yang Wending, 160
Yang Xinzhi, 53, 56, 57
Yang Yuanmao, 157, 159, 160
Yang Yulin, 97-98, 99, 101, 102
Yang Zhenhong, 123
Yangwu clique, xii
Yazhou heqinhui, 125, 126
Yi Zongxi, 160
Yihetuan Movement. *See* Boxer Movement
Yin Ruizhi, 186

Yin Weijun, 181
Yoshida Shōin, 106, 108
Yoshikawa Kōjirō, xiii
You Jiyun, 181
Youth Association, 99, 100
Yu Zuomin, 181
Yuan Shikai, 46, 100, 126, 193, 204, 215, 220, 245, 261, 269; and provisional government, xii, 140, 143, 144, 217-21, 288; support by foreign powers, 15, 23, 27, 262, 264, 268, 269, 271, 277, 286, 287
Yuan Shuxun, 156
Yuenan Guangfuhui. *See* Viet-Nam Quang Phuc Hoi
Yunnan, revolutionary activities in, 182
Yunnan-Guangxi-Vietnam League, 123
Yunnan-Guizhou Society of Fellow-Provincials in Shanghai, 180

Zeng Guofan army, 197
Zeng Yun, 185-86
Zeng Zemin, 184
Zeng Zhaolu, 166
Zhang Binglin, 89-90, 117, 118, 125, 162, 163. *See also* Zhang Taiyan
Zhang Ji, 97, 99, 102, 125
Zhang Muliang, 180, 187
Zhang Peijiao, 166
Zhang Peiyi, 181
Zhang Taiyan, 3, 7-8, 38, 41, 216; on goals of revolution, 28; on language unity, 42-43; on Manchus, 36-37, 44, 45-46, 47. *See also* Zhang Binglin
Zhang Weihua, 181
Zhang Xun, 15
Zhang Yi, 166
Zhang Zaimin, 181

Zhang Zhidong, 51, 63, 89, 156, 240, 244, 247, 249
Zhang Zhijing, 165
Zhang Zhuofun, 185
Zhang Zi, 180, 187
Zhao Erfeng, 167, 170
Zhao Shen, 123
Zhao Sheng, 177
Zhejiang: railway rights movement, 161, 162, 164; revolutionary activities in, 185-86; and silk-reeling industry, 50, 51, 52, 53
*Zhejiang chao*, 9, 39, 44, 98, 99, 155
Zhejiang Student Association, 102
Zheng Guanying, 4
Zheng Quan, 184
Zheng Zhongjing, 181
Zhenhua Xingyahui, 126
Zhongguo geming tongmenghui. *See* Tongmenghui
Zhongguo guominhui. *See* Chinese National Association
Zhongguo tongmenghui. *See* Tongmenghui
Zhou Enlai, 14
Zhou Jianlong, 185
Zhou Laisu, 102
Zhou Shubiao, 158
Zhou Shuren, 104
Zhu Bowei, 181
Zhu Guochen, 166
Zhu Shaoping, 179, 180
Zhu Tengfang, 184
Zhu Zhihong, 157, 165, 166, 167, 168
Zou Daifan, 160
Zou Lu, 176, 185
Zou Rong, 22, 38, 41